T.S. BUCHANAN

D0619680

Psychology for Teaching

A Bear ~~Always~~ ~~Usually~~ Sometimes Faces the Front

Guy R. Lefrancois

University of Alberta

Third Edition

Wadsworth Publishing Company, Inc.
Belmont, California

Education Editor: Roger S. Peterson

Designer: Dare Porter

Production Editor: Sandra Craig

© 1979 by Wadsworth Publishing Company, Inc.

© 1975, 1972 by Wadsworth Publishing Company, Inc., Belmont, California 94002. All rights reserved. No part of this book may be reproduced, stored in a retrieval system, or transcribed, in any form or by any means, electronic, mechanical, photocopying, recording, or otherwise, without the prior written permission of the publisher.

Printed in the United States of America
2 3 4 5 6 7 8 9 10–83 82 81 80 79

Library of Congress Cataloging in Publication Data

Lefrancois, Guy R.
  Psychology for teaching.

  Bibliography: p. 361
  Includes index.
  1. Psychology. 2. Educational psychology.
I. Title.
BF121.L42 1979   370.15   78-16297
ISBN 0-534-00602-7

Photo Credits

Cover, Fredrik D. Bodin, Stock, Boston; Page 1, Elizabeth Crews, Jeroboam; Page 17, Eileen Christelow, Jeroboam; Page 38, Eileen Christelow, Jeroboam; Page 65, Don Dietz, Stock, Boston; Page 98, Bruce Kliewe, Jeroboam; Page 114, Jean-Claude Lejeune, Stock, Boston; Page 146, Karen R. Preuss, Jeroboam; Page 175, Bruce Roberts, Rapho, Photo Researchers, Inc.; Page 195, Steve Meltzer, West Stock; Page 216, Cary Wolinsky, Stock, Boston; Page 247, Cary Wolinsky, Stock, Boston; Page 270, Elizabeth Hamlin, Stock, Boston; Page 289, Karen R. Preuss, Jeroboam; Page 313, Eileen Christelow, Jeroboam; Page 340, Elizabeth Crews, Jeroboam.

Preface to the Third Edition

Eight years ago, the first **Bear** appeared, confidently facing the front – always. **Bear I** described itself as a book that presented educationally relevant theory and research in a clear and interesting manner, a book that was substantive but not encyclopedically detailed, that made more use of humor and illustration than was typical of its academic cousins, and that interpreted and suggested rather than simply reporting and summarizing.

Three years later, **Bear II** reared its ursine head. It had by now realized that only the more stupid of bears did not occasionally look backward, and though it continued to face the front – usually – it sometimes looked in the other direction. **Bear II** was much that **Bear I** had been. It presented no dramatic or violent changes, though it had discarded or deemphasized some of the theories whose relevance had become more obscure rather than more obvious with the passage of time. It also brought with it more emphasis on instructional objectives and evaluation, and a general updating of information.

And now, **Bear III**. Although he neither **always** nor even **usually** faces the front, it is still true that he **sometimes** does. **The Bear** is older and much wiser now, having been approached from the rear on so many occasions. Not paranoiac, simply wiser. But it is still the same **Bear**. It still strives to present useful theory in a clear and interesting manner, and it still makes use of humor and illustration. In other ways, however, it has changed. Not only is there a thorough updating of information wherever appropriate, but there is one entirely new chapter on discipline, Chapter 14. There is an expansion of the treatment of humanistic approaches to education, including such topics as moral development, forgetting, and cognitive approaches to motivation. **Bear III** also includes thirty new cartoons and fifteen new photographs. It is hoped that these changes will make **Bear III** more interesting, more teachable, and more useful than it was when younger.

Yours,

Thank You

To the people whose ideas are acknowledged in these pages; to those whose ideas sneaked in unrecognized; to the countless students who have sat in front of me – especially those who occasionally shout back, and to those who sometimes write; to Richard L. Greenberg, editor for **Bear I** and **II**, whose involvement in this project went considerably beyond the expected; to Roger Peterson, editor for **Bear III**; to Dare Porter, the cover and interior designer; to Tony Hall, the cartoonist; to Sandra Craig, the production editor; to Nancy Flight, the copy editor; to J. D. Ayers, University of Victoria; Michal Clark, California State University, Bakersfield; and Herschel Thornberg, University of Arizona, who reviewed the first edition; to Michal Clark, California State University, Bakersfield; Henry P. Cole, University of Kentucky; Allan M. Dahms, Metro State College; Myron Dembo, University of Southern California; A. J. H. Gaite, University of Oregon; Barry C. Munro, University of British Columbia; Diane Papalia, University of Wisconsin, Madison; Thomas Sherman, Virginia Polytechnic Institute and State University; Hazel Stapleton, East Carolina University, who reviewed the second edition . . . and especially to Ann Pratt of Capital University, Columbus, whose reviewing talents were a joy to me and a real help to the book; to Ted Bayer, State University of New York, Albany; William B. Dragoin, Georgia Southwestern College; A. J. H. Gaite, University of Oregon; Jan Ruthven, Mississippi State University, Gerald L. Larson, Kent State University; Harry Osser, Queens University, Kingston, Ontario; D. T. Sampson, Eastern Washington University; Ignatius J. Toner, University of North Carolina, Charlotte; Ronald D. Zellner, University of Northern Colorado; and Henry Zurhellen, Memphis State University, reviewers of the third edition; and to Marie, Laurier, Claire, and Remi, who make it all worth a great deal more than my while.

Contents

For my first teacher, my father, who taught me to love books and learning, and
For my mother, who taught me to love people and life.

A Science of Humans

1

Humans, the Animals · Humans, the Thinkers · Humans, the Race · Psychology and Education · Educational Psychology · Overview of the Text · Preview of the Text · Summary · Main Points ·

Gibran asks whether the vision of one man
can lend its wings to another.
He does not answer.

And can the pearls of wisdom that have been
gathered by the old people be given
to the young, or must the young always
gather their own?

And if this be so, what then is a teacher?

Advance Organizer This chapter presents some general notions concerning our place in The Scheme of Things. Unfortunately, it says nothing about The Scheme itself, that being left to wiser or more foolish people. The chapter introduces such important concepts as **psychology** *and* **educational psychology,** *and presents a brief preview of each of the remaining fourteen chapters. These chapters are organized into parts according to their major emphases. The first part is simply this chapter: an introduction; the second part presents accounts of the simpler explanations of learning, together with their more obvious educational implications; Part 3 looks at more complex learning, social behavior, memory, and humanistic approaches to education; the fourth part looks at human development; the fifth part discusses individual differences as they are manifested in creative behavior and intellectual functioning; the final part looks at three topics that are of central importance to the teaching-learning process: motivation, discipline, and assessment.*

The archives are old; some of the strange letters carved into the rock tablets have been worn almost smooth in the vast sea of time. Yet they remain the only link between Then and Now—and for a race that has clung so romantically to its past, they are a precious link indeed.

It was a young shepherd who first found the tablets. They were scattered in the remote corners of a cave to which he often went for shelter when the rain came down too hard and too cold. At first he was amused by the strange lines on the faces of the flat stones, but in time he lost interest and put them back in the shadows that they had occupied for countless years.

But one day he brought one of the stones to his home to place in front of his hearth, for it was wide and flat, and on it he could set the hot soup pot without spilling it and without burning another hole in the ancient floor—and the baby was not so likely to trip over such a flat stone and fall into the fireplace.

The stone was there when it was discovered by a hot and thirsty archeologist who stopped for a drink fifty years later. He was led by the now aged shepherd to the cave in the hills, and in time all the tablets were collected in a faraway museum, and stored there in the dark shadows where they remained through several wars and many years. From time to time an enthusiastic graduate student came eagerly to look for a doctoral dissertation in the script on the worn rock faces, eventually lost his enthusiasm, and returned again to the more legible writings of his contemporaries. But some stayed and marveled at the stories on the rocks, and translated them for others to read and marvel at.

Among the many tales told on those stones, there is one that must be told here again. It is the story of Oog, a man who professed to be among the first of the thinkers* of the People. It is a story told by Oog, and it is about him. Oog writes that it occurred to him that a great many children of the People did not know very much. They did not know that they should walk on the top of the hills where their scent

---

* The translation is inexact. It could as easily have been "philosopher," "poet," or "god" as "thinker."

would be carried away into the skies, rather than at the bottom where the scent would find its way to the beasts that lie on the hillsides. They did not know that the huge Bela snake hides among the branches of the Kula berry bushes, not because the snake likes the berries, but because he likes the children. Of this they were ignorant, even as they were ignorant of the skills required to fashion the houses of the People so that the rain would not come in, and of a thousand other things that the People must know. And so the children of the People died like the small rabbits that their mothers cooked; and like the small rabbits, the People continued to make children, but barely managed to keep pace with the heavy losses that they suffered.

It is written on the tablets that for these reasons Oog took it upon himself to gather the wisdom of the People in his mind, and to gather the children of the People at his feet—and he became their teacher. And it is also written that the People soon flourished, grew greatly in number, and chose others who would also be teachers, for there were too many to sit at the feet of Oog. When this happened, Oog withdrew from the tiring business of transmitting the wisdom of the People to its children, and thought instead of how this could be done in a better way. Accordingly, he thought of **education,*** and in time he came to think of **psychology.** And because he was clever as well as industrious, he eventually thought of **educational psychology**.

The story of Oog is therefore the beginning of the story told in this book. It is a story of humans: of adults, of children, and of the attempts that adults make to impart enough of their wisdom to their children to enable them to obtain more of it by themselves, and to survive. The story of humans is the story of *psychology*; the story of the imparting of wisdom is the story of *education*, and the story of this book, since it deals with both of these, is the story of *educational psychology*. We humans are therefore the central theme of this book.

And who and what are we?

Humans, the Animals

We are the species *Homo sapiens*; unattractive, smelly, pugnacious creatures that walk upright, grunting and bellowing. We are only one of many species that live on this planet, and we appear to be among the worst adapted. Our young are helpless for longer than the young of any other species. We have lost most of our hair, and what we have left is little protection against the cold. Our eyesight is weaker than that of most other species, and our sense of smell responds only to the strongest odors. If pursued we can run only a very short distance, and that very slowly. We are remarkably unskilled at climbing trees or digging holes; we cannot live under water, and we swim with less grace than almost any other animal, if we swim at all. We are heavy and awkward and cannot fly—we can't even jump very high. We are singularly unequipped with weapons either for defense or for killing food. It is absolutely remarkable and utterly fascinating that our species has survived at all.

And yet it has. Why?

---

* Boldface terms are discussed in the glossary at the end of the book.

Humans, the Thinkers

If one animal is being pursued by another which is faster and stronger, and which has more highly developed senses, the pursued animal will probably be captured. Yet it may escape by climbing a tree where the predator cannot follow; it may jump into a hole too small for the pursuer, or it may hide somewhere where predators seldom venture. Some of these animals will survive—but most of their energy will be devoted to finding food and avoiding enemies.

If, on the other hand, this animal could amplify its **motor capacities**—make itself stronger, faster, less vulnerable—it might avoid its enemies, and perhaps even find food, more easily. In short, such animals as humans were could best survive by changing their motor capabilities.

This might be accomplished genetically. Through an incredibly slow evolution where only the fittest would survive, humans might eventually come to run faster and perhaps swim naturally with some grace. However, if such a change were left to evolution alone, the fittest of enemies would also survive and, through their offspring, keep pace with changing humans. One can imagine Thros, a Neanderthal caveman, turning to his wife one morning and saying, "Nghaaa! Gor quinted cor cora corraturi potu. Lesj tunc chica ngha quis."*

---

* The translation of this well-known Neanderthal phrase is: "Nghaaa! We have to amplify our motor capacities. They got the kid last night."

**IS THE HUMAN RACE A
BLUNDERING IDIOT?**

The earth is about 4.6 billion years old. Throughout most of its history it was devoid of human life, modern humans being no more than a million years old. And the laws that have governed the countless changes among earth's life forms were, throughout most of that history, the harsh laws of evolution: survival of the fittest (and, conversely, the annihilation or modification of the unfit) and diversification of species. When *Homo sapiens* made its appearance, the course of evolution began to change, for here was an animal intelligent enough to take its physical destiny into its own hands. Yet, beginning with the appearance of the most primitive human, almost a million years passed before the human population reached one billion. That occurred around the year 1830. The next billion, however, took only a hundred years—and the third, no more than thirty! Scientists predict that the next billion will take only fifteen, and that by the year 2000 there will be six billion people on a planet that now has difficulty supporting a mere three billion. Indeed, over half of the earth's present population suffers from malnutrition, and this despite the fact that there are now approximately 1.2 acres of land under cultivation for every human. But scarcity of food is only one of the problems accentuated by dramatic increases in population; drastic critical shortages brought about by increased needs for energy, shelter, recreation, and a great variety of irreplaceable resources are a few of the others. Can technological breakthroughs keep pace with accelerating population growth? Or will the problem be solved by nuclear catastrophe, widespread famine, disease, war, or some other form of madness? Perhaps, if the human race is indeed a blundering idiot.

But humans took the course of evolution into their own hands, to become the first, and perhaps the only, animals to exercise significant control over the world and its future. How does one become stronger? By inventing simple machines— levers, pulleys, wheels, screws, and inclined planes—and by using them to make uncomplicated weapons—bows and arrows, spears, slings, and hatchets. How does one become less vulnerable? By using machines to make both weapons and shelters.

Bruner (1964, 1966) sees human inventions as beginning with the amplification of motor capabilities (the invention of simple machines), followed by amplification of human **sensory capacities** (the invention of telescopes, radio, television, etc.), and culminating in amplification of **ratiocinative** (intellectual) **capacities** (the invention of theory). At present, we appear to be trying to understand and develop our intellectual capacities—and that is one of the functions of psychology.

This physically inferior specimen has survived because of a tremendous advantage that it acquired probably very early in its evolution—the capacity to *think*. Its capacity to think allowed it to foresee the consequences of its actions, leading it to devote the time and energy required to escape from the dangers that beset it at the dawn of civilization. In the same way, it is the child's ability to think which permits sufficient adaptation to the world to ensure survival. *Survival* simply means learning to cope with the world, however structured and socialized it may be. True, the price of nonsurvival, in this sense, is no longer swift and painful death (but it may be incarceration in a mental hospital). Nor has our increasing ability to amplify our capabilities made survival in the world we have created any simpler. Probably it has become even more difficult. We have amplified our capabilities to the point where mushrooming technology is consuming the resources of the planet and replacing them with garbage. Individuals can, in their wisdom, speak of Utopia and environmental control; but the human race often appears to be a blundering idiot.

But now we can do much more than simply think—we can think about our thinking. And that, in large part, is psychology.

Humans, the Race

Psychological literature, particularly when it deals with individual differences, with measuring intelligence, or with personality, tends to stress the differences among people and to account for variations in behavior on the basis of these differences. For **learning**, **developmental**, and **motivation theory**, it is probably more useful to deal with similarities. How much more significant it is that all of us walk upright than that some walk faster than others! In the same way, the fact that we can communicate is more important than the fact that we use more than 5,000 different languages. It is those broad characteristics of human functioning which are relatively common to all that permit the development of a science of humans—a science which among other things, attempts to answer the questions: "Why do we behave?" and "How do we learn?"

Psychology and Education

Psychology attempts to explain human **adaptation** to the environment, and all of the artificial divisions that have been made within the discipline do not alter this fact. Developmental theory looks at sequential adaptation—that is, it looks at the progressive adaptation of individuals at different ages. **Personality theory** looks at social adaptation—the adaptation of individuals in interpersonal relationships. Learning theory looks at nondevelopmental adaptive behavior—the general principles that govern the acquiring of adaptive behavior at any age.

The real business of education is to maximize an individual's adaptability, and all of the divisions that have been made within *that* field do not alter *this* fact. Separate subject areas can only be justified if they enable the student to interact with the world in an appropriate manner. Within subject areas, educational levels differ in the sense that they prepare individuals who are at different levels of adaptation.

When viewed in this way, psychology is obviously a part of education. Indeed, it would be presumptuous to suppose that one could systematically affect the adaptability of an individual without knowing something about the nature of adaptation. And although psychology is young and relatively unsure about many questions, it has much that can be valuable for teachers.

Educational Psychology

Education attempts to maximize human adaptability; psychology deals with the nature of human adaptation; educational psychology applies what is known, or more often, suspected, about human adaptation to the actual practice of enhancing adaptability in individuals. It is, at the simplest level, nothing more than the union of these two areas. Consequently, the psychology useful to an educator is no different from that which might interest a *pure* psychologist (pure may not be the best word)—only the implications are different—and even then, the two will overlap.

Educational psychology has to do primarily with the learning processes. Therefore those aspects of psychology most relevant for education include learning theory, motivation theory, and developmental theory. Such topics as **social learning**, **creativity**, and **intelligence** are also of direct concern and are included in this text, as are **instructional strategies**, **discipline**, and **assessment**.

Learning Theory

Learning theory is a subdivision of general psychological theory. It deals with the question of how **behavior** changes. Indeed, **learning** can be defined as *changes in behavior resulting from experience*. This is why the expressions *learning theory* and *behavior theory* are nearly synonymous.

Behavior theorists are concerned with the explanation, prediction, and control of behavior. Consequently they must assume that behavior is subject to certain rules; that it is affected in predictable ways by experience; that it is not subject to erratic, random forces; that it is, at least to some degree, lawful.

The history of learning theory shows a progression from simple (rather mechanistic) interpretations of human learning to increasingly complex ones. The contemporary divisions within learning theory reflect, among other things, different degrees of complexity in near-chronological order. These divisions, **behaviorism** and **cognitivism,** though often misleading because they tend to restrict interpretations of theories, are nevertheless useful in classifying and organizing positions. The terms as employed in this text, and in most other educational psychology texts, are used to indicate divisions in learning theory that advance different descriptions of human functioning. A third classification, **humanism,** presents a view complementary to the first two approaches.

      Behaviorism The term *behaviorism* denotes those theories that are concerned with the observables of behavior—that is, with the visible aspects of behavior: **stimuli** (that which leads to behavior) and **responses** (the behavior itself). The term was coined by J. B. Watson (1913) in his article "Psychology as the Behaviorist Views It."

      The behavioristic movement in psychology was a reaction against the introspective approach of earlier psychologists like James and Titchener, who had been concerned primarily with feeling and **emotions. (Introspection** is a method of psychological investigation which consists of examining one's own thoughts and emotions and generalizing from them.) What is true of most reactions was also true of behaviorism—the movement in its most rigid interpretation became obsessed with observables to the extent that such words as *emotion* were not only avoided but were redefined in terms of observable, or at least potentially observable, responses. Watson, for example, defined feelings as movement of the muscles of the **gut**—thinking as movements of the muscles of the **throat.**

      Behaviorism, because it is almost exclusively preoccupied with objective things and avoids any speculation about what occurs between stimuli and responses, can explain learning and behavior only in terms of rules that govern the relationships between observed physical events. These rules are largely the result of conclusions derived from studies of animal and human **conditioning**—a subject that receives more attention in the second and third chapters.

      Cognitivism Cognitivism refers to the work of those psychologists who have abandoned much of the earlier concern with external, observable behavioral components. They have, instead, become increasingly preoccupied with the organization of knowledge, information processing, and **decision-making** behavior. Currently evolving cognitive positions include those of Bruner and Ausubel.

Instructional Theory

      Instructional theory, as opposed to learning theory, is concerned not so much with the question of how people learn as with the application of what is known about learning to the process of teaching. While there are no formalized theories of **instruction** as there are theories of learning, a set of instructional strategies can be derived from each learning position. These can be seen as comprising, in a loose sense, a theory of instruction.

Humanism The term *humanism* is employed in psychology to describe an orientation that is primarily concerned with the *humanity* of people—with those characteristics of a person that are assumed to make us most *human*. Humanists deal largely with the affective (emotional) aspects of human behavior. They are interested in explaining our relationship to the world and to other people and in learning how an individual *feels* about things. The theory of Carl Rogers is one example of a humanistic position.

Developmental Theory

Learning theory was described as being concerned with the process underlying changes in behavior. Developmental theory deals with essentially the same questions, but emphasizes *sequential* change. In other words, while learning theory attempts to describe broad characteristics of human behavior, developmental theory describes and compares learning processes at different age levels.

Motivational Theory

Motivational theories deal with the question of *why* we behave. They attempt to identify the particular conditions that instigate behavior and that direct it. Chapter 13 outlines some historical as well as some contemporary approaches to this problem.

Teaching Teaching is often described as both an art and a science. Inevitably, a **textbook** such as this is compelled to deal with the science rather than the art. But where science fails, art should be employed; perhaps even where science is adequate, a measure of art will not be harmful. In treating the science of teaching, there is also a tendency to dehumanize the child, the teacher, and the entire process of interaction between the two. This comes of trying to apply theory in a relatively controlled manner. While working through this text, therefore, the reader would be well advised to stop occasionally and remember that an **organism** is a real live student, a technique is infinitely more complex in practice than it appears in theory, a response is much more than a simple movement, and a stimulus is a conglomerate of sensory impressions. The entire process of teaching can nonetheless be reduced to something simple enough to be both understandable and useful. This reduction is provided in the form of a diagram (Figure 1.1). The model consists of the teacher, the student, the goals of the educative process, and instructional and evaluation procedures. The teaching process begins when the teacher decides what the specific goals for a particular lesson are and what instructional strategies are most likely to lead to these goals. The answer will depend on the student's present level in relation to the goals. The teaching process proper involves employing the chosen strategies. It terminates with evaluation designed to determine whether the goals were attained. This text is primarily intended to increase the teacher's understanding of the

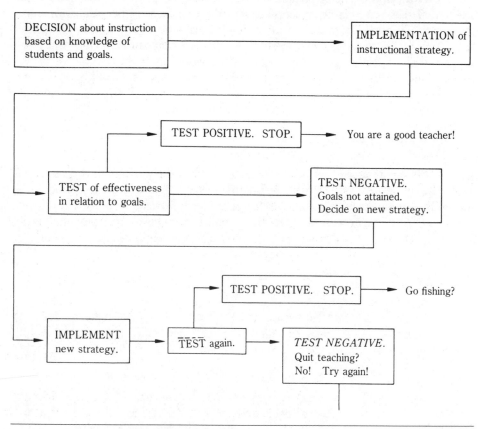

Figure 1.1 *A Teaching Flow Chart*

child. Hopefully this understanding will lead to better decisions relating to instructional strategies, classroom management, evaluation, and other aspects of the teaching-learning process.

Overview of the Text

This text deals with motivation, learning theory, development, creativity and intelligence, social learning, behavior modification, discipline, and assessment. It provides information relating to each of these topics and discusses the practical applications of that information. In some cases, where the extent and importance of the material warrant it, theory and practical applications are covered in separate chapters. The emphasis throughout is on those theoretical positions most relevant for educational practice. Obviously, however, immediate practical relevance cannot be the only criterion. Often theoretical concepts are discussed simply because they amplify other, more directly useful information. The more difficult terms and expressions in each chapter are defined in the glossary at the end of the text.

Preview of the Text

This text consists of fifteen chapters, beginning with an introduction. Interestingly, the introduction comes at the beginning; at the end is an epilogue. In between is the content—the stuff of which textbooks are made. Instead of describing that content in this preview, fourteen behaviors, situations, or problems are described. Each relates directly to the chapter whose number prefaces it. These are hors d'oeuvres, intended to stimulate the appetite for what follows. The reader is invited to return and reread them once he or she has finished the text.

Chapter 2 Early
Explanations of Learning

A dedicated educational psychologist has asked for a volunteer in order to demonstrate a psychological phenomenon. He has placed this humble request with 374 undergraduate students, 373 of whom are going to be observing the demonstration. After several awkward moments, a shaking freshman is propelled to the front of the class by his "friends." The student is asked to sit down and cross his legs. The experimenter then strikes him sharply below the kneecap with a hammer (actually a harmless little rubber mallet). As he swings the mallet, he blows vigorously on a whistle. The procedure is repeated twenty-three times. The twenty-fourth trial is somewhat different. The experimenter bends over as if to strike the patella once more, but instead turns to the class, grins in embarrassed pride, and blows his whistle. The student kicks him squarely in the teeth. Why?*

Chapter 3 Operant Conditioning

In the San Diego Zoo there is a black bear who has delusions of grandeur—it thinks it is a star entertainer. Every time one of the tour conductors approaches its enclosure, it stands and pretends that it is playing a guitar—not unusual behavior in a trained bear, but how was it trained?

---

* PPC** comment: "Perhaps you should change the humor here. Students may miss the point and some instructors might find it offensive."

** A PPC is a prepublication critic—one of several educational psychologists who read the manuscript prior to publication.

Chapter 4
Programed Instruction
and Behavior Modification

An interesting thing about a **bear** is that it always stands facing the front of its tracks. Usually. Well, sometimes.

Chapter 5
Social Learning

In the spring of 1974 a van backed up to the front door of one of California's many Sambo's. The doors flew open and a young man, totally nude, dashed into the restaurant, ran down one aisle, raced up another, and charged back into the van, which immediately *streaked* away. Newspapers, starved for news, covered the incident in exciting detail. And for the next few months, *streaking* became a national pastime. Why?

Chapter 6 Higher
Mental Processes

Joe: I say that if our kids are allowed to spend their school day trying to learn for themselves, they're not going to learn very much.

Pete: You're as old-fashioned as they come, Joe. You want your kid to sit on a bench all day listening to what some teacher tells him. He's got to get involved. He's got to go after knowledge himself. That way he'll be able to use it, and he'll remember it.

Joe: Listen, Pete, most of what a kid learns in school, or anywhere for that matter—unless he's real young—most of what he learns comes from books or people. It's *given* to him. It's much more efficient and effective that way. You think I'm old-fashioned—well, I think you're a faddist.

Who is right?

Chapter 7 Instruction,
Learning, and Forgetting

Luria (a Russian psychologist) presented S (a Russian subject) with a table of fifty single-digit numbers arranged in four vertical columns of twelve digits each, and two additional digits in the thirteenth row. S looked at the table for three minutes. He then reproduced the entire thing in forty seconds; he reproduced the numbers that formed the diagonals in thirty-five seconds; he read off each of the twelve four-digit numbers in the first twelve rows in fifty seconds; in one minute and thirty seconds he converted the entire table into a single fifty-digit number and read it off. Perhaps more striking, after several months had elapsed, with no repetition in the interim, S could reproduce the entire table as easily as he had after first learning it.

Chapter 8 Humanism

An otherwise healthy, and very famous, psychologist suffers from what is referred to in high academic circles as *claustrophobia*. Whenever he finds himself confined in a small space, he perspires profusely and a small voice inside his head whines plaintively, "Mama, mama, mama. . . ." At such moments, the psychologist has a distinct impression that if he were to remain confined for very long, he would suffocate.

Is this impression *real*?

Chapter 9 Human
Development: An Overview

It is often assumed that highly athletic individuals tend to be social and intellectual morons. Indeed, the stereotype of the blundering, drooling, illiterate strongman is almost as deeply embedded in folk wisdom as is the picture of the scholar as a pointy-headed, bespectacled weakling whose coordination is so poor that he can lace his shoes only with considerable difficulty.

How valid are these stereotypes?

Chapter 10 Development:
The Theory of Jean Piaget

A four-year-old child is shown a bouquet of five daffodils and three poppies. "What are these?" he is asked. "Flowers," the child says, intelligently. "What is the name of that yellow flower?" the examiner continues. "A bluebell," the boy says, less intelligently. "Okay. Are there more bluebells than flowers, or fewer, or the same number?" the examiner queries. "More bluebells! More bluebells!" says the child.

Is he stupid?

Chapter 11
Creativity and Intelligence

Galton and Watson had a debate about Johnny West, who had a long nose. The debate started because of Stan Twolips, the milkman, who also had a well-developed **proboscis.** People would look at Johnny's nose and say, "Betcha he got it from ol' Stan." The same people would hear Johnny swear in French and say,

"Betcha he got it from his dad." Galton and Watson wondered whether heredity comes from milkmen and. . . .

Does it?

Chapter 12 Promoting
Creativity and Intelligence

Do you know Johnny West? There is one like him in almost every classroom. Johnny never did very well in school—and teachers never liked him as much as they liked Frank Twolips, who kept his diminutive proboscis mainly in his schoolwork. Johnny and Frank were good friends, but Johnny didn't pay much attention in school. He drew a lot, spent a lot of time trying to invent different ways of doing things, and experimented with substances that he could substitute for ink. It was quite messy.

How many uses can *you* think of for a brick? (Johnny thought of eighty-seven different uses in less than ten minutes.)

Chapter 13
Motivation and Teaching

A grizzled old **rat** who has not been fed for twenty-four hours is released in a large pen. In the far corner of this pen there is a dish of French Canadian pea soup with succulent chunks of salt pork floating lazily on top. The soup is hot and steaming, and its fragrance has spread throughout the pen. Even the experimenter, a bright educational psychologist, has begun to drool. This experimenter is holding a control device in his hand. It has a toggle switch on it. Wires from this device run to a complicated looking black box which is labeled **"Black Box."** Wires run from Black Box to an arm over the rat's pen and down to a tiny electrode implanted in the rat's skull. The hungry rat races toward the bowl of pea soup, but just as he is about to reach it, the experimenter flips the switch. The rat stops, smiles, and appears to forget all about the French Canadian pea soup. Why?

Chapter 14
Discipline and Morality

Frank Twolips' cousin, Elvira, was both a troublemaker and a clown in school. In Mrs. Pott's class she threw spitballs and wiggled her ears (among other things). Eventually Mrs. Pott identified five other hardened troublemakers in her class. By that time the situation had become quite desperate because most of the other students spent a lot of time watching the troublemakers and laughing at them. Eventually Elvira was transferred to another class, where all the children were well behaved. Elvira continued to clown around; children in the new class laughed at her, and she was happy. Before long, however, Elvira's new class was found to contain four previously unidentified troublemakers. Why?

> *Chapter 15 Measurement*
> *and Evaluation*

Can you answer the following, partially deleted, multiple-choice item correctly? Why?

Research has proved that identical twins
a. always have the same . . .
b. never have the same . . .
c. definitely always . . .
d. sometimes . . .

Summary of Chapter 1

This chapter has presented a discussion of humans, of psychology, and of teaching, as well as an overview and a preview of the text.

Main Points in Chapter 1

1. Evolution has equipped humans poorly for physical survival in an animalistic sense. On the other hand, our superior intelligence has allowed us to extend our adaptability by amplifying our capacities. The role of psychology is to explain our adaptation to the environment. The purpose of education is to facilitate that adaptation.

2. Educational psychology deals with human behavior as it relates to the educational process.

3. Learning theory deals primarily with attempts to explain those changes in behavior which result from experience. Commonly accepted divisions among various learning theories are based largely on the different descriptions of behavior advanced by theorists. Behaviorists are concerned with observable behavior and with the conditions leading to behavior. Cognitive psychologists are more concerned with knowing (cognition), information processing, the organization of information, and decision making than with stimuli and responses.

4. Motivational theory deals with attempts to explain the causes of behavior. Developmental theory looks at sequential learning. Instructional theory involves attempts to develop teaching-learning strategies based on psychological theory and principles.

Suggested Readings

For a provocative, though not always scientific, description of the relationship between humans and apes, the reader is referred to:

Morris, Desmond. *The Naked Ape.* New York: Dell, 1969.

The following article by Bruner is of interest not only because it traces our recent evolution but also because it compares the development of the human child to that evolution:

Bruner, J. S. The course of cognitive growth. *American Psychologist,* 1964, 19, 1– 15.

For an entertaining, provocative, highly readable, and pertinent discussion of the role of research in the behavioral sciences, the student is referred to the following:

Agnew, N. McK. and S. W. **Pyke.** *The Science Game: An Introduction to Research in the Behavioral Sciences.* Englewood Cliffs, N.J.: Prentice-Hall, 1969.

Bears are rather large, bobtailed mammals. They walk on the soles of their feet; eat flesh, roots, and other vegetable matter; and have five toes on each foot (Cameron, 1956).

Early Explanations of Learning

When I carefully consider
the curious habits of dogs
I am compelled to conclude
That man is the superior animal.
When I consider the curious habits of man
I confess, my friend, I am puzzled.
(Meditatio)

Advance Organizer My old Uncle Lawrence always stoops as he enters a house. And although it is a graceful and elegant stoop, as stoops go, there is something vaguely inappropriate about it. Innocent, as children are reputed to be, I asked my aunt why my uncle walked so strangely when he came into the house. "Oh, he learned that when he lived in the cabin," she said, dismissing the matter as too unimportant to be worthy of greater elaboration.

Older now, and certainly less innocent, I think I understand what she meant. Presumably my uncle walked as straight as you or I until he had damaged his head sufficiently on the low door frame of his cabin that he had learned to stoop. Later, his stooping behavior generalized to all other doorways.

Early explanations of learning are particularly appropriate for explaining this aspect of my uncle's behavior. Other aspects in which my aunt might have been more interested are less well explained.

September 1930. The grass stood tanned in matted clumps throughout the schoolyard, and a brisk autumn wind swept the morning air through the quiet flat. High above, a single V of Canada geese winged relentlessly southward, their lonesome cries floating softly behind them. The teacher stood on the worn steps of the one-room schoolhouse looking beyond the seared summer grass to the hills where the small patches of pine and spruce stood starkly green among the violent scarlet of wild fruit bushes and the mellow hues of the poplars. It was the first day of school in Pascal, Saskatchewan; the teacher, my father—and *his* first day of school as well.

Pascal was (I say *was* because it no longer *is*) what geography textbooks define as a hamlet: a general store, a post office served by a thrice weekly train, and a small handful of houses. Our home and the school were a generous mile from this metropolis, isolated not only from neighbors but from the world as well, hidden as it was in one of the more remote corners of northern Saskatchewan.

The schoolchildren were a varied lot, roughly a quarter of them being full-blooded Indians; another quarter, Métis; and the remaining half, French. The relative proportions changed from year to year; occasionally a family came, wide-eyed and idealistic, only to be weakened in the face of the country's harsher elements and to leave subdued after the passing of the first winter. Though my father could not have known it as he stood on the school steps that soft autumn morning, he was to stay for thirty-five years.

The children began to arrive when the sun stood several pale blue hands above the horizon. Few of the Indian and Métis families had clocks; they watched to see when the storekeeper's sons left for school, following some twenty or thirty silent paces behind them. They formed a bedraggled file that wound along the river for a half mile, finally to cross it on an old wooden bridge that led up the wagon trail to the schoolhouse where the new teacher waited.

They came and deposited their lard pail lunch boxes in a long row in one of two cloakrooms segregated by sex. Then they found empty desks and sat timidly awaiting the voice of this new teacher, whom they were to call *Stomahghee,* meaning in Cree nothing more complicated than "teacher."

My dad, the new Stomahghee, walked to the front of the class, for that is the place reserved for those who teach. He turned and faced his new charges—forty of them, all shapes and sizes, both sexes, and a great variety of talent, ambition, and previous learning.

What do you say to a new class? What do you do? How do you overcome the first moment of dizzying panic? How do you teach them? And when you have done what you think amounts to teaching, what evidence will there be that they have learned?

Learning

I have an English setter who, in the course of her years with me, has learned a wide variety of behaviors. She has learned to range between fifteen and thirty-five yards when hunting (I never hit anything beyond thirty-five yards—and seldom anything closer than that); she has learned to open a swinging trap door into the garage, to duck as she does by this door, and to jump once she gets through so that the returning door won't hit her where she sits; she has learned to bark at cats and chase them, but to creep up silently on birds and "point" them; she has learned to shake-a-paw, to sit, to lie down, to "speak," and to fetch; and she has learned to recognize all of her people.

What evidence is there that the dog has learned all of these things? The question is only superficially trivial because the answer to it will at least implicitly define both learning and, in part, behaviorism. It appears that the dog has learned because her behavior has changed—and this is the measure of learning in people as well. It is also evident that, at least for parts of the responses described above, changes in the dog's behavior have resulted from experience rather than simply from neurological and physical growth. Behavior changes which are due to experience rather than to maturation are what define learning.

A less global but essentially identical definition of learning is provided by Gagné (1970):

> *A learning event, then, takes place when the* stimulus situation *affects the learner in such a way that his or her* performance *changes from a time* before *being in that situation to a time* after *being in it. The* change in performance *is what leads to the conclusion that learning has occurred.*

Put quite simply, this means that all changes in performance that are brought about by the environment may properly be referred to as learning. This interpretation is essentially identical to that given in Chapter 1, where learning was defined as a *modification in behavior due to experience.*

It is possible, and sometimes useful, to make further distinctions among various kinds of learning. For example, learning that involves muscular coordination and physical skills (**motor learning**) appears to be different from learning involving emotions (**affective learning**) or that involving information or ideas (**cognitive learning**). These three learning distinctions are based upon fairly obvious differences among the reponses involved (Perkins, 1969). Learning may also be classified by reference to the *conditions* which lead to it. This last approach is probably more useful and somewhat simpler to understand. It is the one adopted by Gagné (1965, 1970)—an approach which is presented in this text as an integration of a number of distinct theoretical positions.

The classification of types of learning in terms of the conditions which cause changes in behavior, rather than in terms of external differences among responses, leads one to consider theories of learning in an almost chronological order. This is largely because earlier explanations of human learning tend to be more appropriate for simple types of behavior changes, whereas more recent theories are generally concerned with more complex learning.

The following chapters deal specifically with selected, educationally relevant theories of learning representing the major divisions among learning theories: *behaviorism* and *cognitivism*. Some of their implications are discussed in Chapters 2 through 6. In addition, a more detailed examination of the relationship between learning theories and instructional procedures is presented in Chapter 7. This is followed by a description of an alternative interpretation of behavior, humanism, in Chapter 8.

Behaviorism and Cognitivism

In Chapter 1 distinctions are drawn between two major groups of learning theories: behaviorism and cognitivism. These distinctions center mainly around the preoccupations of the theorists who describe themselves as belonging to each group. *Behaviorism*, for example, includes those theoretical positions which are concerned chiefly with the observable and measurable aspects of human behavior, *stimuli* and *responses*, and with discovering the rules that govern the formation of relationships among these observable components of behavior. *Cognitivism* denotes a preoccupation with such topics as memory, attention, decision making, information processing, and understanding, and a characteristic lack of concern for stimulus-response events per se. These major distinctions, together with the names of some theorists representative of each, are shown in Figure 2.1.

It should be made clear at the outset that there are many different ways of organizing theories of learning. Although this one facilitates the interpretation and understanding of theories, it also tends to oversimplify them. It does so by hiding the differences among positions classified within the same division and by hiding similarities among positions classified in different divisions. It must be kept in mind that, while these terms are convenient descriptive labels indicating different orientations and preoccupations, they are simply that—*labels*. And it is largely true that few theories belong solely in a single division.

The remainder of this chapter presents brief descriptions of three related theories of learning—those advanced by Watson, Guthrie, and Thorndike. Chapter 3

	Symbolic Representation	Variables of Concern	Some Representative Theorists
Behaviorism	S-R	Stimuli Responses Reinforcement	Watson Thorndike Guthrie Skinner
Cognitivism	O	Decision Making Understanding Cognitive Structure Perception Information Processes	Ausubel Bruner Piaget

Figure 2.1 *Theories of Learning*

deals with Skinner's theory of **operant conditioning.** Some implications of this theory are presented in Chapter 4. Chapter 6 discusses two currently evolving cognitive positions—Bruner's and Ausubel's. Chapter 7 examines the educational implications of the theories of Bruner and Ausubel, and Chapter 8 describes Carl Rogers' approach.

Classical Conditioning

If a young human infant is repeatedly tossed high in the air by a sadistic psychologist and allowed to become extremely frightened in the process, the infant may well develop a pronounced fear of that psychologist—and give evidence of that fear by whimpering, screaming, or attempting desperately to crawl away when the psychologist approaches. If, to further complicate the matter, the psychologist yells "Yahoo" every time the child is hurled upwards, the infant may soon react with considerable fear when anyone yells "Yahoo!" This is an easy demonstration to perform, requiring little or no advance preparation, no special equipment, and only a small research grant—and it is a satisfying demonstration, since it illustrates what is generally recognized as one of the simplest forms of animal and human learning. It is an example of **classical conditioning.** The qualifier *classical* is employed simply to differentiate between this specific form of learning and other learning loosely referred to as conditioning in ordinary speech.

Attention was first drawn to the phenomenon of classical conditioning by the Russian physiologist I. P. Pavlov, whose work still dominates much of Soviet psychology. This was the famous Pavlov who noticed that some of the experienced dogs in his laboratory began to salivate when they were about to be fed. This observation might not have been particularly surprising except that the dogs salivated even before they could smell the food—indeed, they seemed to be salivating at the mere sight of their keeper.

This simple observation led Pavlov to his well-known experiments with dogs, buzzers, and food. These experiments involved ringing a bell or sounding a buzzer—both of which are stimuli that do not ordinarily lead to salivation—and then immediately presenting the dogs with food—a stimulus that does lead to salivation. Pavlov soon found that if the procedure were repeated frequently enough, the bell or buzzer alone began to elicit salivation. In these experiments the bell is referred to as a **conditioned stimulus** (CS); the food is an **unconditioned stimulus** (UCS); and salivation in response to the food is an **unconditioned response** (UCR), whereas salivation in response to the bell or buzzer is a **conditioned response** (CR). The model (or **paradigm**) of classical conditioning is presented in Figure 2.2.

Before Conditioning
UCS (food) → UCR (salivation)
CS (bell) → no salivation

Conditioning Procedure
UCS (food) + CS (bell) → salivation

After Conditioning
CS (bell) → salivation

Figure 2.2 *Classical Conditioning*

The relationship of this model to a definition of learning as a change in behavior is clear. The dog's initial performance when it hears the buzzer is demonstrably modified by the experiences it undergoes (i.e., repeated pairing of food and buzzer). The model's relationship to the illustration of the child and the psychologist is also clear. The fact that the psychologist is always present when the infant is airborne serves as a conditioning stimulus. The word *yahoo* is also always present, and may also serve as a conditioning stimulus. The fear reaction is obviously the initial unconditioned response, whereas the sensation of being thrown into the air serves as an unconditioned stimulus.

NEOBEHAVIORISM

Requirements for brevity and clarity have made it impossible for me to deal with all, or even most, learning theories in this book. This insert is to prevent you from mistakenly arriving at the notion that there are only two broad schools of theories, the behaviorist on the one hand, and the cognitive on the other (as they are represented in Figure 2.1). There is at least one other significant group of learning theorists; they are frequently referred to as neobehaviorists. Their concerns are with stimuli and responses, which are also concerns of "pure" behaviorists; but, in addition, they attempt to deal with events that intervene between stimuli and responses—events grouped under the label mediation. Theories such as those advanced by Bandura (see Chapter 5) are largely neobehavioristic.

In more general terms, any stimulus or situation that readily leads to a response can be paired with a neutral stimulus (one that does not lead to a response) to bring about learning of the kind described above. It is important to note that this learning is typically unconscious. That is, the learner does not respond to the conditioned stimulus because he becomes aware of the relationship between it and an

---

VOULEZ-VOUS. . . ?

Most attempts to relate classical conditioning to the classroom have been limited to a discussion of various situations where negative emotional reactions, presumably acquired through classical conditioning, become generalized to various school-related situations: Peter doesn't like pencils, having sat on a pointed one at a tender age and on a tender spot. Ergo, he doesn't like school. Sam, having been frightened by a bearded individual while still an infant, has a profound, unconscious negative reaction to bearded individuals. Ergo, his teacher, a kind but bearded individual, gives rise to the expected reactions in Sam.

Classical conditioning can also account for numerous highly positive emotional reactions. Bill was one of the best students I had in a ninth grade conversational French class. Yet he was one of the poorest students in all other subjects and with all other teachers. He could learn a complicated French phrase after hearing it only once or twice, repeat it with admirable enunciation and accent, and use it appropriately with the many other phrases and isolated words that he had learned. Indeed, by the end of the year he had progressed well beyond the phrase most popular with his friends. "Voulez-vous . . . ?" He and I could converse fluently in French on an impressive range of subjects. Why?

His mother told me why in the course of one of our parent-teacher conferences. When Bill was a child, a distant uncle had lived with them for most of a year and had become an idol for young Bill. The uncle spoke French. Now, although Bill had long since forgotten his uncle, he readily admitted that the thing he wanted most in the world was to be able to speak French. He absolutely loved the language. Was classical conditioning involved?

unconditioned stimulus. Indeed, classical conditioning may be shown to occur not only regardless of the subject's "awareness" but even in relation to responses over which the subject ordinarily has no control. Consider, for example, the fact that a person can be conditioned to urinate in response to the sound of a bell if a fistula (a tube) is inserted into the bladder, air is pumped in through the fistula, and a bell is rung. After this has been repeated a number of times, the subject will urinate when the bell rings. It is unlikely that this occurs because the subject "knows" that the bell *means* that air will be blown into the bladder. Likewise there are conditioning experiments involving constriction or dilation of the blood vessels. These involuntary responses may be brought about by the application of cold or hot packs directly on the skin. A neutral stimulus such as a tone can then be paired with the application of the pack. The tone will eventually come to elicit vasoconstriction or dilation.

Among the numerous investigations of classical conditioning phenomena in humans are studies dealing with sucking behavior in infants (Kasatkin and Levikova, 1935; Marquis, 1931; Wenger, 1936), head turning and eye movements (Koch, 1965), and the eye-blink **reflex** (Brackbill and Koltsova, 1967; Janos, 1965). These studies, together with the illustrations described earlier, clearly demonstrate that classical conditioning typically involves reflexive or involuntary behavior. It is, therefore, particularly relevant in accounting for the origin of many emotional responses (see boxed insert). It is also particularly relevant to the development of such theoretical positions as that of J. B. Watson.

John B. Watson

Watson is recognized as the founder of the behavioristic movement in psychology, not only because he coined the term (Watson, 1913), but also because he developed its basic concepts in his own theorizing. He was greatly influenced by the work of Pavlov and accepted his model of classical conditioning as *the* explanation for learning (Watson, 1916). According to Watson, people are born with a limited number of reflexes—learning is simply a matter of classical conditioning involving these reflexes. Hence differences among people are solely a function of the experiences to which they are subjected—no differences exist initially. This point of view, referred to as **environmentalism,** is discussed in more detail in Chapter 11.

As the founder and chief exponent of behaviorism, Watson was at pains to reject the **"mentalism"** of his predecessors. Indeed, he intended to rid psychology of such terms as *mind, feeling,* and *sensation,* and to render it more scientific by reducing it to a study of the observable aspects of behavior. Accordingly, he defined behavior as consisting of movements (Watson, 1914), since movements are clearly observable. When faced with the problem of explaining such intangibles as "thinking" or "feeling," true to the behavioristic credo he interpreted them in terms of movements (Watson, 1924). He declared, on the one hand, that "feeling" involves movements of the muscles of the gut—a declaration not far removed from the currently popular expression "gut feeling" or "gut-level reaction." On the other hand, he asserted that since speaking involves movements of the muscles of the throat, and since thought is really only subvocal speech, thinking must likewise involve movements of the throat muscles. Since such movements are quite often visible in a sleeping person (who might, after all, be dreaming), the explanation may not be as farfetched as it seems at first glance. Indeed, a large number of psychologists have spent considerable time doing research on subvocal speech.

Watson's influence on the development of psychology in America is perhaps due less to the actual content of his theorizing than to his insistence on precision, rigor, and objectivity. The theory itself, largely because of his zeal for behaviorism and his rejection of any suggestion of mentalism, is relevant only for those simple animal and human behaviors which are explainable in terms of a model of classical conditioning. Not surprisingly, the basic elements of the theory have seldom been completely rejected by other theorists. They have simply been incorporated in larger theoretical frameworks. Watson was the first of the behaviorists—he was not to be the last. Indeed, for the first fifty years after the turn of the century, behaviorism dominated American psychology.

The immense popularity of behaviorism in early twentieth-century American psychology not only was due to the scientific spirit of the times but was related as well to the apparently just and equal view of humans implicit in this approach. If what we become is truly a function of the experiences to which we are subjected, then we are in fact born equal. As Watson declared, any child can become a doctor or a judge.

In fact, however, things are not quite that simple, as is shown in Chapter 11; not everybody can become a doctor or a judge. Nor was Watson's work all as simple as it might appear from this brief description. Although his published work dealt principally with animal research in a purely behavioristic tradition, it later became apparent that his interests went beyond classical conditioning, embracing such exotic subjects as human sexual intercourse—a subject not yet granted scientific acceptance by the work of Kinsey and Masters and Johnson. In this area, Watson was truly a pioneer. Since his wife refused to participate directly in the research, he enlisted the help of his assistant. Connected to various scientific instruments, they spent hours making love. The results of this research are interesting, though not particularly informative. Watson gathered several large boxes of detailed notes on the physiology of the human sexual response. When his wife discovered what was keeping Watson in his laboratory for so many hours, she sued him for divorce, confiscated his notes and records, and effectively ruined his career as a professor of psychology. Watson married his assistant following the divorce, but all universities refused to hire him. In the end he went on to a highly successful career with an advertising agency. Close upon Watson's heels followed Edwin Guthrie—also a champion of behaviorism, but a champion with somewhat different ideas.

Edwin Guthrie

Whereas Watson had been principally concerned with employing a model of classical conditioning to explain a wide variety of human behaviors, Guthrie was concerned with elaborating a single, simple law of learning which was also intended to explain all human and animal learning (Guthrie, 1935, 1952, 1959). Guthrie's law of learning did not make use of the Pavlovian model, although it did not reject it, but asserted instead that whenever a response follows a stimulus it will be learned. In other words, if a person has performed once in response to some stimulation, he will respond again in an identical fashion if the stimulus is repeated. This law has come to be known as the Law of One-Trial Learning—and, accordingly, Guthrie's theory is referred to as the theory of one-trial learning. A model such as Pavlov's paradigm of classical conditioning is easily accommodated by Guthrie's theory. He need simply point out that on the occasion of the first pairing of the conditioned stimulus and the conditioned response, learning has indeed occurred. Prior to this, it is clear that the response was elicited not by the conditioning stimulus, but by the unconditioned stimulus.

A second law completes Guthrie's learning theory. This law maintains that the strength of the association between the stimulus and response is unaffected by practice, but is complete on the occasion of the first pairing. All that practice does is ensure that the response will be performed under a variety of different circumstances.

Guthrie explains the formation of a link between a stimulus and a response as being what he terms "association by **contiguity**." It is because the stimulus and the response are presented in contiguity (simultaneously) that learning occurs. However, stimuli are not usually in contiguity with responses, but precede them. Guthrie circumvents this fact by inventing *movement-produced stimuli* (MPS). He contends that the presentation of a stimulus occasions the appearance of a real but miniature response, which serves as a stimulus for another response, and so on, until the final observable response is emitted. Each of these movement-produced stimuli is in temporal contiguity with the movements that both precede and follow it. Hence the initial stimulus and response are in contiguity through the mediation of the MPS.

In short, Guthrie's system defines learning as involving the formation of **habits,** where a habit is a link between a stimulus and a response. Habits are acquired through contiguity; they require only one presentation of a stimulus followed by the appropriate response, and they are as strong on the occasion of the first pairing as they will ever be. Furthermore, a habit can never be broken. That is, once an S-R bond has been established (and remember that this happens in *one trial*), it will never be rent asunder.

My students are prone to make such devastating and apt remarks as "How incredible," "Rubbish," "Pshaw," and "Go home" when I reach this point in my formal lecture on Guthrie. On occasion I have overheard some less printable remarks.

But Guthrie's system is only superficially incredible. The most obvious criticism is that people do not engage in identical behaviors repeatedly, even when they are placed in the same situations. Guthrie's answer to this is simply that the stimulus situation, which, after all, is not a simple, single stimulus, but a complex of stimuli, is really different. And it is difficult to argue with him on this point. At the same time, however, any behavior theory that can predict responses no better than this is probably of little value. A second criticism of Guthrie's system is that habits do

Habits are replaced —not broken.

appear to be broken—alcoholics sometimes stop drinking, smokers give up cigarettes, fat people stop eating, and schoolchildren eventually stop all sorts of behaviors. Guthrie's rebuttal is that these habits are never broken—they are simply replaced. He then goes on to explain three methods by which a bad habit may be replaced by a better one. Each of these methods has important practical implications for the classroom, some of which are discussed with examples in the following section. A more detailed discussion of techniques for behavior control is presented in Chapter 14.

Breaking Habits

It is important to remember at the outset that within Guthrie's system habits are not *broken,* they are *replaced.* Hence the three techniques described below are simply relatively sensible ways of replacing bad habits with more acceptable ones. Each technique is premised on the assumption that, once the desirable behavior has been elicited in response to the stimulus that initially led to the undesirable behavior, learning will have taken place. The techniques are labeled the **threshold** method, the fatigue method, and the incompatible stimuli method (Guthrie, 1935). Each can be illustrated by reference to the breaking of a horse (not literally but figuratively—Lefrancois, 1972; see Figure 2.3). In the following discussion, each is illustrated by reference to a classroom situation.

The Threshold Method This approach involves presenting the stimulus that ordinarily brings about the undesirable response, but presenting it so faintly that it does not elicit the response. Over successive presentations the intensity of the stimulus is increased, but it is always kept below *threshold*. Eventually, if the procedure is successful, the stimulus will have reached full intensity without ever eliciting the unwanted behavior. At that point, the habit may be considered to have been replaced by another *incompatible* habit—and this incompatible habit may simply be a habit of nonresponding.

Watson (1930) provides a classic example of this procedure in his report of a rather cruel experiment where he conditioned a young orphan boy, Albert, to fear a white rat by making a loud noise every time the rat was presented to the boy. Similar studies by Jones (1924), using rabbits, led to the same results. Eventually little Albert whimpered and cried as he crawled away from the animal. In some cases (Jones, 1924) fear was later extinguished by feeding the child so as to evoke responses of pleasure, while at the same time presenting the animal at the very periphery of the boy's vision. Over successive days the animal was brought closer until finally the boy could eat with hardly a tremor, even when the little beast was on his very lap.

There are numerous classroom applications of the threshold technique. For example, whenever a new subject or problem is being presented to a class—one which may prove so complex as to be frightening—it is often advisable to present it initially for only a short period of time. Exposure can then be lengthened over successive trials until the subject has lost its ability to frighten. As Lefrancois (1972) observed, this is simply a sophisticated version of grandmother's "don't-throw-him-in-the-water-let-him-get-used-to-it-slowly-damn-it" approach. *

The Fatigue Method This second technique for breaking habits involves presenting the stimulus repeatedly in order to elicit the undesirable response so often that the individual can eventually no longer respond. At that point he performs a different response—perhaps simply that of not responding. It follows from Guthrie's theory that the most recent response elicited by a stimulus will be learned. Hence, theoretically at least, the undesirable habit will have been replaced.

It is somewhat more difficult to apply the fatigue method in the classroom. Obviously, many of its potential applications are either barbaric or impractical. A student who is impertinent to a teacher can hardly be made to repeat the imperti-

---

* PPC: "I don't get this. I thought Lefrancois' grandmother was a polite old lady. Should perhaps delete the last two words, damn it."

Author: "She did use that indelicate expression just this once."

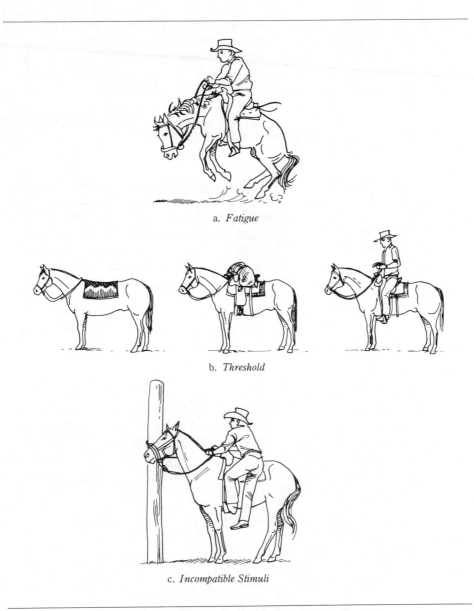

a. *Fatigue*

b. *Threshold*

c. *Incompatible Stimuli*

Figure 2.3 *Guthrie's three ways of breaking habits illustrated with reference to training a saddle horse. In (a), the horse is "broken" in the traditional sense, being allowed to buck until fatigued. In (b), the horse is "gentled" by having progressively heavier weights placed on its back, beginning with a blanket and culminating with a saddle and rider. In (c), the horse is tied down so that it cannot buck when mounted.*

nence until he is so fatigued that he is forced to cease. Nor can a student who has a habit of fighting with others be compelled to fight until thoroughly fatigued.

The fatigue technique has, however, been used extensively in the class-room in situations more closely related to learning—but in a manner that runs directly counter to sound pedagogical procedures. Not infrequently teachers will ask their less able students to stay in after school and write 200 or 500 times, "I will not throw spitballs at my teacher," or "$2 \times 2 = 4$." Although fatigue may well be in-volved in the student's behavior, the responses that are involved are precisely those which he is *NOT* to forget.

The Incompatible Stimuli Method This approach involves presenting the stimulus that would ordinarily bring about an undesirable response, but present-ing it when the individual is unable to respond. For example, a teacher who knows that a conventional presentation of a history lesson will put most of his class to sleep can quite easily present the same lesson when the class *cannot* sleep. This might be done by using a film or other audiovisual device, by acting out parts of the lesson, by presenting some interesting (and perhaps irrelevant) information, or simply by being especially brilliant, amusing, and informative. The same effect could be obtained by making loud, disharmonious noises at intervals throughout the lesson. Unfortunately, while this might keep the students awake, it would probably not serve to focus their attention in the desired direction.

Contiguity and Reinforcement

In attempting to explain the formation of relationships between stimuli, between responses, or between stimuli and responses, the early behaviorists could make one of two choices. They could maintain, as did Watson and Guthrie, that the simultaneous occurrence of stimulus or response events was sufficient to bring about learning. This reasoning is ordinarily referred to as a *contiguity* explanation. A second alternative, and one which was explicitly avoided by both Watson and Guthrie, was to explain the formation of S-R bonds by reference to the *effects* of the behavior. This second explanation, introduced by Thorndike and popularized by Skinner, is labeled a **reinforcement** approach.

The first of the reinforcement theorists, E. L. Thorndike, was also an S-R psychologist. Indeed, he is recognized at the first *experimental* S-R psychologist. Some of the more central aspects of his work are reviewed in the following section.

Edward L. Thorndike

Thorndike referred to his learning theory as a theory of **connectionism** (Thorndike, 1949). It was so called because he defined learning as involving the formation of connections or "bonds" between stimulus and response. Quite simply, learning involves *stamping in* S-R bonds whereas forgetting involves *stamping them out*. A great deal of his theorizing deals specifically with the conditions which lead to the stamping in or stamping out of bonds.

Unlike Watson and Guthrie, both of whom believed that contiguity was an accurate and sufficient explanation for learning, Thorndike maintained that it was the *effect* of a response that led to learning or its absence. Much of the experimental work that he performed with animals (Thorndike, 1911) involved giving the subject some tangible reward for performing a response and then observing what effect this had on the subject's subsequent behavior. The classical experiment involved placing a hungry cat inside a cage and dangling a succulent morsel of fish outside the cage. In order to escape from its cell and obtain the fish, the cat had to pull a looped string or perform some other mechanical feat.

From these experiments Thorndike (1913, 1932, 1933) arrived at two related conclusions about learning. These form the basis of his theory. The first was expressed in terms of a major law—the **Law of Effect.** The second was one of a number of subsidiary laws—the *Law of Multiple Responses.*

The Law of Effect states that responses that occur just prior to a satisfying state of affairs will tend to be stamped in (learned), whereas those which occur prior to an annoying state of affairs will tend to be stamped out. Put more simply, the Law of Effect says that learning is a function of the consequences of behavior rather than simply of temporal contiguity. Thorndike later modified this law by asserting that pleasure is more potent for stamping-in than pain is for stamping-out responses.

Thorndike, as was pointed out earlier, contends that the effect of a response is to strengthen or weaken the connection between it and the stimulus that preceded it. Skinner provides an alternative to this explanation of the effects of reinforcement on behavior: he maintains that the bond is formed between reward and response rather than between stimulus and response. Bitterman (1960, 1969), in reviewing the controversy that has surrounded the Law of Effect, has observed that although the Skinnerian view is more widely accepted, the Thorndikean conception may nevertheless be valid. Indeed, Thorndike's introduction of the Law of Effect in American learning theory is considered one of his major contributions. A second significant contribution, but one that is less relevant here, has to do with his theory of animal and human intelligence (Thorndike, 1898, 1911)—a theory which held that the difference between animal and human intelligence was not based on our unique ability to reason, but rather on our greater ability to form connections between stimuli and responses. In other words, intelligence is primarily a matter of forming associations.

One of the essential differences between Watson's model for learning and Thorndike's is that Watson was concerned primarily with explaining the formation of relationships between stimuli, whereas Thorndike's learning paradigm (*paradigm* is an elegant scientific synonym for "model") deals with the formation of bonds between stimuli *and responses*. In symbolic terms Watson's model is of the S-S variety; Thorndike's is an S-R model.

The Laws of Learning

In order to explain behavior and learning in a more general sense, Thorndike postulated and described three major laws and five additional subsidiary laws. The Law of Effect, already described, is the most important of the major laws.

The Law of Exercise

A second law, the **Law of Exercise,** is based on the notion that the repetition of a stimulus-response connection strengthens it. In short, while practice may not make perfect, it will do much to ensure that what is learned will not be forgotten. It is hardly surprising that the Thorndikean era in education was marked by drill and repetition. These ancient pedagogical techniques had now been granted theoretical respectability.

A third major law, the **Law of Readiness,** recognized that certain responses were more or less likely than others to be learned (stamped in), depending on the learner's readiness. Such factors as maturation and previous learning are clearly involved in determining whether learning is easy, difficult, or impossible. Thorndike considered this third law less important than the other two major laws. Consequently, he provides little information with respect to readiness that is of immediate value to teachers. Current knowledge of children's intellectual and emotional development is of greater relevance, and is discussed in Chapters 9 and 10.

Thorndike's five subsidiary laws are described briefly below.

Multiple Response The Law of Multiple Response is a statement of Thorndike's observation that, when faced with a difficult problem for which they have no ready solution, individuals will engage in a variety of different responses until one produces a satisfying effect. In other words, it is through **trial-and-error** that problems are solved. It was as a result of this law that Thorndike's theory came to be known as the theory of *Trial-and-Error Learning.* As is pointed out later, considerable opposition to this point of view came from the early cognitive psychologists.

Set or Attitude The second of the subsidiary laws is a statement of the fact that people often respond to novel situations in terms of the "**sets**" or "attitudes" that they bring with them. This is not unlike saying that students can be taught to learn as though various aspects of the subject were related, and that they will then proceed to react to new material as though it related to previously learned information. By the same token a student can be given a set to proceed as though the best way of learning were through rote memorization.

This law also implies that cultural background and immediate environment not only affect how a person responds, but are also instrumental in determining what will be satisfying or annoying. For example, it is **culture** that has determined that academic success will be satisfying—even as it is the immediate environment that sometimes determines that popularity will be more satisfying than academic success.

Prepotency of Elements It is interesting to note that in this third subsidiary law, Thorndike anticipated a great deal of current research. Essentially, he was saying that people respond to the most significant or the most striking aspects of a stimulus situation and not necessarily to the entire stimulus complex. Obviously, students cannot, and probably *should* not, respond to all of the sights and sounds that impinge upon them at any given moment. The problem is one of **selective attention,** a problem that is currently receiving considerable study (Zeaman and House, 1963; Cherry, 1953; Cherry and Taylor, 1954; Norman, 1969).

Response by Analogy Thorndike's theory of **transfer** is implicit in this fourth law. Transference involves emitting a previously learned response in the face of a new stimulus (sometimes referred to as stimulus **generalization**). Thorndike believed that the transference of a response to a new stimulus was a function of the similarity between the two stimuli. More specifically, he claimed that stimuli could be conceived of as being composed of elements and that similar stimulus situations had a number of identical elements. The greater the number of such elements, the more likely the individual would be to "respond by analogy." This explanation later came to be known as Thorndike's theory of *Identical Elements.*

Associative Shifting Hilgard and Bower (1966) describe the last of the five subsidiary principles as being closely related to classical conditioning (**stimulus substitution**). In this connection, Thorndike described some procedures for training animals to respond in familiar ways to new stimuli—procedures, in other words, for "shifting" responses from one stimulus to another. It is possible, for example, to train a dog to stand in response to the command "stand" simply by holding food above the dog so that it is compelled to make use of its two hind legs. As it stands, the trainer says, "Stand." Over successive trials, the amount of food is decreased until the dog stands when the hand alone is held out. Eventually, unless it is quite unintelligent, the dog will stand in response to the verbal command if it has been repeated throughout.

Summary and Comparison of Watson, Guthrie, and Thorndike

The pioneering contributions of these three early behavioral psychologists are difficult to assess since their long-range influence on the development of psychology is still being felt. Watson and Guthrie's insistence on objectivity and rigor is probably their outstanding contribution. These criteria are still a measure of the worth of psychological investigations. In addition, they were responsible for elaborating a model of learning that is sufficient to explain at least some simple animal and human behaviors.

Thorndike's contribution is perhaps more widely accepted. He is generally credited with introducing the idea that reinforcement is an important variable in human and animal learning—an idea that, as is made clear in the next chapter, has profoundly influenced the development of psychology.

Admittedly, the present treatment of these three theoretical positions is brief and highly simplified. Only the most salient features of each theory have been discussed. It is possible, nevertheless, to derive a set of *general* educational implications from this chapter. It should be kept clearly in mind, however, that these are extremely general principles, that they are merely suggestions, that they are not always compatible with all three theories, that they are only *some* of many possible implications, and that they could, in many instances, have been derived from theoretical positions discussed later in this text. In addition, a number of suggestions presented in Chapter 7 relate to the theoretical content of the present chapter.

Some Instructional Implications of S-R Theory

"To satisfy the practical demands of education, theories of learning must be 'stood on their heads' so as to yield theories of teaching" (Gage, 1964, p. 269). Presumably the same result would be obtained if students were asked to stand on their heads while the theories remained upright. Unfortunately, however, even as extreme a measure as standing the theories of Watson, Guthrie, and Thorndike on their heads would be unlikely to yield *theories* of teaching. On the other hand, they need be tilted only very slightly in order to produce a variety of *principles* which may be of practical value. Hilgard and Bower (1966) describe a number of these principles (adopted from Hilgard, 1960) which relate directly to a simple S-R theoretical framework. Several are discussed below.

1. The learner should be an active rather than a passive listener or viewer. (Hilgard and Bower, 1966, p. 562)

It should be emphasized that, while *activity* need not involve overt behavior, it is nevertheless true that S-R formulations emphasize the learner's responses. Therefore the point of this principle is that the student should be required to make responses whenever possible.

2. Frequency of repetition is important. (Hilgard and Bower, 1956, p. 561)

Since the formation of bonds is a function of the number of paired presentations of stimuli and responses, repetition should lead to better learning. Even within the context of a theory of one-trial learning (Guthrie) the effect of repetition is beneficial. It leads to the learning of the same response in a variety of stimulus situations, making the response more available and less likely to be replaced. Repetition, from a reinforcement point of view (Thorndike), can be interpreted as providing more opportunity for reinforcement to occur. In addition Thorndike originally believed that bonds were "stamped in" through exercise, although he later conceded that practice was less important than reinforcement.

3. Reinforcement is important. (Hilgard and Bower, 1966, p. 563)

Despite the fact that neither Watson nor Guthrie was particularly concerned with the effects of reinforcement on learning, the notion expressed in this principle is not incompatible with their views. In the first place, reinforcement can be interpreted (within Guthrie's system) as preventing the unlearning of a response. This is accomplished by changing the stimulus situation so that the organism is prevented from making another response to the first stimulus. In the second place, Watson's explanation for learning is not really contradicted by a reinforcement principle. Watson merely describes a "simpler" type of learning. Obviously, Thorndike's theory is in complete agreement with this principle.

A number of additional suggestions for educational practice can be derived directly from each of these three positions. For example, the three suggestions advanced by Guthrie for breaking habits can be applied both to classroom learning and to **discipline** problems. (This is discussed and illustrated in Chapter 14.) Watson's emphasis on the pairing of stimuli suggests a particular type of arrangement of cues for learning. This arrangement would present stimuli in such a way as to pair the desired response repeatedly with the appropriate stimulus. Thorndike's specific consideration of pedagogical problems also contains suggestions for a number of classroom procedures, among which are the following:

1. Punishment is not very effective in eliminating behavior. (Thorndike, 1932)

2. Interest in work and in improvement is conducive to learning. (Thorndike, 1935)

3. Significance of subject matter and the attitude of the learner are important variables in school. (Thorndike, 1935)

4. Repetition without reinforcement does not enhance learning. (Thorndike, 1931)

5. Intelligence tests can be of value in elementary school, although educators should be aware of their weaknesses. (Thorndike, 1927)

Comment on
Educational Implications

The suggestions and principles described above are intended simply to illustrate practical implications that are based directly on theory. The reader is cautioned against either accepting or rejecting these implications before examining the more detailed and inclusive theories of learning that are presented in later chapters.

Summary of Chapter 2

This chapter has presented a description of two major divisions among learning theories: behaviorism and cognitivism. Summaries of three behavioristic theories, those of Watson, Guthrie, and Thorndike, were also presented. In addition, some of the instructional implications of these theories were suggested or illustrated.

Main Points in Chapter 2

1. Learning may be defined as a change in behavior that results from experience.

2. Types of learning may be distinguished in terms of the differences that exist among the behaviors involved (affective, motor, or cognitive) or in terms of the conditions that lead to the learning.

3. The major classification system employed for theories of learning in this text ranks them in terms of their preoccupation with purely objective S-R events (behaviorism) or their concern with cognitive structure and related topics (cognitivism).

4. Pavlov suggested the first model of classical conditioning. He stated that, after repeatedly being paired with an effective stimulus, a previously neutral stimulus will come to elicit a response similar to that caused by the effective stimulus.

5. Watson's behaviorism is based on the notion that learning is a function of the classical conditioning of simple reflexes, sometimes in long complex chains, as in the case of language.

6. Watson may be thought of as the champion of the conditioned reflex and of environmentalism—the notion that individual differences are attributable to experiences rather than to genetics.

7. Guthrie's theory is described as a theory of one-trial learning based on association through contiguity.

8. Guthrie believed that habits could never be broken, but that they could be replaced in one of three ways (he also mentioned a fourth technique, but it is of less practical relevance). These he labeled the threshold method, the fatigue method, and the incompatible stimuli method.

9. E. L. Thorndike introduced the notion of reinforcement in learning theory through the Law of Effect—a law which asserted that responses which are followed by satisfaction tend to become linked to the stimuli that occasioned them. Two other important principles were the Laws of Exercise and of Readiness which highlighted the importance of repetition (drill) and of the learner's capabilities.

10. According to Thorndike, learning involves *stamping in* S-R bonds; forgetting involves *stamping out* bonds. Choice of a response is affected by previous reinforcement but in the absence of previous learning will take the form of trial-and-error. Choice of responses attempted may be affected by set, identical elements in stimulus situations, classical conditioning, or prepotent elements.

11. Among the instructional implications that may be derived from S-R positions are suggestions relating to the value of repetition, reinforcement, and activity.

Suggested Readings

Among the many attempts to apply learning theories to educational practice, the following two have been selected as the most representative and the most practical. Skinner's book is a collection of his papers, some of which are more relevant to other chapters than to this one, but all of which are concerned with teaching. Bigge's book is a description of some selected theories of learning and an attempt to relate these to teaching. The reader is referred to the first four chapters of Bigge's book for an explanation of learning theories which are covered in this chapter, and to the last chapter for an application of these theories to teaching.

Skinner, B. F. *The Technology of Teaching.* New York: Appleton-Century-Crofts, 1968.

Bigge, M. L. *Learning Theories for Teachers.* New York: Harper & Row, Publishers, 1964.

Lefrancois provides a clear and understandable explanation of early theories of learning in:

Lefrancois, G. R. *Psychological Theories and Human Learning: Kongor's Report.* Monterey, Calif: Brooks/Cole, 1972.

Hall and Kelson (1959) list exactly 130 subspecies and types of bears, ranging, alphabetically, from Ursus absarokus, *found in 1914 at the head of the Little Bighorn River in Montana, to* Ursus yesoensis.

Operant Conditioning

All the world's a stage
And all the men and women merely players
(Shakespeare)

Can you speak your own lines, determine your own actions, feel your own feelings? Or is your freedom no more than an illusion— even less perhaps, for we sometimes know what illusions are made of?

Are you free, O noble one? And if not, then are you not blameless? And who, or what, is to blame?

Advance Organizer *Chapter 2 described changes in behavior that are brought about as a result of the simultaneous or near-simultaneous presentation of stimuli or of stimuli and responses. As was noted there, these explanations are sometimes useful for understanding the origins of emotional reactions and also explain why repetition and practice might be important for learning certain tasks. Chapter 3 now moves to an examination of the importance of the consequences of behavior. It might seem obvious that whether our behaviors result in pleasant or unpleasant outcomes will be important in determining whether we do the same thing again or whether we modify our behaviors. What is not so obvious, but of considerable importance for teachers, is precisely how reinforcement or the lack thereof can be employed to bring about and maintain desirable behaviors. But is it ethical to control a person's behavior through the manipulation of behavioral outcomes? The chapter addresses this question as well.*

Rattus Norvegicus

The hero of early twentieth-century psychology was without doubt the white Norway rat. He was elevated to this position largely through the work of

---

RATTUS INTELLECTUOSUS

The intellectual capacities of *Rattus norvegicus* are of considerable importance to the psychologist-cum-rodentologist. Due to difficulties in measurement, the rat's I.Q. has not been firmly established, but he is known to be capable of learning some relatively simple tasks, such as bar-pressing or how to run through a variety of mazes. And observation of his behavior in the wilds has led me to conclude that, though he may not be a genius when compared to a dog or a monkey, he is capable of some rather remarkable achievements.

When I was a boy, living in a remote area of northern Canada, the existence of rats and the necessity of waging constant war against them was a fact of life. It happened, in the fall of 1954, that my father did battle with one of the most destructive and clever rats ever to take up residence in the cellar of our home. The fall of 1954 heralded a long and difficult winter, and rats, like other creatures of the wilds, seemed to foresee the hard times ahead. They moved into people's houses in droves. Among those that moved into our home was a huge brown Norway rat—reportedly a foot and a half long. He was a powerful rat as rats go—and he was the one my father vowed he would catch. Traps were set in all strategic locations. They were baited with cheese, with bread, with raisins and coconut, and even with a little piece of moosemeat. Every night all traps would be sprung. Occasionally one of the younger, less experienced rats would get caught. Every night two or three dozen large potatoes would be carried up a three-foot, smooth cement wall and carted away into the inaccessible regions behind the chimney. Several carrots and an occasional turnip also fell prey to the rats.

Eventually, by dint of sheer persistence, all rats were captured or frightened away except the large one. Potatoes, carrots, and turnips continued to disappear at an alarming rate. My father in desperation purchased a tube of "rat-nip," a poison guaranteed to be extremely attractive to rats and also guaranteed to be sufficient to kill at least a hundred of them. The whole tube of poison was smeared on one potato; it disappeared the very first night and all signs of the big rat also disappeared. Later, mounds of neatly stacked potatoes and carrots were found behind the chimney. All the carrots were carefully laid side by side, the large ends exactly even, and every last one pointed in the same direction. Next to the carrots were twelve unbroken eggs laid in a perfectly straight line.

Skinner—a position which he has begun to relinquish only very recently (and reluctantly) to the human child.

The rat has many advantages as a psychological subject: He is easy to care for and inexpensive to acquire and to feed; he reproduces easily and rapidly in captivity; his experiences can be carefully controlled; he can be rewarded easily and effectively with food; and he is capable of learning such simple, easily observed and measured responses as bar-pressing or running mazes. In addition, even the most devout humanitarian is unlikely to be too upset if procedures unpleasant to the rat are employed without the rat's consent.

The Skinner Box

A **Skinner box** is a small enclosed environment in which an animal such as a rat or a pigeon is placed (see Figure 3.1). From the layman's point of view, it looks like a cage equipped with some relatively sophisticated gadgetry; the psychologist knows that it is not simply a cage—it is an *enclosed environment*. The Skinner box is so constructed as to make it highly probable that the animal inside will perform those responses which the experimenter desires. It is also constructed in such a way that the animal's responses may be measured. In addition, and probably more important, the Skinner box allows the experimenter to determine the effects of **rewards** or punishment on the animal's responses.

A typical Skinner box contains a lever (bar), a food tray, and a food-releasing mechanism. Occasionally a light is placed near the lever, and an electric grid runs through the floor.

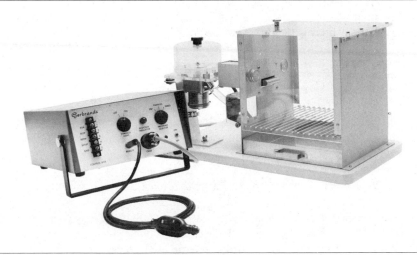

Figure 3.1 *A Skinner box (Courtesy of Ralph Gerbrands Company, Inc., Arlington, Massachusetts)*

By observing the behavior of an animal placed in the Skinner box, one can arrive at a fairly thorough understanding of the **variables** that concerned Skinner, as well as of the learning model which he developed.

Consider, for example, the case of a normal white rat who is placed in the cage. Eventually, in the course of exploring her environment in the manner of any curious rat, she accidentally depresses the lever—and as she does so she hears a click. The experimenter has flicked a switch and a food pellet has been released into the tray. At the same time, the light flashes briefly. The rat scurries over to the tray and quickly devours the pellet. She then returns to her exploration of the cage—and eventually she depresses the lever again, and again she is given a food pellet and the light goes on. After a short while the rat may be seen constantly depressing the lever and running to the food tray. She thinks she has discovered a short-circuited "one armed bandit."

After a time the game changes. The experimenter stops providing food after the rat depresses the lever, but the light continues to go on—and the rat's behavior does not change appreciably. She continues to depress the lever.

Again the game changes—neither food nor light now results from the rat's frantic manipulation of the lever. After a very short while the rat leaves the lever.

Consider a second rat who, like the first, has learned to depress the lever to obtain food, but who doesn't receive a food pellet every time he performs this demanding feat. Sometimes he is rewarded, but sometimes depressing the lever has no effect. Yet he continues to depress the lever rapidly, stopping only to eat the pellet when he hears the telltale click of the food-releasing mechanism. Again, however, the experimenter suddenly stops providing the rat with food pellets. The game is finished, but the rat doesn't know it. He continues to depress the lever tirelessly for several hours. He then goes to sleep, but upon awakening he runs directly to the bar and presses it furiously, smiling as he does so.

Rats and Skinner's Theory

The elements of Skinner's system may be derived from the foregoing examples. The variables involved are the behavior of the animal (his responses) and the behavior of the experimenter, which, as it relates to the Skinner box, involves simply presenting a reward or withholding it. And these two classes of variables, responses and rewards, and the relationships that exist between them form the basis of Skinner's system.

It should be made clear at the outset that Skinner's system is explicitly nontheoretical (Skinner, 1961). In order words, he does not specifically attempt to explain the phenomena that he observes, but simply to organize his observations in ways that will be of practical value.

Respondent and Operant Behavior

To begin with, Skinner accepts the existence of classical conditioning. He claims that there are obviously many responses that not only can be readily **elicited** by a stimulus but also can become conditioned to other stimuli in the manner described by Pavlov or Watson. This type of response he labels **respondent** behavior, since it occurs in *response* to a stimulus.

A second much larger and much more important class of behaviors, however, are those which are not elicited by any known stimuli, but which are simply **emitted** by the organism. These are labeled **operants** since, in a sense, they are operations performed by the organism. Another way of making this distinction is to say that in the case of respondent behavior the organism is reacting to the environment, whereas in the case of operant behavior the organism acts upon the environ-

Classical	Operant
Deals with *respondents,* which are *elicited* by *stimuli*	Deals with *operants,* which are *emitted* as *instrumental* acts
Type S (stimuli) Pavlov	*Type R* (reinforcement) Skinner

Figure 3.2 *Classical and Operant Conditioning*

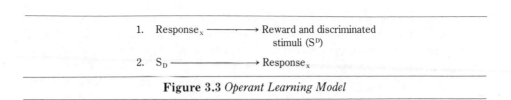

Figure 3.3 *Operant Learning Model*

ment. Skinner further distinguishes between the two by referring to respondent learning as classical or **Type S conditioning** and to operant learning as operant or **Type R conditioning** (see Figure 3.2).

Operant conditioning, since it does not involve stimuli, is somewhat different from Thorndike's conception of learning and the Law of Effect. Whereas Thorndike believed that the effect of reinforcement is to strengthen the bond that exists between the stimulus and the response, Skinner declared that not only is the stimulus usually unknown but, in any case, it is irrelevant to the learning. The link is formed between response and reinforcement rather than between stimulus and response. Essentially, all that happens in operant learning is that when an emitted response is reinforced, the probability increases that it will be repeated. Referring to the rats in their Skinner boxes, the bar-pressing behavior serves as an operant, whereas the food is a reinforcer (see Figure 3.3 for a model of operant learning). Skinner's model of operant conditioning states further that the reward, together with whatever **discriminated stimuli*** were present at the time of reinforcement, are stimuli that, after learning, may serve to bring about the operant. For example, aspects of the sight of the Skinner box from the inside may eventually serve as a stimulus for bar-pressing behavior.

Generalization and Discrimination

Two of the most important phenomena in operant learning are **generalization** and **discrimination**. Not all situations for which a specific operant are appropriate (or inappropriate) will be encountered by an individual while learning. Yet individuals do respond when faced with new situations. The behavioristic theorist explains this by reference to generalization or discrimination. Generalization simply involves making a response that would ordinarily be made under other *similar* circumstances. Discrimination involves refraining from making the response in question because of some significant difference between this situation and other situations for which the response was clearly more appropriate. For example, children may learn very early in life that they will receive their mother's attention if they cry. This type

---

* Also referred to as "discriminative" stimuli. Essentially means those aspects of a situation (stimuli) that differentiate it from other situations.

of behavior is soon generalized from specific situations where they have obtained their mother's attention to new situations where they desire her attention. A wise mother can bring about discrimination learning quite simply by not paying attention to her child in those situations where she does not want to be disturbed. While on the phone, she might completely ignore her child's supplications for attention; soon the child will learn to discriminate between that situation where attention-getting behavior is not reinforced and other situations where it is more likely to be reinforced.

The Prevalence of Operant Behavior

Skinner (1953, 1957) contends that most significant human behaviors fall under the general heading of operant behaviors. This means that there are relatively few readily observable stimuli that lead to human behavior. It also means that reinforcement or its absence will have a great deal to do with the behavior in which an individual engages. Such common activities as writing a letter, telling an anecdote, and lying on a beach may all be considered operants—and as such they are all responses that are, at least to some degree, under the control of their effects.

One can hardly overestimate the relevance for teaching of an understanding of the principles of operant learning. Indeed, a classroom is in many ways like a gigantic Skinner box. It is so engineered that certain responses are more probable than others. For example, it is easier to sit at a desk than to lie in one—and it is easier to remain awake when sitting than when lying. And at the front of a million classrooms stand the powerful dispensers of reinforcement—the teachers. They smile or frown; they say "good" or "not good"; they give high grades or low grades; occasionally they grant special favors, and at other times they withhold or cancel privileges. By means of this reinforcement and punishment, they are **shaping** the behavior of their students.

Drawing an analogy between a classroom, a teacher, and a student on the one hand and a Skinner box, a psychologist, and a rat on the other is somewhat unappealing and perhaps not a little frightening (shades of 1984). Yet the analogy is relevant and potentially useful. Indeed, classroom teachers could often profit immensely from the discoveries of experimental psychologists.

Principles of Operant Conditioning

Skinner's primary preoccupation has been with discovering the relationships that exist between reinforcement and behavior. Most of his research, particularly with animals, has been geared to this end. In addition, he has attempted to point out how one can generalize from the simple behavior of a rat or pigeon to the complex behavior of humans.

The variables he has investigated most extensively, together with his major findings, are discussed below.

Reinforcement

A distinction must be drawn between two related terms: **reinforcer** and **reinforcement.** A reinforcer is a *thing,* or, in Skinnerian terms, a stimulus. Reinforcement, on the other hand, is not a stimulus, but rather its effect. For example, candy may be a reinforcer because it can be reinforcing and because it is a stimulus. The object candy, however, is not a reinforcement although its *effect* on a person may be an example of reinforcement.

Although reinforcement may be variously defined (see, for example, Skinner, 1953), the most widely accepted definition of a reinforcer is *any stimulus that increases the probability that a response will occur.* This is admittedly a circular definition. Nevertheless, it permits a classification of different *types* of reinforcement, and it makes clear that it is the *effect* of a stimulus that determines whether or not it will be reinforcing. This is obviously necessary since the same situation may be highly reinforcing for one person and highly unpleasant for another. First grade students may react in a very positive manner when they are presented with little gold stars in recognition of their work. College students whose professor offered them little stars would probably conclude, and quite rightly, that the professor was demented.

LITTLE GOLD STAR FOR FIRST GRADE STUDENTS

BIG GOLD STAR for COLLEGE STUDENTS

Skinner differentiates between two major classes of reinforcers: *positive* and *negative.* Each of these may, in turn, be *primary, secondary,* or *generalized.* A **primary reinforcer** is a stimulus that is reinforcing without learning. It will ordinarily be related to an unlearned need or drive, as, for example, in the case of food. Presumably people do not have to learn that eating is a good thing.

A **secondary reinforcer** is a previously neutral stimulus that has become reinforcing by virtue of being repeatedly paired with a primary reinforcer. For example, the light in the Skinner box may eventually be sufficient to maintain bar-pressing behavior *in the absence of food.* This is evidently because it has been paired with the primary reinforcer, food, so often that it has become reinforcing.

A **generalized reinforcer** is also a previously neutral stimulus that, through repeated pairings with a number of other reinforcers in various situations, has become reinforcing for many behaviors. Prestige, money, and success are examples of extremely powerful generalized reinforcers.

As was mentioned earlier, each of these reinforcers may be positive or negative. A **positive reinforcer** is a stimulus that increases the probability of a response occurring when it is *added* to a situation. A **negative reinforcer** has the same effect as a result of being *removed from* the situation.

In the preceding Skinner box examples, food is a positive reinforcement—as is the light. If, on the other hand, a mild current were turned on in the electric grid that runs through the floor of the box, and if this current were turned off only when the rat depressed the lever, the turning off of the current would be an example of negative reinforcement.

Punishment

A discussion of negative reinforcement leads directly to a consideration of punishment. Indeed, it is not at all uncommon to confuse the two since both frequently involve noxious (unpleasant) stimuli. In point of fact, however, when each is defined in terms of its effects on behavior rather than in terms of its real or assumed properties, the confusion ceases to exist. Whereas reinforcement, whether positive or negative, increases the probability of a response occurring, punishment does not—and may, indeed have the opposite effect. More about punishment in Chapter 14.

Aversive Control

It should be stressed here again that negative reinforcement and punishment describe two very different situations. The two are often confused because each usually involves noxious or unpleasant stimuli. But, whereas punishment results in a reduction in behavior, negative reinforcement, like positive reinforcement, increases the probability that a response will occur. Thus, a rat may be trained to jump on a little stool by being fed whenever it does so (positive reinforcement); similarly, a rat may be trained to jump on a stool by being shocked when it does not do so (negative reinforcement). In the end the two rats may jump on the stool equally religiously, but research leaves little doubt that the positively reinforced rat will display considerably more enthusiasm for stool-jumping than will the negatively reinforced rat. Indeed, whereas the first rat will run eagerly to the Skinner box, the second may expend considerable energy trying to stay away from the box. In both cases, however, there has been an increase in the probability of stool-jumping behavior when the rat is in the box. In contrast, if the aversive stimulus (electric shock) follows stool-jumping behavior, there will be a marked reduction in the probability that that behavior will occur (punishment). In much the same way, if the rat's food (positive stimulus) is removed following stool-jumping behavior, that behavior is likely to be abandoned. These last two situations simply illustrate the use of punishment in contrast to reinforcement.

Strange as it might seem, the use of negative reinforcement as a means of control is highly prevalent in a majority of today's schools, homes, and churches, as is the use of punishment. These methods of *aversive control* (in contrast to positive control) are evident in the use of low grades, verbal rebukes, threats of punishment, and detention in schools, and in the unpleasant fates that await transgressors of most major religions. They are evident as well in our legal and judicial systems, which are extraordinarily punitive rather than rewarding. "Goodness" is not rewarded positively, though criminality is indeed punished. In fact, the reward for being good frequently takes the form of not being punished. That, in a nutshell, is negative reinforcement.

It is difficult to determine which is most important in our daily lives: positive reinforcement or negative reinforcement. Nor is it always easy to separate the two in practice, daily life being considerably more tolerant of ambiguity than is psychological theory. Consider, for example, that I work in order to obtain the "good" things in life: food, prestige, power, and a soft, wet kiss. It would seem obvious that I am controlled by positive reinforcement. Or is it true, as my grandmother so kindly suggested, that I work to prevent hunger, to escape from anonymity and helplessness, to avoid loneliness? The issue cannot easily be resolved, but it is worth noting that I am much more likely to be happy, whatever that might be, if positive rather than negative contingencies control my behavior. A rat who learns to jump onto a stool to escape a shock may learn to avoid a Skinner box or to escape from it. Indeed, **avoidance** and/or **escape learning** are among the most important consequences of aversive control. A child who performs well in school because of parental and teacher rewards probably likes school; another who performs well in order to escape parental wrath and school punishments will probably have quite different emotional reactions to school, and may *avoid* further noncompulsory schooling or might even consider *escaping* from the present situation.

Aversive control of behavior may have one additional, highly undesirable effect. When Ulrich and Azrin (1962) placed two rats in a situation where they had to turn a wheel to avoid an electric shock, they fell, tooth and nail, upon each other. Although each understood, in a primitive rat way to be sure, that the source of their pain was the wheel and not the other rat, they insisted on behaving in a most unfriendly fashion.

It should be noted that the most dedicated proponents of applied behavioral techniques and principles strongly advocate the use of methods of positive rather than aversive control. This is notably true of B. F. Skinner. What happens in a classroom of fourth graders who are compelled to memorize the Magna Carta (why not?) to avoid detention?

Reinforcement and Punishment

As was shown earlier, there are two types of reinforcement. One involves presenting a pleasant stimulus (positive reinforcement); the other involves removing an unpleasant stimulus (negative reinforcement). In the same way, there are two types of punishment, each the converse of one type of reinforcement. On the one hand, there is the punishment that occurs when a pleasant stimulus is removed; on the other, there is the more familiar situation where a noxious stimulus is presented. Figure 3.4 summarizes these four possibilities, each of which is then illustrated by reference to a classroom situation.

| | Stimulus | |
	Pleasant	Noxious
Added to	Positive reinforcement	Punishment
Taken from	Punishment	Negative reinforcement

Figure 3.4 *Reinforcement and Punishment*

Positive Reinforcement Examples of positive reinforcement in the classroom are so numerous and obvious as to make citing any one appear platitudinous. Whenever a teacher smiles at a student, says something pleasant to him, commends him for his work, assigns him a high grade, selects him for a special project, or tells his mother how clever he is, the teacher is using positive reinforcement. (See Chapter 14 for a more detailed discussion of various kinds of classroom reinforcement.)

Negative Reinforcement Implicit or explicit threats of punishment, failure, detention, ridicule, parental anger, humiliation, starvation, and sundry other unpleasant eventualities comprise the bulk of the modern, well-equipped teacher's arsenal of negative reinforcers. When these follow unruly, nonstudious, or otherwise unacceptable behaviors, they may be interpreted as examples of punishment (the presentation of an unpleasant stimulus following undesirable behavior). When the threat of these possibilities is removed following acceptable behavior, they provide a clear example of negative reinforcement (the removal of an unpleasant stimulus following desirable behavior). Recall that such negative and sometimes maladaptive behaviors as tendencies to escape or avoid situations frequently result from the overzealous administration of negative reinforcement.

Punishment I The first type of punishment involves presenting a noxious stimulus, usually in an attempt to eliminate some undesirable behavior. A classic

No.	Rules of School	Lashes
1.	Boys and Girls Playing Together	4
3.	Fighting	5
7.	Playing at Cards at School	4
8.	Climbing for Every Foot Over Three Feet Up a Tree	1
9.	Telling Lyes	7
11.	Nick Naming Each Other	4
16.	For Misbehaving to Girls	10
19.	For Drinking Spirituous Liquors at School	8
22.	For Waring Long Finger Nails	2
27.	Girls Going to Boy's Play Places	2
33.	Wrestling at School	4
41.	For Throwing Anything Harder than Your Trab Ball	4
42.	For Every Word You Miss in Your Heart Lesson Without Good Excuse	1
47.	For Going about the Barn or Doing Any Mischief about the Place	7

Nov. 10, 1848   Wm. A. Chaffin

Figure 3.5 *Excerpt from a List of Punishments in a North Carolina School, 1848 (Coon, 1915)*

example is the use of the lash in one North Carolina school, in the year 1848 (see Figure 3.5)—a practice which is no longer widely accepted.

Punishment II The second type of punishment involves the removal of a pleasant stimulus. The fairly common practice of detaining students after regular class hours, insofar as it involves removing the apparently pleasant privilege of going home, may be cited as an example of this type of punishment.

The Effects of Reinforcement and Punishment

It may be accepted as almost axiomatic that reinforcement enhances learning. Indeed, it can easily be demonstrated that the behavior of both animals and people can often be controlled largely through the careful administration of reinforcement. That punishment has an equal, if opposite, effect is not nearly so obvious. Indeed, Thorndike was among the first to declare that pleasure was much more potent in stamping in responses than pain was in stamping them out.
In addition to objections based on ethical or humanitarian considerations, there are several pedagogically sound reasons why the use of punishment is almost

invariably discouraged. Among the most obvious is the fact that, since punishment does not ordinarily illustrate or emphasize desirable behavior, but usually simply draws attention to undesirable responses, it cannot be easily employed in a learning situation. A second objection to the use of punishment is that it is often accompanied by highly undesirable emotional side effects, which, interestingly, can often become associated with the punisher rather than with the punished behavior. A third objection is that punishment does not always lead to the elimination of a response but sometimes only to its suppression. In other words, a behavior is not forgotten or extinguished as a result of being punished, but is simply avoided—sometimes only temporarily. A last objection to punishment is a simple, practical one—it often does not work. Sears et al. (1957) cite evidence to support the notion that parents who punish their children severely for being aggressive are more likely than other parents to have aggressive children. And it has been observed that mothers who are unduly punitive when attempting to toilet train their children are more likely to have children who wet their beds. It appears, however, that overpermissive parents are as likely to have problems with their children as are those who make excessive use of physical punishment.

All of which is, indeed, valuable advice, whether it is interpreted by sages or by fools.

Schedules of Reinforcement

Through experiments with pigeons and rats, Skinner attempted to discover: (1) the relationship between type and amount of reinforcement and measures of learning, and (2) the relationship between the way reinforcement is administered and learning. The first relationship cannot easily be ascertained, since type and amount of reinforcement appear to affect different individuals in unpredictable ways. It is clear from numerous experiments that even a very small reward will lead to effective learning and can serve to maintain behavior over long periods. It is also clear that too much reward may lead to a cessation of behavior (satiation). Several guidelines for the use of reinforcement are presented in Chapters 4 and 14. These, however, should be interpreted cautiously.

The second relationship is somewhat easier to determine since it is amenable to direct experimental investigation. The manner in which rewards are administered is usually referred to as the **schedule of reinforcement.** Schedules are invariably either **continuous,** or **intermittent** (also called *partial*). In the first case a reward is provided for every correct response (referred to as every trial); in the second case only *some* of the trials are reinforced, in which case the experimenters have two options. They may choose to reinforce a certain proportion of trials (a **ratio schedule**), or they may arrange their schedule on a time basis (an **interval schedule**). In the first case they might, for example, decide to reinforce one out of five correct responses; in the second case they might reinforce one correct response for every fifteen-second lapse. In either case they still have two options. They might choose to assign reinforcement in a predetermined fashion (**fixed schedule**) or in a more haphazard manner (*variable* or **random schedule**). Or, to really confuse things in proper psychological fashion, they might combine a number of these schedules and gleefully claim that they are using a *mixed* or a **combined schedule.**

They have no more choices, fortunately . . . except maybe one. It is referred to as a **superstitious schedule,** and is explained later in this chapter.

The preceding section may, at first glance, appear somewhat confusing. The reader is advised to read it again slowly. It is really quite simple. Experimenters have two choices; if they choose A, they have no more choices, but if they choose B, they have two new options. Each of these, in turn, offers two further options. And finally, as a sort of *coup de grace,* the last four options may be combined. Figure 3.6 presents a complete summary of schedules of reinforcement.

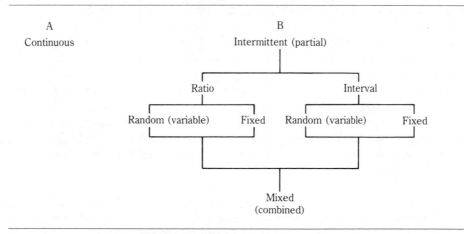

Figure 3.6 *Schedules of Reinforcement*

Schedules and Learning Much of Skinner's work has been directed toward discovering the relationship between various schedules of reinforcement and one of three measures of learning: **rate of learning, response rate,** and **extinction rate.** Not all the results of these studies are reported here, but attention is drawn to the most salient and relevant findings. Probably the most striking thing about Skinner's work is that the relationships he describes appear to be generally valid for a wide range of behaviors in animals (see Ferster and Skinner, 1957). Their applicability to human behavior is discussed later in this chapter.

It appears that continuous reinforcement is most effective with respect to rate of learning. When learning such simple responses as bar-pressing, the rat might become confused, and would almost certainly learn much more slowly if only *some* of its initial correct responses were reinforced. In terms of classroom practice this means that initial learning, particularly for very young children, probably requires far more reinforcement than does later learning. Students often receive this reinforcement in the form of attention or knowledge that they are performing correctly.

Interestingly, although continuous reinforcement often leads to more rapid acquisition, it does not usually result in longer **retention** of what is learned. Indeed, rate of extinction for behavior that has been reinforced continuously is considerably faster than for behavior that has been reinforced intermittently. **Extinction** means the cessation of a response as a function of withholding reinforcement. Extinction rate is simply the time that elapses between the beginning of the nonreinforced period and the cessation of behavior. It is sometimes assumed that longer extinction times are associated with responses that are more firmly embedded in the organism's repertoire.

The use of extinction in schools, often in the form of the withdrawal of attention in the case of unruly attention-seeking behavior, is widespread and effective. Several illustrations are provided in Chapters 4 and 14.

In general, therefore, the best schedule would appear to consist initially of continuous, followed later by intermittent, reinforcement. Among the intermittent schedules, a random ratio arrangement ordinarily results in the longest rate of extinction.

Rate of responding may also be brought under the control of the particular schedule employed. Interestingly, the behavior of pigeons and rats often suggests that they have developed expectations about reward. A pigeon who has been taught to peck a disk, and who is reinforced for the first peck after a lapse of fifteen seconds (fixed interval), often completely ceases pecking immediately after being reinforced and resumes again just prior to the end of the fifteen-second interval. If, on the other hand, the pigeon is reinforced on a random ratio basis, its rate of responding will be uniformly high and constant (often as high as 2,000 or more pecks an hour). (See Figure 3.7.)

Schedules and People So! One can reinforce rats and pigeons in a variety of clever ways and note a number of consistent effects that this has on their ludicrously simple behaviors. From this, numerous graduate dissertations and great

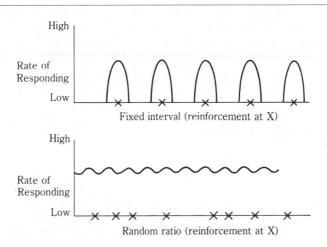

Figure 3.7 *Pigeon Pecking under Two Reinforcement Schedules*

quantities of published research may be derived for the erudition of the scholars and the amazement of the people.

But what of human beings? How are they affected by schedules of reinforcement?

The answer seems to be: in much the same way as animals. Marquis (1941), for example, investigated the behavior of babies who were fed regularly (fixed interval schedule) and of those who were fed on demand. Not surprisingly, infants on fixed schedules showed a marked increase in activity just prior to feeding time. Bandura and Walters (1963) make the related observation that behaviors engaged in by young children who desire parental attention tend to be randomly reinforced—and tend, consequently, to be highly persistent.

There are many examples of the effects of schedules on ordinary people's behavior. The fisherman who frequents the same stream, although he rarely (but occasionally) catches fish, is demonstrating the persistence that results from an intermittent schedule of reinforcement. The small-town student who has led his classes for eight years, but who now finds himself being outdone in the fierce competition of a new school and who ceases to study, may be demonstrating the rapid extinction that follows continuous reinforcement.

Indeed, knowing how schedules of reinforcement affect people's behavior is useful in a variety of practical situations—as the wife who occasionally but not too frequently praises her husband's appearance or his cooking will attest. He will continue to cook and to appear despite long sequences without reinforcement.

Reese and Lipsitt (1970) have reviewed and summarized a great many studies of operant conditioning in infants. These studies have dealt with such diverse behaviors as smiling (Brackbill, 1958), sucking (Seltzer, 1968), eye fixation (Watson, 1966), and vocalization (Weisberg, 1963), to name but a few. Several (for example, Sheppard, 1967; Weisberg and Fink, 1966) have tended to support the contention that the behavior of infants under fixed ratio schedules of reinforcement resembles that of nonhuman species. In other words, the rate of responding tends to be high and constant and to increase as the reinforcement ratio increases. In the same way, the observation that extinction is more rapid in rats following continuous reinforcement appears to be valid for human infants as well (Bijou, 1957; Carment and Miles, 1962; Kass and Wilson, 1966).

Shaping

Shaping, a technique developed by Skinner (1951) to teach animals complex behaviors, is also directly relevant to human behavior. The procedure of shaping involves administering rewards for responses that are not the required terminal response but which approximate what the experimenter desires. The technique is aptly referred to as the **differential reinforcement** of **successive approximations.**

It has been noted (Lefrancois, 1972) that if experimenters wished to train a rat to perform such a complex and impressive behavioral sequence as picking up a marble from one corner of a cage, transporting it diagonally to the opposite corner, returning to the center to think, and then walking casually to the third corner before returning again to the marble, rolling it to the fourth corner of the cage, and then bowing in four directions, they could sit and wait for the animal to emit this complex operant, and then reinforce it. The point made there, however, is that either or both the rat and the experimenters would die of old age before the desired operant appeared.

If, however, the experimenters employed a shaping technique, they might be more nearly successful. Such a technique would involve reinforcing the animal every time it made a move in the desired direction until it had learned this response, and then not reinforcing it again. By reinforcing only *successively closer approximations* tó the desired behavior, it is possible to train an animal to engage in behaviors so complex that they would never ordinarily appear in the animal's repertoire.

Employing a shaping technique together with a secondary reinforcer, I once trained a German short-haired pointer to go to any of three rooms in a house. For some time prior to the actual training, the dog had been conditioned to a secondary reinforcer. Each time she was fed, I snapped my fingers. After a number of training sessions, it was assumed that the sound of the fingers was reinforcing. At that point it was relatively simple to recline on a chair in the manner of an indolent but highly successful animal trainer and to command the dog to proceed to the kitchen. Whenever the confused beast turned in the right direction, *el trainor* snapped his fingers. Eventually the dog ran to the kitchen on command. In like manner she was trained to go to the den and to the bathroom—a convenience which she never quite learned to use properly.

Shaping and People Two related statements may be made about the role of shaping in human behavior. First, the behavior of people is constantly being shaped by its reinforcement contingencies. Second, people frequently, and sometimes deliberately, employ shaping techniques to modify other people's behavior.

The first statement simply recognizes the fact that a great deal of human behavior is modified directionally in small steps by reinforcement. It has often been observed, for example, that as previously reinforcing activities become habitual and less rewarding, they tend to be modified. A motorcyclist derives some considerable reinforcement from the sensation of turning a sharp corner at high speed—but eventually the sensation diminishes and the excitement becomes less. And perhaps, too, as the reinforcement begins to decrease, his speed increases, imperceptibly, but progressively. This is a clear illustration of shaping effected through the outcomes of behavior.

There are numerous examples of shaping in the classroom. Peer approval or disapproval, sometimes communicated in very subtle, nonverbal ways, can drastically alter a student's behavior. The classroom clown would probably not continue to be a clown if no one paid any attention to her. Indeed, she might never have been shaped into a clown had her audience not reinforced her in the first place.

The second statement asserts that people make direct use of shaping procedures, sometimes consciously, in order to control the behavior of others. It is well known, for example, that a person's listeners can often direct a conversation by

means of deliberate or unconscious signs of interest and approval (or the reverse). Indeed, the susceptibility of human speech to external control through reinforcement has led to the demarcation of a special area of research—that of verbal learning (Skinner, 1957). It has been successfully demonstrated, for example, that an experimenter can make a subject utter a preponderance of a specific kind of word in free

Shaping

association (e.g., plural nouns, Greenspoon, 1955; expressions of opinion, Verplanck, 1955) simply as a function of reinforcement. Typically, the experimenter simply says "mmhm" or makes some gesture of approval such as head nodding whenever the subject emits the desired expression.

A last demonstration of shaping must be reported here. Stories are often told about psychology professors whose students condition them to do unusual things in class. I and five fellow students in an undergraduate psychology class provided material for one of these stories in a full semester course. Early in the semester, the class had been introduced to Skinner, operant conditioning, and shaping. Immediately thereafter these six students decided that they would become "head nodders"—head nodders are very reinforcing for professors. To begin with, these head nodders decided that they would reinforce pacing behavior by nodding at the professor's wisdom when he paced. Within four lectures he paced incessantly as he lectured. The experimenters then decided to extinguish this behavior and to reinforce lecturing from one corner instead. This too was accomplished easily and rapidly. The next step was to condition lecturing from another corner. Once this had been done, the experimenters attempted to reinforce what they called "spaces between words." Every time the professor paused, he was to be smiled and nodded at.

This part of the conditioning procedure was never particularly successful, perhaps because the instructor spoke too rapidly. In addition, he probably assumed that the reinforcement was for what he had just said, and therefore hastened on to what he would say next. In any case, he never knew as he paced up and down before the class that he was a walking example of one of his early lectures.

Superstitious Behavior

Recall that a fixed interval schedule provides for reinforcement on the first correct trial after a specified time lapse. In the course of investigating the relationship between schedules of reinforcement and learning, Skinner occasionally employed what is properly a fixed interval schedule of reinforcement without the provision that the learner must perform at least one correct response before being reinforced. This variation is labeled a *superstitious* schedule. Such a schedule reinforces the learner regularly no matter what responses are occurring at the time. Consequently it often leads to the acquisition of strange and sometimes highly persistent patterns of behavior wholly unrelated to the reinforcement. Skinner (1948) reports leaving six pigeons overnight on a superstitious schedule. The following morning one bird was turning clockwise prior to each reinforcement; a second turned its head toward a corner; and two others had developed unnatural swaying motions of the body.

As Skinner (1953) points out, it is somewhat harder to illustrate superstitious behavior in humans. He maintains, however, that those behaviors which have "accidentally" accompanied reinforcement are more likely to occur again. Skinner's own example is that if a man finds a ten-dollar bill in a park, he may well, the next time he walks in the park, hold his eyes just as he was holding them when fortune struck. Indeed, all of his deportment might closely resemble that which accompanied his good fortune.

There is probably considerable unconscious superstitious behavior in most people. People who frown, scratch their heads, purse their lips, or chew their hair (it happens) when trying to think are really not engaging in behaviors that are directly related to thought processes. But they may be displaying the effects of reinforcement which occurred when they happened to be frowning, scratching, or chewing hair.

Biological Constraints

Traditional behavioristic theories have long been premised on the sometimes explicit assumption that *any* operant or respondent could be brought under the control of stimuli (or reinforcement), and that the principles of conditioning were therefore quasi-universal principles, both for nonhuman and for human animals (Herrnstein, 1977). Research suggests that this belief might not be entirely accurate.

The Brelands (Breland and Breland, 1951, 1961) undertook to train a number of animals for display at fairs and conventions. Using Skinnerian shaping techniques, they taught a pig to pick up large wooden "nickels" and deposit them in a "piggy" bank. Similarly, they taught a raccoon to pick up coins and place them in a metal tray, and they taught chickens to pull a loop that would release a plastic pellet onto a slide at the bottom of which the chicken would strike the pellet with its beak, propelling it out to an observer.

Initially the animals responded very well, thrilling audiences with their antics. But with the passage of time, the pig became progressively more reluctant. He would turn over, pick up his wooden nickel, start to bring it back, hesitate, toss it in the air, drop it to the ground, root it with his nose, pick it up, drop it again, and so on. In the end, the pig took so long in getting the coin to the piggy bank that he was not obtaining enough food for his needs.

In much the same way, the raccoon demonstrated increasing reluctance to part with his coins. He would pick them up, rub them in a most miserly fashion (he was eventually displayed as an example of a miserly raccoon), dip them into the tray, bring them out, rub them again, dip them in again, and again rub them. His behavior

.....INSTINCTIVE DRIFT, LEO....?

was highly reminiscent of the behavior of raccoons in the wilds who habitually wash their food prior to eating.

The chicken fared no better. Although she learned her tasks quickly and easily, she soon tired of striking the plastic pellet out of the cage, and began, instead, to drag it back into the cage, and to peck at it. She would pick it up in her beak, pound it on the floor, pick it up again, and pound it again.

The Brelands noticed that these behaviors were highly suggestive of natural, perhaps instinctual behaviors. For each species, the specific behavior (or *misbehavior,* as they termed it) relates to activities associated with finding food or eating it. For that reason, they labeled the phenomenon *instinctive drift* (also sometimes called the *Breland effect*). In essence, instinctive drift may be expressed as a principle which says that, after repeated performance of an arbitrary activity associated with reinforcement, behavior will begin to "drift" toward more instinctive responses, even at the expense of the conditioned response and its contingent reinforcement.

Traditional operant conditioning theory cannot easily explain instinctive drift in view of the fact that the behaviors manifested in these circumstances do not lead to reinforcement but detract from it. Other recent findings are no easier to explain. Williams and Williams (1969) found, for example, that pigeons will learn to peck at an area that is lightened or darkened prior to reinforcement, even though pecking bears no causal relationship to the reinforcement. In fact, after pigeons have "auto-shaped" their pecking behavior to a light that precedes reinforcement, they will continue to peck even when doing so turns the light off and prevents reinforcement. Are auto-

shaped behaviors self-reinforcing? Or are those behaviors that are susceptible to auto-shaping largely instinctual?

As a result of these and related findings, researchers have recently ex-pressed considerable interest in *biological constraints* to learning (see, for example, Seligman and Hager, 1972; Hinde and Hinde, 1973). These constraints are such that certain specific behaviors are very difficult for some species and very easy for others. Thus, a rat can only rarely be taught to depress a lever in order to avoid an electric shock, but it can easily be taught to jump or run in these circumstances (Bolles, 1970). The most obvious explanation relates to the rat's natural response to danger; it fights, flees, faints, or becomes frantic. But it does not calmly approach and depress a lever. In Seligman's terms, the rat is *prepared* to learn a jumping response or an escape response; it is *contraprepared* to learn bar-pressing in these circumstances. A pigeon is prepared to learn a pecking response; a pig, a rooting response; a raccoon, a washing response. And we, human animals, are probably prepared to learn language (Lenneberg, 1969), among many other things.

The study of biological constraints, and of genetic contributions to learning is relatively new (and somewhat controversial). It still offers little that is of im-mediate, practical significance to the teacher. Its theoretical significance may be considerable, however. But does it really invalidate or even seriously threaten be-havioristic theory? The answer should probably be negative. What it does indicate is that the principles of learning developed in behavioristic research are not universally applicable, and that it is important to take into account the genetic and evolutionary history of organisms in attempts to explain their behavior (Skinner, 1977).

Beyond Freedom

If most significant human behaviors are controlled by reinforcement or lack of it, it follows that most of us are controlled by our environments—the freedom of which we are so proud is merely an illusion. And if I awake in the morning and decide to brush my teeth, am I really free to make the choice? Can I either brush or not brush according to the whimsy of the moment? Or am I bound by the dictates of past reinforcement (and/or punishment), real or imagined? A mundane act, surely, that of brushing my teeth. Certainly a very insignificant decision, given the cosmic mag-nitude of other decisions that I can make relative to my destiny. Here I sit generating yards of words in a rather drab office—an activity that is perhaps of greater mag-nitude than the mechanical routine of brushing my teeth. But am I free not to be here? Was I free not to walk out of my warm house into a frigid, snowy, 20-below wind, coax my reluctant car to life, and drive through the frozen poplars to this city where my work awaits? I gave it no thought at the time; but if I had, is it not likely that my actions would have been guided by reinforcement contingencies? And if I had decided not to come to work, thereby convincing my neighbors that here indeed is a free man—a man who does what he pleases and a lazy man to boot—is it not true that I would have done so because the consequences of staying home would have seemed to me more pleasant than the prospect of writing to you? My freedom would still have been an illusion, though a comfortable and pleasing one.

Skinner, in his recent book dealing with freedom (and human dignity, to be sure), asserts that autonomous man is a myth (Skinner, 1971). "Autonomous man," he explains, "is a device used to explain what we cannot explain in any other way. He has been constructed from our ignorance, and as our understanding increases, the very stuff of which he is composed vanishes" (p. 200). It is Skinner's contention that we are controlled by our environment; but, he reassures us, it is an environment of which we are almost totally in control—or at least an environment which is almost wholly of our own making. There is a fundamental difference between the two. An environment over which we have control implies an environment in which we are free, for we can change the reinforcement contingencies of that environment. An environment of our own making, but over which we have no immediate control implies an environment in which we are not free. As a species, we might have controlled our own destiny; but as individuals we do not control our own actions.

This estimate of the human condition has come under severe critical attack from a wide variety of sources—as Skinner had predicted it would. In essence, he has questioned the control exercised by "autonomous" man and demonstrated the control exercised by the environment in an attempt to create a *science* of behavior. The approach itself brings into question the worth and dignity of persons. "These are sweeping changes," Skinner says, "and those who are committed to traditional theories and practices naturally resist them" (1971, p. 21).

The argument, a very fundamental one in contemporary psychology, is essentially between the humanistically oriented psychologists—those concerned more with humanity, ideals, values, and emotions—and experimentally oriented psychologists—those more concerned with developing a relatively rigorous science of behavior. But the two positions are not really incompatible. "Man is much more than a dog," Skinner tells us, "but like a dog he is within range of scientific analysis" (1971, p. 21).

Is the fact that I can deliberately choose to lie to you proof that I am free?

Skinner's Position
and Society

Skinner's "nontheoretical" position is essentially a description of the effects of various schedules of reinforcement on animal and human behavior. He has deliberately avoided drawing inferences from the simple observations that he made. This is the primary reason why his system is relatively impervious to sound, invalidating criticism.

Skinner has, however, discussed at length the possibility of applying a *science* of human behavior for the benefit of humanity (Skinner, 1953, 1961). Such an application would involve a degree of control over human behavior. It is this aspect of his work that has met with the greatest resistance and has led some to speculate that Skinnerian behaviorism can as easily be made a weapon as a tool. The question is really an ethical and moral one. The science exists, imperfect and incomplete as it is—and, to some extent, it is being employed systematically in many areas. Skinner

(1961) describes, for example, how advertising employs *emotional* reinforcement by presenting alluring women in commercials, and how motivational control is achieved by creating secondary or generalized reinforcers. For example, a car becomes a powerful reinforcer by being equated with sex. He describes a society that uses positive reinforcement in the form of wages, bribes, or tips, and that employs drugs, such as "fear-reducers" for soldiers, to control humans.

But all of this began happening before Skinner; and, as he has noted, "no theory changes what it is a theory about; man remains what he has always been" (1971, p. 215).

Skinner and Instruction

Skinner has devoted much thought to problems of instruction. One result has been a renewed emphasis on **programed instruction**—a topic more fully discussed in Chapter 4. Another has been his castigation of education and teaching methods (Skinner, 1965). In an article entitled "Why Teachers Fail," he claims that efforts to improve education seldom involve attempts to improve teaching as such, and that therefore teachers continue to teach the way they themselves were taught. And chief among their teaching methods, for both disciplinary and instructional purposes, are the techniques of aversive control. These are techniques based on the use of noxious stimuli, often for punishment, but sometimes for negative reinforcement.

As alternatives to aversive control, Skinner suggests the obvious—positive reinforcement together with "attractive and attention-compelling" approaches to teaching. In addition, he presents numerous suggestions for the development of a technology of teaching in a book by that title (Skinner, 1968).*

Summary of Chapter 3

This chapter has presented a description of an ordinary rat. It has also examined Skinner's theory, particularly as this theory relates to instruction. Brief reference was made to Skinner's concern with social and educational problems.

Main Points in Chapter 3

1. The white Norway rat (*Rattus norvegicus albinus*) was the hero of early twentieth-century psychology—a psychology whose heroes were well liked.

2. The Skinner box is a cagelike device employed by Skinner to observe the relationship between behavior and reinforcement—ordinarily in rats or pigeons.

---

* Further discussion of the application of Skinner's work to teaching is provided in Chapters 4 and 14.

3. Skinner distinguishes between respondent and operant behavior. The primary difference between the two is that the first results from a known stimulus whereas the second is simply emitted.

4. The model of operant conditioning holds essentially that when an operant is reinforced the probability of its reoccurrence increases.

5. Most significant human behaviors are probably of the operant variety. It is partly for this reason that an analogy between a Skinner box and a classroom is not entirely inappropriate.

6. A reinforcer is any stimulus whose effect is to increase the probability that a response will occur. It may do so by being added to a situation (positive reinforcement) or by being removed from one (negative reinforcement).

7. Despite obvious misinterpretations in numerous textbooks, negative reinforcement is *not* punishment. The effect of punishment is to decrease, not increase, the probability that a response will occur.

8. Reinforcement may be administered continuously or in a random or fixed manner relative to a ratio or interval basis.

9. In general, continuous schedules lead to faster learning, whereas intermittent schedules result in longer extinction periods.

10. Shaping may be employed to teach animals novel behaviors or to alter the behavior of humans in subtle ways. It involves the *differential reinforcement of successive approximations*.

11. A superstitious schedule of reinforcement is a fixed interval schedule without the provision that reinforcement will occur only if there is a correct response. It sometimes leads to the acquisition of strange behaviors, both in animals and in people.

12. Not all behaviors are equally likely to be emitted and learned. Rats, for example, are *prepared* to learn to jump to escape an electric shock. They are *contraprepared* to learn bar-pressing in this situation. The recognition of these *biological constraints* on learning limits the generality of behavioristic principles.

13. It is possible that we are not free, that we are controlled by our environment and have only an illusion of freedom.

14. Skinner's concern for the application of a science of man is evident in his discussion of both social and instructional problems.

Suggested Readings

For one of the simplest, yet fairly comprehensive, explanations of the theory of B. F. Skinner, the reader is referred to the following very short book:

Keller, Fred S. *Learning: Reinforcement Theory* (2nd Edition). New York: Random House, 1969.

For more detailed explanations of Skinner's position in increasing order of comprehensiveness and difficulty, the reader is referred to the relevant portions of each of the following three books:

Hilgard, E. R. and G. H. **Bower.** *Theories of Learning* (3rd Edition). New York: Appleton-Century-Crofts, 1966.

Hill, W. F. *Learning: A Survey of Psychological Interpretations* (Rev. Edition). New York: Chandler Publishing Company, 1971.

Logan, F. A. *Fundamentals of Learning and Motivation* (2nd Edition). Dubuque, Iowa: Wm. C. Brown, 1976.

> *Skinner provides a highly readable and very important behavioristic estimate of the human condition:*

Skinner, B. F. *Beyond Freedom and Dignity.* New York: Knopf, 1971.

> *An active polar bear is thought to be able to fast for very long periods of time without losing its strength. Eskimos once believed that a bear could go without food so long that it would eventually be light enough for a single man to lift (Perry, 1966).*

4
Programed Instruction and Behavior Modification

An interesting thing about a bear is
that it always stands facing the front of its
tracks. However, only very stupid bears
never look back over their shoulders. Is
hindsight really better than foresight?

Advance Organizer Chapters 2 and 3 dealt with classical and operant conditioning, respectively. From your point of view as a teacher, these explanations of learning are best viewed not as competing alternatives but as complementary theories. Each offers some important insights into different aspects of human behavior. In addition, operant conditioning theory has led very directly to the development of specific methods for managing instruction and student behavior. Most obvious among these methods is programed instruction, described in the first part of this chapter, and behavior modification, the subject of the last part of the chapter.

Two students sit side by side in a seventh grade class—Johnny West, who has a long nose and a low I.Q., and Frank Twolips, whose nose is like his dad's but whose I.Q. is very high. Johnny reads at a fourth grade level; Frank reads as well as an average eleventh grader. Both are reading a science textbook. It is a well-written seventh grade textbook. Frank Twolips is absolutely bored; Johnny West is completely confused. Since neither of these conditions represents an optimal learning situation, any attempt to change them might be desirable.

One obvious solution is to have the teacher spend time with Johnny explaining this confusing text to him, spend time with Frank amplifying and enriching the content of the text, and spend a little time with all other Franks and Johnnys in the class. Then, of course, the average seventh grade students must also be taken care of. Obviously, teachers will be able to implement this solution only on those days that have seventy-two hours, or in those classes where the pupil-teacher ratio is no more than 1 to 10.

A second solution is to "track" the seventh grade class. This involves calling the bright group "bluebirds," the middle group "robins," and the low group "larks," and putting each group in a separate room. The euphemistic labels are used to avoid offending parents and making life more painful for the lower groups. Interestingly, it seldom takes first grade students more than a week to discover that "larks" are dumb and "bluebirds" are smart.

Separating a class into tracks is only the beginning of the solution. Unfortunately, it is also often the end. Bluebirds read the same material as larks; they simply do it faster. Larks write the same examinations as bluebirds; they simply don't do it as well. The misfortune is that, despite some notable exceptions, this cynical description of tracking is generally warranted.

Programed Instruction

A third solution—programed instruction—has been available for some time. The term may be used in a general sense to describe any organized **auto-instructional device**—that is, any device that presents information in such a way that the learner can acquire it without the help of a teacher. In this sense, textbooks are a kind of programed material. A more specific definition of the term, however, limits it to include only material that is specifically designed to be auto-instructional *and* that is constructed according to one of two patterns or some combination of these. The patterns, *linear* and *branching,* refer specifically to the arrangement of the material which is to be learned. They are described below.

The originator of programed instruction is generally considered to be Sidney Pressey, the inventor of the teaching machine (Pressey, 1932). This early teaching machine offered the student problems together with multiple-choice answers. It caused little excitement in educational circles, partly because of our natural resistance to innovation, and partly because of the depressed economic conditions of those times. The man most responsible for the excitement that later surrounded programed learning was B. F. Skinner (1954). A major modification of programed material was later introduced by N. A. Crowder (1961, 1963). Skinner is usually associated with the **linear program,** whereas Crowder introduced the **branching program.**

MAINSTREAMING

At present one school age child out of every eight suffers from some *handicapping* condition (U.S. Census data), these conditions ranging from deafness, blindness, physical disability, and disease to emotional disturbances, learning disabilities, and mental retardation. Traditionally, the seriously handicapped seldom found their way into regular classrooms, and have therefore not been of great concern to the general educator; "special" education was designed to provide specifically for the needs of the handicapped.

Two recent events have changed much of this. First, educators (and those responsible for educational policy) began to recognize that many individuals who had been labeled "emotionally disturbed" or "mentally retarded" and who had therefore not been admitted into regular classrooms were capable of learning and functioning effectively when given access to these classrooms. At the same time, a relatively new classification of "handicapped" children was introduced: *the learning disabled.* The category, often loosely described, generally includes those individuals who do not have obvious "handicaps" (blindness, deafness, or mental retardation, for example), and who have therefore not been eligible for special classrooms, but who have not functioned well in regular classrooms. Thus there is on the one hand a recognition that some "special" children have been mislabeled and that, even if they haven't been mislabeled, they can benefit from regular classroom experiences; on the other hand, educators now recognize that there are a number of children in regular classrooms for whom "special" attention would be highly desirable.

The current effect of these observations is manifested in *mainstreaming.* In effect, to mainstream is to place into the regular classroom (into the "main" stream, so to speak) those individuals who might otherwise be placed in special classrooms. And at present mainstreaming does not appear to be simply an alternative means of dealing with "handicapped" children, but, following the passing and implementation of major laws, will soon be mandatory in most jurisdictions. What this means is that teachers will be faced increasingly with the task not only of identifying children with handicaps, but of providing, usually with the help of specialists, appropriate educational experiences for them whenever possible. Regular teachers will be required to exercise their assessment skills and knowledge more carefully to avoid the mislabeling that has been quite prevalent. And most important, regardless of labels employed (perhaps even in their absence) it is the regular classroom teacher who will be asked to design individual educational programs (termed I.E.P.) for each child. The impact of mainstreaming on teacher education programs and on teacher behavior will be considerable.

Linear Programs

The Skinnerian program is based directly on operant conditioning principles. It is, in fact, probably the best known and most systematic attempt to apply theoretical knowledge to the practical aspects of educating. A linear program is one where all learners move through the same material in exactly the same sequence, in the manner intended by God. It provides for individual differences by allowing students to proceed at their own rate. This is one of the advantages most often claimed for programed instruction.

In terms of an operant conditioning model, a program can be seen as an arrangement of material that will lead the student to emit a correct response and will also provide reinforcement for that response. Viewed very simply, the student's response is an operant, and the knowledge that he has responded correctly is a reinforcer. Linear programs have certain characteristics designed to ensure that a student will *almost always* answer correctly. Among these characteristics are the following:

1. The material is broken down into small steps. These are referred to as **frames.** Each frame consists of a minimum amount of information, so that this information can be remembered from frame to frame. Frames are ordered in logical sequence. Theoretically, the objective is to *shape* the learner's behavior through *successive approximations*. Hence the small amount of information in each frame and the requirement that most learners answer most frames correctly. Knowledge of being correct is assumed to provide reinforcement.

2. Students are required to make frequent responses—usually one in every frame, and often as many as four or five in one frame. The responses should, theoretically, be constructed by the students. They will, however, be given a variety of **prompts** to ensure that they answer correctly. Among commonly employed prompts are the following (Taber et al., 1965). They are illustrated so as to be self-explanatory.

Formal Prompts

Partial Response Prompt

     a. Johnny West inherited his long nose from Stan Twolips. Physical characteristics are determined largely by her_____.   [heredity]

Rhyming Prompt

     b. Although it is a little rare, *Ursus* is a word for

——————————.   [bear]

Literal Prompt

     c. Carmine is a color. A picturesque word for the color of blood is _____ (red).   [carmine]

Frame-structure Prompts

     d. Scientists are very intelligent. Physicists are very

——————————.   [intelligent]

     e. Doraboturs live in dark _ _ _ _ _ _.   [holes]

Thematic Prompts

Picture Prompt

a. A dorabotur is an _____.*   [animal]

Context-setting Prompt

b. Science Fiction. Manleonic drives are used to propel ships through _____.   [space]

Synonym and Antonym Prompts

c. Rats learn best when they are rewarded or _____.   [reinforced]

d. Heat causes expansion. Cold causes _____.   [contraction]

Research on the role of prompts in programed instruction suggests that, although they may serve to ensure that the correct answer is given, and although they usually lead to rapid learning (Cook and Spitzer, 1960; Cook, 1963; Levine, 1965), prompts may often be overused. Anderson and Faust (1967) have demonstrated, for example, that the excessive use of formal prompts may serve to inhibit rather than to enhance learning.

3. The third characteristic of linear programs is that they provide immediate **knowledge of results.** Students know at once whether they have answered correctly. This knowledge is assumed to act as reinforcement. Ammons (1956) reviewed the literature on the effects of knowledge of results. He concluded the evidence supports the notion that knowledge of results improves learning. Kaess and Zeaman (1960) have demonstrated that positive feedback (i.e., knowledge that one is right) is probably more effective than negative feedback (knowledge that one is wrong). Since linear programs attempt, through the use of prompts and small frames, to ensure that few errors are made, most of the feedback will be positive.

Branching Programs

The Crowder system for constructing branching programs differs from Skinner's linear system in a number of ways. To begin with, not all students go through the program in exactly the same way. Students who give all responses

---

* PPC: "The dorabotur illustration does not show the small, scoop-shaped appendage on each forefoot, essential for removing sand from lidless eyes. Is this not a critical attribute of doraboturs, and should it not be shown?"

Author: "Neither doraboturs nor artists are perfect."

correctly go through the shortest possible way. Students who make errors receive remedial instruction and further clarification in the course of the program. Typically learners who answer incorrectly are sent to a **remedial frame** or sequence of frames and eventually return to the one where they made their first error. They then proceed from there (see Figure 4.1). This necessitates a second difference between linear and branching programs. The former require that learners construct their own answer; the latter ask them to choose among alternatives. Directions to the next frame can then be determined by the nature of the response given, as well as by whether the response was correct. A third distinction between the two is that branching programs typically have much longer frames. Sometimes an entire page is one frame requiring one response.

Linear and branching programs are obviously not so different that they cannot be used in combination. Indeed, such combinations can enhance the advantages of each.

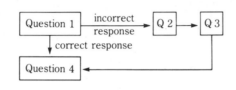

Figure 4.1 *A Branching Program*

Effectiveness of
Programed Instruction

Schramm (1964) reviewed 165 studies on programed instruction. He concluded that programs do teach, but that there is no evidence they do so better than more conventional forms of instruction, including simply reading books. In addition, the studies he reviewed showed that short programs where the frames were rearranged randomly were almost as effective as programs arranged in supposedly logical order. Perhaps the extreme simplicity of many linear programs may serve to explain this finding.

Feldhusen (1963) also reviewed studies dealing with programed instruction. He concluded that programs were really ineffective since they did not teach any better than carefully written narrative material.

A third review (Lange, 1972) looked at 112 separate studies. In 41 percent of these, programed instruction was found to be significantly superior to conventional instruction; 10 percent found conventional instruction to be superior, and 49 percent found no difference between the two.

Dale (1967) asserts that programed instruction is in fact one of the major contributions to education made by Skinner and his followers and that much of the importance of this contribution derives from programed instruction's emphasis on the clarification of instructional objectives. It appears reasonable to assume, as well, that much of the demonstrated ineffectiveness and inefficiency of programs is due to poor program construction. Pressey and Kinzer (1964) report a simple experiment where 1,110 words from Skinner and Holland's introductory psychology program were reduced to 360 words of textual material. Students required approximately two minutes to read the textual material, whereas the corresponding programed material required twenty-two minutes. There was no appreciable difference between the two groups on a later test. Pressey's subsequent argument against clumsy, voluminous, "thousand-frame" programs is well taken. While programs are by no means the

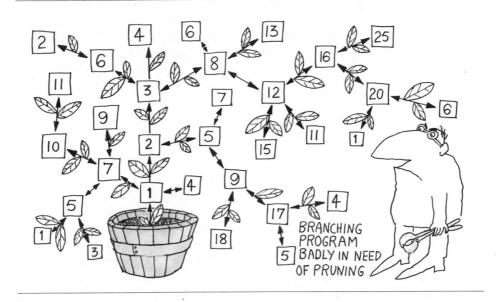

educational panacea they were once touted to be, there is little doubt that many principles and forms of programed instruction will profoundly affect educational practice for some time to come.

Evaluation of Branching and
Linear Programs

Research has not shown either type of program to be clearly superior to the other (Silberman et al., 1961), but it has shown that their use can serve to provide teachers with considerably more time for individual instruction. This is, in fact, one of their major potential contributions. As adjuncts to conventional and/or creative teaching methods, they are quite compatible with the more humanistic and less mechanistic goals of education.

In short, programs do teach—not that they necessarily teach better or more quickly than teachers, nor that they really provide for individual differences. Even branching programs can provide for only a very limited number of alternatives unless they are removed from a printed format and employed in the form of **computer-assisted instruction (CAI)**. Perhaps they will prove useful as adjuncts to more conventional forms of teaching, a use that is strongly advocated by Pressey. While it is difficult to estimate how frequently programed materials are used in contemporary schools, Komoski (1965) provides information that may indicate that their use is declining. The number of programs available for purchase declined from 352 in 1963 to 291 in 1965. With the continued development of CAI, however, it is not at all unlikely that programs will be more widely used in the future.

Teachers should also remember that some of the principles of programed learning can be usefully employed in more conventional classroom procedures. Such strategies as presenting small units of information, providing for a great deal of student involvement through responses, and giving immediate knowledge of results can be worthwhile. Attempts to structure lessons in as logical a sequence as is required in programs, while relatively time-consuming, can be highly conducive to learning.

CAI

The impact of the technological revolution on education includes the use of computers for instructional purposes. Obviously, computers may be useful in schools for such routine and clerical tasks as registering students, storing data, solving schedule problems in large schools, issuing report cards, and so on. It is not as immediately obvious that the computer may also assist in instructional programs. Although CAI is not in widespread use, largely because it is expensive and materials are lacking, it is explained briefly below.

The computer has several distinct advantages over more conventional in-structional media. These include its almost unlimited storage capacities (**memory**), its accurate and rapid **retrieval** of information, its problem-solving capacities, and its versatility in terms of possible modes of presentation. In addition, Stolurow (1968) claims that of all instructional media the computer is the only one that communicates on a completely individualized basis. It does so by modifying its responses depending upon the person using it. Conventional programed instruction, on the other hand, does take into account individual rates of learning but, even in the case of branching programs, cannot allow for a sufficient variety of individual differences.

Basically a CAI system includes a computing center together with a number of student terminals. Typically the learner interacts with the computer program by means of a typewriter keyboard and/or a videoscreen that reacts to a light pen. The machine in turn communicates with the learner via audio and/or video systems.

A CAI system can be put to several uses. One of the most common involves nothing more than the solving of computational and logical problems. The instructor continues to teach as usual. The students employ the computer only as a computational device for problems assigned by the teacher.

A second use involves drill and practice. A CAI system may be used to provide practice for such subject areas as mathematics or language learning. Unlike problem solving, this function requires that the system be specially programed.

Stolurow (1968) discusses a third application—the *inquiry* function. This involves using the computer as a source of information. To gain this information, the student must communicate the appropriate questions to the computer, usually by means of the typewriter keyboard.

A fourth, intriguing application involves the use of computers for simulation and for games. This requires the formulation, in program form, of some relatively complex model or situation with which students interact and about which they may be asked to make certain decisions. Such skills as are involved in problem analysis, decision making, and logical inferential processes may be taught and practiced through the simulation of problem situations.

Finally, a CAI system may be used for tutorial instruction. This may be described as the application of computer facilities for *teaching,* in the sense of imparting skills and information, rather than as an information center, or a computational tool, or for simulation or practicing skills. As a tutorial device, a computer can quite easily be used to present complex branching programs; or it may simply present information much as a textbook does. It is quite possible to use computers in unimaginative, conventional, and highly wasteful ways.

As was pointed out earlier, computers are not widely used in education, particularly as instructional systems (although their use is increasing). This is partly because of a lack of instructional materials (programs), and partly because computers are expensive. In computer **jargon,** the problem is really one of **software** (programs are software), although the cost of **hardware** (electronic equipment) is a problem too. Interestingly, the software problem with regard to CAI exists because there is little reliable information about alternative instructional procedures and their relative merits (Stolurow, 1964, 1966, 1968; DeCecco, 1968; Kelly and Cody, 1969). One of the major early contributions of computers to education might be to stimulate interest in research on instruction.

Examples of Programs

Following are two illustrative programs. The first is a linear program that presents some Piagetian terminology. Although it is covered in Chapter 10 as well, the reader might profit from going over this material rather carefully. The second program is more irreverent. It is included as an illustration of a branching program.

Linear: Piagetian Jargon

Objectives After reading this program you should be able to define and give examples of:

1. **adaptation**
2. **functioning**
3. **assimilation**
4. **accommodation**
5. **invariants**
6. **structure**
7. **schemas**
8. **stages**
9. **content**

Directions Fold a sheet of paper or use a strip of cardboard to cover the answers, which are given in the right-hand margin. With these answers covered, read frame 1 and write your answer in the blank provided. Move the paper down so as to check your answer before proceeding to frame 2.

1. Jean Piaget has developed a theory that deals with human adaptation. It is a developmental theory of human _____.

adaptation

2. As children learn to cope with their environment and to deal effectively with it, they can be said to be _____ to it.

adapting

3. Adaptation therefore involves interacting with the environment. The process of adaptation is one of organism-environment _____.

interaction

4. One of the central features of Piaget's developmental theory is that it attempts to explain _____ through interaction.

adaptation

5. Interaction takes place through the interplay of two complementary processes: one involves reacting to the environment in terms of a previously learned response. This process is called assimilation. Assimilation involves a _____ learned response.

previously

6. Whenever a child uses an object for some activity that he has already learned, he is said to be *assimilating* that object to his previous learning. For example, when a child sucks a pacifier he is _____ the pacifier to the activity of sucking.

assimilating

7. A child is given a paper doll. She looks at it curiously, and then puts it in her mouth and eats it. She has _____ the doll to the activity of eating.

assimilated

8. Assimilation is one of the two processes that are involved in interacting with the environment. It is part of the process of _____.

adapting or adaptation

9. Adaptation involves two processes. The first is assimilation. The second is called accommodation. It occurs whenever a change in behavior results from interacting with the environment. Accommodation involves a _____ in behavior.

change or modification

10. When children cannot assimilate a new object to activities that are already part of their repertoire, they must _____ to them.

accommodate

11. Johnny West was presented with a very long pacifier on the occasion of his first birthday. Prior to that time he had been sucking a short "bulb" pacifier. The long pacifier matched his nose. He had to elongate his mouth considerably more than usual in order to suck this new pacifier. Johnny West had to _____ to the new pacifier.

accommodate

12. If Johnny West had been given his old, short pacifier, he could more easily have _____ it to the activity of sucking.

assimilated

13. Adaptation is defined in terms of the interaction between a person and the environment. This interaction takes the form of two complementary processes: _____ and _____ .

assimilation and accommodation

14. Assimilation and accommodation are ways of functioning in relation to the world. They do not change as a person develops. Adults still interact with the environment in terms of activities they have already learned (assimilation), and they change their behavior in the face of environmental demands (accommodation). This does not mean that adults eat paper dolls, however. What it does mean is that a person's ways of functioning do not _____ from childhood to adulthood.

change

15. Activities which do not change are *invariants*. Assimilation and accommodation can be referred to as _____ _____ .

invariants (Did you see the prompt?)

16. The twin invariants of adaptation are assimilation and _____ .

accommodation

17. These are also called *functional* invariants, since they are activities related to human functioning. Adaptation involves _____ . Functioning involves assimilation and accommodation.

functioning (Too easy?)

18. When a Frenchman is given a bowl of pea soup and a spoon, he probably _____ the spoon and soup to the activity of eating.

assimilates

19. When the same noble Frenchman is given a pair of chopsticks, it is probably necessary for him to _____ the activity of eating to these novel instruments.

accommodate

20. A short review before continuing: adaptation involves the interaction of the functional invariants, assimilation and accommodation. These are called invariants because as ways of interacting with the environment they do not change from childhood to adulthood. Accommodation involves modifying some activity of the organism in the face of environmental demands. Assimilation is the use of some aspect of the environment for an activity that is already part of the organism's repertoire. These terms are employed in the developmental theory of _____ .

Jean Piaget (I hope you got this one correct!)

Using les chopsticks

21. Why is it that people behave in certain ways in the face of environmental demands? Part of the answer is that the activities with which they respond are part of their repertoire. Another way of putting this is to say that the activities that a person has learned comprise intellectual *structure*. Structure is a term that refers to the "mental" component of behavior. For every act there is a corresponding mental _____.

structure

22. If Johnny West sucks pacifiers, it is because he has some sort of structure that corresponds to the activity of sucking. From the fact that people behave we can infer that _____ exists.

structure

23. When an object is being assimilated to some activity, it is really being assimilated to structure. Structure is the mental counterpart of an _____.

activity

24. If aspects of the environment can be assimilated to structure, then those aspects of the environment to which a person accommodates must cause a change in _____.

structure

25. Assimilation can be defined as the use of existing structure. Accommodation involves changes in _____.

structure

26. If a child can stick out her tongue, it is partly be-

cause she has some _____which corresponds to
tongue-sticking-out behavior.   structure

       27. What sort of intellectual structures are children
born with? They are obviously born with the ability to perform
some very simple acts such as sucking, looking, and so on.
These are called re _____.   flexes

       28. The primitive intellectual structure of a child is de-
fined in terms of _____.   structure

       29. Changes in reflexive behavior involve changes in

_____.   structure

       30. Such changes involve the process of _____

_____.   accommodation

       31. The exercising of a reflex without changing it sig-
nificantly involves the process of _____.   assimilation

       32. All activity involves both assimilation and accom-
modation. This is because new behaviors are always based on
old learning, and because even the use of a very familiar activity
can be interpreted as involving some change in structure. That
change might simply involve a higher probability that the same   assimilation
response will occur again. All activity involves both _____   and
_____ and _____.   accommodation

       33. The name given to the intellectual structure of a
young child is schema. A schema can therefore correspond to a
reflex. The intellectual component of reflexive behavior is called

_____.   schema

       34. Schemas are related not only to reflexes but also
to any other behavior. A schema is usually named in terms of a
behavior. For example, there is a sucking schema, a looking
schema, a reaching schema, and so on. Schemas are units of
intellectual _____.   structure

       35. It is obvious that structure, since it corresponds to
behavior, must have something to do with assimilation and accommodation. In fact, objects in the environment are assimilated
to structure. This simply means that people react toward
them in terms of activities they already know. Accommodation,
on the other hand, will involve a change in _____.   structure

       36. One last term—*content.* Content is simply behavior!
Why not call it behavior? Paraphrasing Dr. Seuss: Are they not
like one another? I don't know, go ask your mother. In any case,
behavior is called _____.   content

       37. Again, behavior is called _____.   content

       38. Now you have it:

          adaptation   invariants
          assimilation   structure
          accommodation   schema
          functioning   content

If you don't know what each of these is, either the program is bad, you were
not paying attention, or . . .

Bear Hunting: A
Branching Program

Objectives: After you have read this program you should be able to:

1. recognize a forest
2. recognize a bear's tracks
3. recognize a bear
4. discharge a firearm
5. run very rapidly in all directions

Note Since the program has not been completed, only the first two objectives may be attained.

Directions Read each frame very carefully; reread it if it appears confusing. Then select what you think is the best answer for the question asked, and follow the directions that correspond to that answer.

1. A forest is a collection of trees. It is a large collection of trees, just as a city is a large collection of people. A wood is a small collection of trees, just as a town is a small collection of people. A bush is a collection of small trees. Where are there collections of small people? Never mind. Bears are often found in large collections of trees.
    If you were looking for a bear, would you go to:
    (a) a large collection of people?
    (b) a forest?
    (c) an ocean?
    If you answered (a) go to frame 10.
    If you answered (b) go to frame 3.
    If you answered (c) go to frame 7.
    2. Correct. Good. Now that you have found a forest, you must find some tracks. Remember, a bear's tracks look like this:

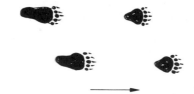

After you have found the tracks, follow them. Somewhere, a bear is standing in them.
    If you find these tracks:

should you go
(a) N?
(b) S?
(c) E or W?
If you said (a) go to frame 8.
If you said (b) go to frame 12.
If you said (c) go to frame 4.

3. You are correct. Bears are found mostly in forests. Occasionally, however, bears are also found elsewhere. You should keep this in mind. The best way of finding a bear is to do two things: First, look for a forest; second, look for a bear's tracks. They look something like this:

The best way of finding a bear is to:
(a) look for an ocean.
(b) look for its tracks.
(c) look for a forest.
If you answered (a) go to frame 7.
If you answered (b) go to frame 9.
If you answered (c) go to frame 2.

4. Your answer is incorrect, but it may not be unwise. If you are afraid of bears, you might even consider going south. Go to frame 12 to see what would happen if you went south.

5. It appears obvious that you are afraid of bears. Your instructions are to go directly to Chapter 15 (do not pass Go, do not collect $200, heh, heh). You are asked to read about **counterconditioning,** paying special attention to Wolpe's **systematic desensitization.** If you can afford to, you might consider hiring this textbook author as a therapist. If you can't afford it, hire someone else.

6. Good! Good! You should do something else. But first you must return to the large collection of people and purchase a firearm. That is a polite word for gun. Having done that . . .

(Turn now to frame 13.)

7. You are not paying attention. Go back to frame 1 and start again.

8. Good. You noticed the arrow. You may eventually get a bear. It is interesting, don't you think, that a bear always stands facing toward the front of its tracks. This makes it a lot easier to find it. After you have found the bear, you will have to make a decision:
Will you
(a) stop and pray?
(b) run home?
(c) do something else?
If you said (a) go to frame 11.
If you said (b) go to frame 5.
If you said (c) go to frame 6.

9. That is not correct. If you begin to look for a bear's tracks before finding a forest, you may never find either track or bear. Go back to 3.

10. That is not correct. A large collection of people is a city. Bears are not usually found in cities, but they are often found in large collections of trees, or forests. You might waste a lot of time looking for bears in cities. Now go back and read frame 1 again.

11. Piety is an admirable quality in a student, but it is not the desired response. You might seriously consider, at this point, whether or not you really want to hunt bears. If you are sure that you do, you are instructed to begin again with frame 1.

12. Stop! You are going in the wrong direction. A bear faces toward the front of its tracks. That is an important point. Now you may go back to frame 2, or you might want to rest for a minute before continuing. You may do so, but you should probably begin at frame 1 when you are well again.

13. This incompleted program is included here simply as an illustration of a branching technique. Frustrated would-be bear hunters are invited to consult their local branch of the national organization of guides and outfitters.

Behavior Modification

In a general sense, **behavior modification** refers to the application of learning principles in deliberate and systematic attempts to change behavior. The majority of these principles have been derived from Skinner's work with operant conditioning and from extensions of that work. Thus behavior modification as an applied science is essentially a collection of behavioristic methods, many of which are extremely pertinent for teaching behavior.

The remainder of this chapter describes five major behavior control techniques and illustrates each with respect to the classroom. Chapter 5 describes a social learning theory which, as will become evident, is also very closely related to Skinner's operant conditioning and to behavior modification.

Extinction

The elimination of a response by withdrawing the reinforcement that maintains it is an example of **extinction.** No longer releasing a food pellet when a rat depresses the lever, after the rat has learned bar-pressing, will lead to the extinction of that behavior. Obviously, the only behaviors for which this procedure is appropriate are those which are maintained by positive reinforcement over which the experimenter or teacher has control. I recall quite clearly and with some embarrassment an unsuccessful attempt to apply extinction procedures with a stubborn English setter. The dog had just moved to a new, well-carpeted home, along with her owners, and had discovered that she was no longer welcome in the house. In fact, I had been told in a very clear manner that either the dog stayed out, or I did. Since I have a marked preference for living in houses when in cities, I proceeded to build the chagrined dog an elaborate (and expensive) wire kennel in the back yard. That night the dog was placed in her new quarters and the master retired—for a while. An unhappy English setter can make a great deal of noise—this English setter was not happy.

Elementary problem, surely. If the dog were allowed to leave the kennel, this would reinforce her behavior. If she were not allowed to leave, then, of course, this very undesirable behavior would soon be extinguished. Therefore, let her howl.

The first neighbor to phone said, "What in heaven's name do you think you're doing?"—to which I replied, "I'm using an extinction technique." For some reason this answer was less than satisfactory. An hour later the dog was in the house and the author was on the couch.

Positive Reinforcement

The use of positive reinforcement to modify behavior is implicit in a great deal of what teachers do. Whenever teachers praise a student, give a high mark, grant a special privilege, smile, pay particular attention, or ask an interested question, they may be reinforcing a student's behavior.

Where the deliberate and systematic use of positive reinforcement is particularly effective, a behavioral deficit is usually involved. In other words, positive reinforcement is most often employed not where there is *undesirable* behavior, but where the desired behavior has not been learned. Numerous examples of this technique used in relation to children have been reported (Hart et al., 1964; Allen and Harris, 1966). Azrin and Lindsley (1956) report a successful attempt to bring about

Teacher reinforcements

cooperative behavior through reinforcement. Training involved having pairs of children play a "game." Each child was given a stylus and told simply that the game was to place this stylus in one of three holes that were in front of the child. Children were also told that a jelly bean would occasionally fall into a cup between them. The apparatus was so constructed that reinforcement (the jelly bean) occurred only when children who faced each other placed their styli in corresponding holes at about the same time. Cooperation was required of them not only in deciding which hole to use and when, but also in sharing the candy. Within ten minutes, all teams learned to cooperate without instruction to do so.

Counterconditioning

This forbidding term signifies a relatively simple behavior control technique. It can be defined as the eliciting of a desirable response in the presence of the stimuli that ordinarily evoke undesirable responses. The assumption is that the original behavior was conditioned; hence the term *counterconditioning* for its removal.

Several specific methods of counterconditioning can be suggested. The most obvious are the three that Guthrie describes in relation to the breaking of habits (see Chapter 2). It will be recalled that these were the *fatigue* method, the *threshold* method, and the method of *incompatible stimuli*. In each of these an attempt is made to bring about a desirable response for a stimulus that would ordinarily elicit a less desirable response; each is therefore a procedure for counterconditioning. The fatigue method involves repeated presentation of the stimulus; the threshold method involves presenting the stimulus very faintly, and the method of incompatible stimuli involves presenting the stimulus when the response cannot occur.

Another example of counterconditioning is a **psychotherapeutic** technique developed by Joseph Wolpe (1958) and labeled *systematic desensitization*. * In essence this method does not differ from Guthrie's threshold technique; in detail of application, however, Wolpe provides some useful suggestions. The most usual approach to systematic desensitization is to train the patient to relax. Hypnosis is sometimes employed to this end. The patient then lists or describes all of the situations that lead to the response to be eliminated. For example, she may be a teacher with a severe fear of snakes. The undesirable response is the fear reaction; the stimuli that lead to this

behavior may include, in addition to snakes, such objects as worms, crocodiles, spiders, and perhaps even inanimate snake-like objects such as pencils or pieces of chalk. Snake fear is not a simple complaint, particularly in a teacher who, above all people, needs to react with anything but fear to pencils and chalk.

All of these stimuli are then arranged hierarchically in terms of the degree of fear that they elicit. The patient, who by now can relax completely at a moment's notice, is asked to imagine the stimulus. As soon as an anxiety response is elicited,

* To further amplify psychological jargon, this technique is also called *reciprocal inhibition*.

however mild, the procedure is stopped and the patient is asked to relax. The intention here is to replace the fear response with a response of relaxing—relaxation being incompatible with fear. The relationship between the threshold approach and this is obvious. The procedure is so designed that successively presented stimuli are always below threshold for the fear response. After four months of therapy, and a sizable fee, the patient can go home a happy woman—and remain happy until she picks up her first venomous snake.

Social Imitation

As a behavior modification technique, social imitation is the deliberate use of models to bring about desirable behavior or to eliminate less desirable responses. A very clear example of the systematic use of social imitation both for eliminating undesirable behavior and for bringing about socially acceptable responses is provided by two highly successful international organizations: Alcoholics Anonymous and Weight-Watchers. In both these organizations individuals describe their experiences, thereby serving as models to be emulated by other members of the group.

"Here I stand before you on the greatest day of my life. It was exactly a year ago tonight that I went home absolutely drunk out of my mind. I tell you! And then, when I got there, the dog barked and growled at me like I was some stranger, and the kids hid behind their mom's legs, they was so scared. Yessir, I tell you! And my Mrs., she never said a word to me. I tell you! I was a bum, a bum!

"Look at me now, will ya? I tell you! I come home tonight and the dog just come a runnin' and licked my face, and the kids, I tell you! And my Mrs.! Today I am proud. I am someone in the community, I tell you!"

Weight-Watchers follows a similar pattern. A 298-pound person stands in front of a large hall full of other fat people—an impressive sight from either direction.

"I am proud, I sure am. A year ago today I weighed myself, and then I started watching my weight, folks, and now look at me . . . !"

Discrimination Learning

Discrimination learning in behavior modification involves becoming aware that certain behaviors are acceptable in some situations, but not in others. Deliberate training in discrimination may well involve the use of both punishment and reward— punishment for the undesirable behavior and reward for desirable behavior. On the other hand, there are instances where either punishment or reward alone could bring about the same discriminations. Consider, for example, the case of a cow learning to find her own stall. The problem is essentially one of discriminating between her stall and others. One way to bring this learning about is to hit her soundly on the rump when she makes a false move. Another way is to feed her only in her stall. A third and more frequent practice is to hit her when she makes the wrong move and feed her when she finally makes the right one. A child learning to say "dad" when he sees his daddy and not to say "dad" when he sees someone else is in the same position as the cow. The reward he receives for a correct response may come from his father or mother or from anyone else around. For making an incorrect response he may simply be ignored. This would amount to nonreinforcement. Alternatively, he may be punished by the laughter that his behavior occasions or by his father's unintentionally cold behavior toward him.

Classroom Applications
of Behavior Modification

The foregoing is not intended to be an exhaustive list of behavior modification techniques. Obviously such a list would need to include simple S-R control techniques and could conceivably include such topics as methods for increasing creativity and programed instruction, among others. These are simply five relatively useful, therapeutically oriented techniques described by Bandura and Walters (1963) and by Bandura (1969). Although these authors discuss them in relation to therapy, they can be usefully applied to ordinary classroom practice. This is made clear in the following sections. These sections explain and illustrate each of the five techniques in relation to learning.

Extinction: The Elimination
of a Response through the
Withdrawal of Reinforcement

A student has acquired the habit of saying punctuation marks when he reads. For example, he says, "Stan comma the milkman comma has a long nose period." His classmates laugh when he does this, obviously reinforcing him. An extinction procedure might involve instructing the class not to laugh when the student reads. If, however, someone occasionally titters, thereby providing intermittent reinforcement, the behavior might become much more difficult to extinguish. In this case it might be better to ignore the student and hope that the reinforcement will eventually cease. Hope, too, has its place in teaching.

The situation described above can be interpreted as both a discipline and a learning problem. Obviously it is relatively rare for the removal of a behavior that is maintained by positive reinforcement to constitute a clear example of learning. This is especially true since classroom learning usually involves the *acquisition* rather than the elimination of responses.

I experienced a situation similar to that described above while I was teaching in a senior high school. One of the students persisted in being late for school almost every morning. At recess he was always asked why he had been late. He would then very politely, and with obvious sincerity, describe the terrible ailment which had kept his mother from making breakfast for their family of ten, or the severe wound that he had suffered on his now well-bandaged hand. On occasion he would tearfully explain that his alcoholic father had locked him in his room, or that he had stopped to rescue an old lady whom he had found in a ditch on the way to school.

I eventually realized that I was being had. After this, I rapidly extinguished the behavior, save for the occasional relapse, by failing to show surprise or concern at any of the student's fabrications. My concern had probably been the reinforcer.

Positive Reinforcement:
Bringing about Desirable
Behavior through Reinforcement

Positive reinforcement is centrally involved in classroom learning. Its systematic application, however, requires that two related questions be answered:

1. Under what stimulus conditions will the desirable response be emitted?
2. What reinforcement will be employed?

The first question may be answered in a number of ways. There are specific pedagogical devices such as programs, techniques such as Ausubel's reception learning (see Chapter 6), and the commoner day-to-day classroom routines that involve explaining, asking, showing films, demonstrating, and experimenting.

The second question also gives rise to several answers. Reinforcement can be extrinsic (external) or it can be intrinsic (internal). Obviously, extrinsic reinforcement is more likely to be under the control of the experimenter than is intrinsic reinforcement. The former consists of such things as praise, tokens, stars, grades, or promotions. The latter is defined in terms of the *satisfaction* that the student gets from learning.

Intrinsic Reinforcement Although intrinsic reinforcement is not under direct teacher control, the teacher can nevertheless structure learning situations in ways that are more or less likely to lead to satisfaction. Presenting students with tasks that are too difficult is likely to lead to anything but satisfaction with learning. The opposite is true as well. Excessively simple tasks are not self-reinforcing.

The teacher's use of external rewards provides another source of influence on intrinsic reinforcement. If rewards are initially administered for behaviors related to learning, it follows that the process of learning will acquire the characteristics of a generalized reinforcer. In fact, it is customary in those structured teaching programs which are based on reinforcement principles (for example, Meacham and Wiesen, 1969; Hewett, 1968) to advocate the use of external rewards only in the initial stages of the program. It is assumed that intrinsic reinforcement will eventually suffice to maintain the behavior.

Extrinsic Reinforcement Among the extrinsic reinforcers most commonly employed are those mentioned above: praise, tokens, stars, grades, or promotion. Another very important, and apparently very effective, source of reinforcement is defined by the *Premack Principle* (Premack, 1965). This principle states that behavior which ordinarily occurs very frequently can be employed to reinforce less frequent behavior. Parents and teachers use this principle constantly. A child is allowed to play outside *after* eating supper; a student is permitted to read a library book *after* completing an assignment.

Bijou and Sturges (1959) classify extrinsic reinforcers into five categories: consumables, manipulatables, visual and auditory stimuli, social stimuli, and tokens. It is interesting, and potentially valuable, to consider the use of each of these in the classroom. *Consumables* are relatively inconvenient. A teacher walking around a classroom with a bag of cookies, dispensing these as she observes desirable student behavior, might occasion some concern among parents. *Manipulatables,* which include objects such as toys or trinkets, can be employed successfully, particularly with young children. *Auditory* and *visual* stimuli that are reinforcing are less likely to be readily available to a teacher. Such reinforcers are defined as signals that have been given reinforcing properties. For example, if a teacher told students that she would ring a bell every time she was happy with them, the bell would be an auditory reinforcer. This is not to be confused with *social reinforcers,* which generally take the form of praise or approval, and which are by far the most prevalent and powerful reinforcers available to a teacher. In this connection it should also be kept in mind that peer approval is often as powerful or more powerful a reinforcer than teacher approval. *Tokens,* checkmarks or stars, are sometimes employed as direct extrinsic reinforcement for desirable behavior. In a *token* system, it is not uncommon to arrange for tokens to be exchanged for other reinforcers: consumables, manipulatables, or perhaps time for some pleasant activity.

Seven Principles for Using Reinforcement Michael (1967) describes seven principles that should be kept in mind when attempting to control behavior through its consequences. Some of these have been discussed earlier, but all are important enough to bear repeating.

The first is that the consequences of behavior, whether rewarding or punishing, are defined only in terms of their effect on the learner. Teachers cannot always assume that a stimulus that they consider pleasant for a student will, in fact, strengthen behavior. Peer approval, for example, is generally strongly reinforcing. For a very inhibited student, however, peer approval and the attention it generates may be quite punishing. Nor can a teacher simply ask students what is reinforcing for them. This might well render some reinforcers almost meaningless. If, for example, students were to indicate that praise was reinforcing, subsequent praise might be interpreted as less genuine and hence less reinforcing.

The second principle states that the effects of reinforcement are automatic. That is, the teacher need not explain to students that if they learn well they will receive some specific reinforcement, which will then lead them to study even harder. The point is that if students do learn, and consequently are reinforced, they will probably study even harder without ever having discussed this marvellous phenomenon with their teacher.

A third principle stresses that reinforcement or punishment should be related very closely to the terminal behavior. In other words, teachers must have some short-range goals clearly in mind so that they can reinforce behavior that matches those goals.

The fourth principle is concerned with consistency. This is not intended to mean that reinforcement must occur for every correct response. It does mean, however, that a specific behavior should not be reinforced one time and then punished the next.

A related principle, the fifth, is that consequences should follow behavior very closely. Delayed reward or punishment, for children as for animals, is much less effective than immediate response consequences. Adherence to this principle is very clearly one of the major strengths of programed instruction, where learners receive knowledge of results immediately. Another implication of this principle is that the period of time between giving a quiz and returning the results should be kept as short as is practically possible.

Sixth, Michael claims that the amount of reinforcement necessary for behavioral change is usually underestimated. This is particularly true for the early stages of learning. The sixth principle says that reinforcement must be potent. If, in fact, teacher praise is highly valued by a student, that student will probably require less praise than another who does not value it so much.

The seventh principle relates to the structuring of a learning situation. It maintains that the student's work should be so programed that there are many clear steps, each of which can be reinforced. Obviously, traditional programed instruction

Material should be arranged in small steps.

can meet this requirement much more easily than can a classroom teacher who is responsible for a relatively large number of students.

A simple illustration of the use of rewards in a learning situation was provided by a ninth grade typing teacher in a remote rural school. The teacher had contracted with the class to give students fifteen minutes of free time if they learned to type at a rate of fifty words per minute. An additional fifteen minutes was to be given for every five words per minute above fifty. No rural school has since developed a group of such proficient ninth grade typists. This may have been due to the fact that the contract was interpreted to mean that the entire class would get fifteen minutes for each typist scoring fifty. On a warm morning in June when the lake lay calm and inviting, not a single student showed up in class. Most of us can still type.

Counterconditioning: The
Eliciting of a Desirable Response
in the Face of a Stimulus that Is
Associated with Undesirable
Behavior

Guthrie's techniques for breaking habits illustrate three different methods of bringing about counterconditioning. Each of these can be readily employed in relation to discipline problems. It is somewhat more difficult to apply them to learning-oriented situations since counterconditioning is defined as the replacement of an undesirable response with a desirable one. To some extent this involves learning as well. The illustrations of counterconditioning given here, however, relate primarily to discipline problems.

Fatigue The fatigue technique can be interpreted as involving punishment since the continued repetition of a response eventually becomes highly unpleasant. It is probably not employed very often by parents or teachers, and, in view of the frequently negative effects of punishment, probably should not be employed at all (see Chapter 3 for a discussion of punishment). Guthrie gives an example of the use of the fatigue method with a little girl who refused to stop playing with matches. Her mother forced her to light countless matches until the girl was completely satiated—but still she was made to continue, until near exhaustion. Her behavior toward matches was apparently changed after this.

Threshold Method A teacher who has in her class a child with an intense fear of teachers—a child who howls vociferously whenever he sees a teacher—can probably make good use of this technique. It is readily apparent that the student's behavior poses a discipline problem, inasmuch as a howling child in a classroom is not a highly recommended instructional aid. The elimination of this behavior might eventually be achieved by having the teacher stand outside the classroom, in plain view of the students, but far enough away not to elicit howling. Over successive days, the

teacher is allowed to move closer and closer to the school, all the while observing the children playing on the other side of the windows. She should pay particular attention to the involvement of the problem child in the play behavior which surrounds him. The teacher would be well advised to stand a few feet further back when the student appears to resent her very gradual approach. A clever and well-trained teacher may eventually succeed in approaching close enough to be able to crawl through a window and rejoin her now healthy charges.*

A somewhat less facetious illustration of the threshold method is mentioned in Chapter 2. It involves the rather common-sense practice of presenting difficult material in class periods that are deliberately kept short and interesting. The intention is clearly to keep the presentation somewhere below the boredom threshold. Subsequent related lessons may then be lengthened without ever bringing about the problems associated with restlessness and inattention.

Incompatible Stimuli A relatively frequent discipline problem in today's schools involves student inattentiveness in class. Applying the technique of incompatible stimuli to this problem would involve carrying on classroom activities when inattentiveness is impossible, or at least unlikely. One way of doing this might be to have parents present in the classroom as observers, or to invite the principal, also as an observer. Neither of these approaches is very likely to be practical very often, however. A third solution might be to have the teacher present a stimulating, attention-compelling lesson. Given enough such presentations, a few bad ones are much less likely to create a real problem.

---

* PPC: "Could we have a more realistic example?"
Author: "Read on."

Social Imitation: The Systematic
Use of Principles of Imitation to
Modify Behavior

The deliberate use of principles of social imitation in the classroom can be of great value. Several illustrations follow immediately. In addition, Chapter 5 presents a more detailed discussion of social imitation, and Chapter 14 looks at the use of social imitation in relation to discipline.

The task of teaching a child to operate a tool in an industrial arts workshop or to execute a movement in a physical education class can often be accomplished more effectively and quickly by demonstrating the required procedure. In the same way a student can be taught some aspects of writing, how to pronounce foreign words, how to convey emotion in a drama class, or how to conduct a debate. In many cases other students can serve as models instead of the teacher.

Social imitation

Two features of modeling procedures make them particularly useful in the classroom. The first is that the effects of reinforcing a single model, as Bandura and Walters have shown (1963), are transmitted to the observers. For example, a student who is highly praised for using humor in a written assignment is very likely to serve as a model for other students. The second is that the use of this technique need not involve either the teacher or the students as models. Among the variety of symbolic models available to the teacher are books, films, television, and records, as well as verbal and written descriptions and instructions.

> *Discrimination Learning:*
> *Learning to Distinguish*
> *between Situations Where*
> *Specific Behaviors Are*
> *Permissible and Those Where*
> *the Same Behaviors Are*
> *Inappropriate*

Learning The formation of discriminations is of paramount importance in classroom learning, as in social learning. This is less a behavior control technique, however, than a simple description of one type of learning. From the teacher's point of view, the formation of simple discriminations is especially important in the teaching of reading. Such letters as b and d or p and q require rather fine discriminations. The most common technique for initiating the discrimination is probably simply to tell the student how the stimuli differ. It is obvious that the consequences of responding appropriately to these discriminated stimuli will be reinforcing, whereas incorrect responses will tend not to be reinforced and, therefore, not to be learned.

A Case Study Illustration
of Behavior Modification

The following is an edited version of a case study report of the actual application of operant conditioning techniques in the classroom. The report was written by Eileen C. Klein (reprinted by permission). It is presented here as an illustration of the role that theory can play in practice.

> *The purpose of this nonclinical experiment was to modify the behavior of a boy who showed no respect, within a classroom, for the conversational rights of others. Positive reinforcement through reward promised to be an effective means of producing the desired responses in this social learning situation because the same method had been eminently successful during the fall term in curbing, within the same child, the tendency to meet every unpleasant peer encounter with physical aggression. To provide an opportunity to witness the effectiveness of the social learning principles presented by Bandura and Walters (1963), the strategy included the use of models.*

> **Significant Facts from Case**
> **History**
> *Rob is the only son and third oldest child of a family of four children. The children and parents immigrated to Canada from Germany in 1966. At that time, when the oldest daughter was enrolled in school, the mother and children could speak no English. The mother tongue is still spoken in the home. Rob entered school a year and a half ago.*

Because of language difficulty, he spent the first year in a readiness type program, but he is now coping successfully with the regular first grade course. He is a cheerful, healthy seven-year-old. Results of Wechsler tests administered last May indicate average intelligence.

Description of Undesirable Behavior

When compared to the types of behavior which psychologists and therapists attempt to modify in the application of their theories, Rob's behavior appears more troublesome than deviant. It was considered an appropriate study because it is with the annoying type of behavior that nonprofessionals must deal daily, without the benefit of assistance from more qualified people. Furthermore, it appeared ideal for testing theories, because one aspect of the particular behavior was more easily manipulated to accommodate an experiment.

On January 26th, a record was kept of the number of times Rob made audible interruptions of general classroom routines. During that day he did not once raise his hand to ask for attention. The twenty-five interruptions were classified as follows:

a. Direct interruptions of a student speaking to the class in a formal situation —6.
b. Direct interruptions of the teacher speaking to the entire class in a formal situation —4.
c. Calling out answers to class-directed questions —10.
d. Speaking to gain the teacher's attention when she was working with a small group of which he was not a part —5.

"Interruptions" as used here is a general classification of unsolicited remarks and questions such as, "I rode a horse lots of times" —"Mickey is using red pencil" —"Can I mark the calendar tomorrow?" Not tabulated, of course, are the number of times he spoke in informal and small group situations where it was not considered necessary to await permission.

Strategy and Observations

The following Monday morning, a process of extinction of undesired responses was begun. For two days, with no previous explanation of what was being done, all unsolicited remarks or questions were completely ignored or answered by the teacher with, "I'm sorry, I'm not listening to you." When he became insistent and walked over to the teacher, repeating his remark, she closed her eyes. Detailed care was taken to anticipate his every real need, so that his general progress and comfort would not be jeopardized. Tuesday, after school, it was explained to Rob, in very basic English, that he could be heard but was not being acknowledged, and the reasons for taking turns speaking were reviewed.

On Wednesday there was an observable change in Rob's behavior. He appeared to be consciously keeping his hands under the table, and he began to speak in a louder, more demanding voice. When his remarks met with the same lack of response, he attempted to gain attention by tapping his foot and annoying his classmates. This behavior, too, was ignored by the teacher, and the other children appeared to imitate the adult model.

By Thursday afternoon Rob had lapsed into a very sullen silence and would not reply even to questions specifically directed to him.

On the second Tuesday a program designed to facilitate the emergence of acceptable patterns of behavior was begun. Rob appreciates any kind of cartoon drawing, so the introduction to the printing lesson that day involved two cartoon-type pictures: "This is a watchbird watching an arm-lifter" and "this is a watchbird watching a no-arms." The children printed, "See the watchbird" on special yellow paper with a place for an illustration. Rob's drawing showed the watchbird scowling at a boy with no arms, but fingers were sticking out from behind the figure. Throughout the day he made no attempts to speak but did reply to questions addressed to him. Other children were acknowledged with, "Yes, we want to hear you. Your hand was up."

The next day the science lesson was on evaporation and condensation. Rob had a much clearer understanding of this science concept than most of his classmates and in the discussion following the experiments he appeared very eager. He started to speak out in reply to a question, then stopped himself, but sat with his brows raised eagerly. Permission to speak was given by saying, "Yes, Rob, you raised your eyebrows and that's almost the same as raising your hand." That afternoon he was called upon to speak four times because he had raised his brow. He appeared very happy with the proceedings.

It was his turn to clean chalkboards after school that day and Gef was asked to stay behind to help. A game was played wherein each boy, in turn, was told to erase a given number of words from his section of board. Before he could erase, he had to raise his hand and say, "May I?" If he forgot either step, extra words were written on the chalkboard. Rob entered into the game spiritedly and showed no reluctance in making the desired response. Both boys were praised, at first continuously, then at variable intervals for their behavior, and it was arranged that Rob should win.

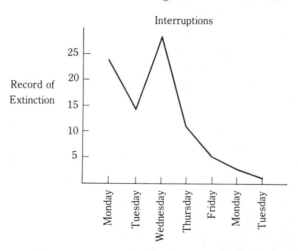

At 9:05 the next morning Rob raised his hand and requested permission to get his running shoes. He had shoes to wear beside his desk, but he was rewarded with praise for having asked in the correct manner and allowed to go for the runners. He showed obvious pleasure when, upon his return, Gef whispered, "Good boy, Rob." That day he raised his hand seven times and was continuously rewarded with instant recognition and praise. On one occasion when he started to speak, stopped himself, and raised his hand, he was given the good watchbird cartoon to keep.

Rewards for exhibiting the desired responses during the ensuing three weeks were dispensed on a variable-ratio schedule, and consisted largely of praise given either immediately or at the end of the day. Twice he received special privileges as reward. Most effective of all as stimuli for eliciting the desired responses were remarks of approval from the peer group. Observations two months later show a satisfactory modification of behavior. Rob occasionally reverts to his former behavior, but a shake of the head is sufficient to remind him to raise his hand.

Summary of Chapter 4

This chapter has presented descriptions of two major areas in educational theory and practice in which operant conditioning principles are centrally involved: programed instruction and behavior modification. The characteristics and effectiveness of branching and linear programs were described, and examples of each were provided. In addition, five major behavior modification techniques were described, with special emphasis on their applicability to the classroom.

Main Points in Chapter 4

1. A number of different methods are available for dealing with individual differences. Among them are increased individual attention and tracking. For practical reasons, these are seldom as effective as one would wish.

2. Programed instruction is a third alternative for coping with differences among students. Theoretically, the fact that it allows learners to progress at their own rate makes it suitable for both slower and faster learners.

3. A program is essentially a sequential arrangement of information in small steps (frames), each of which requires the learner to make a response. Immediate feedback (knowledge of results) serves as reinforcement.

4. Skinner is largely responsible for current interest in programed instruction. He is responsible for the development of linear programs. Crowder is credited with the development of branching programs.

5. A linear program requires all learners to progress through the same material in exactly the same sequence. It also requires them to construct their own responses.

6. A branching program requires learners to select an answer and then directs them to the next frame on the basis of that answer. Those who answer all items correctly progress through the program in the shortest number of frames possible. Those who make errors are provided with further explanation and/or information.

7. Research has not shown that either branching or linear programs are superior. It has shown, however, that programs do teach. Pressey claims that they do so most effectively as adjuncts to other methods of instruction.

8. Bears always face toward the front of their tracks.

9. Behavior modification involves the systematic application of operant learning principles in attempts to change behavior. The five behavior modification techniques discussed here are: extinction, positive reinforcement, counterconditioning, social imitation, and discrimination learning.

10. Extinction involves the elimination of a response through the withdrawal of reinforcement.

11. Positive reinforcement as a control technique makes use of various kinds of reward for controlling responses.

12. Counterconditioning involves bringing about a desirable behavior in response to a stimulus that previously elicited an undesirable behavior. Guthrie's three methods for breaking habits are examples of counterconditioning.

13. The deliberate use of social imitation in order to modify behavior is particularly evident in groups when individuals serve as explicit models for other members of the group.

14. Discrimination learning involves learning to make different responses to similar situations, where not doing so would lead to inappropriate behavior.

15. Each of these techniques can be applied to classroom situations.

Suggested Readings

The following two books of readings on programed instruction should be of particular value to the student who wishes to explore this area more carefully:

DeCecco, J. P. *Educational Technology: Readings in Programmed Instruction.* New York: Holt, Rinehart and Winston, 1964.

de Garzia, A. and D. **Sohn** (Eds.). *Programs, Teachers and Machines.* New York: Bantam Books, 1962.

For practical instruction on how to write programs, the reader is referred to the very useful and readable book:

Markle, S. M. *Good Frames and Bad: A Grammar of Frame Writing.* New York: John Wiley, 1964.

The potential impact of the computer on education, and the relationship of this impact to the behavior and preparation of the classroom teacher is examined in the following:

Hicks, B. L. and S. **Hunka.** *The Teacher and the Computer.* Philadelphia: W. B. Saunders, 1971.

The systematic application of the principles of operant conditioning to problems in the classroom is detailed in a number of excellent references. A short book by Meacham and Wiesen is especially valuable in pointing out the many sources of reinforcement that are available to the classroom teacher and their possible effects on pupil behavior. The O'Leary and O'Leary book contains a large number of articles relating to the use of behavior modification techniques in the classroom.

Meacham, M. L. and A. E. **Wiesen.** *Changing Classroom Behavior: A Manual for Precision Teaching.* Scranton, Penn.: International Textbook Company, 1969.
O'Leary, K. A. and S. G. **O'Leary.** *Classroom Management: The Successful Use of Behavior Modification.* New York: Pergamon Press, 1972.

An area in which the principles of operant conditioning and of social learning are being applied with highly promising results is that of educating emotionally disturbed children. The following book by Hewett provides an excellent introduction to this area:

Hewett, S. *The Emotionally Disturbed Child in the Classroom.* Boston: Allyn and Bacon, 1968.

Seals are the staple food of the polar bear. Infant seals are particularly easy to capture when they are still in the aglos *(calving dens). The* aglo *is a small ice cave hollowed out by a mother seal and accessible only from the water. It is covered with a three-to-five-foot layer of snow and a thick cover of ice. The polar bear can scent* aglos *from remarkable distances. Having found one, the bear rapidly excavates the overburden of snow with quick blows of paws, and then attempts to break through the ice by rearing up and smashing downward with both front paws. If the ice is too thick, the bear may move back a short distance, run toward the aglo, leap high in the air, and come thundering down with all four paws, crashing noisily through the ice. It is then a simple matter to reach inside and pull out the squirming infant (Perry, 1966).*

5
Social Learning

Imitation is the sincerest form of flattery.
(Charles Caleb Colton)

Imitation is nature's cheapest trick!

Advance Organizer There is much more to learning than contiguity and reinforcement or punishment. We learn from reading, watching television, listening, and observing. And we probably learn from many other things and in many other ways as well. This chapter looks specifically at the ways in which models influence our behavior, paying particular attention to the acquisition of socially acceptable behavior as a function of imitation. The underlying theoretical explanation is based principally on operant conditioning theory (Chapter 3), and some of the more obvious educational implications of this social learning theory are described in the section on behavior modification in Chapter 4, and in the chapter on discipline (14).

In a Monday issue of the local newspaper there appeared a brief front page news item: a woman in Rome had killed her young son by tossing him from the top floor of a twelve-story building. She had then attempted to commit suicide by jumping down after him, but had succeeded only in injuring herself severely. In the Wednesday issue of the paper that same week, there appeared a similar story which described an event in Naples. A woman had killed her three sons by throwing them into a well and had then attempted to commit suicide by jumping in after them. She was reported in serious condition, but was expected to live.

Coincidence? Perhaps, but it is remarkable how often news of some bizarre (and sometimes not so bizarre) happening is followed shortly by a report of a similar event elsewhere. A campus riot is given national front page and television coverage; a rash of riots sweeps campuses across the country. A man keeps his wife hostage and holds police at bay for three days; another keeps his entire family hostage for a week. A sniper shoots three people in New York; another shoots four in Detroit. A Cuban hijacks a plane to go to Havana; 300 of his compatriots do likewise.

It is also remarkable how fads and expressions sweep through countries: overnight (almost) men begin to wear their hair long or short; the miniskirt is in, then out; everyone is saying "yeah" or "outasight"; things are "cool" or "neat" and people are "beautiful."

Other phenomena, while not nearly so remarkable, serve, perhaps, to illustrate the same thing. In this culture most men wear shoes, shirts, jackets, and ties (on occasion); women wear dresses and skirts; women tend the home and men work outside for a living (this is changing); it is taboo to touch strangers (or even friends) unless the stranger happens to be one's husband or wife; regardless of any inclination to the contrary, virtually everyone stands for the national anthem; when pleased, audiences clap their hands, and when displeased, they boo.

Some of these are illustrations of normal, socially acceptable (even socially *expected*) behavior. Some are illustrations of deviant behavior, and some are illustrations of controversial behavior. All, however, are examples of imitation, a process that many social learning theorists consider to be central to socialization. Processes involved in imitation (or **observational learning**) are described by Bandura as:

> *One of the fundamental means by which new modes of behavior are acquired and existing patterns are modified . . . . (Bandura, 1969, p. 118)*

These processes are described, elaborated, and illustrated in this chapter.

Definition of
Social Learning

Social learning involves the acquisition of those behavior patterns which society expects. Socially acceptable behavior varies from culture to culture. In many parts of India it is highly acceptable (even desirable) to openly bribe superiors or government officials with gifts, money, meals, flattery, or favors. In the Western world the practice, while quite common, is not sufficiently socially acceptable to be carried on openly. In Korea students are expected to bow to their professors and to offer them gifts. On this continent, a student who bowed to his professor and offered him gifts would embarrass them both, would be ridiculed, and could end up in a psychiatric ward.

Not only does socially acceptable behavior vary from culture to culture, but it also varies from one person to another even within one culture. This is highly obvious in caste societies, where the behavior of members of different castes toward one another is carefully prescribed through social rules. Even in a relatively class-free society such as ours, the behavior of people in service occupations (clerks, receptionists, taxi drivers, waiters, etc.) is determined largely by the social expectations of their roles. And the behavior of the sexes toward each other is, when socially appropriate, highly dependent on the patterns of behavior that our culture considers suitable for each. Socially acceptable behavior also varies for different age groups.

A third characteristic of socially accepted behavior patterns is that they are partly determined by the immediate situation. Some behavior patterns are socially acceptable in one situation and quite unacceptable in another—for the same individual. An employee can offer her boss a drink when the boss comes to her home. When the boss comes to her office, however, she should probably refrain from saying, "Have a drink, Charlie?"

The point of these illustrations is that social learning does not involve simply learning a set of behaviors that *are* acceptable; it also involves learning under what conditions they are *not* acceptable. In other words, effective social learning involves a great deal of generalization and discrimination.

Probably one of the most important tasks of the home, in the early years of a child's life, and of the school in later years, is to foster the development of behaviors that are appropriate for the child. This really involves transmitting the culture of a society to a child and teaching him behaviors appropriate for his sex and for his social class (see McNeil, 1969).

The central question from a learning theory point of view is: How does the child learn socially acceptable behaviors? A number of answers have been given to this question. The concept most common to these answers is that of *identification* or *imitation*.

Identification and Imitation

A distinction has often been drawn between the processes of identification and imitation. In essence, **identification** is said to be the more general and more inclusive term. It is commonly employed by psychoanalysts (for example, Freud) to describe the total process of attempting to assume the role, attitudes, feelings, and behaviors of another person. The term *imitation*, on the other hand, is employed to describe the simple process of copying the behavior of others. Recently Bandura and Walters (1963) and Bandura (1969) have suggested that no distinction need be drawn between the two, that the processes described for both are identical, and that therefore the words are simply different terms for the same phenomenon.

Put simply, learning through imitation, sometimes referred to as observational learning, involves acquiring new responses or modifying old ones as a result of seeing a model do something.

Miller and Dollard

One of the earliest well-known attempts to include imitation in a theory of learning was made jointly by Neal Miller and John Dollard in their book *Social Learning and Imitation*. Basically, theirs was a reinforcement theory much like Skinner's, but with one crucial difference. This had to do with their concept of reinforcement. Reinforcement, they believed, results from the reduction of a **drive.** Hence *drive,* rather than *reinforcement,* becomes the central notion in this theory. By *drive* is meant any aroused state of the organism that leads it to action. Drive is attached to a specific stimulus: hunger, pain, excitement, joy, and so forth. The behavior it leads to will become learned if it results in a reduction of drive. Hence reinforcement always results from the removal or reduction of drive. The role of imitation in this model of learning is a simple one. Miller and Dollard assume that the behavior of others serves as a *cue* for an individual's response only after the individual has been reinforced for imitative behaviors often enough that she has acquired a generalized habit of imitating. For example, a child may engage in a number of responses in the presence of others. Some of these responses will match the responses of others and may be reinforced. If this occurs often enough, the child may eventually learn to imitate.

This simplified account of Miller and Dollard's basic position is included as an introduction to the more highly developed and more research-based position recently advanced by Bandura and Walters.

Bandura and Walters

The social learning theory advanced by Bandura and Walters (1963) and Bandura (1969) is also based on a model of operant conditioning. The system is principally concerned with reinforcement and imitation as they relate to the control of behavior. Much of the work done by Albert Bandura and Richard Walters (who died a few years ago at an early age) deals with the development of personality variables in children through the process of imitation. Much of their experimental work deals with the development of sex roles, of **aggression,** and of dependency in children. In addition, they have been highly concerned with **behavior modification,** a subject discussed in Chapter 4.

The learning position they advance is most easily understood in terms of what Bandura (1969) calls behavior control systems. He describes three such systems.

Behavior Control Systems

Stimulus Control A relatively large number of human behaviors are under direct stimulus control. These include reflexive acts such as withdrawing the hand from a hot stove or jerking the leg when the patella is struck. In both these instances, the stimulus determines that the behavior will occur.

A larger and more important class of behaviors under direct stimulus control includes all responses acquired through classical conditioning, whether through contiguity or through association with reinforcement. For example, a child may learn to react with fear to the sound of a dog growling, after being bitten by the dog. The fear is acquired because of the initial contiguity of the sound and the pain. After learning occurs, the fear reaction is under direct control of the stimulus, *dog growling*.

A third class of behaviors controlled directly by stimuli includes instrumental acts that come under control of a stimulus because of the stimulus is always present at the time of reinforcement. An example of this kind of response is given by Bandura (1969, p. 24). It involves learning to make a response in an experimental session only when a green light is on, but never when the red light is on. Eventually the green stimulus is *discriminated* from the red one and acquires control over whether the response will occur.

Outcome Control The second behavior control system takes into account those responses which are controlled by their consequences. This type of system assumes that the feedback an individual receives as a consequence of behavior will determine whether or not the behavior is likely to take place again. Consequences of behavior, usually in the form of reinforcement or nonreinforcement, will, in this case, control behavior.

Symbolic Control The third behavior control system involves what Bandura (1969) labels central mediational processes. These are processes involved in organizing information, in interpreting stimulus and response events, in forming hypotheses about the kinds of responses most likely to lead to reinforcement, and in making decisions with regard to behavior. In short, central mediational processes are cognitive (intellectual; see Chapter 6) processes.

Bandura and Walters' (1963) orientation was initially behavioristic and remains largely unchanged in later writings (Bandura, 1969), partly because of the role played by operant conditioning principles in their model. The concept of **mediation,** however, is not rigidly behavioristic. It has had to be introduced because a simple operant conditioning model appears inadequate to explain imitation. The typical operant conditioning model assumes that, once an operant has been reinforced in the presence of a discriminated stimulus (cage, light, verbal command), it will be repeated upon recurrence of the stimulus. What typically happens in observational learning, however, is that, even after imitation has been reinforced on numerous occasions, the presentation of a model (stimulus) may not lead to a response until considerable time has elapsed. In order to account for the effectiveness of the stimulus in eliciting a matching response after a time lag, it is assumed that mediating processes can, in a sense, serve as stimuli and, at the same time, represent anticipation of reinforcement. The importance of intrinsic, as opposed to extrinsic, reward for learning through observation cannot be overestimated. This type of reinforcement, labeled **vicarious reinforcement** by Bandura and Walters, accounts for the formation of a great many response patterns in both children and adults. This is discussed further in the next section.

The Theory in Capsule

Bandura and Walters' position may be summarized in the form of three statements:

1. Much human learning is a function of observing the behavior of others.
2. It is probably correct to assume that we learn to imitate through being reinforced for so doing and that continued reinforcement maintains imitative behavior.
3. Imitation, or observational learning, can therefore be explained in terms of operant conditioning principles, provided it is correct to say that people can, through mediation, "imagine" both reinforcement consequences and the behavior of models.

The following questions, directly related to these statements, are particularly relevant:

1. How prevalent is observational learning?
2. What are the sources of reinforcement in observational learning?
3. What, in behavioral terms, are the specific possible results of this kind of learning?

Answers to these questions form the remainder of this chapter.

Prevalence of Imitation

Copying the behavior of others is a relatively widespread practice. At the beginning of this chapter a number of behaviors were mentioned as being examples of imitation. All of these involved humans imitating humans in advanced Western cultures. It is interesting to note differences in patterns of imitation among cultures and the occurrence of imitation among animals and across species. Bandura and Walters (1963) cite an illustration of imitation in a primitive culture, that of the Cantalense. Here a young girl is given miniature working replicas of all the tools her mother uses: broom, corn-grinding stone, and so on. From the moment she can walk she follows her mother and imitates her actions. There is little or no direct teaching.

Most of the significant social learning accomplished by girls in that culture results from direct imitation.

Another culture where learning occurs through observation is that of the Canadian Ojibwa Indian, who, until the turn of this century, depended almost exclusively upon trapping, hunting, and fishing. In Ojibwa tribes, young boys followed their fathers around traplines as soon as they were physically able. For the first few years they simply observed—again there was no direct teaching. When the boy was old enough, he would fashion his own weapons and traps and set his own snares as he had seen his father do. Whatever he bagged would be brought back to his father's lodge. If he had a sister, she would have learned how to prepare hides, meat, and fish; how to make clothing; how to erect shelters; and how to do the many other things she had seen her mother doing. Now, if she were old enough, she would take care of her brother's catch, prepare his meals, and make his clothing.

In more technological societies such as ours, it is almost always virtually impossible to provide children with miniature working replicas of the tools used by their parents—nor is it possible for children to observe their parents at work. It would appear, then, that observational learning, while it might be of some academic interest, could hardly be of much practical value for teachers. This however, is false. The reason why has to do with the meaning of the term *model*.

Models

The term *model* may refer to an actual person whose behavior serves as a stimulus for an observer's response. Or it may, as is more often the case in our society, refer to a **symbolic model.** Symbolic models include such things as books, verbal or written instructions, pictures, mental images, cartoon or film characters, religious figures, and, not the least important, television. These are probably more prevalent than real-life models for children of a technological society. This is not to deny that peers, siblings, and parents serve as models, or that teachers and other well-behaved people are held up as **exemplary models.** ("Why don't you behave like Dr. Lefrancois? See how nicely he sits in church with his eyes closed. He's praying for us, dear man.") It is probably true that much social learning involves direct observation of real-life models.

Animals, like people, appear to be susceptible to the effects of imitation. Among the many studies one might cite to support this contention is that of Herbert and Harsh (1944), who demonstrated that cats can learn remarkably rapidly after watching other cats perform learning tasks. I can also cite a rather striking phenomenon peculiar to some breeds of dogs, among which is the English setter (an undocumented phenomenon, to be sure, but one that can easily be verified). It appears that dogs can learn very quickly how to bark like other dogs. The first time this became apparent, the English setter had been left in a kennel where basset hounds were bred. An English setter will sometimes bark politely when the situation fully warrants it, but on most occasions it is a quiet animal. When this setter returned from the kennel, however, she howled and bayed very impolitely and very much like a basset.

I spent almost an entire week barking politely in response to the setter's baying, in order to show her how a setter should behave. It is highly likely that *observational learning* was sufficient to account for this behavior. Further corroboration of this notion was obtained some months later when the setter was left in a different kennel—one where chihuahuas were raised. There is nothing quite so disgusting as a large dog yipping like a chihuahua.

The most often cited examples of animals imitating humans involve monkeys or chimpanzees. When reared in human families, these animals, not surprisingly, typically adopt many human behaviors.

There are fewer instances of people adopting the behavior of animals. Despite the fact that people can be squirrely, can act like mules, occasionally go ape, or are pigs or turkeys, it is unlikely that the behaviors that lead to the labels are acquired through the observation of animals. Indeed, it is considerably more likely that human models are involved. There are a number of instances reported, however, of children who have been abandoned by their parents and who have subsequently learned to behave like the animals with whom they roamed. A number of such children have been brought up by wolves (**feral children**) and have learned to eat carrion, to walk on all fours, and to howl at night (Singh and Zingg, 1942).

Sources of *Reinforcement in Imitation*

An easy answer to the question "Why do people imitate?" is simply that they imitate because to do so is reinforcing. The next question is not quite so simple. What are the sources of reinforcement in imitation?

Imitation may be reinforced in three ways. The first way is most applicable to the early learning of children. It involves direct reinforcement of the learner by the model. It is not at all uncommon to hear parents exclaim over the behavior of their children simply because "he's doing it just like Daddy!" Nor is it uncommon to hear a child draw his parents' attention to the fact that he *is* doing it just like Daddy—and that is pretty strong evidence that the child has learned to expect reinforcement from the model.

A second source of reinforcement is inherent in the consequences of the behavior, particularly if it is socially acceptable behavior that is instrumental in attaining a goal. Even though a child may learn to say "milk" as a function of imitation, and partly as a function of her model's reinforcing her, she is not likely to go on saying "milk" unless someone gives her milk when she says it. It is in this sense that the consequences of behavior learned through observation can be reinforcing.

A third source of reward is termed *vicarious* reinforcement. It involves deriving a second-hand type of satisfaction from imitating. It is as though the observer assumes that if a model does something he must do it because he derives some reinforcement or pleasure from his behavior. Therefore, someone else who engaged in the same behavior would receive the same reinforcement. Interestingly, an observer may engage in even quite ineffective and unreinforced behavior over a prolonged period of time. The fact that the behavior is maintained is taken as evidence that some sort of vicarious reinforcement is involved. Studies have shown that the administration of reward or punishment to a model has an effect on the behavior of observers similar to that which the direct administration of the reward or punishment would have. One such study (Bandura, 1962) involved exposing three groups of children to three different models. All models behaved aggressively toward an inflated plastic doll. The first model was rewarded for so doing, the second was punished, and the third suffered no consequences. The subjects' subsequent aggressive responses were observed. It was noted that there was a significant difference in mean number of responses between the model-rewarded and the model-punished group. The effect of reward and punishment on the models was transferred *vicariously* to the subjects.

Effects of Imitation

Superficially, imitation seems to consist of little more than copying the behavior of a model. A closer examination of the responses involved, however, permits the division of imitative behavior into three categories. These categories were suggested by Bandura and Walters (1963) and reaffirmed later by Bandura (1969). They are labeled the **modeling effect,** the **inhibitory-disinhibitory effect,** and the **eliciting effect.**

The modeling effect involves the acquisition of new responses. The *inhibitory* and *disinhibitory* effects involve the **inhibition** or the disinhibition, respectively, of deviant responses, usually as a result of seeing a model punished or rewarded for the behavior. The *eliciting* effect involves behavior that is neither novel for the observer nor deviant. It is manifested when the observer engages in behavior related, but not identical, to that of the model.

The three effects of observational learning or imitation are examined and illustrated in the following three subsections.

The Modeling Effect Whenever an observer acquires a new response (or set of responses) as a result of seeing a model emit that response, the *modeling* effect is illustrated. It is unlikely that imitation in adults will take the form of learning novel responses since most behavior patterns have already been acquired.

The acquisition of novel aggressive responses has been extensively studied in laboratory situations (Bandura, 1962; Bandura, Ross, and Ross, 1963). Subjects have usually been nursery school children. The typical experiment involves exposing the subjects to a real-life model, or a cartoon or filmed model, engaged in novel aggressive behavior directed toward a large inflated plastic doll. The model might punch the doll, strike it with a hammer, kick it, or sit on it. Control groups are exposed to the same model sitting quietly with the doll (rather than on it). The results of experiments such as this almost invariably illustrate the modeling effect. Children exposed to aggressive models are not only more aggressive than control groups when left with the dolls, but also usually demonstrate precisely imitative aggressive responses that are in all likelihood novel to them.

These experiments involve eliciting aggressive behavior through observation in laboratory situations. In addition, the aggression is generally directed toward an inanimate object. It might be argued that this is a far cry from aggression against real people in real life. Ethical considerations, however, prevent the use of babies rather than dolls in these experiments. It is therefore very difficult to illustrate the acquisition of meaningful aggressive responses experimentally. But considerable anecdotal evidence suggests that children whose playmates are highly aggressive will also tend to be aggressive. Even very brief exposure to an aggressive model may result in the imitation of that model's behavior by a formerly docile child. My young son is a case in point. There was no finer, better behaved child until one of his mother's friend's children visited him. The visitor was an overaggressive child. He kicked me on the left shin twice, knocked my young daughter over repeatedly, and pulled the dog's tail. After he left, my son knocked his sister over, pulled the dog's tail, and kicked me in the left shin. By the time this last novel aggressive response had been emitted, my desire to observe the modeling effect in a real situation had been satisfied. That response was therefore treated quickly and effectively with a psychologically and practically sound aversive stimulus.

Numerous nonaggressive responses are also transmitted through imitation and are examples of modeling. The initial learning of socially appropriate behavior in primitive cultures such as that of the Cantalense or Ojibwa people provides one illustration. The learning of a language is also an example of modeling. This is particularly obvious in the case of an adult learning to speak a foreign language. Not only the sounds that are foreign to her, but also the arrangement of sounds that she already knows, must be acquired through a conscious attempt to imitate her teacher. (Whether that teacher is a person, tape, book, or record really makes no difference since the last three are *symbolic* models.)

Motoric activities such as walking are probably learned largely through imitation. A local psychologist is reported to have attempted to demonstrate this with his young daughter. For the first eighteen months of her life, she was not allowed to see anyone walk. Her mother was required to enter the daughter's room on all fours. The father did likewise. Whenever the child was out of her room, all members of the family crawled on all fours. Visitors seldom stayed long. Apparently the child had not even attempted to walk by the age of eighteen months. The experiment has not been published and cannot be documented, but it could be replicated.

The Inhibitory or Disinhibitory Effect This second effect of imitation is particularly interesting to people who are concerned about deviant behavior. The inhibitory effect is the suppression of deviant behavior in an observer, usually as a result of seeing a model punished for engaging in that same behavior. The disinhibitory effect is the opposite. It occurs when an observer engages in previously learned deviant behavior, usually as a result of seeing a model either not punished or rewarded for the same behavior. As experimental evidence of disinhibition, Bandura and Walters (1963) cite those studies of film-mediated aggression in children where the aggressive responses are not novel, but merely represent the emission of previously learned behavior that is ordinarily suppressed. The evidence is quite clear that exposure to aggressive models has a disinhibitory effect on young observers. This is revealed by the number of aggressive responses they engage in compared to the number engaged in by the control groups.

An interesting and highly relevant experiment, cited earlier, was carried out by Bandura (1962) to show the effects on the observers of punishing the model, rewarding him, or neither punishing nor rewarding him. In addition, after the experiment all subjects were offered incentives for repeating the model's behavior. As was expected, subjects who had observed models punished for being aggressive engaged in fewer aggressive responses than did subjects whose models were neither punished nor rewarded. The really striking finding, however, was that offering the subjects rewards completely wiped out all differences between the groups.

One of the implications of this study is of special significance in explaining why punishing misbehavior frequently fails to deter other transgressors. One of the implicit reasons for incarcerating criminals is the hope that others will take heed and cease committing crimes. In other words, the intention is to inhibit criminal behavior by punishing a model. It follows from the Bandura experiment, however, that as long as subjects have their own incentives for criminal behavior, the model may just as well be rewarded as punished as far as deterrence is concerned. Whether or not this observation is valid, society can continue to justify its behavior toward criminals on the grounds that perhaps the offender's own criminal activities will cease, or simply on the grounds that criminals deserve to be punished.

A striking and sobering series of experiments has been conducted to illustrate that socially unacceptable behavior in adults can be disinhibited through the use of models (Walters et al., 1962, 1963). The experiments involved asking adult subjects to participate in an experiment dealing with memory. Subjects were first shown one of two films: the first group saw a scene from the film *Rebel without a Cause* in which two youths engage in a fight with knives; the second group saw some adolescents engaged in art work. All subjects were then asked to help with another experiment. This one involved administering a series of shocks to students in order to study the effects of punishment on learning. The subjects ostensibly involved in the learning experiment were confederates; those who thought they were helpers were in fact subjects. The subjects were made to sit in the confederate's chair and were administered one or two mild shocks, so that they would realize what the punishment was really like. They were then seated at a control panel that consisted of two signal lights, one red and one green, a dial for selecting shock intensities, and a toggle switch for administering the shock. Instructions were simply to administer a shock whenever the red light went on, since it indicated that the subject had made an error.

The general results of these studies indicate that exposure to films with aggressive content significantly increases aggressive behavior of subjects as revealed in the number and intensity of the shocks they are willing to give. (The confederates did not actually receive any shocks since one electrode was always disconnected prior to the experiment.)

The results of studies like these, if generalizable, may have profound significance for interpreting and predicting the probable effects of violence on television—particularly in view of the fact that the average male viewer by age sixty-five will have spent nine full years of his life in front of a television set (Johnson, 1969). That is approximately 9,000 eight-hour days.

The Eliciting Effect A third effect of imitation involves eliciting responses that do not precisely match those of the model and that are not deviant responses, but that are related to the model's responses: they belong to the same class of behavior. For example, a man might serve as a model of generosity if he works hard for civic organizations, church activities, and home-and-school functions. A number of his neighbors might be moved, through his example, to be generous in different ways. One might give money to his son's teacher; a second might volunteer himself for a church raffle; a third might give freely of his advice. None of these observers imitates the model's behavior precisely, but each of them emits a response that is related to it in that it involves being generous.

Another clear example of the eliciting effect is provided by the behavior of teachers, who are, as is well known, highly underpaid. Being underpaid, they cannot take full advantage of the summer holidays so generously given to them by the people whose children they teach. Many teachers have to spend their summers working.

Teachers are quiet, God-fearing, well-behaved pillars of conservative communities—they have to be, since they are the self-chosen transmitters of a quiet, God-fearing, well-behaved culture. Sadly, they occasionally find themselves working, sometimes at hard labor, with rough, unwashed, and uncouth individuals— individuals whose short-sentenced conversations are liberally sprinkled with four-letter words. Only extremely rarely does a teacher in such circumstances manage to serve as an effective model of God's, the Queen's, and the President's English. More often he becomes the "observer" and adopts his co-workers' manner of speech.* Evidence that this change illustrates the eliciting effect is found in the fact that the teacher's behavior is seldom a direct imitation of the language around him, but is often an embellishment of that language. The improvement is probably derived from expressions that had been effectively inhibited by a teacher-training program.

Social Learning
and Imitation

The greatest advantage that learning by imitation has over other forms of learning is that it provides a complete behavioral sequence for the learner. There is no need for successive approximations, for trial-and-error, or for association by contiguity. Nobody would be put behind the wheel of a car and allowed to learn to drive by trial-and-error alone. One might, on the other hand, learn to drive through the presentation of one or more models: exposure to a person driving, a driving manual, or a series of verbal instructions. In this as in many other types of learning it would be foolhardy to permit people to learn only by doing.

Educational Implications
of Social Learning Theory

The relevance of social learning theory for teachers was discussed briefly in Chapter 4. Among other things, it was noted that learning in the classroom can often be facilitated by the presentation of appropriate models. Indeed, it is not incorrect to maintain that a good deal of the "excellence" (whatever that lovely term might mean) that a teacher succeeds in developing in her students results from the models of "excellence" that she provides for them. These models go considerably beyond the behaviors that she herself exhibits, but include as well examples of other students' work, of the work of experts, or simply verbal descriptions of instructional goals.

But the relevance of social learning theory for teaching goes some distance beyond whatever it might say concerning the presentation of models and their likely influence on the behavior of students. Not only does social learning theory highlight

---

* PPC: Apples are like that too.
Author: "Apples?"

again the importance of reinforcement, but it points as well to the possibilities that a knowledge of social imitation offers for a classroom management (less euphemistically referred to as classroom discipline). Chapter 14 describes in more detail the application of specific behavioristic principles, derived from social learning theory, for classroom management. Suffice it to mention here that the inhibition and/or disinhibition of socially deviant behavior can often be understood and (hopefully) controlled through the manipulation of some of the variables involved in imitative learning.

One final point needs to be made in this chapter. Our presentation has thus far offered a relatively uncritical description of behavioristic theory and its application. For a variety of reasons, some of which might well be intuitively apparent to you, behavioristic approaches to education have not met with universally uncritical acceptance. In fact, their increasing popularity in the late 1960s and early 1970s is largely responsible for the elaboration of what are frequently referred to as alternatives to behaviorism. These alternatives are generally labeled *humanistic,* and are described in some detail in Chapter 8. One of the important points made in that chapter is that humanistic approaches to education do not constitute alternatives in an either-or sense. That is, a well-intentioned teacher need not make a choice between being a behaviorist or a humanist. Hopefully we are all capable of humanistic feelings and concerns; but we can still make use of the offerings of behaviorism wherever appropriate.

Summary of Chapter 5

This chapter has described social learning as involving the acquisition of socially appropriate behavior patterns. The role of imitation in this type of learning has been stressed. Discussion has centered around Bandura and Walters' description of social learning, which is based on imitation and reinforcement. Three effects of imitation have been defined and illustrated: the modeling effect, the inhibitory-disinhibitory effects, and the eliciting effect. Applications of this work to behavior modification are detailed in Chapter 4.

Main Points in Chapter 5

1. Since a great deal of human behavior appears to result from the observation of models, an awareness of the effects of imitation is important for teachers.

2. Social learning is defined as the learning of socially expected, and therefore socially appropriate and desirable, behavior. It is complicated by the fact that even within one culture behaviors that may be appropriate in one situation are not necessarily appropriate in other, highly similar situations. Hence, a great deal of discrimination learning as well as generalization is involved.

3. Most theories of social learning assume that identification or imitation is a central process in the determination of behavior. These terms are treated as synonymous here, although a distinction is sometimes made between them. Essentially, imitation (or observational learning) involves: (a) a model who engages in some behavior; and (b) an observer who, *as a result of observing the model,* engages in similar, though not necessarily identical, behavior.

4. Miller and Dollard advanced one of the first behavioristic theories of social learning based on imitation. Their position is essentially that the behavior of models often serves as a *cue* for *imitation* because imitation has been reinforced through *drive reduction* in the past. This position can be seen as a basis for the Bandura and Walters formulations.

5. Bandura and Walters' theory of social learning accounts for behavior in terms of three *behavior control systems.* Bandura (1969) maintains that behavior is controlled: (a) directly by stimuli, (b) by its consequences, and (c) through the symbolic mediational processes that are involved in observational learning.

6. Observational learning is not limited solely to learning among humans but is also involved in animal learning. In addition, there is some evidence of cross-species imitation.

7. It is important to note that the term *model* does not refer exclusively to a *person* who might serve as an example for another. Symbolic models are highly prevalent in technologically advanced societies. They include verbal and written instructions, fictitious characters in books or films, television, and so on.

8. The sources of reinforcement that are attendant upon observational learning include direct reinforcement by the model, reinforcement as a consequence of behavior, and vicarious reinforcement. This latter reinforcement is manifested when the punishment or reward an observer thinks a model has received affects the observer's behavior. It is an intrinsic source of reinforcement, and, as such, is of considerable importance in the theoretical explanation of observational learning.

9. Imitation is not a simple process, but involves three distinct effects. These are identifiable in terms of the nature of the response elicited. The *modeling* effect involves the learning of novel responses. The *inhibitory* or *disinhibitory* effects are illustrated when deviant behavior is disinhibited or suppressed as a function of imitation—usually as a function of response consequences to the model. The *eliciting* effect involves the emission of responses that are related to those made by the model, but are neither identical to them nor deviant.

10. The greatest advantage that observational learning has over other forms of learning is that it provides the learner with a relatively complete behavioral sequence. Trial-and-error would not only be very inefficient for social learning, but could even be disastrous.

11. People's tendency to imitate is sometimes made use of by propaganda artists, PR people, and other would-be shapers of behavior. One such technique is commonly referred to as the *bandwagon* approach, or the *keep up with the Joneses* push.

Suggested Readings

For an easy and readable approach to the process of socialization, the reader is referred to the following book by McNeil. Among its virtues are a great many interesting and provocative photographs.

McNeil, A. B. *Human Socialization.* Belmont, Calif.: Brooks/Cole, 1969.

Chapters 1, 2, and 5 of the following short book by Bandura and Walters should help to amplify and explain much of the foregoing chapter:

Bandura, A. and R. **Walters.** *Social Learning and Personality Development.* New York: Holt, Rinehart and Winston, 1963.

A more detailed and more comprehensive account of the social development theory of Bandura and Walters is provided by the following:

Bandura, A. *Principles of Behavior Modification*. New York: Holt, Rinehart and Winston, 1969.

Bears are extremely confident and capable climbers, particularly when young. With increasing weight, however, they trust only the stoutest of branches, although a fall is not likely to prove disastrous. Polar bears, for example, can climb an almost sheer ice wall, and will then routinely jump down from heights of fifteen to twenty feet. And this in spite of their ponderous weights. One bear reportedly dove more than fifty feet into the water to escape hunting dogs, and then set off in the direction of the closest land mass—an impressive twenty-two miles away (Perry, 1966; Matthews, 1969).

6
Higher Mental Processes

Nothing is so unique, so personal,
or so well remembered as that which a child
has discovered for himself.

How many children will discover
the atomic structure of the universe? How
many will discover what they already have in
their own minds? And what is a teacher?

Advance Organizer Decision making, problem solving, analyzing and synthesizing, evaluating, and other manifestations of the cognitive *functions that are involved in what we ordinarily think of as* thinking *qualify as higher mental processes. This chapter presents two theoretical approaches to cognitive functions, each with explicitly different instructional implications. Bruner's theory argues for discovery-oriented learning; Ausubel's makes a strong case for a more didactic approach. The merits of each are examined. And the origin and meaning of the expression* advance organizer *are finally revealed.*

Mazes are complicated arrangements of pathways and barriers. There are many of them in everyday life. Most modern university buildings are mazes since they are deliberately constructed with many barriers and pathways. University administrators and architects usually consult psychologists when planning new buildings in order to ensure that complicated mazes are built in them. The university mazes are used as screening devices. Many freshmen students cannot find their classes until the courses are well under way; it is assumed that these students are not really intelligent enough to go to a university (and perhaps become professors).

A smaller and somewhat simpler version of these mazes is employed in the psychological laboratory under more controlled conditions. Great discoveries about learning are made by psychologists using rats as subjects. The rat is released at one end of the maze; food is located at the other, but between the rat and the food are numerous barriers (see Figure 6.1). A measure of the rat's learning over successive trials is obtained by counting the number of errors it makes in choosing the correct path to the food. This type of situation is obviously analogous to that of a student who

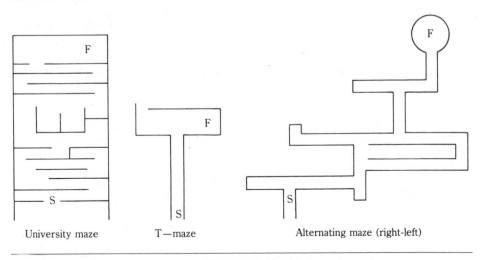

University maze   T—maze   Alternating maze (right-left)

Figure 6.1 *Mazes*

enters a building (entrance to the maze) and proceeds down various hallways in an attempt to get to an educational psychology class (the reward). Psychologists almost always know beforehand what the rat in the maze will do; given the proper circumstances, however, rats have sometimes behaved in surprising ways. For example, a well-fed rat who is placed in a maze but who finds no food in it *nevertheless learns something about the maze*. Indeed, it appears to develop a remarkably accurate "cognitive map" of the area in the absence of drive or reward (Tolman, 1955). This type of learning poses problems for rigid behavioristic explanations.

An even more striking example of some sort of higher mental process in the rat is provided by the alternating maze experiments. One example of a simple alternating maze is given in Figure 6.1. In this maze the correct turns are right, left, right, left, right, left. If a rat is allowed to learn this maze and then is placed in a left-right, left-right maze (the opposite), the rat will learn the alternate much more quickly than it would otherwise have done. The contention that it has developed some sort of mental *representation* of the pattern is strengthened by evidence from the studies involving more complex transfers (e.g., right, right, left; right, right, left; to left, left, right; left, left, right). It is this evidence of behavior that cannot be explained with a simple S-R model that has led to the development of the so-called cognitive theories—theories that are less concerned with behavior and with the formation of sensory and motor associations than with more "central" processes, such as problem solving, decision making, and perception. Two examples of cognitive positions are discussed in this chapter—Bruner's and Ausubel's. The first is treated extensively, the second less so, because much of what it contains is implicit in Bruner's position.

Bruner and Ausubel Compared

The theories presented by Bruner and Ausubel are similar in some respects; in others they are quite different. Both are concerned with the organization of cognitive material, neither is behavioristic, and both have very specific educational implications. The major difference between the two, other than the terminology, is that Bruner advocates that learners should organize material for themselves as a result of having been provided with opportunities to discover relationships inherent in the material, while Ausubel advocates that, in most instances, the material can be organized more profitably by the teacher and presented to the student in relatively final form.

Bruner

Orientation

Jerome Bruner's writings of the last twenty years may be interpreted as tentative suggestions for theories relating to conceptualization (Bruner, Goodnow, and Austin, 1956; Bruner, 1957a), perceptual processes (Bruner, 1957b), instruction (Bruner, 1961b, 1963, 1966), and development (Bruner, Olver, and Greenfield, 1966; Bruner, 1964, 1965, 1968). Unfortunately, Bruner has not systematically integrated these scattered writings, and neither the subjects he has treated nor his approach to them has served to unify his work. Indeed, it may be said that he is a cognitive theorist only insofar as he deals with topics of the "cognitive" variety. In some respects his theorizing retains elements of behaviorism.

Bruner's work was described as comprising "tentative" suggestions for theories. The contention that he has not really presented a theory (Piaget, 1967) is not entirely inappropriate. More precisely, he presents descriptive but often unrelated models of some aspects of human functioning. For the sake of simplicity and clarity, and in order to highlight the educational relevance of Bruner's work, only those aspects of it that may be said to comprise a relatively unified theory of conceptualization and perception have been selected and organized in this chapter.

Conceptualization

In everyday terms, to conceptualize is to think. In more psychological terms, to conceptualize is to form or to be aware of concepts, whereas to think is to relate and alter concepts—hence the relationship between thinking and conceptualization.

A **concept** may be defined as an abstraction that represents objects or events having similar properties. *Purple* is a concept. As a concept it represents all wavelengths that are interpreted as similar because of their physical properties (as perceived by humans). *Human* is a concept. The concept *human* relates to all organisms that have two legs, two eyes, a brain, and so on—in other words, to all organisms which are similar in specified ways.

One way of interpreting human functioning in relation to the environment is to describe it in terms of humans' understanding of that environment. As is pointed out in Chapter 9, developmental psychology is primarily concerned with describing children's increasing ability to understand their world. This is further clarified through a consideration of the work of Jean Piaget (Chapter 10).

If this discussion is related to the initial definition of concepts, it is clear that, at least to some extent, people's understanding of their world is related to their conceptualization of it—that is, to the representations that they have for their environment. A discussion of the formation of concepts is thus central to both learning and developmental theory. Indeed, Bruner's "learning theory" may be described as a theory of conceptualization. In his own terminology, however, a more appropriate label for the theory would refer to **categorization.**

Categorization

The terms *categorization* and *conceptualization* are synonymous, since to categorize is to form concepts. In other words, a category *is* a concept. And there are few clearer ways of defining a concept than simply by describing a category.

A **category** is, in one sense, a representation of objects or events that have similar properties. For example, *bird* is a category. It is a category that represents animals with feathers, wings, two legs, and beaks. In another sense, a category is a *rule*. It is, to begin with, a rule for classifying things as being equal, since whenever two objects are placed in the same category the inference is implicitly made that they are in some ways equal. Two objects that are both placed in the category *bird* are equal in the sense that they both have feathers, wings, two feet, and one head. (Indeed, they are both birds, and one bird equals another.)

Categories and Attributes

As a rule, a category specifies some characteristics of the objects or events which it comprises. The category *bird* may be described as a set of four rules, as follows:

1. In order to be a bird, an object must have feathers, two legs, one head, etc.

2. It must have the head somewhere above the shoulders; the wings must be symmetrical and rest one on either side of the body; the feet must be in contact with the ground when the beast is standing on it; etc.

3. Even if the object has only one or two feathers, it might still be a bird.

4. In order to be feathers, objects must possess certain characteristics. Heads are defined by specific properties, and legs must also conform to certain standards.

These four groups of rules may be more generally described (Bruner et al., 1956) in terms of the conditions they specify relative to **attributes** and **values.** An attribute is a property or characteristic of an object or event. It is a property that can vary from one object to another, and which can therefore sometimes be employed in defining a category. Values are the variations that are possible for an attribute. For example, the attribute *red* can vary continuously from a yellowish orange to deep carmine; the attribute *sex,* on the other hand, ordinarily varies dichotomously—it is either male or female.

Categories, as rules, specify:

1. The attributes an object must possess

2. The way in which the attributes will be combined

3. The importance of various attributes, singly or in combination

4. The acceptance limits for values of the attributes

The definitions presented earlier in relation to the category *bird* illustrate these four general specifications for membership in categories.

Criteriality Whenever an attribute is employed as part of the definition for a category, it is said to be **criterial.** Obviously, not all of an object's properties are essential for it to belong to a category. Some birds have tufts of feathers on the back of their heads; others are completely bald. Yet both are birds. Therefore the absence or presence of feathers on the head is irrelevant for the category *bird*.

Categorization and
Human Functioning

The preceding discussion of conceptualization might be partly justified as an intriguing intellectual exercise. But within the present context it is largely irrelevant unless it can be related more directly to human behavior. Bruner's attempt to do this has taken the form of several assumptions. First, he assumes that interaction with the world always involves categories. Such activities as **perception,** conceptualization, and decision making can all be described in terms of the formation and utilization of categories. Second, by explaining why it is *necessary* for people to categorize, Bruner shows how this process is relevant for human behavior. He does so by describing five achievements of categorization (Bruner et al., 1956). Each is listed, explained, and illustrated below.

First, categorization reduces the complexity of the environment. When an individual can respond to different objects as though they where the same, what would otherwise be an extremely bewildering array of isolated objects or events becomes much simpler. A large group of people is perhaps a collection of arms, legs, mouths, and so on; but in addition it is something as simple as a crowd. A downtown building may well consist of bricks, mortar, glass, steel, wires, ducts, openings, a top, sides, a foundation, and unknown contents, but in the casual observance of an uninterested and otherwise-occupied passerby, it is just another building.

Second, categorizing permits the recognition of objects. Indeed, Bruner goes so far as to say that it is only through the use of categories that any object will be recognized. If it does not fit in any way into any category, then it cannot be identified—nor can the perceiver's experience of it ever be communicated. It is, in the words borrowed by Bruner, "doomed to be a gem serene, locked in the silence of private experience." In effect, an object is recognized because it is *like* other objects of its class. A pen is identified as a pen not only because it is elongated and because it can be employed to make marks on papers and walls, but principally because it is, in these respects, like all other objects that are arbitrarily called *pens*.

Third, categorization reduces the necessity for constant learning. It does this in two ways: first, by permitting the recognition of objects without any actual *new* learning, and second, by permitting the individual to *go beyond the information given* (Bruner, 1957a). This last achievement is of primary importance in Bruner's system. It is also immediately relevant to his views on instructional procedures— views which are elaborated in Chapter 7.

There are two ways in which, by means of categorizing, an individual *goes beyond the information given*. The first involves the recognition of an object. There is nothing about a thing per se that says what it is; all it possesses is a particular arrangement of properties that indicate what class of objects it may be equated with (i.e., how it may be categorized). Its identity derives from its class membership, and

is based on redundancies or similarities among members of that class. Hence the identification of an object involves going beyond the information obtained directly from that object; it involves making use of information relating to similarities and differences among a number of objects. A child may be assumed to know that a piece of chalk *is* chalk not simply because of its properties, but more precisely because it is like other pieces of chalk and not like pens.

The second way in which categorization permits going beyond the information given is this: Whenever an object is placed in a category (i.e., is identified), implicit in the process of categorizing is a whole set of inferences about the object. For example, when an object as simple as a piece of chalk is categorized as being chalk, the perceiver can now make the further inference that this same object can be used to make marks on a blackboard, that it is relatively light, that it is nontoxic but quite unpalatable, and so on. And all of these are attributes of the object that she need not perceive directly. Therefore, she is in fact going beyond the limited data which are immediately available to her.

The last two achievements of categorization are closely related to the first three. First, categorization provides directions for instrumental activity. In other words, recognizing an object implies deciding what behaviors (instrumental acts) are appropriate for it. It is obvious that the instrumental act of running from an angry bear follows from the recognition that this is indeed not only a bear, but an angry one. Even such a mundane act as putting on a shoe demands that an object be recognized as a shoe. For this particular act, the ability to recognize a foot is also helpful.

Finally, categorizing permits individuals to relate objects and classes of events. This, again, serves to reduce the complexity of the environment. In order to learn by what other means events and objects may be related, it is necessary to understand one additional Brunerian concept—that of *coding*.

Coding Systems

It is an intuitive fact that not all categories are at the same level of generality. There are, on the one hand, those highly specific categories that are defined by relatively detailed descriptions of their members' attributes. Such concepts as *pear, apple, lemon,* and *orange* are highly specific. On the other hand, there are the much more general (the Brunerian term is *generic*), and consequently more inclusive, categories such as *consumables*. And generic categories include more specific categories, in the same way as the class *consumables* includes pears, apples, lemons, and oranges. In between the two there may be many other categories, each becoming more inclusive as it becomes more generic and less defined by specifics. Figure 6.2 presents one simplified example of a **coding system** that comprises the illustrations used above.

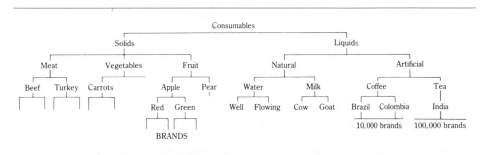

Figure 6.2 *A Coding System*

The formation of generic codes for human thought processes is important because of its role in **retention, discovery, learning,** and **transfer.** Bruner contends that, in order to remember some given specific, it is often sufficient to recall the coding system into which it falls. Remembering, for example, that a substance called baloney (also spelled as though it were really bologna) is a meat enables one to remember that it is edible, since that is one of the characteristics of this coding system. A somewhat more remote illustration makes the point clearer. Being told only that a banana is a fruit is tantamount to being told that a banana is edible, that it grows, that it originates from a seed, and so on. This example also illustrates the role of coding in discovery and in transfer. Imagine, for example, a naive explorer who finds a banana. Since she does not know what it is, she cannot categorize it. (More precisely, since she cannot categorize it, she does not know what it is.) But because a banana bears a vague resemblance to an orange (that *is* vague), the explorer can tentatively place it in the category *fruit.* In effect, she says, "Maybe this is a fruit," scratching her head in a superstitious manner as she utters this piece of brilliance. Suddenly she becomes a discoverer *by virtue of being able to employ this coding system,* for she now can say, nodding sagely, "If it *is* a fruit, it may be edible." Being a resourceful person, as explorers are, she will then eventually devise a direct test of her prediction.

THEORIES AS CODING SYSTEMS

Coding systems are not limited to such obvious hierarchical arrangements as depicted in Figure 6.2. Indeed, it is not inaccurate to say that languages are coding systems consisting largely of rules governing the use of the symbols comprising the language. Similarly, theories, whether in the hard sciences or in other fields such as psychology and education, are also coding systems. In fact they are coding systems deliberately devised to enable the individual to go beyond the information given. Consider, for example, the theory of operant conditioning. Any situation involving reinforcement or learning can now be subsumed under this particular coding system. A teacher who wishes a student to learn some given specific need not have taught this specific to others in order to arrive at some strategy for bringing about the learning; he simply generalizes from his knowledge that reinforcement leads to learning and arranges for the desired behavior to be accompanied by reinforcement. In effect, he devises strategies based on an implicit coding system that might be represented as in the diagram below. Note that the representation serves as a summary of some of the salient features of operant conditioning theory. Note also that operant theory is this schematic representation is really a subset of the larger set, behavioristic theories (which in turn is really a subset of the more inclusive set, learning theories, which in turn fits into the general field of human psychology, which is part of the behavioral sciences, which are in turn part of the natural sciences, and so on). In short, then, it is possible to conceive of all knowledge as being arranged in coding systems that are related one to the other. The extent of their relatedness, their clarity, and their comprehensiveness is directly related to the ease with which an individual can make intuitive leaps among disciplines.

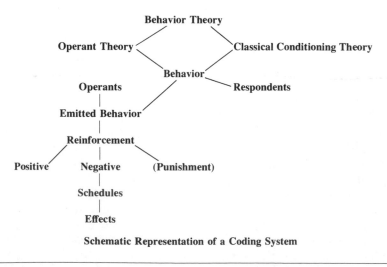

Schematic Representation of a Coding System

Coding systems are also related to transfer; this too is implicit in the preceding discussion. Transfer is ordinarily defined as the use of a behavior or a concept that was learned in relation to one object or situation, in a new situation. Clearly, placing a new object in a coding system facilitates transfer in that it not only allows the new object to be related to others, but also suggests responses toward it.

A discussion of those learning conditions most conducive to the formation of generic codes is presented in the next chapter. That chapter also includes a more detailed discussion of discovery and generic coding systems.

Perception

Conceptualization and perception are assumed to involve identical processes of categorization. Indeed, Bruner makes no clear distinction between the two, except to claim that conceptualization is somewhat more removed from immediate sensory data than perception is.

The preceding section of this chapter is as clearly applicable to perception as to conceptualization. For the sake of clarity, however, the point can be made that perceptual processes, as described in this section, are concerned with the identification of stimulus input.

Bruner's theory clearly states that to identify an object is to place it in the appropriate category. Misperception is therefore a function of improper categorization. To perceive correctly, on the other hand, requires not only that one have learned the appropriate category, but also that one know what cues to use to place objects in that category. In addition, it is helpful to know what objects are most likely to occur in the environment. In other words, a student will not recognize a piece of chalk until he has learned what chalk is (learned the category), and until he has learned that shape and color are probably the best cues for categorizing chalk. If, furthermore, he knows that chalk may often be found lying peacefully on the ledges below blackboards, he is very likely to recognize a piece when he sees it. His recognition would be less immediate if he saw the chalk lying on his dinner plate instead.

Adequate perception is assumed to depend on how accessible the appropriate category is. Bruner (1957a) contends that the more accessible a category is, the less input is required, the wider a range of values is accepted, and the more likely other categories are to be ignored. Such things as the individual's ongoing activities and his immediate needs and expectations directly affect category accessibility. A hungry man looking for a restaurant, and expecting to find one in a shopping center, is very likely to perceive it correctly when he sees one.

At the same time, misperception sometimes results when an overaccessible category masks another, better-fitting alternative. Consider, for example, the thousands of cows (may their souls . . .) who are shot each year by avid nimrods— nimrods whose "moose," "bear," or "what have you" category is so accessible that very little input, of almost any range of values, is accepted as "fitting." And the much more appropriate category "cow" is completely masked. Consider also, the many hunters who are shot each year by avid nimrods. . . .

Neurological Basis

In order to integrate his theory of categorizing, Bruner suggests that the human organism must possess a neurological system having at least four characteristics. The specific functioning of this system is not detailed (Bruner, 1957b). The four characteristics are described as neurological mechanisms.

1. The first is labeled a **match-mismatch mechanism.** It is obvious that in order to categorize one must know whether input matches or does not match predetermined criteria. In order to recognize a blue object, it is not sufficient to know that an object must be blue if it is to be called a "blue object"; one must also know that when she sees blue she *is* seeing blue, and when she sees *not blue,* it is *not blue* that she is seeing. Well, anyway.

2. Neurological functioning must also involve some sort of **gating** process. Bruner, like most theorists, considers it axiomatic that a person cannot attend to all stimulation. Some must therefore be "gated" out.

3. The third mechanism involves the *grouping* and *integrating* of stimulus input in order to form categories. In this connection, Bruner assumes that our neurological systems are capable of organization that parallels categories and coding systems.

4. The last neurological mechanism gives meaning to the notion of category accessibility. It is labeled *access ordering* and is intended to make possible the arrangement of categories in terms of their accessibility.

Summary of Bruner's Theory

The following is a simplified statement of those aspects of Bruner's theory which are presented in this chapter:

1. Learning involves the formation of categories and coding systems.

2. These in turn permit accurate perception, promote discovery, facilitate transfer, and aid memory.

A second, explicitly cognitive, position—that of David P. Ausubel—is presented next.

Ausubel

Theoretical Orientation

Ausubel (1963, 1965, 1968; and Robinson, 1969) has advanced a cognitive theory of learning that is specifically intended to deal almost exclusively with what he calls *meaningful verbal learning.* He admits this theory is not based on a great deal of empirical evidence, but he expects it to be substantiated. More important from the point of view of educational psychology, it consists of a search for the "laws of meaningful classroom learning."

Meaning

An object has meaning, according to Ausubel, not when it elicits fractions of the responses associated with other objects (a behavioristic notion), but rather when it elicits an image in the "content of consciousness" that is equivalent to the object. Similarly, a concept acquires psychological (also called *real*) meaning when it is equivalent to an idea that is already present in the mind. In both cases meaning depends on the existence of some "equivalent" representation in the mind. In other words, for a stimulus or concept to have meaning, there must be something in the learner's "consciousness" to which it can be equated. This "something" is labeled **cognitive structure.** Put more simply, the word *car* has meaning for an individual only when it can be related to a mental representation of what cars are.

Cognitive Structure

Cognitive structure consists of more or less organized and stable concepts (or ideas) in a learner's "consciousness" (presumably in the brain or cortex, since the word *mind* is generally avoided like the very plague). The nature of the organization is assumed to be hierarchical, with the most inclusive concept at the apex, and increasingly specific concepts toward the base. (In effect, this is simply a description of a coding system using different terms.) In line with this notion of cognitive structure, Ausubel contends that material is ordinarily organized from the apex downward—that is, from the most inclusive to the most specific. Therefore, instruction should proceed from the most general and inclusive toward details of specific instances. This contention is clearly and explicitly in contradistinction to Bruner's claim that learners should be presented with specifics and allowed to "discover" their own organization (coding system). The relative merits and implications of these apparently opposing views are examined later in this chapter.

Subsumption

In describing cognitive structure Ausubel only occasionally employs the more familiar terms *concept* or *idea*. Usually he employs the expression **subsumer.** A subsumer is, in effect, a concept or an idea; but the term has the added advantage of implying a concept which incorporates or includes (subsumes) other concepts— and this is precisely what Ausubel means. It is, indeed, subsumers arranged in hierarchical fashion that define cognitive structure. It is then appropriate to describe learning and forgetting in terms of a process that is labeled **subsumption.**

LANGUAGE AND HIGHER MENTAL PROCESSES: THREE VIEWPOINTS

This chapter deals with some "higher mental processes," but not explicitly with language. Can the two be separated?

Whorf (1940, 1941), one of the early proponents of the Whorfian hypothesis, thinks not. In its most extreme form, the Whorfian hypothesis maintains that language is necessary for thought. Early evidence to support this belief often alluded to "primitive" cultures where apparent cognitive or perceptual differences were reflected in language. Some believed that Eskimos could "see" twelve or more different kinds of snow because they had words for each different kind. The evidence is not convincing. It is likely that we can "see" all of these snows; it is simply not important or useful for us to have different terms for each of them.

Bernstein (1958) also argues that language is centrally implicated in thought processes (see Chapter 9). The language of lower-class children is systematically different from that of upper-class children (in England). These differences are reflected in school achievement as well. But do they cause lower school achievement? Perhaps, given the heavy language orientation of contemporary schools.

Piaget (see Chapter 10), too, points to the striking correspondence between the development of thinking and the development of language. Unlike Whorf, however, he (and Vygotsky, 1962), is careful to point out that the understanding of certain concepts often *precedes* the development of relevant terms and expressions. For example, children must understand the logical properties of dimension before such words as *bigger, smaller, shorter* and so on become meaningful.

Given that there is virtually unquestionable evidence of thinking among nonhuman animals and preverbal children, it is clear that language is not necessary for thinking. But even if it is not necessary, it is still true that language is extremely important in thought and in communication in societies such as ours. More about language in Chapter 9.

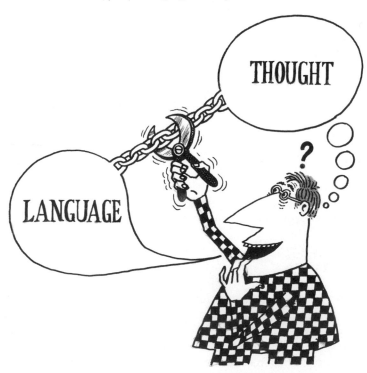

Can they be separated?

To subsume is to incorporate meaningful material into existing cognitive structure. More simply, to subsume is to learn, and the meaningfulness of what is learned is a direct function of the appropriateness of the existing subsumers. A subsumer is appropriate to the extent that it can incorporate the material being learned. Totally unfamiliar material—unfamiliar because there is nothing like it in existing cognitive structure—is meaningless. Highly familiar material is, by the same token, highly meaningful.

Derivative and Correlative Subsumption Subsumption may take one of two forms. If the new material is so similar to existing structure that it could have been derived directly from it, **derivative subsumption** is said to take place. If, on the other hand, the new material is an extension of structure in that some of it is entirely new, **correlative subsumption** is said to take place. For example, as a man drives down an unfamiliar road he goes around many new corners—but it is likely that each of these is so similar to other corners that he has known, and which are therefore incorporated in his cognitive structure, that he can subsume them easily and quickly. They are *meaningful* for him. Even if he comes across a very different corner—for example, a "pigtail" turn—one of those simultaneously curving and elevating artificial ramps such as are sometimes found on mountain roads—it will also be meaningful to him, but in quite a different way. The first kind of corner involves derivative subsumption since it can be clearly understood in terms of previous knowledge; the second requires correlative subsumption since it is partly new. One important difference between the two processes is that the learning involved in each will be remembered for different lengths of time.

Memory

Within Ausubel's system the ability to remember is a function of whether new material can be dissociated (separated) from existing structure. After learning (subsumption), the newly subsumed material becomes increasingly like the structure to which it was incorporated—in Ausubel's terms, it loses its **dissociability.** And when it has finally reached the point of zero dissociability, it can no longer be recalled. Again in Ausubel's terms, it is said to have undergone **obliterative subsumption.** In short, learning involves derivative or correlative subsumption; **forgetting** involves obliterative subsumption. And derivative and correlative subsumption may be further differentiated in terms of the speed with which they reach zero dissociability (obliterative subsumption or forgetting). Very familiar material is forgotten most quickly, since it is already very much like the subsuming structure. An ordinary turn cannot be recalled even one minute after it has been passed. On the other hand, unfamiliar material is remembered longer, as in the case of the "pigtail" turn. Whereas derivative subsumption occurs quickly, but leads to rapid forgetting, correlative subsumption may require more time for the actual learning but is retained for a longer period of time.

MEANINGLESS LEARNING

"Learning involves the subsumption of meaningful material within existing cognitive structure, through derivative or correlative means." This particular pearl of psychological wisdom is undoubtedly meaningful to you, but only because you know through previous learning what derivative and correlative subsumption are, what meaningful material is, and what type of beast cognitive structure is. Attempting to teach what learning is to a group of people who do not already know each of these terms would be quite fruitless if the above phrase were employed. In short, the learning would be meaningless.

It is remarkably easy for teachers to fall into the trap of asking students to learn material which is inherently meaningless for them because they do not have the required background information. One widely cited example of this involves the use of various white middle-class-oriented readers for children from ghetto neighborhoods or, as was the case in the Arctic until recently, for Eskimo children. These children, who had never seen a city, an automobile, a telephone, or an indoor toilet were asked to learn to read sentences similar to: "John goes for a drive," "Firemen, policemen, and college professors are our friends," and "When you cough or sneeze or sniff, be quick my lad with your handkerchief."

Do you remember learning that a demagog is "an unprincipled politician who panders to the emotions and prejudices of the populace"? That the center of the earth is "in a state of igneous fusion"? That the closest star is "several billion light years away"?

An Illustration of Subsumption

If Ausubel's theory is a valid description of human verbal learning, then any classroom illustration of such learning is describable in terms of a process of subsumption.

Consider the following excerpt from a typical lesson prepared by a teacher well grounded in educational psychology:

Teacher: Class, for you I am wishink demonstrate wan example . . . somethink important for sure. That is wan Blurk. (Teacher holds up a green blurk. It remotely resembles a kadiddle with the legs removed, but it is really more like a kind of querellor. In fact it has been used as a querellor by some people.) This ban wan green blurk. It lookink like the kadiddle wit leggs offit, but really lookink more like querellor. People kin usink like querellor.

It is likely that correlative subsumption is involved in learning about the blurk. Notice how cleverly the teacher drew a comparison among a blurk, a kadiddle, and a querellor. Concepts related to these last two are obviously well anchored in the students' cognitive structure. Hence it becomes easier for them to assimilate this new material. Also, because this is correlative subsumption, since the new material is an extension of preestablished subsumers, the students will forget the blurk very slowly. In other words, zero dissociability will be reached only after a long process of obliterative subsumption.

Consider, on the other hand, this second illustration, also an excerpt from a well-prepared lesson:

*Teacher: Here we have, my dear students, an example of a **book**. You will notice that it has a cover made of soft material, and that in between the two halves of the cover are many pages. This is a textbook in educational psychology. It can be said that these pages are filled with the wisdom of many very wise men. I repeat, this is a book.*

The process of learning what the object is that the teacher is demonstrating would probably involve derivative subsumption, since "book" is already a well-established concept in cognitive structure. Because of the great similarity, at least superficially, between this book and any other, it is subsumed quickly and easily, and reaches zero dissociability very rapidly. That is, very soon it is impossible for students to dissociate (remember) this book as opposed to any other book.

Implications of Subsumption Theory

The educational implications of Ausubel's position are considerable. They derive not so much from his new discoveries about learning as from the applications he advances. His emphasis on meaningful verbal learning through a process of reception, as opposed to discovery learning, is discussed in some detail later in this chapter, as are his recommendations for enhancing the development of cognitive structure in students.

Among the most important of the instructional techniques that Ausubel investigated and described is the use of what he calls **advance organizers.** These are concepts or ideas that are given to the learner prior to the material actually to be learned. They can take various forms, but their intended function is always to enhance the learner's ability to organize the new material, and consequently to learn and to remember it. Chapter titles and section headings in a text such as this one are examples of advanced organizers. As such they serve (presumably) to indicate to the reader what the succeeding content is and, in some cases, how it relates to other content. In the same way, introductory paragraphs frequently contain no new material, but serve instead to remind the learner of certain ideas that are important in terms of their relationship to the new material. As a further practical illustration, this text offers advance organizers, so labeled, prior to each chapter.

Instructional Applications

Instructional implications may be derived from any theoretical position that deals with human learning. (See, for example, Bigge, 1964; Hilgard and Bower, 1966; or Skinner, 1968.) In some cases the implications are remote. In others, they

ZEBRAS AND ASSES

As part of a science lesson, a teacher wishes to familiarize his students with a variety of cows. His students already know what cows are; they also know colors. But they do not know that an Aberdeen Angus cow is a sleek-looking black cow. He tells them so. Is this likely to be meaningful learning? What type of subsumption is involved?

This same teacher now wishes to teach his class what a zebra is. He tells them what it is; he compares it with horses, donkeys, mules, and—being resourceful—asses; he then shows them a picture of a zebra. What type of subsumption is involved here?

Why would the simple statement that a zebra is a herbivorous, black and white African animal be relatively meaningless for these cosmopolitan white children who have never seen a zebra in books or on television?

are explicit; this is true of the theories of Bruner and Ausubel. The implications of each of these positions are discussed in the remainder of this chapter. This discussion takes the form of an examination of a long-enduring and largely unresolved educational controversy—a controversy between the passionate believers in teaching by discovery and their equally passionate opponents.

The following section presents Bruner's views first, then Ausubel's, and finally a reconciliation of the two. The length of the section reflects the amount of *real information* which exists about the relative effectiveness of the two approaches. It does not reflect the amount of ink that has been devoted to discussing their merits. Here probably more than anywhere else are prime examples of exercises in gifted irrelevance—some of it is less gifted.

Bruner—Discovery Learning

Consistent with his theoretical framework, Bruner strongly advocates the use of discovery in schools. **Discovery learning** can be defined as the learning that takes place when students are not presented with subject matter in its final form, but rather are required to organize it themselves. This is assumed to involve *discovering* relationships that exist among items of information.

Why Discovery?

Relating this definition more directly to Bruner's theory of categorizing, one sees that discovery is really the formation of categories or, more often, the formation of coding systems. This is so since both categories and coding systems are defined in terms of relationships (similarities and differences) that exist among objects and events.

The most obvious characteristic of the discovery technique as a teaching method is probably that after the initial stages it requires less teacher guidance than do other methods. This does not imply that the teacher ceases to provide any guidance once the problem has been presented to the learner. Rather, it implies not only that the guidance provided will be less directive, but also that students will assume more responsibility for their own learning.

Since discovery learning is largely reflected in the formation of generic codes, its merits are those inherent in coding systems. It will be recalled that Bruner maintains that generic (general) codes facilitate transfer and retention. Consistent with this, he also maintains that discovery facilitates transfer and memory. In fact, these are two of the four advantages he claims for the discovery approach (Bruner, 1961a). Increased transferability is manifested in what he calls *intellectual potency*—an ill-defined but attractive term. The other two advantages are related to problem-solving ability and to motivation. Bruner contends that the frequent use of discovery methods leads a learner to acquire skill in problem solving (in Brunerian terminology, a learner acquires the *heuristics* of discovery). With respect to motivation, he believes that discovery leads to a shift from reliance on extrinsic reward to reliance on intrinsic reinforcement. Since the act of discovery is itself highly pleasant, an external reward is assumed to be unnecessary. Numerous successful discovery experiences make the learner want to learn for the sake of knowing.

Discovery and the
Formation of Generic Codes

The relationship between discovery learning and the formation of generic codes is described in the previous section. The point made there is that discovery involves the formation of coding systems. It follows from this that those conditions which are most likely to lead to the formation of generic codes are also most likely to favor discovery. Bruner describes four such conditions: *set, need state, mastery of specifics,* and *diversity of training*.

Set refers to the predisposition that individuals have for reacting in certain ways. A discovery-oriented person is one whose customary approach to a problem involves looking for relationships among items of information. Obviously, one way of affecting set is through the use of instructions. For example, a student can be encouraged to memorize subject matter as though it consisted of isolated bits of information simply by being told to do so. The same effect can also be produced by *testing* only for knowledge of isolated bits of information. On the other hand, students can be encouraged to look for relationships among items of information either by being instructed to do so or by being told that they will be examined on their understanding of these relationships.

Need state refers to the arousal level (excitation or alertness) of the learner. Bruner contends that a moderate level of arousal is more conducive to the formation of generic codes than a too-high or too-low level. In support of this he cites an

experiment involving maze-transfer in hungry rats (cited in Bruner, 1957). One group of rats was assumed to be under conditions of high drive—they had not been fed for thirty-six hours; the other group was fed twelve hours before the experiment. The task involved having the rats learn a left-right alternating maze (L-R-L-R-L-R) and then transfer this learning to the opposite maze (R-L-R-L-R-L). As expected, the hungrier rats did less well, presumably because their activation levels were too high. There is some question, however, about the similarity between maze-transfer in rats and the formation of generic codes in people. Nor has it been clearly established that a very hungry rat is in a state of arousal comparable to that of an excited human being. However, on the basis of the relationship that is presumed to exist between arousal level and learning (see Chapter 13), and in view of the negative correlation between anxiety and measured I.Q. (Sarason et al., 1960), it is not unreasonable to accept Bruner's contention.

Degree of mastery of specifics refers to the extent of the learner's knowledge of specific relevant information. Bruner argues that discovery (which is really the formation of generic codes) is not a fortuitous event. It is more likely to occur when the individual is well prepared. The wider the range of information learners possess, the more likely they are to be able to find relationships within that information. Bruner's fourth variable, *diversity of training,* is related to this. The point made here is that a learner who is exposed to information in a wide variety of circumstances is more likely to develop codes to organize that information.

GUIDED DISCOVERY

There are a number of subjects taught in schools that seem to lend themselves more readily to discovery-oriented techniques than others. It is generally accepted, for example, that some (though by no means all) scientific principles can be discovered by students in guided discovery situations where sufficient background information and the appropriate experimental equipment are provided. Similarly, children on field trips can "discover" a variety of phenomena, although understanding and interpreting these phenomena (and even noticing them in the first place) often requires considerable guidance. The beginning teacher should not make the mistake of assuming that teaching through discovery implies letting students go out on their own with no more than the simple instruction "Discover. . . ." Not only must the processes of discovery be taught—through experience as well as through more didactic procedures—but the student must frequently be given guidance while in the process of discovering. The guidance need not ruin the discovery nor destroy its magic.

Even such prosaic subjects as geography can be taught through discovery. Bruner (1961) describes in some detail how a class of elementary school children is led to discover important geographical features. Among other things, they are asked where they would establish a settlement if they were exploring an area for the first time. Their reasons for settling in certain areas rather than others gradually led them "to discover" that at the confluence of various rivers and near natural harbors there should be major settlements. Thus, studying geography becomes a question of discovering relationships between the environment and humans rather than simply of memorizing maps and related data.

Can the principle of the combustion engine be discovered by an eighth grade class? Yes, it can. Can you design a guided discovery lesson that could be employed for this purpose?

A Speech

Bruner's writings lend themselves particularly well to speech-making before parent and teacher organizations, school superintendents, and other groups of educators. This is partly because there is widespread conviction that any approach to education that is not discovery oriented must be passive, benchbound, meaningless rote learning. In case the reader should ever be asked to present a talk to an eager group of educators, the following is offered as an introduction to one of the most stirring after-dinner speeches of this decade:

Mr. Mayor, Mrs. West, Mr. Twolips, ladies, and gentlemen. It is my very great pleasure to have been invited to speak to you this evening on the occasion of the publication of my book. I feel a little like a cow as I stand before you, heh! heh! You know, the cow who turned to the farmer one cold winter morning and said, "That's what I appreciate, a warm hand." Heh! Heh! (Pause for laughter.)

But all joking aside, ladies and gentlemen, I will speak to you of a very serious topic . . . the education of our children —our little Franks, our John Georges, our Johnny Wests with the long nose. These are our most prized possessions. They are the children with whose minds we must be so careful. We must develop and expand those minds; we must increase their intellectual potency; we must teach them creative *(emphasis here) ways —I repeat,* creative *(emphasis again —perhaps pause for short burst of spontaneous applause) . . . . Yes, we must teach them creative ways of solving the problems they will face in this difficult world. We must teach them to appreciate their knowledge. And what better way of doing this than to allow them to* discover *that knowledge.* Discovery, *ladies and gentlemen,* discovery is the means whereby we shall open up the wondrous storehouse of treasures that a child's mind can be, and whereby we shall teach our children to value the mind, since it is *personally their own. And what can be more uniquely personal of all that a child knows than that which he has discovered for himself. (Pause for a long round of applause, nodding your head gravely and sagely as you do so.) A great author by the name of Lefrancois once said that learning which is not discovery oriented (gesture dramatically throughout this line) must be benchbound, meaningless, passive rote learning —and that is the truth! (End the line pounding the podium with your fist and pause again for the applause.)* [Readers are invited to complete this speech for themselves.]

*Specific
Educational Implications*

Bruner's eloquent plea for the use of discovery-oriented techniques in schools is advanced in several articles and books. Among the better known are "The Act of Discovery" (1961a) and *The Process of Education* (1961b). This last book, while not firmly based on the evidence of research data, provides a number of specific suggestions for educational practice that have received a great deal of attention. They include the following:

1. ". . . the curriculum of a subject should be determined by the most fundamental understanding that can be achieved of the underlying principles that give structure to that subject" (p. 31).

Knowledge of underlying principles and, accordingly, of the structure of a subject is assumed to facilitate the formation of generic coding systems, since these are based on organizing principles. For example, it is obviously much easier to arrive at some concept that relates blondes, brunettes, and redheads once it has been discovered that they are all people. Indeed, it is the "peopleness" of individuals that allows them to be reacted to in similar ways, and that permits going beyond the information given. Bruner's argument with respect to curriculum is that, unless its organization is such that it facilitates the formation of structure (coding systems), it will be learned with difficulty, it will not lend itself to transfer, and it will be remembered poorly.

2. ". . . any subject can be taught to any child in some honest form" (p. 52).

Bruner's adversaries have been quick to point out that not any subject can be taught at any age. For example, proportion can probably not be understood by a four-year-old. Bruner's reply to this is that the statement should be reinterpreted and examined in terms of the possibility of teaching *aspects* of any subject at any age level. Perhaps some aspects of proportion *can* be taught to a four-year-old. The important question is: How can teaching be made effective for very young children? Bruner's (1966) answer is that the form can be simplified and the mode of presentation geared to the simplest representational systems available. Since children progress from motoric or sensory (**enactive**) representation to representation in the form of relatively concrete images (**iconic**), and finally to abstract representation (**symbolic**), it follows that the sequence in teaching should be the same. In other words, if it is possible to present a subject so that a child can first experience it, then react to a concrete presentation of it, and finally symbolize it, that is the best instructional sequence.

3. A spiral curriculum which develops and redevelops topics at different grades is ideal for the acquisition of generic codes.

Bruner argues in several places (1961b, 1966) that spiral curricula seem to be ideally suited to the development of coding systems. Not only the repetition that they necessitate, but also the careful organization of subject matter in terms of principles, and the characteristic progression from the simplest to the most complex understanding possible, parallel the ideal development of a coding system. To begin with, learners are exposed to specific, simple instances of concepts. As they discover relationships among these, they are progressively exposed to higher-level, more general concepts, which include their earlier learning. The result, theoretically, is the formation of structure that is highly conducive to transfer, recall, and discovery.

4. ". . . a student should be given some training in recognizing the plausibility of guesses" (1961b, p. 64).

Bruner speaks, in this connection, of the intuitive leap—the educated guess, which is something more than a blind attempt, but something less than simply going beyond the information given. The latter involves making predictions on the basis of what is known about similar instances. An intuitive leap is less certain than that. Bruner argues persuasively that to discourage guessing is tantamount to stifling the process of discovery.

5. Aids to teaching (audiovisual, etc.) should be employed.

One reason advanced to support this recommendation is that audiovisual aids provide students with direct or vicarious experiences and thus facilitate the formation of concepts. This relates directly to Bruner's suggestion that the best instructional sequence is often one that progresses in the same direction that the child learning to represent the world does—that is, from enactive to iconic and finally to symbolic.

Ausubel— Expository Teaching

Why Reception Learning (or Expository Teaching)?

The most outspoken defender of expository teaching is undoubtedly David Ausubel. Part of his defense is contained in the following passage:

> *Beginning in the junior high school period, students acquire most new concepts and learn most new propositions by directly grasping higher-order relationships between abstractions. To do so meaningfully, they need no longer depend on current or recently prior concrete-empirical experience and hence are able to bypass completely the intuitive type of understanding reflective of such dependence. Through proper expository teaching they can proceed directly to a level of abstract understanding that is qualitatively superior to the intuitive level in terms of generality, clarity, precision, and explicitness. At this state of development therefore, it seems pointless to enhance intuitive understanding by using discovery technics (Ausubel, 1963, p. 19).*

He argues not only that expository teaching *can* lead to a high level of understanding and generality, but also that discovery approaches are extremely time-consuming, without being demonstrably superior. In a review of the literature on discovery learning, he and Robinson (1969) conclude that research supporting such learning is virtually nonexistent. "Moreover," they state, "it appears that enthusiasts of discovery methods have been supporting each other by citing one another's opinions and assertions as evidence and by generalizing extravagantly from questionable findings" (1969, p. 494).

Much of Ausubel's defense of what he terms **reception learning** takes the form of an attack on discovery learning. To this end he lists a number of **assumptions** which discovery enthusiasts are assumed to make. He then proceeds to invalidate them. The reader who is interested in this entertaining, though highly prejudiced, argument is referred to the appropriate sections of three of Ausubel's books (1963, 1968; Ausubel and Robinson, 1969). The reader should be cautioned, however, that many of the assumptions attributed to advocates of discovery learning are seldom made by them. The following are three of these so-called assumptions, none of which is central to a discovery position, and none of which is seriously argued by its advocates:*

1. All real knowledge is self-discovered (1969, p. 485).
2. Meaning is an exclusive product of nonverbal discovery (1969, p. 486).
3. Expository teaching is authoritarian (1969, p. 491).

Ausubel's concern with reception learning stems in part from the fact that most classroom learning seems to be of that type. In addition, meaningful verbal learning, with which his theory deals, occurs mainly in the course of expository teaching. He argues that this type of teaching is not passive—nor does it stifle creativity or encourage rote learning. Indeed, meaningful verbal learning is anything but "rote." It involves relating new material to existing structure, while rote learning involves ingesting isolated bits of information.

Ausubel advances some general recommendations for the planning and presentation of subject matter. These take the form of a discussion of the variables involved in subsumption.

*Variables in
Meaningful Learning*

Organizers An **organizer** (also referred to as **advance organizer**) is a complex set of ideas or concepts that is given to the learner *before* the material to be learned is presented. It is meant to provide stable cognitive structure to which the new learning can be anchored (subsumed). Another function of an organizer is to increase recall (prevent loss of dissociability). The use of advance organizers is called for, then, under two circumstances. The first is when students have no relevant information to which they can relate the new learning. The second is when relevant subsuming information is already present but is not likely to be recognized as relevant by the learner (Ausubel and Robinson, 1969, p. 145).

Ausubel describes two different types of organizer—one to be employed when the new material is completely novel, and the other when it is somewhat

---

* This technique is labeled the "straw man" approach. In all fairness to Ausubel, it must be pointed out that in a recent book (Ausubel and Robinson, 1969), he and his coauthor also discuss some of the advantages of a discovery approach.

familiar. The first is termed an **expository organizer** since it presents a description or *exposition* of relevant concepts. The second is called a **comparative organizer** since it is likely to make use of similarities and differences between new material and existing cognitive structure.

Expository Organizer: I have employed several expository organizers in the first chapter of this text. These take the form of descriptions of educational psychology, of learning theory, and of other topics, which are then presented later.

Comparative Organizer: A comparative organizer might be used to advantage in teaching a child what a Korug is (a Korug is the fruit which results from crossing a pear tree with an orange tree and painting the graft blue). The teacher might simply begin by discussing fruit and trees, thereby enabling the student to recall relevant information from existing cognitive structure.

Recall that this chapter presented a comparison of Bruner and Ausubel prior to the actual presentation of their theories—another advance organizer. Of necessity, a textbook is primarily expository (though parts of it may lead to a type of guided discovery). Hence the frequent use of organizers in most textbooks.

Discriminability A major variable in determining the stability of what is learned is the discriminability of the new material from previous learning. Ausubel defines retention in terms of the ease with which new learning can be dissociated from old learning. He observes that information closely resembling previous knowledge (derivative subsumption) is quickly forgotten (zero dissociability), whereas dissimilar input (correlative subsumption) tends to be retained longer (higher dissociability). It follows from this that teaching techniques which highlight the *differences* between new material and old learning will lead to longer retention. At the same time it is still necessary to relate the new to the old in order to facilitate

---

ADVANCE ORGANIZERS

Ausubel (1960), in an experiment designed to demonstrate the value of advance organizers, divided a group of college students into two groups with equal ability to learn unfamiliar material (based on a short test following their exposure to new material). One of the groups was then given relatively abstract material on the differences and similarities among metals and alloys; the other group was given no related information. Subsequently both groups were given information on steel without any direct reference to any of the material about metals and alloys. Three days later both groups were given a multiple choice test on steel. The group that had been exposed to the comparative organizer (metal and alloy material) did significantly better on the test.

Similar strategies can be employed profitably in schools. I once observed a student teacher introduce a lesson on boreal forests by discussing the relationship of climate, elevation, terrain, and vegetation. Whether his use of this comparative organizer was deliberate or not, it was effective. It provided students with an opportunity to recall information that was later relevant to understanding the new lesson.

Can you think of several good advance organizers for lessons in your area of specialization? (Do you have an area of specialization?)

subsumption. Hence the comparison of information in terms of similarities and differences should be of benefit in both learning and retention.

Finally, Ausubel suggests that the *stability* and *clarity* of the subsuming idea are directly related to the ease with which new material can be both incorporated with it and dissociated from it.

Readiness The variable *readiness* refers in part to the learner's existing cognitive structure, but also to developmental level. In this connection Ausubel (1963) finds Piaget's description of stages, particularly in terms of a concrete-abstract dimension, valuable in determining the most effective mode of instruction. More recently (Ausubel and Robinson, 1969), he accepts the notion that because of the readiness factor, an inductive discovery technique may be superior to an expository approach for students still in the concrete operations state (seven or eight to eleven or twelve years of age). (See Chapter 10 for a discussion of Piaget's theory.)

A Speech

Ausubel's work also lends itself well to speechmaking before groups of educators. It is particularly well documented and is characterized by both reason and passion. In the event that the reader is a proponent of expository as opposed to discovery learning, the following introduction to a rousing Ausubellian speech is provided:

> *Mr. Mayor, Mrs. West, Mr. Twolips, ladies and gentlemen. At the end of this evening, ladies and gentlemen, I shall turn to you like a cow on a cold winter morning and say, "That's what I really appreciate, a warm hand." Heh! Heh! But enough levity, for these are serious times in which we live. A great writer by the name of Lefrancois—I'm sure you're all familiar with his work—this great man wrote: "Man has amplified his capabilities to the point where his mushrooming technology is consuming the resources of his planet and replacing them only with garbage. Individuals can, in their wisdom, speak of Utopia and environmental control; but the human race often appears to be a blundering idiot." (Pause for an ovation.) These are indeed serious times in which we live. That's why, ladies and gentlemen, it is so terribly important that we give our children the best of possible educations. This is no time for fads. This is a time for proven methodology! (Pause again for a satisfying burst of applause, nodding in wisdom as you do so—now continue emphatically.) While one's educational convictions should be argued with passion, it seems a sensible requirement that they should also be informed with* reason.* *And those who would have us believe that children can effectively and efficiently learn in schools if they are allowed to discover for themselves are not tempering their arguments with reason (applause). They are, in fact, unreasonable! (Pound the podium at this point, and pause for the cheering that will follow.)* [The reader may wish to complete this for an oratorical contest.]

---

* From Ausubel and Robinson, 1969, p. 478.

Making Learning Meaningful

Ausubel's emphasis on reception as opposed to discovery learning is partly based on his belief that the most desirable kind of learning is "meaningful" as opposed to "rote." This does not imply that discovery techniques do not lend themselves to meaningful learning. Indeed, as the following section makes clear, Ausubel concedes that discovery techniques may profitably be used to test the meaningfulness of learning. On the other hand, didactic approaches do have some obvious advantages, particularly in terms of the efficient use of the learner's time.

Meaningfulness is defined in terms of the relationship between new learning and existing cognitive structure (existing knowledge). This has a number of implications for teacher behavior, some of which are implicit in the preceding discussion on advance organizers. In the first place, meaning may derive directly from associations that exist among ideas, events, or objects. Obviously, however, this meaning is not present unless the learner is aware of the association. For example, students can quite easily learn to pronounce and spell words that are meaningless to them because they do not relate to any of their ideas about the things they represent. An Eskimo child who learns to read by using an American text is often put in the frustrating situation of learning "meaningless" words. This situation also illustrates that meaning derives not only from relationships among ideas and objects, but also from associations that exist between the learner's past experiences and the material being learned. It is clear that a new concept will have meaning if it relates to the learner's past experiences as well as to other ideas currently being learned.

The important point here is that meaning is not an intangible property of objects or concepts themselves. Ausubel contends that no idea, concept, or object is meaningful in and of itself: it is meaningful only in relation to a learner. The implication for teaching is, therefore, that the teacher should present no new material until the learner is ready in the sense of having appropriate cognitive structure to understand it. Consequently much of the teacher's effort will be directed toward providing the student with background information, frequently through the use of advance organizers.

Reconciliation

It is unfortunate that it should seem necessary to reconcile the two apparently divergent views presented in this chapter. The juxtaposition of the two positions in order to highlight the controversy between them is something of a pedagogical device. At least part of the reconciliation consists in pointing out that discovery and expository approaches are simply two different emphases. One need not be definitely superior to the other—nor is there any need for one to be used to the exclusion of the other. Further reconciliation can be derived directly, surprisingly enough, from Ausubel and Robinson (1969, pp. 483–484) where they cite the "legitimate claims, the defensible uses, and the palpable advantages of the discovery method" (p. 483). These include the following:

1. Discovery may have advantages for transmitting some subject-matter content at the *concrete operations* stage. It ceases to have these advantages when the learner has a large store of information to which new content presented in an expository fashion can easily be related.

2. Discovery can be used to test the meaningfulness of learning. Such a test would involve asking the learner to generate instances where the learning (for example, a principle) would be applicable.

3. Discovery learning is necessary in problem solving since it is desirable to have students demonstrate whether they understand the problem-solving methods they have learned.

4. Ausubel concedes, also, that transfer might be increased where generalizations have been discovered by the learner rather than being presented in final form.

5. Finally, the use of discovery might have superior effects in the establishment of motivation for learning. This is partly because discovery learning is highly regarded by contemporary society and is therefore greatly rewarded. It may also be because what is self-learned is intrinsically satisfying.

It should be kept in mind that, although Ausubel accepts the possible superiority of a discovery approach in the foregoing instances, he remains a strong advocate of greater emphasis on the more didactic instructional procedures. He maintains not only that most learning is, in fact, of the reception variety, but also that any alternative would be highly inefficient in terms of the time involved, the cost incurred, and the benefits to the learner. Indeed, it seems obvious that relatively little school learning can be discovered by a student, not only because it would take too long, but also because students are seldom capable of discovering much that is significant. Even those subjects which ostensibly lend themselves to discovery approaches can frequently be mastered as well and faster if the information is given to the learner in relatively final form. Ausubel contends that, after the age of eleven or twelve, the learner possesses enough background information to be able to understand many new concepts very clearly if they are simply explained. At this age, asking a student to "discover" such a concept is largely a waste of time.

Relevant Research

Since numerous studies have investigated the relative merits of discovery and exposition, it should be possible to evaluate the two without relying solely on opinion, conjecture, and/or theoretical speculation. Unfortunately, however, the research does not consistently support either. Typically, one or more of three different criteria are used to evaluate the results of studies designed to compare teaching techniques. These criteria are speed of learning, retention, and transfer. Interestingly, when comparing speed of learning and retention, one finds that expository approaches tend to produce higher scores (Craig, 1956; Haslerud and Meyers, 1958; Wittrock, 1963). With regard to transfer the results have sometimes been equivocal (Craig, 1956; Wittrock, 1963). More recently, however, Guthrie (1967) has shown that discovery facilitates transfer.

GRAY POSITIONS

Disturbing as it might be for those who prefer the uncomplicated comfort of a black or white position, in a great many instances it is impossible to employ only one instructional approach to the complete exclusion of others. Johnny, intensely motivated to *discover* the nocturnal habits of that noble barnyard fowl, the turkey, runs to the local library and finds a learned *exposition* on the turkey. From this exposition he learns a bewildering amount. *Discovery* learning? In contrast, Frank's teacher, a recent reception learning convert, presents a brilliant exposition of the nocturnal habits of turkeys to his benchbound students. During the course of this exposition, it occurs to Frank that turkeys have been unnecessarily and unjustly demeaned in recent times, as is evident in the popular expression "you turkey!" In the course of his inspired musings, he *discovers* that there is little reason not to rank turkeys with eagles as birds worthy of our respect and admiration. *Reception* learning?

The confusion that might result from considering these illustrations may be lessened by the realization that, in a simplified sense, learning is what students do, and teaching is what teachers do. A teacher who emphasizes discovery will attempt to arrange the teaching-learning situation in such a way that students are encouraged to experiment, to think, to gather information, and, most important, to arrive at their own personal organization of that information. Teachers who emphasize expository teaching will be more concerned with organizing information so that it is immediately meaningful for students, and, for that reason, becomes a stable part of their existing cognitive structure. In the end, however, it is the student who learns. And, in spite of teacher emphasis, students may discover new information and new relationships for themselves, or may discover no more than a structured exposition ready to be learned and assimilated as is.

The state of the research on the relative merits of discovery and reception learning is such that the most reasonable recommendation seems to be one advanced by DeCecco (1968, p. 475):

> *For the teacher the realistic and scientifically sound question should always be for what purposes and for which students and under what learning conditions should I employ any one method or combination of methods in instruction.*

Its imprecise nature reflects precisely the imprecision of the conclusions derived from that research.

Summary of Chapter 6

This chapter has described two positions that attempt to account for higher mental processes. The first was Bruner's theory—a theory of learning and perception; the second was Ausubel's—a theory of meaningful verbal learning. The educational implications of these theories were then discussed at length.

Main Points in Chapter 6

1. Bruner's writings deal with a number of topics but offer no single unified theory. The work presented in this chapter relates to perception and learning.

2. Bruner's learning theory may be described as one of conceptualization. However, since conceptualization involves the formation of categories, it is more appropriately labeled a theory of categorization.

3. A category may be thought of as a concept, a percept, or a rule. As a rule it specifies the properties an object must possess to be included in the category. The Brunerian term that is almost synonymous with property is *attribute*.

4. An attribute is considered to be criterial if it is employed in categorizing an object. Noncriterial attributes are termed irrelevant.

5. Categorization is assumed to reduce the complexity of the environment, make possible the recognition of objects, and eliminate the necessity for constant learning. In addition it permits an individual to go beyond the information given.

6. Categorization involves going beyond the information given in that, whenever an object is recognized, there is implicit in the act of categorizing it the possibility of making inferences about its unseen properties.

7. Hierarchical arrangements of related categories are referred to as coding systems. A coding system is so arranged that the most generic category is placed at the top of the hierarchy, whereas the more specific categories form its base.

8. Coding systems are assumed to be important for retention, discovery, and transfer. Perception involves categorizing in the same way as conceptualization does. To perceive accurately requires not only having appropriate categories, but also knowing what cues to employ in placing objects in those categories.

9. Category accessibility, defined largely in terms of the amount and nature of input that is required for perception, is instrumental in determining perceptual readiness.

10. The neurological basis for Bruner's theory is borrowed largely from Hebb. In this connection Bruner describes a match-mismatch mechanism, a gating process, a grouping and integrating mechanism, and an access-ordering process.

11. Ausubel's theory may be described as a cognitive attempt to explain meaningful verbal learning. It is concerned largely with arriving at laws of classroom learning.

12. Ausubel defines meaning as involving *cognitive equivalence*. Meaning therefore presupposes the existence of related cognitive structure.

13. Cognitive structure consists of hierarchically organized concepts (called subsumers) arranged much as categories are arranged in Bruner's coding systems.

14. To learn is to subsume material to existing cognitive structure. This may take the form of deriving material from pre-existing structure (derivative subsumption), or it may involve material that is an extension of what is already known (correlative subsumption).

15. Forgetting is defined as a process of obliterative subsumption. It occurs when new materials can no longer be dissociated from cognitive structure (zero dissociability).

16. Discovery approaches to instruction require the learner to structure information by discovering the relationships that exist among concepts or principles. In expository (reception) learning the material is presented in final form.

17. Bruner, an advocate of the discovery approach, argues that discovery leads to the formation of codes which are more generic, and which therefore lead to higher degrees of transfer and longer retention. It also increases motivation and leads to the development of problem-solving skills.

18. The acquisition of generic codes is thought to be affected by four general conditions: set (predisposition to learn in a given way); need state (degree of arousal); mastery of specifics (amount and detail of learning); and diversity of training (variety of conditions under which learning takes place).

19. Among specific educational recommendations advanced by Bruner are a series of explicit suggestions in his book *The Process of Education* (1961). These include statements in favor of a spiral curriculum, the teaching of difficult subjects in simplified but honest form to younger students, the organization of a curriculum around themes or underlying principles, the encouragement of plausible guesses, and the use of aids in teaching.

20. Ausubel's recommendations with regard to reception learning are justified in part by the observation that discovery learning is highly time-consuming and often impossible.

21. The theory of meaningful verbal learning described by Ausubel presents three general observations related to teaching. These are that *advance organizers* can be of value in teaching, that *discriminability* affects retention, and that *readiness* must be taken into account in presenting subject matter.

22. Discovery methods and expository teaching are not mutually exclusive. Research evidence does not clearly favor either; there is a time and a place for both.

23. Ausubel concedes that discovery may have advantages for teaching in the early grades, for testing meaningfulness and problem solving, for ensuring transferability, and for establishing intrinsic motivation.

24. Research suggests that expository techniques favor rapid learning and long retention, whereas discovery facilitates transfer.

Suggested Readings

Contemporary approaches to learning theory, such as are represented by Bruner and Ausubel, are too recent to have been reviewed and summarized as older theoretical positions have been. For this reason it is usually necessary to refer to original sources for detailed information. The three references cited below are the clearest available presentation of Bruner's theoretical position on learning and perception:

Bruner, J. S. On perceptual readiness. *Psychological Review,* 1957, 64, 123–152.
Bruner, J. S. "On going beyond the information given," in *Contemporary Approaches to Cognition.* Cambridge: Harvard University Press, 1957.
Bruner, J. S., J. J. **Goodnow,** and G. A. **Austin.** *A Study of Thinking.* New York: John Wiley, 1956.

The psychological theories of Ausubel are best explained in:

Ausubel, D. P. *Educational Psychology: A Cognitive View.* New York: Holt, Rinehart and Winston, 1968.

The application of Bruner's theoretical position to education, together with his arguments for discovery-oriented techniques in schools, are presented in the following well-known paper:

Bruner, J. S. The act of discovery. *Harvard Educational Review,* 1961, 31, 21–32.

An elaboration of views that are essentially identical to those presented in the preceding article is contained in the following short book:

Bruner, J. S. *The Process of Education.* Cambridge: Harvard University Press, 1961.

A provocative and potentially useful attempt to develop a theory of instruction is described by Bruner in:

Bruner, J. S. *Toward a Theory of Instruction.* Cambridge: Harvard University Press, 1966.

The much-feared grizzly bear (Ursus horribilis) *weighs around 900 pounds at maturity. Many "experts" consider the grizzly to be a species of the brown bear* (Ursus arctos). *Their prodigal strength is attested to by the fact that one bear moved an 850-pound trap one quarter of a mile and then escaped (Soper, 1964).*

7
Instruction, Learning, and Forgetting

> I've a grand mind for forgetting, David.
> (Robert Louis Stevenson)
>
> It may be that the art of forgetting is more valuable than the art of learning. Wise, clear-minded people are those who have been successful in not cluttering their minds with the trivia that confuses the minds of simpler people.

Advance Organizer This chapter serves as a major summary of much that has preceded it. Gagné's description of learning categories can be interpreted as a hierarchical arrangement of learning theories, from simplest to most complex. But the usefulness of his approach is not so much that it integrates a great deal of information, but that it presents specific suggestions relating to the conditions under which each type of learning can be facilitated.

The second part of the chapter deals with what is known (or suspected) about human memory, and presents some suggestions for improving ability to recall.

I (Lefrancois, 1972) once presented an illustration of the two basic characteristics of human functioning: reactivity and plasticity. The illustration was obviously fictitious (although one reviewer assumed that it wasn't, and commented "How ludicrous," making it clear in the process that the "ludicrous" was quite unacceptable in a textbook). It involved asking the reader to consider the following situation: A student (male) is asked to volunteer for a psychological demonstration and is brought to the front of a classroom. He is then asked to turn his back to the instructor, who unceremoniously proceeds to plant a good swift kick in the seat of his pants. The student's immediate behavior is an example of *reactivity*. His subsequent refusal to turn his back again illustrates *plasticity*. And although this illustration is absurd (*c'est la comédie de l'absurde*), it makes the point clearly. The human organism is reactive—it can respond to the environment even as the student responded to the initial directions. But more important for its survival, it is also plastic—the nature of its reactions can change. Clearly, reactivity and plasticity are closely related, since the latter simply denotes a change in the former. It is equally clear that plasticity involves learning.

The illustration, absurd as it is, makes a third point—one highly relevant to this chapter. The professor's activity is a clear and simple example of *instruction*. Consider what happened. First the professor gave a series of directions (i.e., "I need a volunteer. You! Come to the front."). These may be seen as setting the stage for learning. Once the learner was ready, the lesson was delivered. Finally, its effectiveness was examined in terms of the changes it had produced in the learner. And although teachers don't ordinarily employ quite such direct methods in attempting to reach their instructional goals, the process of instruction is, in a general sense, identical. It may be defined as the arrangement of the learning situation in such a way that learning is facilitated.

This chapter discusses the implications of learning theory for instruction. No attempt is made to provide an exhaustive listing of all the recommendations that could be derived from every theoretical position. Indeed, the chapter is not meant as a guide to the nitty-gritty of classroom practice. Rather, it is meant to provide some *general* guidelines premised on theory. These guidelines are presented in terms of a discussion of the *conditions of learning* (Gagné, 1965, 1970, 1974). The topics of forgetting and transfer are then discussed.

Instruction

Gagné makes two useful distinctions regarding the arrangement of the learning situation. One involves what he calls the *management of learning;* the other involves *conditions of learning.* The former deals with questions of motivation, the direction of interest and attention, the evaluation of the outcomes of learning, and the reporting of these outcomes. These questions are assumed to be relatively independent of the content to be learned or of the conditions necessary for learning. The arrangement of *conditions* for learning, however, involves procedures that are closely related to the content.

The Arrangement of Content

Various theoretical positions offer different, though generally compatible, implications as to the best way of arranging content for instructional purposes. Bruner's theory explicitly recommends that knowledge be self-discovered. Content should be so organized that relationships become apparent to learners *as a result of their own activity.* On the other hand, Ausubel recommends that the teacher should, in most cases, present the material in relatively final form—that is, with all pertinent relationships clearly pointed out. Despite the apparent incompatibility of these two approaches, in the end they both advocate an arrangement of content that highlights relationships.

A more specific approach to the organization of content stems from the work of Gagné (1962, 1968), who hypothesized that in any area there is a hierarchy of knowledge. This hierarchy is such that in order to understand higher levels, or to solve problems at the apex of the content structure, it is necessary to have mastered a number of subordinate capabilities. Indeed, the hierarchy as a whole is so constructed that each level is a prerequisite for succeeding levels. One example of such an arrangement for a problem of conservation (see Chapter 10) is presented in Figure 7.1.

With regard to content organization, Gagné's hypothesis implies that the instructional sequence should parallel the hierarchy of knowledge in any given area. If the satisfactory performance of one task demands that several others be mastered first, it is evident that instruction must logically proceed from the subordinate to the final task. Such terms as **task analysis** or *task description* (Gagné, 1962) are often used to describe a procedure for ordering subject content in hierarchical fashion.

Research evidence does not clearly support the hypothesis that each level in a hierarchy must be *mastered* before the learner proceeds to the next. Although this assumption has frequently been made (Crowder, 1960; Gagné, 1965; Gagné and Paradise, 1961; Ausubel, 1963), research conducted by Merrill (1965) tends to disprove it. Indeed, a "two-stage" correction/review procedure is as effective on a later test of retention as is mastery of each level. This finding does not contradict the implication that subject matter should be organized in hierarchical fashion. It simply suggests that the mastery of each successive level is not always a prerequisite for later learning.

Instructional Objectives

There is currently much concern with what is being called "teacher accountability." The phrase implies that teachers should in some way be held accountable for their performance in the classroom—accountable perhaps to students, perhaps to parents, but most certainly to the administrative authorities that hire and fire them. Unfortunately (or perhaps fortunately) there is no easy way of assessing teacher performance per se. Instead, teacher performance tends to be judged in terms of students' performances. While it is easy to understand the administration's wish to monitor the teacher's behavior and its effects more closely, it is also easy to understand why a large number of teachers are reluctant to conform to increasing demands for manifested competence. Some subjects are more difficult to teach and to learn; some students learn more slowly or more rapidly; and some teachers are better at their profession. A teacher strike in Miami, Florida, was in fact a reaction against an administrative decision to incorporate evidence of student learning into a merit pay structure.

Related to this, a large number of school authorities now require that teachers specify instructional objectives for their courses. This is the case in Colorado and in California, for example. This, of course, does not make instructional

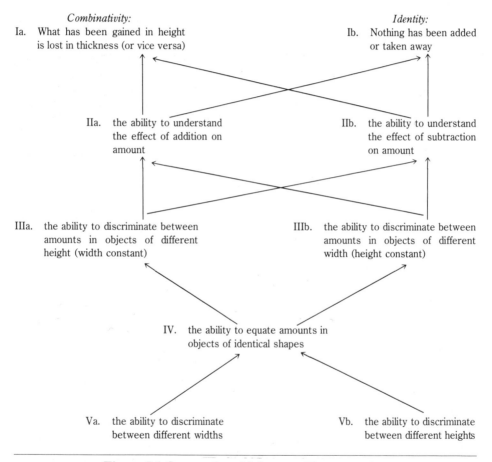

Conservation Behavior —The realization that amount does not change unless something has been added or removed

Combinativity:
Ia. What has been gained in height is lost in thickness (or vice versa)

Identity:
Ib. Nothing has been added or taken away

IIa. the ability to understand the effect of addition on amount

IIb. the ability to understand the effect of subtraction on amount

IIIa. the ability to discriminate between amounts in objects of different height (width constant)

IIIb. the ability to discriminate between amounts in objects of different width (height constant)

IV. the ability to equate amounts in objects of identical shapes

Va. the ability to discriminate between different widths

Vb. the ability to discriminate between different heights

Figure 7.1 *Conservation of Substance: Hierarchy of Subordinate Capabilities (reprinted from Lefrancois, 1966, by permission)*

objectives any more or less important for the teacher and student; they have always been important. But it does make it more important for the teacher to learn how to formulate objectives properly.

Instructional objectives are simply statements about the type of performance that can be expected of students once they have completed a lesson, a series of lessons, or a course. It is important to note that objectives do not describe the course itself, but instead describe very specifically the intended *performance* of students. Since performance implies behavior, the phrase *behavioral objectives* is often used interchangeably with the phrase *instructional objectives*.

Mager (1962) has described in detail the characteristics of useful instructional objectives. First, the objectives must describe clearly what the learner must be able to *do* following instruction. In other words, an instructional objective is a statement of the instructor's goals couched in behavioral terms—that is, worded in terms of the actual, observable performance of the student. This type of instructional objective serves not only as a description of course goals, but also as a guide for instructional strategy. Perhaps equally important, it also serves as a guide for measurement and evaluation of student and teacher performance, about which more is said in Chapter 15.

Consider, for example, the following statements of instructional objectives:

1. The student should understand evolutionary theory.
2. The student should be able to state the two Darwinian laws of evolution and give examples of each.

The second statement is much more useful for a number of reasons. It specifies exactly what students must *do* in order to demonstrate that they have reached the course goal; it provides the teacher with specific guidelines for determining whether course goals have been reached; and it suggests what must be taught if course goals are to be reached. The first statement, because of its use of the rather ambiguous term "understand" and the global phrase "evolutionary theory," does none of the above. It is clearly open to misinterpretation. Similarly, such terms as "to know," "to appreciate," and "to master" are rarely found in good, unambiguous statements of objectives, unless the nature of knowing, appreciating, or mastering is also spelled out.

A second quality of meaningful statements of objectives is that they frequently establish specific criteria of acceptable performance. Consider the following:

1. The learner will be able to translate a simple passage from French to English.
2. The learner will be able to translate a simple passage from French to English without the use of a dictionary. The passage will be taken from the prescribed text, and the translation will be considered correct if there are no more than five errors for each one hundred words of text, and if the translation is completed in no more than twenty minutes for each one hundred words.

The second statement is much more precise than the first and, again, is much more useful both for the instructor and the learner. It specifies not only the nature of the expected behavior but also the constraints under which it is to be performed in order to be considered acceptable.

There is little doubt that writing good instructional objectives is a time-consuming task. There is also little doubt that carefully prepared objectives can be of tremendous assistance to teachers in planning instructional strategies and in evaluating their performance and that of their students. In addition, if statements of behavioral objectives are given to each student at the beginning of courses, units, or lessons, they can be of tremendous value to the learner. Indeed, Mager (1962) states, "If you give each learner a copy of your objectives, you may not have to do much else" (p. 53).

Categories of Learning

Before one can specify instruction techniques for different types of learning, one must obviously differentiate the types. One way of accomplishing this would be to examine learning theories to discover more precisely what each is concerned with. Such an approach would reveal, for example, that the early behaviorists dealt largely with a very simple type of stimulus-response learning, and that some later theorists were more concerned with the formation of concepts. Carrying out this analysis for a wider array of theoretical positions might ultimately lead to the type of classification described by Gagné (1974) and Melton (1964), among others.

Gagné (1974) classifies human *learned* capabilities into five major domains: intellectual skills, verbal information, attitudes, motor skills, and cognitive strate-

gies. These five domains represent, in effect, outcomes of the learning process. Intellectual skills differ from the other four categories in that they are concerned with the *how* of learning; the other four domains are more concerned with the *what* of learning. In other words, intellectual skills are centrally involved in acquiring and processing information, and can best be understood from a learning theory point of view; in contrast, verbal information, attitudes, cognitive strategies, and motor skills relate more to content than to process. In Gagné's (1974) words, intellectual skills pertain to *knowing how;* the other domains relate to *knowing that*.

The practical usefulness of Gagné's recent theorizing derives largely from his analysis of the *conditions* most conducive to learning the capabilities represented by each of the five major divisions. Knowledge of these conditions, although that knowledge still remains incomplete and sometimes speculative, can be of tremendous value in suggesting appropriate instructional strategies. Accordingly, each of these categories is described in the following five subsections, together with the conditions believed to be conducive to their learning.

Intellectual Skills

Among the most important of the five categories of learned capabilities is intellectual skills, for it is largely through the exercise of these skills that learners are able to acquire verbal information, attitudes, and so on. Indeed, Gagné's (1965, 1970) initial theoretical formulations dealt exclusively with what he now terms the intellectual skills; in those earlier writings, the intellectual skills were simply labeled categories of learning.

As was mentioned earlier, intellectual skills refer to *knowing how*. These are the skills involved in acquiring information, discovering rules, solving problems, and so on. In another sense, they are the outcomes of the learning processes described by the learning theorists discussed in earlier chapters of this book. Each is related to the others in hierarchical fashion, and each is distinguished from the others largely by the conditions required for the specific learning. The eight categories are hierarchical in the sense that the higher-level types of learning are assumed to depend on lower-level capabilities. In other words, just as knowledge within a given content area may be described in terms of a hierarchical arrangement of subordinate capabilities, so may classes of learning skills. One must have mastered lower levels before progressing to higher ones.

The instructional implications of the foregoing paragraph may be summarized as follows:

1. Content in a given area should be arranged in hierarchical fashion so that simpler abilities and concepts which are necessary for later learning are mastered first.

2. Instructional goals should be analyzed in terms of the types of learning involved in their attainment. Instructional procedures may then be premised on knowledge of the *conditions* required for those types of learning.

Gagné's (1965, 1970) eight categories of intellectual skills and the conditions requisite for each are discussed in the following section.*

Type I: Signal Learning

The simplest type of learning, and consequently the lowest one in the hierarchy, is labeled **signal learning.** It is defined as the acquisition of involuntary behaviors through a process of classical conditioning. As Gagné describes it, Type I learning includes primarily diffuse emotional reactions. It is particularly appropriate for explaining the acquisition of fear responses in young children. One example of signal learning is provided by Landreth and Read's (1942) description of a sixteen-month-old boy who developed a pronounced fear of doctors as a result of painful inoculations. Involuntary fear reactions to dentists or to the sound of a drill are present in many adults and may be similarly explained.

According to Gagné, the conditions essential for Type I learning include the availability of a stimulus that will elicit the initial response. Two other important variables are under external control. The first is *contiguity* between conditioned and unconditioned stimuli. The second is *repetition*. Both are assumed to be important for signal learning.

Type II: Stimulus-
Response Learning

Stimulus-response learning is defined as the formation of a single bond between a stimulus and a response. It differs from signal learning in that the response is precise and voluntary. It is not a diffuse and involuntary emotional response. Operant or **instrumental conditioning** (Kimble, 1961) and trial-and-error learning (Thorndike) are examples of Type II learning. In this connection, Gagné (1970) describes a dog learning to "shake hands" in response to the appropriate verbal command. A young child is thought to acquire language partly through stimulus-response learning (Gagné, 1970).

In order for this type of learning to occur, the learner must be capable of performing responses that result in reinforcement. In addition, a number of external conditions relate directly to the learning. One is a short time lapse between the response and reinforcement. In general, the shorter the delay, the faster the learning. Another seems to be repetition. Evidence suggests that one of the functions of repetition is to facilitate the discrimination of the relevant stimulus.

---

* It should be noted that the first four of these skills are of less importance for school instruction than the last four. Accordingly, Gagné's more recent classification describes only five classes of intellectual skills, the first four being combined under the general label "simple types of learning" (Gagné, 1974, p. 56).

Type III: Chaining, and
Type IV: Verbal Association

The third and fourth types of learning are highly similar in that both involve the formation of those stimulus-response sequences known as **chains.** Type III learning relates to the simpler of the two types—chains involved in motor learning. Type IV refers to the formation of verbal chains. The acquisition of any complex motor skill exemplifies Gagné's Type III learning, whereas developing the ability to use words in sequence illustrates Type IV learning.

The conditions necessary for Types III and IV learning are also similar. To begin with, the learner must have previously acquired the ability to execute each stimulus-response unit in the chain before connecting them. This is an internal condition. Several external conditions must also be met. In the case of motor chains, these are:

1. The links (S-R connections) in the chain must be presented in contiguity and in the appropriate sequence.

2. Both reinforcement and repetition are usually of some importance, although it appears that a chain may be acquired on one single occasion if the previous conditions have been met. That is, if the learner has acquired each separate link, and if these are presented in sequence and in contiguity, repetition and reinforcement may be unnecessary.

Similar conditions are considered essential for the formation of verbal associations. The responses in the chain must be performed in the proper sequence and in close temporal contiguity. Both repetition and reinforcement in the form of knowledge that the responses are correct are also important.

Types III and IV learning are more apparent in school situations than are the first two types. This is not to imply that some degree of signal learning is not involved in school. Furthermore, the formation of stimulus-response connections (Type II) is a necessary condition for Types III and IV. Among the numerous examples of school-related motor chains are such activities as using a pencil, turning pages in a book, using scissors, printing, and writing. Verbal chains are even more prevalent in schools since a large part of the day-to-day activity in a classroom is verbal and since a great deal of verbal interaction involves habitual (memorized) verbal chains.

Type V:
Discrimination Learning

The learning of discriminations involves acquiring the ability to differentiate among similar inputs in order to respond correctly to those inputs. Such learning requires the formation of related chains. A common example of motor discrimination is provided by the task of selecting the appropriate key from among a number of similar but different keys. If the process is not one of trial-and-error (as it sometimes is), the individual may be assumed to have learned to discriminate among keys.

A discrimination problem

One condition necessary for the learning of discriminations (also called multiple discriminations when more than two chains are involved) is the presence of the related individual chains. Several external conditions are also important. To begin with, each of the stimuli that is to be discriminated must be presented in order to elicit the chain appropriate for it. Both confirmation (reinforcement) and repetition also appear to be essential. They ensure that the discrimination will not be forgotten due to the *interference* of other, related learning. Moreover, in order to reduce interférence, measures should be taken to emphasize the discriminability of the stimuli.

Discrimination learning is complex, but it is prevalent in much school learning. It is involved in learning to make different responses to printed letters, numbers, or words; in learning to differentiate between classes of things, and in learning to identify similar objects. These are but a few of its uses.

Type VI: Concept Learning

Whereas to discriminate is to respond to differences among stimuli, to learn a concept is to respond to similarities. Such responding appears to depend on the ability to represent stimulus input internally. In humans this representation often takes the form of language. Experiments (for example, Kendler and Kendler, 1961) have shown that children who have not yet acquired the relevant verbal chains for representing stimuli cannot easily form concepts. Thus, the presence of previous learning in the form of verbal chains is an important internal condition for the learning of concepts. Among the external conditions that facilitate concept formation, Gagné (1970, p. 181) lists the following:

     1. Stimulus objects are presented simultaneously in order to elicit their corresponding verbal chains. For example, the concept "odd" may be taught by presenting the child with three objects, two of which are identical while one is *odd*.
     2. The procedure goes on to present a variety of objects where, for each presentation, one is always *odd*. In the example cited above (Gagné, 1970) a reward (candy) is placed under the *odd* object.
     3. The learner's grasp of the concept is verified by asking for additional examples of the concept.
     4. Reinforcement is provided. In the example cited, the reinforcement (in the form of knowing that a correct choice has been made) is provided by placing the candy under the *odd* block.

     Gagné maintains that the importance of concept learning for formal education can hardly be overemphasized. Indeed, it is because of the presence of concepts that a learner can *generalize* from one situation to another. Obviously students cannot be presented with all the different instances for which they will need a response. For example, if one of the instructional goals of a mathematics program is that students should be able to subtract 1,978 from 2,134, from 7,461, from 1,979, and so on, each of these instances need not (and probably *can* not) be taught separately. Instead, a concept or a combination of concepts (see Types VII and VIII) is employed.

Type VII: Rule Learning

     This combination of concepts may take the form of a rule. A rule is defined by Gagné as "a chain of two or more concepts" (1970, p. 57). It is a chain that enables an individual to respond to different situations in similar, *rule-regulated* ways. Spoken language offers numerous behavioral illustrations of rules. A child who says, "He jumps, cats jump, men jump, and rabbits jump," is obviously applying the rule that a verb preceded by a plural subject does not ordinarily end in *s*.
     As in the preceding cases, the formation of rules depends upon the presence of simpler types of learning. Several external conditions are also important. These Gagné describes in the form of a generalized instructional sequence, which he summarizes as follows (Gagné, 1970, p. 203):

     Step 1: Inform the learner about the form of the performance to be expected when learning is completed.
     Step 2: Question the learner in a way that requires the reinstatement (**recall**) of previously learned concepts that make up the rule.

Step 3: Use verbal statements (cues) that will lead the learner to put the rule together, as a chain of concepts, in the proper order.

Step 4: By means of a question, ask the learner to "demonstrate" one or more concrete instances of the rule.

Step 5: (Optional, but useful for later instruction): By a suitable question, require the learner to make a verbal statement of the rule.

The educational implications of rule learning are considerable, particularly in view of the fact that much of what is learned in school consists of rules. Consider even as simple a statement as "Mammals give birth to live young." The *idea* that mammals do indeed give birth to live young can only be understood if the *concepts* "mammals, birth, and live young" are meaningful and if the verbal chain involved conveys that meaning. The sentence "Mammals give birth to live young" is really a verbal expression of a rule.

Type VIII: Problem Solving

Problem solving, a category labeled "higher-order rules" in Gagné's more recent writings, refers to the "thinking out" of a solution to a problem by combining old rules in order to form new ones. It is the main reason for learning rules in the first place. Numerous examples of problem solving may be drawn from the daily activities of ordinary people. Whenever no previously learned rule is appropriate for the solution of a problem, problem solving may be said to take place (providing, of course, that the problem is solved). A child who is learning to tie a shoe* may

---

* PPC: "Shouldn't that be a shoelace?"

Author: "Picky, picky."

combine several rules in order to succeed. The idea that laces go into holes and the notion that intertwined laces tend to cling together are rules that may be combined to form the *higher-order* rule: "Laced shoes with intertwined laces may be considered to be tied." Less mundane examples drawn from mathematics (i.e., show that $21(a + b) = 21a + 21b$), from Maier's (1930) pendulum problem, and from Katona's (1940) work are provided by Gagné (1970). Maier's problem involved constructing an apparatus that could be used to mark the floor in a room at a designated point. The subject was provided with poles, wire, chalk, and several clamps. Katona's work included some of the well-known matchstick problems where subjects are required to form a specified number of squares by moving a given number of matches in a prearranged design.

A condition clearly necessary for problem solving is the presence of the appropriate rules in the learner's repertoire. Gagné (1970) also lists three external conditions that appear to be necessary for problem solving.

1. The rules required for the solution of the problem must be active at the same time or in close succession.

2. Verbal instructions or questions may be used to elicit the recall of relevant rules.

3. The direction of thought processes may also be determined by verbal instructions.

Partial Summary

The preceding discussion of Gagné's classification of intellectual skills serves to show how educational implications are derived from learning theory. On the one hand, his writings delineate the conditions that appear to be essential for learning to take place. These conditions suggest the employment of specific instructional strategies. On the other hand, his basic assumption that both content and learning types are hierarchical also gives rise to important implications, some of which have been discussed earlier. It should be pointed out, however, that not all the varieties of learning described by Gagné are dependent upon simpler types. Gagné does not believe (as does Mowrer, 1960) that Type I is necessary for Type II. In addition, *either* Type III or Type IV is necessary for Type V, but not both. The hierarchical relationship may be summarized as follows:

> *Problem solving (VIII) depends upon rules (VII), which are derived from concepts (VI), which require as prerequisites the learning of discriminations (V). Discriminations depend upon either verbal associations (IV) or motor chains (III), both of which are derived from stimulus-response connections (II). Signal learning (I) is simple, unconscious, involuntary and emotion related. It depends on no simpler learning.*

In addition to the intellectual skills, for which specific learning conditions can be described, there are four other major domains of learned capabilities. Each of these is also important in schools, and the acquisition of each can be facilitated through manipulation of conditions external to the learner.

Verbal Information

A great deal of the school learning that is of most direct concern to teachers takes the form of verbal information. In effect, verbal information is nothing more or less complicated than what is generally described as *knowledge* (Gagné, 1974). Its identifying characteristic is that verbal information can be expressed as a sentence, or at least as an implied sentence. Thus the statement *"Ursus Arctos* are the true bears," or the single word *bear* are both expressions of verbal information, both presumably having meaning for whomever expresses them. This is not meant to imply that verbal information is always learned and stored verbally. Much of our verbal information is derived from pictures and illustrations, perhaps from visions and dreams, surely from our own behavior and that of others, as well as from the countless observations that we make in the course of our daily activities.

Gagné describes the three principal functions of verbal information as follows: First, specific items of verbal information are frequently requisite for the acquisition of other verbal information. It is clear that the sentence "Turkeys are noble" will remain meaningless until the learner understands what turkeys are and what the word *noble* means. Both of these items of information are examples of

verbal information. Second, verbal information is very often of immediate practical value—more than that, it is indispensable to ordinary conversation. The names of objects, their relationships and uses, their meanings—all represent items of verbal information. Without a body of common verbal information, not only would we be incapable of communicating verbally with each other, but we would find ourselves quite confused by such simple things as street lights and all the other trappings of our cosmopolitan societies.

The third important function of verbal information is, quite simply, that it makes thinking possible. It is little wonder that schools devote so much time and energy to deciding what bodies of knowledge (verbal information) should be transmitted to students, and how it can best be transmitted.

Many of the conditions which Gagné describes as being desirable external conditions for the acquisition of verbal information are similar to those described by Ausubel. Thus he mentions the importance of advance organizers and of meaningful context, such as is sometimes provided by placing information in sentences. In addition, verbal information can often be made more meaningful by means of images, charts, illustrations, and other pictorial representations (see, for example, Figure 7.1). Other useful instructional strategies are geared toward ensuring that learners pay attention, and that recall and generalization are facilitated. Thus, variations of tone and emphasis in oral presentation, the use of attention-compelling instructional aids such as slides and films, and other stimulus variations can serve important functions as attention-directing and motivational features of the instructional process (see Chapter 13 for a more complete discussion of motivation in the classroom). Similarly, a number of specific strategies may be employed to enhance recall of learned material and generalization from one situation to another. These strategies are discussed in the final major section of this chapter.

Cognitive Strategies

Our intellectual functioning is directed by more or less complex, difficult-to-describe personal strategies. These strategies govern how we go about paying attention, organizing, learning, and remembering things. In a simpler sense, they result from the development of such elusive capabilities as are involved in learning how to think, to create, to discover, or to remember. It is to the cognitive strategies that school officials most often pay the greatest lip service; and it is to the cognitive strategies that teachers often devote the least amount of time. Verbal information, intellectual skills, motor skills, and, to some extent, attitudes, can somehow be grasped directly, translated into meaningful form, and taught. Cognitive strategies cannot easily be described. Nor can they easily be taught. But indications are that they can be developed, though the processes by which that is accomplished are neither simple nor direct. Problem-solving skills, for example, are not taught by presenting students with a handful of related problems. The intellectual skills involved in solving specific problems might be taught in that manner, but the general

cognitive strategies associated with successful problem solving can only be developed after a long period of presenting students with a variety of problems,
some novel and challenging, so that they, in the end, develop and organize their own
cognitive strategies.

Given the importance of the "thinking" and "creative" skills involved in
cognitive strategies, an entire chapter of this text is devoted to them (see Chapter
12).

Attitudes

Our educational systems have a number of grand goals common to most
educational systems throughout the world. We want to develop students who love
life and learning, who respect those people, institutions, and ideas that we respect,
who want to be good citizens. In short, we want to develop students with positive
attitudes. In fact, however, our educational systems teach attitudes only incidentally;
they are geared more specifically toward teaching motor skills, verbal information,
intellectual skills, and, to some extent, cognitive strategies. Why? Because an attitude is not an easy thing to teach, being, in effect, a personal affective (emotional)
reaction. In brief, an attitude is a positive or negative predisposition that has important motivational components. A positive attitude toward school, for example, implies not only liking school, but endeavoring to do well in school, to be liked by
teachers, to conform to the explicit and implicit goals of the school.

At a simple level, attitudes are affected by reinforcement. It is clear that
those students who have been most successful in school will usually have more
positive attitudes toward school than those who have not been successful (i.e., have
not been reinforced). And although this observation is, in fact, obvious, teachers do
not always behave as though they were fully aware of it. Quite simply, if you want
your students to have positive attitudes toward whatever it is you are trying to teach
them, it is imperative that they meet with success (reinforcement) rather than
failure, particularly in their initial encounters with you and your subject.

Gagné (1974) refers to Bandura's description of imitative learning as one of
the principal indirect methods for "teaching" attitudes (see Chapter 5). Steps in the
instructional sequence include selecting an appropriate model, preferably one with
whom the student identifies (teachers are powerful models); arranging for the model
to display personal choices reflective of those attitudes that are to be established;
and drawing attention to the model's consequent reinforcement. If, for example, a
teacher describes some small act of honesty that she engaged in and for which she
was subsequently reinforced either directly or simply through "feeling good" about
her behavior, she might have gone some distance toward developing positive attitudes toward honesty in her charges. Lest this sound too simplistic, however, let
me hasten to point out that attitudes are subtle, pervasive, and powerful predispositions to think, act, and feel in certain ways; they are established in many ways and
places (i.e., out of school); and they are not nearly as easily modifiable as the
preceding discussion might imply.

Motor Skills

Motor skills are the many skills in our repertoires involving the execution of sequences of controlled muscular movements. Writing, typing, driving, walking, talking, dancing, and digging holes for outdoor toilets are motor skills. Some of these are important for school; others aren't. Many of them can be facilitated through appropriate verbal instructions (i.e., "This is how you should sit in front of your typewriter . . . address the ball . . . grasp the shovel . . . hold the pencil . . . point your nose"); still others can only be learned and perfected primarily through practice. Like other skills, motor skills are highly susceptible to reinforcement. Not only is reinforcement involved in determining whether a learner is likely to want to acquire a skill (in other words, whether or not the learner's attitude will be positive), but it is intimately involved in determining how well and how rapidly the skill will be learned and perfected. A typist would learn very slowly if she could not see the results of her work. Not only could she not correct her mistakes, but she would also receive little reinforcement for a good performance.

A Review

Table 7.1 presents a summary of Gagné's classification of learning outcomes and of external conditions that appear to facilitate these outcomes. Knowledge both of conditions and of outcomes can be of considerable value to teachers in helping them arrive at appropriate and effective instructional strategies. But the learning sequence is, in many respects, much more complex than our somewhat simplified, learning-oriented discussions might imply. Gagné (1974) recognizes this greater complexity in a model of the act of learning, presented in Figure 7.2. This model takes into consideration the importance of motivational and attention-compelling factors, as well as retention and transfer. Motivation is discussed in Chapter 13; retention and transfer are subjects of the remainder of this chapter.

Memory

Recall that learning was defined as a relatively permanent change resulting from experience. Evidence of learning can therefore be derived from observations of relevant changes in behavior or performance. By the same token, evidence of learning requires the involvement of memory since memory consists of the lasting effect that experiences have on us. Put another way, it is because we have memories that we can give evidence of having *learned* who we are, how to speak, what a shovel is, or how to do a problem in advanced calculus. In short, storing attitudes, impressions, skills, strategies, or information in memory is an integral part of the learning process. And knowledge of the nature of that process can be of considerable value in guiding the instructional process.

Table 7.1 Gagné's Five Major Domains of Learning Outcomes, Some
Illustrations, and Some Suggestions Pertinent to the Instructional Process

---

Outcomes of Learning (Major Domains)	An Example of Each	Some Suggested Conditions for Facilitating Outcomes
1. Intellectual Skills Problem Solving (Higher-Order Rules)	Learner determines the optimal order of topics in an instructional sequence through experimentation	Review of relevant rules; verbal instructions to aid in recall of rules; verbal instructions to direct thought processes
Rules	Learner demonstrates that metals expand when heated and contract when cooled	Learner is made aware of desired learning outcome; review of relevant concepts; concrete examples
Concepts	Learner classifies objects in terms of size (shape, function, position, color)	Examples presented; learner actively involved in finding examples; reinforcement
Discriminations	Learner distinguishes among various printed letters of the alphabet	Simultaneous presentation of stimuli to be discriminated; reinforcement (confirmation); repetition
Simple Types (Types I–IV)	Learner arranges words in sentence-like sequences	Contiguity; repetition; reinforcement
2. Verbal Information	Learner recalls information in writing or orally	Advance organizers; meaningful context; instructional aids for motivation and retention
3. Cognitive Strategies	Learner devises novel method for digging small holes	Frequent presentation of novel and/or challenging problems
4. Attitudes	Learner selects among a choice of activities (subjects, teachers, schools)	Models; reinforcement; verbal guidance
5. Motor Skills	Learner types (swims, walks, runs, flies)	Models; verbal directions; reinforcement (knowledge of results); practice

---

A Model of Memory

Human memory has often been compared to a filing cabinet. The analogy presents several useful parallels. First, in the same way that material must be recorded before it is filed, so we must learn before we can store in memory. Second, even as material placed in a large filing system would be extremely difficult to retrieve if it were not properly labeled and arranged, so material stored in memory can be very difficult to retrieve in the absence of proper cues. Third, in much the same way that a filing clerk continually makes judgments concerning the relative importance of various items that might be filed, discarding a great many and filing only the most important, we do not commit to memory a great many trivial and unimportant events. Sadly, there are a number of important events that appear not to get filed as well.

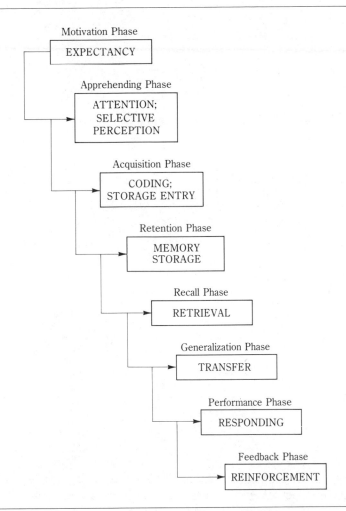

Motivation Phase
EXPECTANCY

Apprehending Phase
ATTENTION;
SELECTIVE
PERCEPTION

Acquisition Phase
CODING;
STORAGE ENTRY

Retention Phase
MEMORY
STORAGE

Recall Phase
RETRIEVAL

Generalization Phase
TRANSFER

Performance Phase
RESPONDING

Feedback Phase
REINFORCEMENT

Figure 7.2 *The Phases of an Act of Learning, and the Processes Associated with Them (from* Essentials of Learning for Instruction *by Robert M. Gagné. Copyright © 1974 by The Dryden Press, a division of Holt, Rinehart and Winston, Inc. Reprinted by permission of Holt, Rinehart and Winston.)*

Psychologists have identified three levels of memory, each serving different functions and each with different characteristics: sensory memory, short-term memory, and long-term memory (see Figure 7.3).

Sensory memory is no more than the immediate sensory recognition of a stimulus. If I read you a list of numbers in a dry, professorial monotone, without any prior instructions, and then ask you to repeat the numbers some ten seconds later, it is unlikely that you will remember very many, if any, of the numbers. But if I

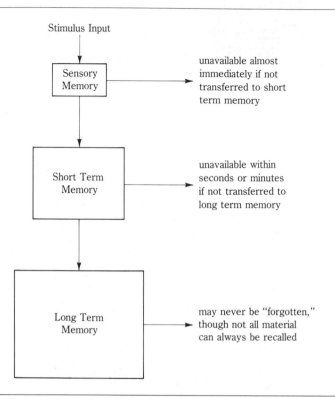

Figure 7.3 *A Model of Memory*

interrupt my reading and ask immediately, "What was the last number I read?", you would in all likelihood respond correctly. In fact each of the numbers is stored in sensory memory for a very short period of time, but if it is not transferred to long-term memory, it will no longer be available for recall after a very short time lapse.

Short-term memory lasts just a few seconds longer than sensory memory, but it too involves material that is quickly forgotten unless it is transferred to long-term storage. A typist busily copying a letter will ordinarily not remember the words he is typing. Indeed, in most cases, he will simply recognize a word, automatically execute a skilled sequence of motor movements which result in the word's appearance on the paper, and promptly forget the word; it registers only in sensory memory. On occasion, however, he might have to stop and ask his employer to decipher a word. Now he must keep the word in mind long enough to return to the typewriter and type it. Again, however, he will forget it promptly. Simple, immediate sensory recognition of a stimulus defines sensory memory; a short-term holding in memory of a stimulus defines short-term memory. We use our short-term memories for those many items of information that are immediately useful, but that

would unnecessarily clutter our minds were we to try to commit them to long-term memory.

Long-term memory refers to a relatively permanent storage of information. Accordingly, most of what is taught in schools is intended for long-term storage. Its characteristics are therefore of central concern for the instructional process. These may be described briefly as follows.

Characteristics of Long-Term Memory

First, by definition, what is stored in long-term memory is relatively stable. Whereas short-term memory involves an active, ongoing process and is easily disrupted by external events, long-term memory is passive and not easily disrupted. If I read you a list of six digits and ask you to repeat them immediately, you will in all likelihood be able to do so, although you will probably have forgotten all digits within a few minutes (unless they are rehearsed and thus committed to long-term memory). If, while you are reciting the digits, I interrupt you with a simple question or request (for example, "Tell me your name"), it is likely that the disruption will be sufficient to obliterate any remaining memory of the digits you were in the process of recalling. In contrast, if you know the names of the months today, you are not likely to forget them tomorrow.

A second feature of long-term memory is that memory appears to be partly *constructive* rather than entirely *reproductive*. That is, what we remember is often a distortion of what was originally learned. In recalling a scene, for example, we tend to remember some of the major elements and to "fill in" whatever is missing. Thus, to some extent, we construct as well as reproduce. That to a large extent explains the well-known unreliability of eyewitnesses. In some of my introductory clases, I have often brought in a stranger under a variety of pretexts, and later asked the class to describe the stranger. A class of several hundred students will invariably run the entire range of physical characteristics, a large number of them being quite convinced that their descriptions are accurate. The problem may be as much one of faulty perception as of faulty memory.

Teaching for Retrieval

Several other characteristics of long-term memory are of particular pedagogical significance: Material that is meaningful is more easily learned and is remembered for longer periods of time than is insignificant material (Ausubel and Robinson, 1969). In much the same way, events that are particularly striking tend to be recalled more easily and more clearly. Less striking events may be recalled easily over long periods of time if they are frequently rehearsed. A common psychological expression for the rehearsal of material that has already been committed to memory is "overlearning." Overlearning serves as insurance against forgetting. Students are often asked to overlearn multiplication tables; some of us overlearn telephone numbers, social security numbers, and related items.

Whereas short-term memory is of very limited capacity, long-term memory stores appear to be almost limitless. Short-term memory, frequently measured by having individuals repeat digits that they have just seen or heard, appears to be limited to seven discrete items of information (Miller, 1956). Psychological research has not yet demonstrated that after a lifetime of learning our "memories" become so overcrowded that we then find ourselves incapable of learning new material until we have forgotten some of the old. But what does seem to happen on occasion is that old and new learning interfere with each other, making retrieval difficult.

It should be noted as well that there is no substantive evidence that anything which is learned is ever forgotten. Indeed, there is evidence to the contrary. Wilder Penfield (1956) stimulated the brains of some of his patients during surgery and elicited remarkably detailed and precise "memories" of very distant events— memories that would not be available to normal waking memory. Our problems with memory may well not be those of forgetting so much as those of not being able to recall. There is a difference.

Other findings from memory research that are of particular relevance for our purposes are concerned largely with the characteristics of material that can easily be remembered. As noted earlier, organized and meaningful material appears to be easier to learn and remember than disorganized and meaningless material. Similarly, visual material frequently has an impact on memory that is seldom equalled by verbal materials. Standing (1973) showed subjects 10,000 pictures. Later he showed them some of these same pictures paired with other pictures the subjects had not seen. Under these circumstances, subjects were able to recognize as many as 90 percent of the pictures they had seen. It is not surprising that most of the powerful memory aids described later in this chapter make extensive use of visual imagery.

Why We Forget

Knowledge of the characteristics of long-term memory can be of considerable value for teachers, as is shown later in this chapter. So too can knowledge of why we forget, and of what can be done to impede the process. Although no one knows precisely what the physiology of memory is or what happens when forgetting takes place, a number of theories have been advanced to explain these processes.

Fading Theory This theory holds that material which is not brought to mind frequently enough (not used) tends to fade from memory. I know at this moment that the oldest recorded age at which a woman has given birth to a live infant is 57. This fact was brought to my mind as I perused *The Guinness Book of World Records* in search of a record that I might break. Swallowing 257 live goldfish at one sitting seems somehow more difficult than having a baby at age 57. I probably won't try either. And unless I repeat this information again, or have it brought to mind by someone or something, I probably won't remember it next year at this time. It will have faded.

Distortion Theory Not only does material fade from memory with the passage of time, but that which doesn't fade entirely is often distorted. In Ausubel's terminology, the material becomes subsumed under other material, becomes similar to it, and is in the end indistinguishable from it. It is now difficult for me to remember a specific sunset accurately, because I have seen so many that even the most striking ones have become distorted until in my memory of sunsets there isn't a single one that looks very different from any other. It's sad but true. My sunrises fare better, probably because I haven't seen as many.

Suppression Theory It appears that people tend to forget events that are particularly unpleasant. The prevalent explanation for this phenomenon derives from the work of Freud, who maintained that unpleasant memories filter into the subconscious mind where the individual is not aware of them but where they continue to have some effect on the person's emotional life. This theory is supported by the observation that the memories most adults have of their childhood are predominantly pleasant.

Interference Theory The most popular current theory of forgetting, and one that has direct relevance for teachers, is based on the notion that interference from previous or subsequent learning is a prevalent cause of forgetting. When previous learning interferes with present learning, **proactive inhibition** is said to occur; **retroactive inhibition** takes place when subsequent learning interferes with previous learning. Teachers frequently have difficulty learning the names of new students, particularly if they have been teaching for a long time and have known many students with similar names. It becomes easy to confuse old names with new but similar faces. By the same token, once teachers have learned the names of all their present students, they sometimes find it difficult to remember names of students from years past. The first case illustrates proactive interference; the second, retroactive interference.

Poor Retrieval Theory Some psychologists also maintain that forgetting can often be accounted for in terms of the inability to retrieve from memory rather than in terms of simple loss from memory, distortion, suppression, or interference. In other words, individuals appear not to remember simply because they are unable to find a way of recalling an item of information from memory; they do not possess good retrieval cues.

Implications of Forgetting Theories

In summary, information may appear to be forgotten because it has faded through disuse; because it has been distorted, suppressed, or interfered with; or because the individual does not have the proper retrieval cues. One of the important functions of a teacher is to transmit information, attitudes, and skills that will not all be forgotten. Knowledge of why people forget can help in this task. If students forget because of disuse, teachers can provide repetition and review to *remind* students of important items, and to bring about overlearning. The effects of distortion can be partially overcome by taking pains to point out similarities and differences between new and old learning as advocated by Ausubel and Bruner. Hopefully, you will not provide your students with experiences that need to be suppressed. In any case, you would probably be ill advised to attempt to prevent suppression or to bring back to memory those experiences that have been suppressed. Spacing learning and organizing it to make use of similarities and differences may help overcome the effects of interference. Finally, organizing material may partially overcome the retrieval problem, particularly if the organization facilitates the identification of relationships.

Specific Memory Aids

In addition to these general pedagogical principles, there are a number of well-known strategies and techniques for improving memory. Most of these make use of specific retrieval cues, and are referred to as *mnemonic devices*. Rhymes, patterns, acronyms, and acrostics are common mnemonic devices. "Thirty days hath September . . . " is a simple rhyme without which many of us would not know how many days hath November. Similarly, the year in which Columbus sailed the ocean blue is nicely revealed in its little rhyme. The number "five million five hundred and fifty-one thousand two hundred and twelve" is considerably more difficult than the number 555-1212. Triple five, double twelve may be even easier. This mnemonic aid makes use of patterns, and is commonly referred to as *chunking.* Quite simply, large units of information are grouped into chunks.

Acronyms are letter cues that help one to recall relatively complex material. NATO, WAC, and UNESCO are popular acronyms. Roy G. Biv, the ordered colors of the visible spectrum, is another popular acronym. Acrostics are similar to acronyms except that they generally make use of words or sentences where the letters or the first letter of each word represents an item of information to be remembered. Without the bizarre sentence "Men very easily make jugs serve useful nocturnal purposes," I would have considerable difficulty recalling the planets in order from the sun.

There are a number of more complex mnemonic devices. These have been described in detail by Higbee (1977), and are reviewed briefly here. All have one thing in common: they make extensive use of imagery. Recall that visual material appears to have a greater impact on memory, and can be retrieved much more easily than most verbal material.

The simplest of these devices, more properly referred to as systems, is the *link system*. It requires the subject to visualize the item to be remembered and to form a strong visual association (link) between it and other items to be remembered. It is easily illustrated with reference to a grocery list. (Once you have mastered this system, you need never write a grocery list again.) Suppose the list contains the following items: bread, salt, ketchup, dog food, and bananas. Visualize the first item. The picture that comes to mind first should be concentrated on since it is likely to come to mind again when you think of bread. It might be bizarre, or it might be a simple image of a plain loaf or slice of bread. Now visualize the second item, salt, and form a visual link between the first image and the second. You might, for example, see a slice of bread perched delicately on a large silver saltshaker. The saltshaker is dripping with ketchup being poured from a bottle held by a hungry dog with a banana in its ear. In most cases, you need not spend more than a few seconds with each image, nor should these be rehearsed while you are learning the list. The system does work amazingly well, although it has a number of disadvantages. One is that it is sometimes difficult to remember the first item on the list. In that case, it might also be impossible to remember any of the other items, since they are linked one to the other. This problem can be overcome by forming a visual association between the first item and a location that is likely to remind you of the item. You might, for example, see the loaf of bread reclining in a grocery cart.

A second disadvantage of the link system is that, if one of the items is not recalled, none of the subsequent items are likely to be recalled. A variation of the link system, labeled the *loci system,* serves to overcome this disadvantage. In effect, the loci system simply forms associations between items to be remembered and places that are very familiar to the learner and that can therefore be visualized very clearly. Rooms in a familiar house make good loci (*locus:* Latin, meaning "place"). A grocery list such as that given above can quite easily be "placed" in the rooms of a house simply by forming strong visual images of the objects in each of the rooms. The advantage of this system is that if you cannot remember what you placed in the hallway, you can always go to the bathroom.

The effectiveness of the loci system has been experimentally demonstrated. Bower (1973) explained the method to a number of subjects and then presented them with five lists, each containing twenty unrelated words. Presentation was auditory, with one word being presented every five seconds. Subjects who had learned the method recalled 72 percent of the words; those who had not been taught any method recalled only 28 percent of the words.

One final mnemonic system is described here. It is by far the most powerful, although it requires considerably more effort. Indeed, if you master this system, you could become a professional mnemonist. At the very least, you will impress your grandmother. The *phonetic system,* so called because it makes use of associations between numbers and sounds, allows an individual to recall items in order, backwards, by twos, threes, fours, or, perhaps even more impressive, to recall any specific item (for example, the fourteenth item listed).

The first step in learning the system involves making an association between numbers and consonants. Vowels do not count in the system. Traditionally, the number 1 is represented by a letter such as *t* or *l,* since each has a single downstroke; the number 2 might be an *n,* since it has two downstrokes; *m* is 3; 9 is *p,* since they resemble each other. Once you have associated a letter with each digit, you can then form words that, in effect, represent numbers. Thus the number 13 might be "tam," "tome," or "team" (remember that vowels do not count); the number 21 might be "nut" or "net"; and so on. The next step is simply to form a strong visual image of each of the words that correspond to numbers 1 through 25, for example. Having done so, you can stand on stage and have your audience describe or show you 25 items as these are recorded by your assistant, in order, on a large chalkboard. Having formed strong visual associations between each of these items and your number-linked words, you can then recall all 25 items in any order, or any specific item by number of appearance.

This must have some classroom implication. Surely.

Transfer

Among the most important suggestions for enhancing recallability of information are those relating to the use of similarities and differences among items of information, a topic touched upon in the section on generalization and discrimination in Chapter 3. These topics are frequently treated under the heading of transfer, where the term *transfer* simply refers to the effects of old learning on new learning. Transfer can be either positive or negative. Positive transfer occurs where previous learning facilitates new learning and is sometimes clearly evident in learning second languages. It is considerably easier, for example, to learn Latin if one knows French than if one knows only English. The similarities between French and Latin facilitate positive transfer. Negative transfer occurs when previous learning interferes with present learning and is, in fact, very similar to proactive interference (and to obliterative subsumption as well). Negative transfer occurs, for example, when you or I go to Bermuda, rent a motorcycle, and discover that all the traffic is on the wrong side of the street.

One of the obvious ways of teaching for positive transfer while at the same time eliminating some negative transfer is, as was suggested above, to relate new material to old material, emphasizing similarities and differences. The similarities should aid in facilitating positive transfer; knowledge of differences should minimize negative transfer.

Summary of Chapter

This chapter has presented a summary of Gagné's classification of five major types of learning outcomes. The conditions necessary for each were described. The nature of human retention and forgetting was discussed, as were a number of suggestions for facilitating learning and recall.

Main Points in Chapter 7

1. Learning and instruction may be defined and illustrated by reference to human reactivity and plasticity. Learning is defined as a change in reaction (plasticity) that may be brought about by arranging the learning situation (instruction).

2. Statements of instructional objectives should specify what the learner must do as well as the criteria of acceptable performance.

3. Gagné classifies learning outcomes into five major domains: intellectual skills, verbal information, cognitive strategies, attitudes, and motor skills.

4. Intellectual skills were initially classified into eight hierarchical *types*. Later classifications provide for only five types, the lowest four levels of the original hierarchy being included in a single category labeled simple types. Intellectual skills are the "how-to" skills. They are hierarchical in the sense that higher-level skills are dependent upon lower-level skills. The original eight categories, from simplest to most complex, are described in the following eight main points.

5. Type I: *Signal learning* may be defined as Pavlovian classical conditioning. It involves diffuse emotional reactions.

6. Type II: *Stimulus-response learning* is concerned with the formation of single S-R bonds through operant conditioning or trial-and-error.

7. Type III: *Chaining* deals with the formation of sequences of motor S-R links.

8. Type IV: *Verbal associations* are chains of verbal expressions.

9. Type V: *Discriminations* result from the ability to respond differentially to similar stimulus input.

10. Type VI: *Concepts,* on the other hand, result from the ability to respond to similarities.

11. Type VII: *Rules* are statements of relationships among related concepts.

12. Type VIII: *Problem solving* involves the combination of single rules to form higher-order rules which may be employed to solve complex problems.

13. Verbal information includes what we commonly refer to as knowledge. Such information can be expressed in sentence form, and is indispensable to ordinary conversation as well as to ordinary daily activities.

14. Cognitive strategies are concerned with high-level activities such as are involved in learning how to think and to create.

15. Attitudes are affective predispositions to make certain choices or to behave in certain ways, given a choice of behaviors. They therefore have important motivational properties.

16. Motor skills involve the execution of controlled sequences of muscular movements, such as in typing, writing, or hanging twenty on a skateboard.

17. Contemporary models of human memory describe three types of storage: sensory memory involving little more than the momentary recognition or apprehension of a stimulus; short-term memory, useful when material need be remembered only for a very short period of time; and long-term memory, which, by definition, involves material that is stored and available indefinitely. Long-term memory is of more importance than sensory or short-term memory for educational purposes.

18. Material that is stored in long-term memory tends to be relatively stable, although it changes over time. Meaningfulness, organization, visual imagery, rehearsal, and overlearning all contribute in important ways to ensuring that material will be remembered and recalled.

19. Theories of forgetting maintain that information may be forgotten because it is unused, distorted, suppressed, interfered with, or because the individual has a poor retrieval system.

20. Mnemonic devices include rhymes, patterns, acrostics, and acronyms. More complex mnemonic systems are the link system, the loci system, and the phonetic system. The latter might make you into a professional mnemonist if that is one of your ambitions.

21. Positive and negative transfer can be respectively facilitated and inhibited by highlighting similarities and differences beween old and new learning.

Suggested Readings

Gagné's classification of human learning and his explanation of the conditions required for the various types of human learning are succinctly explained in the following books. The second is a very useful book for teachers.

Gagné, R. M. *The Conditions of Learning* (2nd Edition). New York: Holt, Rinehart and Winston, 1970.
Gagné, R. M. *Essentials of Learning for Instruction.* Hinsdale, Ill.: Dryden Press, 1974.

A highly readable, informative, and practical discussion of human memory and mnemonic aids is provided in:

Higbee, K. L. *Your Memory: How It Works and How to Improve It.* Englewood Cliffs, N.J.: Prentice-Hall, 1977.

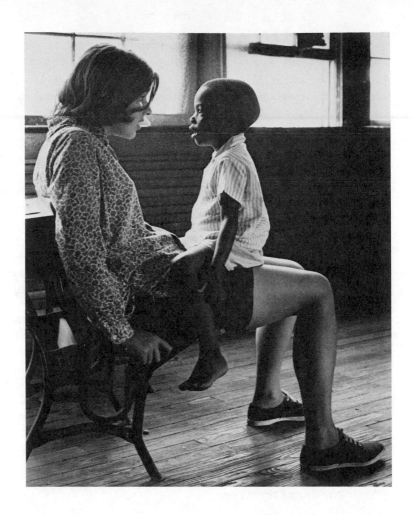

Homo sum; humani nil a me alienum puto.
(I am a man; I count nothing human
indifferent to me.)
(Publius T. Afer Terence)

And would it be inhuman, Publius T., to count
nonhuman things indifferent?

Advance Organizer Humanism presents both an objection to what is sometimes interpreted as the mechanistic, dehumanizing, and inhumane emphasis of "traditional" approaches to psychology and education, and a plea for the adoption of new attitudes, concepts, and approaches in these areas. This chapter presents an account of some of the most fundamental characteristics of humanistic approaches to understanding people and to teaching. The most important point it makes is that humanism and behaviorism are not necessarily incompatible. You can be all the good things that humanism implies and still make use of the knowledge offered by other approaches. Chapter 14, which deals with discipline, serves to illustrate and clarify this point further.

In three different passages of this text the point is made that a science of humans tends to dehumanize people—in Chapter 1, in the Epilogue, and here. The point is especially appropriate here, since the approach discussed in this chapter attempts to *humanize* people.

The theory presented first is a summary of those aspects of the writings of Carl Rogers which deal with personality and behavior. Unlike the theories discussed earlier, it is based not so much on objective data as on the answers to such questions as: What do individuals think about the world? How do they feel? How do they perceive their relationship to others? Thus it contrasts sharply with the more "rigorous" approaches of other theorists—and may be of considerable value to the prospective teacher in suggesting ways of looking at and relating to the student. Following the presentation of Rogerian theory, several "humanistic approaches" to education are discussed.

Nature of the Theory

The theory itself has been described by various authors in terms of three fairly inclusive labels. The first is Rogers' (1951) own **client-centered therapy**—a label that describes several aspects of the system. It indicates, first, that the theory is a therapeutic one. That is, it is designed to be useful for a counselor who deals with various behavioral and emotional problems. Second, the label highlights the major difference between this and other approaches to **counseling**—namely, that the counseling procedures revolve around the client. It proposes a client-centered as opposed to a **directive** (see Ellis, 1962) approach to **therapy.** The counselor's role is accordingly deemphasized; it is no longer one of giving advice or solving problems *for* clients. Instead, the therapist sets the stage so that clients themselves define their problems, react to them, and take steps toward their solution. (The process is actually much more complex than it may seem from the preceding statements. The interested reader is referred to Rogers, 1951.)

The second label is **phenomenology,** a term that denotes concern with the world as it is perceived by an individual rather than as it may actually be. Rogerian theory is phenomenological in that it is concerned primarily with the individual's own view of the world—that is, with the world as a person sees it rather than as it appears to others.

The third label is **humanism.*** Humanism in literature, philosophy, and psychology has historically been concerned with human worth, with individuality, with humanity, and with individual right to determine personal actions. Accordingly, the development of human potential tends to be highly valued, while the attainment of material goals is de-emphasized. Rogers' description of self-actualization as the end toward which all humans strive is a clear expression of humanistic concerns. In addition, his encouragement of client-centered therapy is compatible with the humanist's emphasis on self-determination. Indeed, the question of self-determination versus external control, together with a consideration of the ethical and practical problems of applying a *science of behavior,* was the subject of a debate between Rogers and Skinner (1956)—a debate that is reviewed briefly below.

Behavior Control— Rogers and Skinner

Although the written debate between Rogers and Skinner does not resolve any issues, it serves to clarify what the issues are. They center around the application of behavior control techniques for personal control in social groups, for educational procedures, and for control by governments. Skinner pleads eloquently for abandoning techniques of aversive control (see Chapter 3) and for consciously and openly applying techniques of positive control toward the betterment of society. This same topic was the subject of his novel, *Walden II* (1948)—an account of a fictitious society developed through the application of a behavioral technology. Rogers raises as one point of disagreement between them Skinner's underestimation of the problem of power: Skinner assumes that techniques of social control will be employed in the better interests of society. Rogers raises as a second point Skinner's apparent failure to specify goals for a behavioral technology. He dismisses Skinner's claim that, if behavioral scientists experiment with society, "eventually the practices which make for the greatest biological and psychological strength of the group will presumably survive" (Skinner, 1955, p. 549). Rogers contends that a society's goals should be concerned primarily with the process of "becoming," achieving worth and dignity, being creative—in short, the process of **self-actualization.**

The debate resolves no issues. But it does indicate that the conflict is between a position that favors human control (for our benefit) through the thoughtful application of a science of behavior, and one which seems to assert that science should enhance our capacity for *self-determination.* Some of the theoretical basis for this latter position is presented in the following section.

---

* The humanistic movement in psychology is currently gaining momentum through the writings of such people as Maslow and Bugental and is sometimes referred to as third-force psychology.

Rogers' Theory of
Personality and Behavior

The following discussion is based primarily on the eleventh chapter of Rogers' *Client-Centered Therapy* (1951). There Rogers presents an integrated account of his position in the form of nineteen propositions. The first thirteen are systematically listed and interpreted here, particularly as they relate to the schoolchild. The last six are summarized more briefly. This "list" of propositions is not meant to be memorized. The technique is employed to provide structure to an area that has traditionally been amorphous and sometimes vague. Rogers is sufficiently representative of other writers in the humanistic tradition that an understanding of these propositions is likely to lead to a better understanding of the rationale underlying the various approaches to humanistic education described later in this chapter.

1. *Every individual is the center of a continually changing world of experience.* This, the fundamental assertion of the phenomenologist, recognizes two features of human functioning that are particularly important for the teacher. First, it states that the significant aspects of the environment, for any individual, consist of the world of private experience. Second, it implies not only that the individual's phenomenological world is private, but that it can never be completely known by anyone else. Consider, for example, the simple complaint of a child to his mother in the unreal space which follows waking from a nightmare: "Mama, I'm scairt." The fear that the child expresses is a real and significant aspect of his world—and his mother may draw on her own stored-up memories of past fears in order to imagine how her son feels; but she cannot really *know* his fear. The phenomenological world is private. Not only is it private, but some aspects of it are not known even by the individual himself. That is, the **phenomenal field** (the individual's world) consists not only of those aspects of the world to which the individual is now attending, but also of all other now-present stimulation.

2. *The organism reacts to a field as it is experienced and perceived. This perceptual field is, for the individual, reality.* This proposition makes the point that reality *is* the phenomenal field, and since this field is defined in terms of the individual's private experience, *reality* is also private. It follows, then, that what is *real* for one individual is not necessarily real for another. Indeed, much of the disparity in behavior among people in similar circumstances may be attributed to the fact that their concepts of reality differ. A student who likes her teacher, no matter how unbearable that teacher appears to other students, has a likable teacher in her phenomenal field—and her behavior toward that teacher will necessarily reflect this "reality." This is partly why, to understand the behavior of individual students, one must be aware that they in fact perceive their worlds in different ways. And it is probably no accident that the teacher who seems to understand students best is often described as emphathetic (able to intuit how others feel) and human (this is, after all, a humanistic concern).

3. *The organism reacts as an organized whole to this phenomenal field.* This proposition is of particular theoretical relevance. In the first place, it explicitly rejects what are considered to be the oversimplistic explanations of human functioning

advanced by behaviorists (also referred to as atomists, since they tend to reduce or atomize behavior). In essence, Rogers' objection to an S-R explanation for behavior is that it reduces an extremely complex, dynamic, and continually changing process to an unrealistic fragmentation of itself.

In the second place, this proposition implies that behavior is purposive. In other words, the "organized" activity of an organism in response to its field tends toward the attainment of goals. Its purposive activity may involve a variety of alternatives for attaining a goal, the directing force being the goal rather than some aspect of the activity itself. This poses a second problem for a simple behavioristic interpretation of goal-directed behavior—one which more recent research attempts to circumvent by introducing the concept of S-R chains and mediating processes (see, for example, Osgood, 1957; Staats and Staats, 1963; Gagné, 1970).

4. *The organism has one basic tendency and striving—to actualize, maintain, and enhance the experiencing organism.* Propositions 1 through 3 describe reality as it appears to each individual, and assert that individual behavior will be influenced by reality as the individual perceives it. The point has also been made that behavior is goal-directed. Proposition 4 provides a definition for the term *goal* as Rogers uses it.

This proposition specifies that it is not necessary (or, indeed, useful) to list a variety of needs, drives, or goals to account for human behavior, but that we strive for only one goal, that of self-actualization. Rogers admits that "it is difficult to find words for this proposition" (1951, p. 488). Indeed, having found a central word, namely *self-actualization,* he is now left with the problem of defining it. A commonly accepted, generic definition is that self-actualization involves becoming whatever one can become through activities determined by oneself (Maslow, 1954). In other words, to actualize oneself is to develop one's potentialities. Rogers attempts to clarify this definition by describing some characteristics of the process of self-actualization. It is, first, a directional process—directional in the sense that it tends toward maturation, increasing competence, survival, reproduction, and so on. Interestingly, all of these are *goals:* each has, at some time, been described as a more or less important motivation-related end for human functioning. For Rogers, however, these goals are merely tendencies that characterize an overriding process. Self-actualization is also directional in that it is assumed to move toward increasing "self-government, self-regulation, and autonomy." At the same time it moves away from "heteronymous control, or control by external forces" (Rogers, 1951, p. 488). This is one reason for the basic incompatibility of behavior control in a Skinnerian sense with the process of growth in a Rogerian sense.

In summary, Rogers contends, as do most humanists, that humans have an inner, directing need to develop themselves in the direction of healthy, competent, and creative functioning. This notion is absolutely basic to an understanding of the humanist's view of people as being essentially good and as forever striving toward a better state. It leads logically to the Rogerian belief that occasional less-than-healthy functioning is a result of the environment. The idea is not new, Rousseau having proclaimed it passionately many years ago.

5. *Behavior is basically the goal-directed attempt of the organism to satisfy its needs as experienced, in the field as perceived.* Proposition 4 may be interpreted as the

single most important motivational concept in the Rogerian system. Proposition 5 also relates to motivation, but does so in a more limited sense. Rogers defines needs as physiological tensions that result from lacks. For example, hunger gives rise to contractions of the stomach, which may or may not be felt. When perceived, these needs will be reacted to in the context of the individual's phenomenal field. In other words, an individual attempts to satisfy needs by reacting to reality as it is perceived. A child who needs affection, for example, and who, because of past experiences, has learned to expect that teachers will be affectionate, may react accordingly. A Rogerian illustration of this is that a thirsty man will try just as desperately to reach a mirage as a real oasis.

6. *Emotion accompanies and in general facilitates such goal-directed behavior, the kind of emotion being related to the seeking versus the consummatory aspects of the behavior, and the intensity of the emotion being related to the perceived significance of the behavior for the maintenance and enhancement of the organism.* Proposition 6 looks like a highly complex statement, but it is, in fact, relatively simple—it is merely long.

It asserts, first, that goal-directed behavior is accompanied by emotion or feeling, and that the nature of this emotion will be a function of whether the individual is still searching for the goal or has already reached it. Specifically, goal-seeking behavior is assumed to be accompanied by more intense and less pleasant emotion, whereas the emotion associated with consummatory responses (having reached a goal, an organism may be said to consume it) is generally pleasant and calm. The proposition further states that the intensity of the emotion relates directly to the perceived significance of the activity—a point of view highly similar to that held by arousal theorists (see Berlyne, 1960, 1966). Rogers also assumes that emotions accompanying goal-seeking behavior usually enhance it. When too intense, however, they can have the opposite effect. This is in line with Hebb's view of the relationship between arousal and performance (see Chapter 13).

The relationship between goal-related behavior and emotion is illustrated by a typical classroom examination situation. The goal that is perceived as being of some importance by most students is to succeed on the examination. The process of studying for the examination may be viewed as one goal-directed behavior, and it is a behavior that is often accompanied by some degree of emotion. The actual writing of the test is usually accompanied by much greater emotion, probably because it is an activity more clearly and more directly related to the goal. The behavioral label for the emotion felt by the students might be "competitiveness" or "anxiety." Almost certainly, some students will do less well on this test than their knowledge or ability warrants—simply because of what Sarason and Mandler (1952) have called "test anxiety." Frequently, however, the more anxious students may do better (Spielberger, 1966). Indeed, the relationship between anxiety and performance on tests seems to be a function of a complex and indefinite interaction between the type of test, the student's I.Q., and general anxiety. It follows from Proposition 6 that the degree of emotion will be a function of the perceived significance of the activity. For example, students whose parents demand a high standard of performance from them, and who consequently place a high value on academic success, are likely to feel relatively intense emotion in a test situation. On the other hand, students who do not care are less likely to become emotionally involved.

7. *The best vantage point for understanding behavior is from the internal frame of reference of an individual.* This is logically so since the individual behaves in relation to reality, and since reality is personally defined (in terms of phenomenal field). Rogers contends that much of our inability to understand behavior stems from our failure to recognize that responses are meaningful only from the organism's own point of view. As an illustration he explains that the explorer who describes the "ridiculous foods" and "meaningless ceremonies" of a primitive people can label them "ridiculous" or "meaningless" only from the perspective of his own culture. In the same sense, we tend to interpret others from our personal point of view. One can gain a much clearer understanding of what appears to be maladaptive behavior, for example, by knowing why some people engage in such behavior, how they feel about it, how they react to the world, and so on. But since they alone perceive the world as they do, complete understanding can only be obtained through communication. And the major emphasis of client-centered counseling is to facilitate communication by reducing defensiveness and encouraging "openness" so that both the counselor and the client can understand the client's *field* more clearly.

8. *A portion of the total perceptual field gradually becomes differentiated as the self.* This is the first of six propositions that deal with the development of the self—an extremely important concept, particularly since its actualization appears to be the highest individual *good* within the context of Rogerian theory.

The self is a somewhat nebulous concept, ordinarily symbolized by such terms as *I* or *me*. It is assumed not to be present at birth, but to develop slowly, perhaps partly as children become aware of their own functioning. Some clarification of the term and its development is provided by the next two propositions, which are discussed together here as in Rogers' own treatment of them.

9. *As a result of interaction with the environment, and particularly as a result of evaluational interaction with others, the structure of self is formed—an organized, fluid, but consistent conceptual pattern of perceptions of characteristics and relationships of the "I" or the "me," together with values attached to these concepts.*

10. *The values attached to experiences, and the values which are a part of self structure, in some instances are values experienced directly by an organism, and in some instances are values introjected or taken over from others, but perceived in distorted fashion, as if they had been experienced directly.* The first of these two propositions describes one aspect of the development of self—that which results from evaluational interaction. As an individual receives feedback about himself from others, he incorporates this information into his concept of "self." Most children at a very early age receive signs from parents and others indicating that they are lovable and good. Consequently, notions of *themselves* as being good become part of their perceived self. In the same manner, a child may learn that she is *cute* from the verbalized comments of others; she may also learn that she is anything but cute ("My, my, look at that kid's nose, will you!"). As a result of receiving high grades, a student may develop a concept of self that includes the belief that he is intelligent. Conversely, he may come to think of himself as being stupid if the evaluational information he receives is negative.

The second of these propositions describes two sources of information that are related to the development of the self. In the first place, there are the child's direct experiences—experiences of being loved and wanted and of feeling good as a result; experiences of being hurt and the consequent realization that the *self* does not like to be hurt; experiences of gratification (e.g., eating) together with the realization that gratification is pleasant. These *direct* experiences lead to the development of an awareness of self. But, in addition, the child also experiences self-related events indirectly, and often distorts these into an awareness of self. The child who, through direct experience has learned that she is lovable, but who is told by her mother, "I don't like you when you do that," may *introject* an image of not being liked in her perception of herself. Indeed, many of an individual's direct and indirect experiences are incompatible with one another and lead to conflicting notions of the self. Consider, for example, the student whose indirect experiences have led him to believe that he is academically gifted (i.e., his mother has often said to him, "You are academically gifted, son"), but who constantly fails in school. The resolution of this conflict may take several forms. One, of course, involves perceiving the situation correctly. An alternative would be for him to accept the introjected value, but to distort his perception of direct experience. He might, for example, conclude that he is, indeed, quite brilliant but that the teacher does not like him. Or again, he might seek additional information in order to resolve the dilemma.

A related discussion of conflict and its resolution is provided by Festinger's theory of *cognitive dissonance* (1957, 1962). This theory of motivation attempts to account for some aspects of human behavior in terms of the assumption that incompatible cognitions generally lead to behavior that is designed to eliminate the conflict. Rogers contends that the seeds for later maladaptive behavior are often found in the early failure to resolve the conflicting pictures of self that emerge from directly experienced and introjected values.

11. *As experiences occur in the life of the individual, they are either* (a) *symbolized, perceived, and organized into some relationship to the self;* (b) *ignored because there is no perceived relationship to the self-structure;* (c) *denied symbolization or given a distorted symbolization because the experience is inconsistent with the structure of the self.* The three parts of Proposition 11 are essentially self-explanatory. Parts (a) and (b) refer to the process of attending. Rogers claims that experiences which satisfy a need *and* are congruent with the image that the individual has of himself will be attended to. The hungry man perceives himself as being hungry and will therefore attend to such food-related experiences as the sight of a restaurant or the sound of a silver dinner bell. The man whose image of himself does not include immediate awareness that he is hungry will simply not attend to those stimuli since they do not relate to his perceived self-structure. On occasion, however, when experiences that cannot be "gated out" are inconsistent with self-structure, they may be denied or distorted. This point was also made in relation to Proposition 10, but it is repeated here in order to emphasize the stability of people's self-concepts and their reluctance to have them altered. A person who considers herself to be extremely unattractive is very likely to disbelieve (distortion) someone who tells her that her freckles are becoming, since this is inconsistent with her image of self. This illustration also serves to show that the distortion occurs not because the experience presents derogatory information, but simply because it is contradictory. Indeed, in this case the experience is considerably more flattering than the self-concept.

12. *Most of the ways of behaving which are adopted by the organism are those which are consistent with the concept of self.* Consider, for example, the man who thinks of himself as a gifted orator and who has been invited to address the local chapter of the Ear Realignment Association. Proposition 12 predicts clearly that, in line with his image of self, this individual will accept the invitation. The same proposition predicts that the person who conceives of himself as inhibited and verbally crippled would be likely to turn down such an invitation. In both of these cases, and indeed in most instances of human behavior, the activity selected is compatible with the self-image.

Consider what happens, however, when the image of self is somewhat distorted—when, for example, the person who believes himself to be a gifted speaker has derived this notion not from direct experience (i.e., applause following past orations) but from the words of his wise and ancient grandmother: "You shpeak so vell Ludwig, you mus be a gud spichmakerrr." In line with his self-image, he accepts the invitation, but as the day approaches, he becomes afraid—*not consciously, but organically.* The fear is not symbolized (Proposition 11), since it is

incompatible with his self-structure; but, being present, it exerts an influence on his behavior. This individual may suddenly find himself physically ill in a literal sense. How can a sick man be expected to address a large audience of ear realigners? Indeed, to refuse to do so, *when ill,* is quite congruent with this man's image of self-as-great-orator. In Rogers' words, "The behavior which is adopted is such that it satisfies the organic need, but it takes channels which are consistent with the concept of self" (1951, p. 588). This, the organism's attempt to satisfy a "real" need that is not consistent with the image of self, is assumed to be one of the primary sources of neurotic behavior in humans.

13. *Behavior may, in some instances, be brought about by organic experiences and needs which have not been symbolized. Such behavior may be inconsistent with the structure of the self, but in such instances the behavior is not "owned" by the individual.* This proposition is intended to account for the possibility that individuals will engage in behavior that is not completely compatible with their self-images. It appears to contradict the preceding proposition, which asserts that the behavior of an organism conforms to its concept of self. It must be noted, however, that the contradiction disappears with the claim that such behavior (inconsistent behavior) is not "owned" by the individual. By this Rogers means that when individuals act in direct contravention of those values which they perceive as part of the self, they are often not even *aware* of their behavior—or, if they are, they would stoutly maintain that "I was not

myself" or that "I was beside myself." This, indeed, is the usual response of the man at breakfast whose wife is relating to him what he did "last night."

14– 19. The remaining six propositions deal primarily with adjustment and mental health, a topic that is obviously relevant for teachers. They are not, however, as necessary to an understanding of the Rogerian view of humans as were the first thirteen propositions. The central features of Propositions 14 through 19 are summarized briefly in the remainder of this section.

To begin with, Rogers contends that maladjustment often results from a conflict between organic needs and behavior that would be more congruent with the self-concept. This belief was also implicit in Proposition 13. The resulting conflict may give rise to what Rogers terms *psychological tension*. A reduction in this tension may often be effected through a partial restructuring of the self.

In line with this, Rogers maintains that good psychological health results from being able to incorporate all experiences in a manner consistent with the self. This state of congruency between experiences and self-image is termed *integration*. Accordingly, one of the goals of therapy is to bring about the development of an integrated self.

As a corollary to the preceding discussion, Rogers presents the proposition that rigidity and inflexibility of self-concept often result from the presence of *threat* in the environment. An individual who perceives an ascetic way of life as highly desirable may be so threatened by the incessant temptation presented by society that she will withdraw completely into a rigid, closed, and "protective" self. It follows that, in the absence of threat, the self-structure becomes more flexible and more subject to change. In a healthy, "open" person, this change often takes the form of a rejection of previously introjected and distorted values. The achievement of an open, flexible, and integrated self is, indeed, one of the goals toward which the process of self-actualization tends.

Evaluation of Rogerian Phenomenology

To summarize: This view of behavior is, in many ways, an obvious and intuitively correct one. That is, it is obvious that each individual perceives the world in a manner not experienced by anyone else. It is also obvious that, in order to understand others completely, it may be useful to adopt their point of view. Admittedly, however, some aspects of the propositions are not so obvious—nor are the generalizations about human behavior necessarily as *general* as Rogers implies. The approach is clearly "soft-nosed." Its merits in the progress of science building may, nevertheless, be considerable since such theorizing can sometimes generate fruitful ideas. It has also had considerable impact on counseling and teaching.

The important question now should not be: "Is this a correct view of humanity?" but simply: "Is this a useful way of looking at humanity?" Indeed it is—and indeed, so are other positions.

Instructional Implications

In line with this model Rogers presents a strong and eloquent plea for what he calls *student-centered teaching* (Rogers, 1951)—a philosophy of teaching focused upon self-discovered learning (Rogers, 1969).

He criticizes traditional approaches to instruction on several counts. These include the assumption that all students are equally ready for learning, that they can learn in the same amount of time, and that the teacher is the best judge of what is meaningful and necessary for students.

As an alternative, Rogers suggests that teachers should serve as a *learning facilitators,* and that they will undertake this role successfully to the extent that they are genuine, accepting, and empathetic. These are characteristics of successful counselors and teachers.

In effect, the principal implication of a Rogerian view of human functioning is more philosophical than pedagogical. This theory advocates an essentially humanistic view of people—one that accepts individuals for what they are, one that respects feelings and aspirations, and one that holds that every person has the right to self-determination. Such a view of the student would, indeed, lead to child-centered schools.

Humanistic Education

The thinking exemplified in Rogers' theorizing has become part of the so-called third-force psychology—the other two forces being behavioristic S-R theory

---

BEHAVIOR CONTROL À LA ROGERS

As an alternative to Skinner's behavioral technology, Rogers proposes the following five-point model for a concept of the control of human behavior (Rogers and Skinner, 1956, pp. 1063–1064):

1. It is possible for us to choose to value man as a self-actualizing process of becoming; to value creativity, and the process by which knowledge becomes self-transcending.
2. We can proceed, by the methods of science, to discover the conditions which necessarily precede these processes and, through continuing experimentation, to discover better means of achieving these purposes.
3. It is possible for individuals or groups to set the conditions, with a minimum of power or control. According to present knowledge, the only authority necessary is the authority to establish certain qualities of interpersonal relationship.
4. Exposed to these conditions, present knowledge suggests that individuals become more self-responsible, make progress in self-actualization, become more flexible, and become more creatively adaptive.
5. Thus such an initial choice would inaugurate the beginnings of a social system or sub-system in which values, knowledge, adaptive skills, and even the concept of science would be continually changing and self-transcending. The emphasis would be upon man as a process of becoming.

and Freudian theory. Most representatives of third-force psychology have not advanced psychological theories, however. Rather, they represent a movement that is pervaded by two beliefs: the first is concerned with the uniqueness and importance of the human individual; the second is a rather strong reaction against overly mechanistic and dehumanizing approaches to understanding humans.

The humanistic movement in psychology has a corresponding movement in education, represented by such writers as Kohl (1969), Dennison (1969), Simon et al (1972), Gordon (1974), Postman and Weingartner (1971), and many others, and by a variety of approaches to education, many operating under the guise of free schools, open classrooms, process education, and community-centered education. The rationale for these "new" education methods is based in part on a genuine concern for the welfare of children and a firm belief that the approach is better for that welfare, and in part on the conviction that present methods of schooling leave much to be desired. Thus, Dennison (1969), in his description of an alternative to traditional schooling, speaks not only of the profound beneficial effects of that alternative on the *lives* of students, but castigates as well (in a very polite manner) the "military discipline, the schedules, the punishments and rewards, the standardization" of more conventional approaches (p. 9). His book, however, like many similar books, is not in itself a criticism of existing educational methods, but rather an attempt to describe another approach that might be better. "There is no need to add to the criticism of our public schools," Dennison informs us. "The critique is extensive and can hardly be improved upon" (1969, p. 3).

Description of an
"Open" Classroom

Dennison's account of one alternative is interesting and can be of value to beginning teachers. It is, to begin with, an alternative that emphasizes student-centered and intensive but relaxed teacher-pupil contact—a feature made possible in his situation by the fact that the teacher-pupil ratio was extremely low. It is also an approach that deemphasizes schedules—an approach that is premised on Rousseau's

---

HOW SHOULD I TEACH?

The school system that hires you (and that can also fire you) will almost inevitably operate within a relatively well-defined set of regulations governing the conduct of teachers in classrooms, prescribed curricula, reporting and testing procedures, disciplinary actions, and so on. Yet, in the final analysis, your approach to teaching will be determined by no one but yourself. No person need be bound to violate personal conviction. And if you firmly believe in the importance—even the sanctity—of the right of all students in your care to be treated as human beings and to be allowed to develop in such a way as to enhance their human qualities, it might happen that you will be frustrated by the system (or by your interpretation of that system) and that you will look for alternatives. In that case you would be well advised to read some of the references annotated at the end of this chapter.

notion that time is not meant to be saved but to be lost (Dennison, 1969, p. 13). The philosophy of the school, as expressed by Dennison, rests on the beliefs that a school should be concerned with the *lives* of its children rather than with education in a narrow sense, that abolishing conventional classroom routines can lead to important insights concerning the role of emotions and other features of the human condition, and that running an elementary school *can* be a very simple thing once it is removed from "the unworkable centralization and the lust for control that permeates every bureaucratic institution" (p. 9).

It is impossible, in this short section, to fully convey the atmosphere that appears to permeate the school of which Dennison speaks (at least to convey it as he has in his own words). Indeed, it seems futile and perhaps misleading to describe the school as one that had no administrators, no report cards, no competitive examinations, and extremely modest facilities; as one where every child was treated with "consideration and justice"; as one where the lives of the children and their unfolding was the primary concern. While this is an accurate description of the school, it is only a partial description and therefore misleading. As Kohl (1969) points out in his book, it is difficult to say exactly what an open classroom is (p. 15). Similarly, it is difficult to say what freedom is or to draw the line between chaos and student-determined order, between rebelliousness and the legitimate expression of individual rights, between nonproductive time wasting and the productive waste (or use) of time for noncurriculum-defined activities.

If one accepts that many of today's schools have become overly rule-bound, excessively authoritarian, highly regimented, and relatively dehumanizing, top-heavy bureaucracies, then the teacher clearly has the responsibility of exploring alternative approaches to education. It is worth keeping in mind that many of these alternatives are possible within the present structure of schools (as Kohl clearly points out). At the same time you should realize that traditional methods within well-established structures are much simpler and safer, as far as the teacher's relationships with parents and principal are concerned. Are they really as comfortable? Are they as effective? Are they as rewarding? And are they as human?

Principles of
Humanistic Education

General descriptions of "humanistic" classrooms are often of limited value to the prospective teacher, particularly in relation to the nitty-gritty of classroom activity. Such descriptions pay less attention to the details of the instructional process than to the personal qualities of teachers and to teacher attitudes toward children. In short, while advocates of humanistic approaches to teaching present appealing and sometimes highly convincing arguments for humanizing the teaching-learning process, they too often leave the novice teacher woefully short of methods and strategies. Unfortunately, they also often leave the novice with the impression that the traditional classroom and the more humanistic classroom are quite incompatible—that, to be more specific, the latter must eventually replace the former.

Two important points need to be made here. First, humanistic education *should not* present the teacher with a bundle of educational strategies and instructional tactics. The most important contribution that humanistic concerns can make to teacher preparation must surely be in the area of attitudes rather than methods. The humanistic educator strives toward a real caring for persons, toward open and effective communication, toward genuineness, empathy, and warmth. True, there are a number of writers, self-described as humanists, who present teachers with very specific strategies and pointed advice concerning how they should behave so that students will perceive them as being genuine and really caring. But there is a large difference between really caring and being sufficiently genuine that your concern is openly communicated, and the deliberate practice of textbook strategies designed to make you appear that way.

The second very important point is that the concerns of humanistic education and those of the more "traditional" schools are basically quite compatible. All schools are concerned with the present and future welfare of students; all recognize the worth and the rights of the individual; all pay lip service to such human and humane values as openness, honesty, selflessness, and altruism. The conflict between humanistic and traditional approaches exists where the pressure of large numbers, regimentation, anonymity, and the striving for academic success leave little time and energy for unpressured communication, the exploration of values, or the development of affect and self. As was noted earlier, however, there is nothing that absolutely prevents you from being a humanistic teacher in a traditional classroom situation.

Humanistic approaches to education are highly varied, although current literature suggests that they do have a number of things in common. Knowledge of these commonalities might be of value for teachers. More detailed information than can be included here might be of even greater value; hence the expanded list of suggested readings at the end of this chapter.

Most humanistic approaches share a number of common emphases, chief among which is a greater attention to thinking and feeling than to the acquisition of knowledge. In this respect, they are sometimes quite different from more traditional approaches. Postman and Weingartner (1971), eloquent advocates of a *Soft Revolution,* present a number of provocative suggestions for effecting change in the direction of greater freedom and creativity. Many of their suggestions are intended for students rather than for teachers, however, and many are more radical than is typical of humanistic literature in general.

A second common emphasis of humanistic approaches relates to the development of notions of self and of individual identity. Representative of this emphasis are books by Borton (1970), Satir (1972), and Purkey (1978). Borton presents a highly humanistic, three-phase teaching model designed to identify student concerns, that students might be *reached, touched* as individuals, and still *taught* in a systematic fashion quite compatible with traditional schools. Labels for these three phases form the title of the book, *Reach, Touch, and Teach*. Purkey, also concerned with the developing self-concepts of students, draws an interesting and useful distinction between teachers (and teacher behaviors) that are *inviting* and those that are *disinviting*. One of his major premises is that there are more students who are disinvited than disadvantaged, disinvitation often being communicated to the child through apparent teacher indifference and through failure to respond to students as persons. A teacher *invites* students by communicating to them (in any of many different ways) that they are valuable, able, self-directed; by expecting behaviors and achievements of them that are compatible with their worth and their self-directedness; in short, by having and communicating highly positive feelings about students. Examples of *disinvitations* are included in the accompanying boxed insert.

A third major emphasis is on communication. Gordon's (1974) Teacher Effectiveness Training (TET) program is illustrative of this emphasis. It presents teachers with specific advice concerning methods of bringing about good teacher-learner relationships, and is premised on the notion that teachers should be taught the principles and skills of "effective human relations, honest interpersonal communication [and] constructive conflict resolution" (1974, p. ix).

A final emphasis shared by most humanistic approaches relates to the recognition and development of personal values. Students are encouraged to know themselves and to express themselves; to strive toward feelings of self-identity; to actualize themselves. Simon et al. (1972), for example, present teachers with seventy-nine specific strategies geared toward the elaboration and clarification of values in students.

These four common emphases (affect, self-development, communication, and values) lend themselves to a number of instructional methods more readily than

---

DISINVITED STUDENTS

Purkey (1978) presents a strong argument for the encouragement of teacher behaviors that *invite* students to see themselves as valuable, responsible, worthwhile, and important persons (see text). It would be naive to assume that all teachers have attitudes toward students that lend themselves to *inviting* behaviors. Below are some samples of experiences that are clearly *disinviting* in that they label students as irresponsible, incapable, or worthless (and sometimes all three). (From Purkey, 1978)

—The teacher said I didn't want to learn; that I just wanted to cause trouble.
—She told the class we were discipline problems and were not to be trusted.
—The teacher put me out in the hall for everyone to laugh at.
—They put me in the dummy class, and it had SPECIAL EDUCATION painted right on the door.
—The teacher said to me in front of the whole class: "I really don't think you're that stupid!"
—When the principal hit me he said it was the only language I understood.
—She said I was worse than my brother, and I don't even have a brother.
—My name is Bill Dill, but the teacher always called me "Dill Pickle" and laughed.
I transferred to a new school after it had started. When I appeared at the teacher's doorway, she said, "Oh, no; not another one!"

do the more traditional emphases (mastery of academic content, good citizenship, sportsmanship). Thus group process approaches, rooted in sensitivity and encounter group movements (sometimes referred to collectively as "growth groups"), are a common instructional approach in humanistic education. In groups students may be encouraged to express their feelings more openly, to discover and clarify these feelings, to explore interpersonal relationships, and to articulate their personal value systems. Various communication "games" may be employed to enhance the "genuineness" and "openness" of interpersonal relationships. Role-playing games also offer different means of exploring affect and human relationships.

None of these "humanistic" techniques is described in detail here. The omission is deliberate. Indeed, to describe these techniques would be highly unethical, and quite incompatible with the human goals of humanistic education. The danger is far too great that a teacher with insufficient and perhaps inappropriate training and background would unwittingly inflict serious psychological damage on students through inexpert and ill-advised attempts to implement "growth group" activities in the classroom. The American Psychological Association's (1973) ethical code for growth groups makes it clear that the classroom teacher, educated in the usual fashion, is hardly qualified to conduct "groups" in the classroom. And even if he or she were fully qualified, and fully aware of the implicit dangers, the use of group process techniques in the classroom requires a degree of compulsion that would still be incompatible with the APA code of ethics.

The preceding is not intended to be a wholesale condemnation of growth groups in the classroom. There are a number of group activities (for instance, some role-playing games) that can profitably be employed by any teacher. But public expressions of deep inner feelings such as are often required in growth groups, while they should be encouraged under some circumstances, should never be "required" of the learner in the context of group and social pressure.

It should be kept in mind that humanism is more an educational philosophy than an assortment of instructional methods. As such, it offers the teacher a number of worthwhile goals, and encourages the development of attitudes that cannot help but affect the instructional process. In the end, it is quite unnecessary to copy the models and the advice presented by the more visible of humanistic educators; what is necessary is that you genuinely care about the people as persons. The rest will follow.

Watson—A Last Word

It may seem inappropriate to conclude a discussion of humanism by referring to the recognized initiator and principal ideological proponent of the position usually considered most directly antithetical to humanism. It is interesting to note, however, that some of the writings of John B. Watson describe the society that Rogers and Skinner advocated years later. Indeed, parts of the following excerpt from Watson could have been written by either Skinner *or* Rogers. As far back as 1930, Watson concluded a book with a section entitled "Behaviorism as a Guide for All Future Experimental Ethics." The entire section is quoted below (Watson, 1930, pp. 303– 304):

> *Behaviorism ought to be a science that prepares men and women for understanding the principles of their own behavior. It ought to make men and women eager to rearrange their own lives, and especially eager to prepare themselves to bring up their own children in a healthy way. I wish I could picture for you what a rich and wonderful individual we could make of every healthy child if only we could let it shape itself properly and then provide for it a universe in which it could exercise that organization—a universe unshackled by legendary folk-lore of happenings thousands of years ago; unhampered by disgraceful political history; free of foolish customs and conventions which have no significance in themselves, yet which hem the individual in like taut steel bands. I am not asking here for revolution; I am not asking people to go out to some God-forsaken place, form a colony, go naked and live a communal life, nor am I asking for a change to a diet of roots and herbs. I am not asking for "free love." I am trying to dangle a stimulus in front of you, a verbal stimulus which, if acted upon, will gradually change this universe. For the universe will change if you bring up your children, not in the freedom of the libertine, but in behavioristic freedom—a freedom which we cannot even picture in words, so little do we know of it. Will not these children in turn, with their better ways of living and thinking, replace us as society and in turn bring up their children in a still more scientific way, until the world finally becomes a place fit for human habitation?*

Summary of Chapter 8

This chapter has presented a description of the phenomenological, person-centered, humanistic view of human functioning advanced by Carl Rogers. In addition, a comparison was made between the views of Rogers and Skinner on behavior control. The implications of Rogerian theory for schools were also examined as were some of the general principles of humanistic education.

Main Points in Chapter 8

1. Carl Rogers' theory may be described as phenomenological in view of its concern with what is termed the *phenomenal* as opposed to the *real*. The phenomenal world is the environment as it is perceived by one individual.

2. The theory is also humanistic, particularly in terms of its concern for the individual together with the belief that self-actualization is a prime motivating force.

3. Rogers' notions regarding the desirability of self-determination are opposed to Skinner's expressed concern with control through the application of a science of behavior (namely, the principles of operant learning).

4. Rogers summarizes his theory of behavior and personality in the form of nineteen propositions. The substance of the most important of these is contained here in summary points 5 through 12.

5. An individual's "real" world is the phenomenal world (what a person perceives). Only the individual can fully know it.

6. Individuals react in an integrated and purposive manner toward the phenomenal world. The direction (purposiveness) of their behavior is determined by a tendency toward self-actualization.

7. One way of defining self-actualization is to say that it involves a continuing effort to achieve the maximum development of an individual's potentiality. The process is assumed to be related to healthy and creative functioning.

8. Emotion accompanies the attempt to obtain a goal. It increases with the importance of the goal and becomes less intense and more pleasant when the goal is reached.

9. The development of the "self" results from interactions with the world (direct experience) and from values about the "me" that are borrowed from the actions of other people (indirect experience). Occasionally the values derived from these two sources are incompatible and result in conflict.

10. People tend to perceive and react to those aspects of the environment that are congruent with their perception of "self."

11. One source of neurotic behavior is conflict between real organic needs and behavior that corresponds to the self-image.

12. Healthy, adaptive behavior is related to a nonthreatening environment and a flexible and open self-structure.

13. The most important education-related implication of Rogerian theory is that, in order to promote full healthy functioning, schools should be student centered. The instructional procedures that Rogers sees as best for these schools are discovery oriented.

14. Kohl, Dennison, Barton, and others describe humanistic alternatives to contemporary education. The major emphases of humanistic approaches relate to the development of self, the clarification of values, openness, honesty, and self-determination.

Suggested Readings

In order to arrive at a clear understanding of the Rogers-Skinner debate the reader is advised to refer to Skinner's Walden II *for a description of his position and to follow that with Krutch's* The Measure of Man. *Walden II describes a society based on the principles of operant conditioning. Krutch, in a strong reaction to Skinner's controlled society, presents a humanistic point of view. These two readings can then be followed by the classical Rogers-Skinner debate.*

Krutch, J. W. *The Measure of Man*. Indianapolis: Bobbs-Merrill, 1953.

Rogers, C. R. and B. F. **Skinner.** Some issues concerning the control of human behavior: a symposium. *Science,* 1956, 124, 1057–1066.

Skinner, B. F. *Walden II*. New York: Macmillan, 1948.

Rogers' own attempt to apply his theories and beliefs to education is expressed in:

Rogers, C. R. *Freedom to Learn*. Columbus, Ohio: Charles E. Merrill Books, 1969.

Additional insight into humanistic psychology is provided by interviews with Maslow, Murphy, and Rogers in:

Frick, W. B. *Humanistic Psychology: Interviews with Maslow, Murphy, and Rogers.* Columbus, Ohio: Charles E. Merrill Books, 1971.

Two intriguing and stimulating first-person accounts of alternatives to traditional education are detailed in:

Dennison, George. *The Lives of Children: The Story of the First Street School.* New York: Random House (Vintage Books), 1969.

Kohl, Herbert R. *The Open Classroom: A Practical Guide to a New Way of Teaching.* New York: Random House (Vintage Books), 1969.

Among numerous humanistic books for teachers and students are the following:

Borton, T. *Reach, Touch, and Teach: Student Concerns and Process Education.* New York: McGraw Hill, 1970.

Gordon, T. *T.E.T. Teacher Effectiveness Training*. New York: Peter H. Wyden, 1974.

Postman, N. and C. **Weingartner.** *The Soft Revolution.* New York: Delacorte Press, 1971.

Purkey, W. W. *Inviting School Success: A Self-Concept Approach to Teaching and Learning.* Belmont, Calif.: Wadsworth, 1978.

Satir, V. *Peoplemaking*. Palo Alto, Calif.: Science and Behavior Books, 1972.

Simon, S. B., L. W. **Howe,** and H. **Kirschenbaum.** *Values Clarification: A Handbook of Practical Strategies for Teachers and Students.* New York: Hart Publishing Co., 1972.

9
Human Development:
An Overview

The childhood shews the man,
As morning shows the day.
(John Milton)

But does it not sometimes storm on
the evening of a sun-filled morning? And can
even the wisest of human grandmothers
explain or predict these happenings?

Advance Organizer It would appear axiomatic that in order to teach children it is necessary to understand them. Certainly, in order to train dogs we have found it highly useful to have some knowledge of the ages at which they are most likely to profit from our efforts, as well as of the methods to which they are most likely to respond. But even with dogs we have found remarkable individual differences not only among different species, but also among individual dogs within a single species. So it is with children. This chapter presents a selective summary of some of the most important findings and concepts in the study of child development. It is important to keep in mind, however, that our discussion is necessarily limited to that mythical but convenient invention, the Average Child. Your children are not likely to be "average"; they will need to be understood as individuals. Nevertheless, knowledge of the average may prove to be of considerable value in understanding the individual.

Little is known about the courtship behaviors and mating rituals of bears; about turkeys, considerably more is known, though much of that information has cleverly been kept secret. In any case, it is quite irrelevant for our purposes.

About the mating behaviors and courtship rituals of humans, there is a great deal of speculation and an impressive collection of scientific observations. Too, there are numerous, though not necessarily effective, recipes, medications, aids, and collections of advice. But that too would be of little relevance or interest.

Of more immediate relevance is the recent discovery that pregnancy is caused; it does not just happen (Lefrancois, 1977). The process of development begins with the cause, eventuates in birth, and terminates at death.

The period with which developmental psychology is most concerned, however, usually begins at birth and ends around the age of sixteen. The study of human development attempts primarily to describe and explain the systematic changes that an individual undergoes in the course of **ontogeny.** These include physical, motor, intellectual, and personality changes. They are often dealt with separately, although they are known to interact in significant ways.

This chapter gives a brief historical overview of the emergence of child study as a psychological undertaking and describes, in fairly general terms, some of what is known or suspected about human development. This description takes the form of *eleven principles.* The next chapter deals exclusively with one theoretical account of development—that advanced by the man who is without doubt the most significant living developmental psychologist, the Swiss Jean Piaget.

In order to clarify the issues involved in this discussion, four terms need to be defined: **growth, maturation, learning,** and **development.**

1. *Growth:* refers to quantitative physical changes, such as increases in weight or height.

2. *Maturation:* a global, relatively nebulous term; refers to changes that are assumed to result from a natural process. Refers to physiological changes that are reflected in increased competence (e.g., development of small-muscle coordination) rather than to more "psychological" changes.

3. *Learning:* refers to changes that result from experience rather than from natural processes.

4. *Development:* refers to the total process of development of an individual's capacities to adapt to his or her environment. Includes processes defined by the terms growth, learning, and maturation.

The Origins of the
Study of Child Development

Children in the Western world have not always held as high a position in the affection of adults as they do now. Indeed, there appears to be a remarkable correspondence between the economic wealth of a nation and the love that is lavished on its children. Wealthy countries have historically prized their children most (Johnson and Medinnus, 1969). This is difficult to accept in view of the popular notion that the members of poor families love each other deeply—a notion which may well be true where poverty does not mean not having enough food, but simply means not having enough money to buy good clothes or television sets. This, however, is a far cry from living on the edge of starvation.

Anthony Ashley Cooper, seventh Earl of Shaftesbury, describes in vivid detail the conditions children worked under in coal mines in nineteenth-century Europe (Kessen, 1965). He paints a picture of misery and poverty so terrible that it can only have resulted from an almost complete lack of love between parents and children. Boys and girls, sometimes as young as five or six, worked for fourteen or sixteen hours a day in small tunnels deep underground. The lighting, ventilation, and drainage were extremely bad. More often than not, the children worked in three or four inches of water. Many of the coal seams had ceilings as low as twenty-four inches, so that they were forced to work crouched over. Much of the work consisted of placing chunks of coal in baskets, which were then pulled out of the tunnels by means of a girdle and chain. This cruel contraption was a belt fastened around the child's middle. At the front was a ring to which a chain was attached. The chain passed between the child's legs and was fastened to the basket behind him. The baskets were then hauled out, with the child usually crawling on all fours. Great raw wounds often developed where the chain rubbed against the inner thighs.

While the conditions under which children are allowed to work (or indeed, whether they are allowed to work at all) is one indicator of their parents' attitude toward them, there are other indexes as well. For instance, the practice of abandoning children also indicates lack of affection. This practice was highly prevalent in eighteenth-century Europe. One foundling home in Dublin, for example, received 10,272 children in the last quarter of that century. It is significant that of these only forty-three survived till age five (Kessen, 1965, p. 8).

The very high mortality rate among children is significant because it reflects the relative newness of pediatrics as a branch of medicine. In fact, children appeared so unlikely to benefit from medical attention that physicians all but completely neglected them until this century. The probability that a child would succumb to one of the many childhood diseases, in the absence of inoculations and of even the most rudimentary knowledge about the transmission of illness, was very high indeed. Before 1750 the probability of surviving to age five was one in three (Kessen, 1965, p. 8). This was undoubtedly another reason for lack of affection between parents and children. The chances that the child would die were too high to justify becoming emotionally involved with it. The risk of heartbreak was too great.

Several historical events helped to further the development of a science of child study. To begin with, it is assumed that as recently as the nineteenth century children in Europe were cared for less than they are now, and that this was partly because economic conditions made child labor desirable. In addition, the undeveloped state of child medicine made infant death probable. It follows, then, that the reasons for changes in parental attitudes should be linked with changes in medicine and in economics. Medicine made great strides at the beginning of the present century. Consequently infant mortality rates are very low and parents can afford to become attached to children with only a small risk of losing them. In addition, the industrial

revolution made child labor largely unnecessary. Consequently attention could now be focused on the question of what to do with children who were no longer needed in the labor force. This attention took the form of increased interest in education and, more important, of increased interest in children on the part of people in other disciplines. As a result of the work of such men as Darwin (e.g., *A Biographical Sketch of an Infant*, 1877) and Freud, people slowly became aware of the value of studying child development. Children have now become worthy of study in their own right; they have even been at least partly successful in replacing the rat as a subject of psychological investigation.

This section does not describe in detail the theoretical positions that consti-tute the history of developmental psychology, but only names and defines them. A treatment of the issues with which they deal, and of the controversy they engen-dered, is implicit in the discussion of principles of development which forms the balance of this chapter.

Developmental theories have centered around a number of controversial questions: the nature-nurture question, the question of whether children learn through activity or whether they are passive receivers of knowledge, and the ques-tion of the nature of the difference between a child and an adult, together with the related question of the nature of a child's intellectual processes. The first question (nature-nurture) is examined in some detail in Chapter 11. The second (active or passive) and the fourth (nature of intellectual processes) are covered, at least im-plicitly, in the learning part of this text. The third question (the difference between a child and an adult) forms the basis of the discussion in this chapter.

Most early developmental positions can be categorized according to whether they assume that heredity or environment plays the more crucial role in development. The former assumption is made by *preformationistic* or *predeterministic* orientations. The latter is made by all of the positions that fall under the heading of *environmental* (**tabula rasa**) approaches (Hunt, 1961; Ausubel, 1958).

Preformationism

Preformationism is the position that assumes that whatever children will be as adults they already are at birth. In other words, there are no real differences between the child and the adult. The child is a little man or woman, miniature, to be sure, but complete in every significant detail. The only developmental changes pos-sible are therefore quantitative ones; children will simply become more of what they now are.

This position is really of no more than historical interest since it is generally accepted that there are some real and important qualitative differences between children and adults. Manifestations of preformationistic ideas in some aspects of contemporary theories are interesting to note, however. Theories of human instincts are essentially preformationistic in the sense that an instinct is defined as an un-learned behavior pattern, perfect and fully developed on the occasion of its first appearance.

Predeterminism

The predeterministic approach resembles preformationism in that both as-sume that heredity is the deciding factor in development. **Predeterminism,** how-ever, maintains not that the child is a miniature adult, but rather that the sequence of development is predetermined. In other words, while there is a progression in the unfolding of a child's capacities, that progression is due to genetic rather than environmental factors. There are many examples of predeterministic approaches, the most important being the theories of G. Stanley Hall and Arnold Gesell.

The sense in which G. Stanley Hall's theory is predeterministic is this: He described ontogenetic development (from birth to death) as involving a series of stages highly similar to those through which the human species is thought to have progressed. The often-quoted phrase that expresses this notion is: "Ontogeny recapitulates **phylogeny**." Simply stated, this means that the development of one individual from conception to death will resemble the development of the entire species. As evidence for this theory, Hall describes the evolution of a child's interest in games, claiming that these parallel the development of human occupations. The child is, in sequence, interested in games corresponding to each of the following: an arboreal existence (e.g., climbing on chairs and tables); a cave-dwelling existence (e.g., crawling into dark, close spaces); a pastoral existence (e.g., playing with animals); an agricultural existence (e.g., tending plants and flowers); and, finally, an industrial existence (e.g., playing with vehicles). This, for Hall, was more than a simple description of developmental phenomena; it was an explanation of them. A second, much more recent example of a recapitulation-like doctrine is found in the writings of Jerome Bruner (1964, 1968). As was pointed out in Chapter 1, Bruner describes human evolution as having involved three major classes of inventive behavior: the first concerned with amplifying motor capacities, the second with sensory capacities, and the third with ratiocinative (intellectual) capacities. The interesting thing about this view of evolution is that it provides a framework for describing the development of a child. Bruner points out that a human child progresses through a series of stages representing the world that roughly parallels the sequence of human inventions. First, the world is represented in terms of the activities of looking, seeing, smelling, hearing, tasting, manipulating, walking around, and so on. This is termed **enactive** representation. It corresponds to our early preoccupation with motor capabilities; it is a stage of motoric intelligence (see Chapter 10, Piaget). The second representation system involves images—pictures that resemble the real. This is termed **iconic** representation. It corresponds to our invention of amplifiers of sensory capacities. The last, and most sophisticated, of human representational systems corresponds to the amplification of ratiocinactive capacities. It is termed **symbolic** representation. The difference between a *symbol* and an *icon* is that icons (or images) bear a real resemblance to the objects they represent, whereas symbols are completely arbitrary.

The developmental system that Bruner has begun to describe (1964, 1966, 1968) is highly similar to Jean Piaget's. However, it is somewhat more concerned with the role of language—our most advanced system for symbolic representation— in information-processing and problem-solving behavior at different ages.

Arnold Gesell's *theory of maturation* provides a third example of a predeterministic approach. Gesell, one of Hall's students, rejected the doctrine of recapitulation but accepted the notion that development is determined by innate factors. Maturation is the rather global term used to define the cause of developmental changes. The central assumption is that this course is predetermined and will unfold according to a genetically controlled plan.

The Tabula Rasa *Approach*

Whereas both predeterministic and preformationistic approaches hold that heredity is the crucial factor in development, the *tabula rasa* (blank slate) approach advanced by the British philosopher John Locke stems from the opposite orientation. It assumes that environment is the determining force in human development. Probably the clearest example of this approach is found in the work of J. B. Watson (see Chapter 2). His *environmentalism* was, in fact, an almost complete rejection of the importance of genetic factors in development.

Contemporary behavioristic positions, while not as openly environmentalistic as Watson's, tend to be much more concerned with experiential factors than with genetic ones. This is true of the more cognitive positions as well. It is not, as is probably evident, an "either-or" question. Both nature and nurture, as is made clear in Chapter 11, are involved in human development.

Language Development

It is the ability to communicate through **language** that most clearly separates us from other beasts. Language is the repository of all our knowledge and wisdom, except for what is stored in individual minds—and even that may be at least partly in language forms. Not only is information stored in language, it is transmitted through language as well. But language accounts for even more than storage and transmission; it is a means for transforming knowledge. The universality of meaning and the sharing of human experience are both accomplished largely through language. It is the chief medium of instruction in schools; hence its importance can hardly be overestimated.

Language and Communication

Language is not synonymous with **communication.** Animals communicate, but they do not have language. A dog who looks at its master, walks to its dish and barks, looks at its master again, and then begins to growl is communicating very effectively. Animals that are not domesticated also communicate. Pronghorn antelope convey alarm by bristling their rump patches; white-tailed deer do the same by waving their long tails. Pheasants attract rivals by crowing; elk, by bugling; and moose, by grunting. Hebb (1966) refers to this type of behavior as communication through reflexive activity. The behavior of the dog described above, however, is an example of purposive communication—but it is still not language. To communicate is to transmit or convey a message. It requires a sender and a receiver. To communicate through language is to make use of *arbitrary* sounds, gestures, or symbols in a purposive manner in order to convey meaning. Further, the use of language involves sounds or other signs that can be combined or transformed to produce different meanings. A parrot, for example, can mimic a word or even a phrase, and may be taught to say this phrase when its utterance will appear purposive. A parrot that says "You bore me" after a guest has been talking incessantly for two hours may appear to be using language in a purposive manner. But the parrot cannot transform this phrase to "Bore me," or "You," with the intention of communicating a different meaning. That would be language as opposed to simple communication.

The Early
Development of Language

It is interesting that in the course of children's babbling they may emit every sound used in all of the world's languages. How these sounds become organized into the meaningful patterns of the language is a matter for speculation. One relatively reasonable and clear account of early language learning can be based on an operant conditioning model. This explanation maintains that, while babbling, a child will emit wordlike sounds, which will tend to be reinforced by adults. As the frequency of these specific sounds increases, parents or siblings may repeat the child's vocalizations and thus serve as models for the child. Eventually, through reinforcement, children learn to imitate the speech patterns of those around them (see Chapter 12). Were it not for this imitation and reinforcement, frequency and variety of speech sounds would probably decrease. This is borne out by the observation that deaf

---

LAD

The operant conditioning model advanced to explain children's acquisition of language is partly correct, but it is also inadequate. The incredible rapidity with which children acquire *syntax* (knowledge of grammar) during their third and fourth years, coupled with the fact that they make only a fraction of all the mistakes that they would be expected to make were they learning through reinforcement alone, makes it unlikely that operant conditioning will provide a complete answer. And the nature of their errors frequently reveals that the errors result not so much from lack of proper models or lack of reinforcement, but rather from the application of rules that they have derived, unconsciously, but without direct adult tuition. The irony is that the rules are themselves correct, but the vagaries of our language present so many exceptions that children cannot apply these rules generally; they must also learn the exceptions. Thus children who say "I eated," "I was borned," "I dood it," and "I runned fast," are displaying that they are fine grammaticians even if they have not completely mastered the language. Chomsky (1957, 1965), among the most noted of contemporary linguists, has undertaken considerable research in an attempt to explain children's development of language. His conclusions, simplified, are that children are, in effect, "linguists extraordinaire," that their behavior is similar to that of a person who is *inventing* grammar for the first time, that linguists can learn much about language simply by listening to children, and that the child's rapid acquisition of an incredibly complex syntax can only be explained on the basis of prewired neurological mechanisms. In other words, the child is neurologically predisposed to learning the forms of a language. This neurological predisposition (prewired—in other words, innate) he labels a Language Acquisition Device, *Lad* for short. While there is no substantive evidence of Lad's existence, it is a theory that, for the time being, fits the facts as they are now known.

children make sounds much like those made by normal children until around the age of six months. After that they utter few sounds, particularly repetitive ones.

Prior to the age of six months a child's utterances are completely unsystematic and erratic. As such they defy analysis. After six months there is an increase in the number of controlled repetitions of sounds, until eventually evidence is provided that specific sounds are being associated with a certain object or with a group of objects. These first "meaningful" sounds are not necessarily words as we know them.* By the age of one, the average child can speak or understand three words (Smith, 1926). By the age of two, that number will have increased to over 300, and by six, the child's vocabulary may consist of well over 2,500 words. Since it is very difficult to get an accurate count of all the words a child speaks or understands, these figures are considered to be very conservative estimates, particularly for higher ages.

The acquisition of language is an extremely complex process. It involves much more than simply learning the names of concrete or abstract entities. It consists also of learning the grammar that governs sequence and transformations in the language. And it is grammar that gives language its tremendous power. Consider the simple sentence: "Stan Twolips struck Johnny West." The same referents in different order convey a drastically altered meaning: "Johnny West struck Stan Twolips." This is only one possible transformation—perhaps Johnny Twolips struck Stan West or Stan West struck Johnny Twolips, or they both struck. . . .

By the time an average child arrives at school the development of language and grammar is well under way. One of the school's most important functions is to enhance that development, since a child's language sophistication is very closely related to functioning in school.

Language and Behavior

Several Russian psychologists (for example, Luria, 1961; Vygotsky, 1962; Sokolov, 1959) have conducted intensive investigations into the role of language in the regulation of behavior. Luria (1961), for example, describes an experiment where a subject is asked to squeeze a balloon when a light goes on. In the first stage, language has an *impulsive* function. It can initiate action, *but it cannot stop it*. Once the child has been told "squeeze," or once a light has gone on to signal the beginning of the act of squeezing, the word *stop* will not cause children to stop but will make them squeeze harder. At approximately a year and a half, language acquires an *inhibitory* function as well. It is not until the child is four or more years old that *covert* speech (thought, in other words) acquires a complete regulatory function. It can then both initiate action and terminate it prior to its natural ending.

The relationship of language to behavior in a broad sense is somewhat more difficult to isolate, since so much human activity is inextricably linked with speech. It

---

* For example, the author's son's first word was *buh*—this meant light.

is relatively simple and revealing, however, to look at the relationship between verbal ability and achievement and intelligence.

Language and Intelligence

The **correlation** (see Chapter 11 for an explanation of this term) between verbal ability and measured intelligence is very high. This may be partly because most measures of intelligence are highly verbal—that is, they require that subjects at least understand verbal directions. In many cases, they are also asked to make oral or written verbal responses. In addition, many of these tests measure extent and sophistication of vocabulary. The very construction of intelligence tests, then, probably accounts for at least some of the high correspondence that exists between language and intelligence. On the other hand, the fact that verbal ability is given such a central role in these tests is an indication of the belief that intelligence is largely verbal.

Language and Achievement

Bernstein (1961) attributes at least part of the difference in achievement between lower-class and upper-class children to the language differences between them. The lower-class child has a much more restricted language background than the upper-class child. The former uses what Bernstein calls *restricted language codes;* the latter uses what he calls *elaborate codes*. Restricted codes are characterized by short, simple expressions—for example, "Shut the door." An elaborate code makes wider use of modifiers and explanation for example, "Johnny, would you please shut the door. The draft is hitting the baby and she might catch cold." It is understandable that children from "restricted" backgrounds would begin school at a much lower level of language development. Various correlational studies leave no doubt that the relationship between language and school achievement is very high. This is obviously partly because most school subjects require some transaction through language, whether it be written or oral.

Principles of Development

This section provides an overview of some of the present knowledge and current beliefs in developmental psychology. The overview takes the form of a description of eleven summary principles of development. The "principles" are concluding of explanatory remarks that have been made by various authors in various places or that have been included in sections or chapters of textbooks entitled, surprisingly enough, *Principles of Development*. It should be clearly understood that these "principles" are only some of the many such statements which could have been included.

Principle 1

Development is influenced by both heredity and environment. Both the meaning and the truth of this principle are obvious. What is not so obvious is the extent to which each of these factors contributes to development. While a more detailed discussion of this principle is included in Chapter 11, an illustration of the effects of heredity and environment is given here.

Consider the well-known case of Johnny West. Johnny has red hair. His red hair is rather striking. That is really not very unusual in itself, but what is more extraordinary is that Johnny looks remarkably like the milkman, Stan Twolips. Both Johnny and Stan have extra-long noses.

People occasionally remark on how Johnny doesn't look like his dad, but he sure talks like him. This is odd, since Johnny's mom had not met his dad until Johnny was two years old. People look at Johnny's nose and say, "Betcha he gottit from ol' Stan." Such is the power of heredity. The same people hear him swear in French and say, "Betcha he gottit from his dad." That is the influence of environment. This does not mean, of course, that environment comes from fathers and heredity from milkmen. What it does mean is . . . aw, forget it.

More seriously, the relative influences of heredity and environment on development have been extensively studied, particularly with respect to such characteristics as intelligence. Ironically, it is in areas such as these that the separate effects of nature and nurture are least obvious and most difficult to differentiate one from the other. Chapter 11 presents a relatively detailed examination of this area.

Principle 2

Development takes place at different rates for different parts of the organism. This is not intended to mean that the left foot grows rapidly for a short while, then the right foot, and then one arm—although from personal experience I know that some people do grow like that, and sometimes their development gets arrested at embarrassing stages. It does mean, however, that physical growth as well as some aspects of personality, and of cognitive or perceptual ability, may grow at different rates and reach their maximum development at different times.

The development of cognitive ability and of personality traits has recently been shown to be governed by this principle. Bloom (1964) found that for each personality trait there is a characteristic growth curve. By the age of two and a half, half of a child's future height will have been reached. Half of a male's aggressiveness is thought to be established by age three, and, more significant, fully two-thirds of a

---

EARLY EXPERIENCES

A host of well-respected psychologists have believed for some time that the effects of early deprivation, if sufficiently severe and prolonged, are for the most part irreversible. They maintain that a child who is isolated from others, deprived of intellectual stimulation, and otherwise raised in an extremely barren environment can be expected to be retarded in intellectual, motor, and emotional development. They would also expect such a child's future potential for learning and adjusting normally to society to be severely limited.

In an interview (*Saturday Review*, 1973), Jerome Kagan discussed his observations of a Guatemalan tribe in which children are isolated in windowless bamboo huts for the first year of their lives. Children have considerable physical contact with their mothers, but they have no toys or verbal interaction. As expected, these children are noticeably retarded at an early age. Kagan describes them as "quiet, somber, motorically passive, and extremely fearful [and] on tests of maturational and intellectual development they are four or five months behind American children." In addition, they do not begin to talk until the age of two and a half or three. By the age of eleven, however, these same children are gay and alert and, according to Kagan, they are *more* impressive than American children on tests in which familiar words and materials are employed. Apparently the severe isolation these children experience in the first year of life does not affect their potential for future development.

Does this one study provide sufficient evidence to conclude that early experiences are not particularly important for later development? How severe must isolation be before its effects are irreversible? Are there individual or racial differences in the effects of deprivation on children? Is there a critical period during which deprivation will have lasting effects? And if the effects of deprivation don't last, do those of early enrichment?

person's intellectual capacity has already been developed by age six.* Hence development is not a uniform process for all features of an organism. To understand it, investigators are compelled to look at different aspects of development and at their interaction.

The description of growth curves for development has led Bloom (1964) to postulate a law that, if valid, is of major importance for education. It is given here as Principle 3.

Principle 3

Variations in environment have greatest quantitative effect on a characteristic at its period of most rapid change and least effect on the characteristic at its period of least rapid change (Bloom, 1964, p. VII). This principle is most clearly illustrated in the area of physical growth. It is evident, for example, that changes in environment are not likely to affect the height of subjects over twenty. On the other hand, dietary changes for children under one could conceivably have a very significant effect on future height.

In the area of intellectual development, several studies tend to confirm this principle. There is the now famous study reported by Lee (1951), which examined the intelligence test scores of American blacks living in Philadelphia. Of three groups of blacks who had all been born in the South, one had moved to Philadelphia prior to grade one, the second at grade four, and the third at grade six. The first group showed much greater increases in intelligence test scores than the last two. In addition, the greatest changes occurred during the first few years. Other studies (see, for example, Deutsch, 1964; Pines, 1966; Lefrancois, 1968) have demonstrated that it is possible to accelerate children's development through direct manipulation of the environment. The implications for teaching are obvious. Stimulating educational experiences, particularly if they provide children with success and not with failure, may exert a lasting influence on intellectual development.

Principle 4

Development follows an orderly sequence. In fetal development the heart appears and begins to function before the limbs reach their final form; the lips and gums form prior to the nasal passages; the tail regresses before the permanent tooth buds are formed, and so on.

In motor development, children can lift their chins from a prone position before they can raise their chests; they can sit before standing, they can stand before

---

* Statements such as these are hypothetical approximations at best. The important point is simply that major personality and intellectual characteristics appear to be strongly influenced (and perhaps partly determined) by early childhood experiences.

creeping, and they can creep before walking (Shirley, 1933). Learning to move in a prone position, they go through fourteen distinct sequential stages (Ames, 1937).

In intellectual development, the same principle can be seen to apply, although the sequences are less obvious and the stages less distinct. Piaget's theory (Chapter 10) is premised on the assumption that human development is characterized by distinct sequential stages. Piaget's analysis of the evolution of play behavior in children offers one example of sequential development in a nonmotoric, nonphysical area. The illustration selected deals specifically with the evolution of game rules in the child (Piaget, 1932)—an evolution Piaget describes as comprising two aspects, both of which exhibit the orderly sequence of Principle 4.

There is, on the one hand, the child's actual behavior in game situations; on the other, there are verbalized notions of rules. These do not necessarily agree. The following descriptions are based upon observations of children playing the game of marbles.

Stage I (1 to 3 years): During Stage I children behave as though there were no rules. Their marble games are those of free play.

Stage II (3 to 5 years): At around the age of three children begin to imitate aspects of the rule-regulated behavior of adults. They think they are following rules, but in reality they are making their own. My son, when three, delighted in throwing toy cars across the room and then shrieking, "Sixteen points." When his sister did likewise he occasionally allowed her to earn "sixteen points," but more often than not he insisted that the car either went too far or not far enough. The rules changed continuously but aspects of the behavior were rule-bound in a loose sense (e.g., the notion of points is derived from adult games).

Stage III (5 to 11 years): In the third stage children play in a genuinely social manner. Rules are mutually and rigidly adhered to by all players. They are never changed.

Stage IV (from 11 or 12 years): The fourth stage is marked by a more complete understanding of the purpose and origin of rules. They are occasionally modified in the course of playing games.

Interestingly, while these four stages describe the way children play games, they do not describe the child's verbalized notions of rules. These follow a different sequence:

Stage I (1 to 3 years): The verbal notions of rules at this stage correspond to behavior. Children know no rules and play according to none.

Stage II (3 to 5 years): At Stage II, children's play behavior is in accordance with rules, but these change continually. They make them up as they go along. If asked about rules, however, they describe them as being external and unchangeable, and readily admit that new rules would be quite unfair.

Stage III (5 to 11 or 12 years): Whereas children at this stage follow rules rigidly without ever changing them, they believe that rules come from other children, and that they are, in fact, changeable.

Stage IV (from 11 or 12 years): Both in behavior and in thought, rules are now completely understood and can be modified.

These observations are a typical example of the method Piaget employed in gathering data for the development of his theory. Two points crucial to an understanding of that theory are comprised in the next two principles.

Principle 5

Development is continuous rather than discrete. In other words, stages of development are not separate but follow one from the other with no clear-cut break. It follows, then, that the ages assigned to various steps in a developmental sequence are simply approximations.

This principle also recognizes the fact that, as a continuous process, development is relatively smooth and orderly. There are occasional spurts in various areas, but in the main the child's competence increases gradually enough that changes often go unnoticed by parents and teachers. Nevertheless, knowledge of children's capabilities and interests at different ages can be of considerable value for teachers in suggesting appropriate activities, instructional methods, and so on.

Principle 6

There is a great deal of variability among individuals. This is related to the high plasticity of the human being, to different genetic characteristics, and to the effects of different environments on children. It remains true, nevertheless, that valid generalizations about children as a group can be made. It is extremely important to note that these generalizations apply to children as a group and not to any specific individual child. There is no normal, average child; the average child is a myth invented by grandmothers and investigated by psychologists.

Principle 7

Any breaks in the continuity of development will generally be due to environmental factors. An obvious contradiction of this principle is provided by the effects that prolonged or severe illness can have on development. This, however, can probably be considered an environmental factor. In essence the principle states that major disturbances in a developmental sequence can usually be accounted for in terms of experiential factors. On the one hand there is the possible enriching effect of optimal environment on development (Fowler, 1962, 1967; Worth et al., 1966). On the other hand there are the possible deleterious effects of impoverished environment. Spitz (1945, 1946), for example, studied the effect of maternal deprivation on children in institutions. He found that, in general, institutionalized babies have an extremely high mortality rate, *despite good medical attention,* and that they are considerably retarded in motor and intellectual development. While the Spitz studies have been severely criticized (Pinneau, 1955), there is much corroborative evidence

Lefrancois said there is no such thing! Hee hee!

to suggest that the effects of impoverished environments on children are highly harmful, and to some extent irreversible (Bowlby, 1952; Dennis, 1960). The Dennis study, for example, describes children brought up in very barren environments in an orphanage in Tehran. At the age of four, only about 15 percent of the children could walk. Surprisingly, most of those who could not walk did not creep or crawl but "scooted" instead—that is, they propelled themselves sitting down, pushing with their hands and pulling with one foot. It appears that the sequence of motor development can be altered through environmental changes.

Much more significant for education are studies reporting attempts to remedy the effects of early deprivation. Without doubt the most ambitious of all these attempts is Project Head Start in the United States, a massive program aimed at the slum-area preschool child. It is not yet clear from the numerous reports now being published whether the Head Start programs are effective in closing the educational gap. Many of the programs for slum children have had to be too concerned with the child's physical needs to spend much time on more cognitive activities. Hence tests do not always show changes that have taken place, since they measure the wrong thing. (See Pines [1966] for a readable and interesting account of Project Head Start.)

Principle 8

Correlation and not compensation is the rule in development. There is a popular notion that contradicts this principle. It is widely believed that individuals who are intellectually gifted are, of course, not nearly so well endowed in other areas. The "egghead" is believed to be a blundering social idiot; he is certainly unattractive and frail; his vision is weak; he is completely useless at any kind of task requiring even the smallest degree of dexterity; his breath smells, and his teeth are crooked.

The athlete, a handsome and virile brute, is remarkably stupid; he spells his name with difficulty; he cannot write a check without a lawyer to correct it; he reads children's comic books and laughs uproariously at very unfunny events.*

In actual fact these stereotypes are less representative of reality than one might think. The person who excels in one area is more likely to excel in others. This is supported by data from the Terman et al. (1925) studies. The corollary is that people who are less than gifted in one area tend to be below average in other areas as well—and this too is true. While there are obvious exceptions to this principle, it nevertheless serves as a useful guide in understanding the overall development of children.

Principle 9

Development proceeds in stages. ** This principle is often stated in developmental literature (for example, Mussen, 1963; Hurlock, 1968). In reality it is nothing more than a statement of a popular belief. In fact, it is probably as reasonable to assume that development *does not* proceed in stages, but progresses, rather, in a slow continuous fashion (Principle 5). But it appears reasonable within the context of Piaget's theory to describe development as being stage-bound. Bruner's stages of representation also appear reasonable; Freud's psychosexual stages are marked by their own individual characteristics, and both Sears' and Erikson's stages represent developmental landmarks. The interesting point is that these stages are not parallel. They are all expressions of different points of view, and they all describe different features of child development. Therefore, while it might appear reasonable to say that development proceeds in stages, it must in all honesty be made clear that the stages are simply inventions made by theorists to clarify and order their observations.

One such set of stages is Piaget's. It describes intellectual development:

Stage		Age
1. **Sensorimotor**		0 – 2 years
2. **Preconceptual**		2 – 4 years
	Preoperational	
3. **Intuitive**		4 – 7 years
4. **Concrete operations**		7 – 11 years
5. **Formal operations**		11 – 15 years

---

* PPC comment: 'Some students may take this seriously."
Author: "Don't."
** This does not contradict Principle 5. Development is, in fact, continuous; but the continuum may be examined in terms of stages.

A less forbidding, more intuitive classification is Hurlock's:

Stage	Age
1. Prenatal	Conception – 280 days
2. Infancy	0 – 10 to 14 days
3. Babyhood	2 weeks – 2 years
4. Childhood	2 years – adolescence
5. Adolescence	13 (girls) – 21 years
6. Adolescence	14 (boys) – 21 years

Three additional stages could be added to Hurlock's list:

Stage	Age*
Adulthood	21– 25 years
Middle age	25 – 30 years
Old age	30 years – death

A third classification of developmental stages is provided by Erikson. It describes what he labels "psychosocial crises." Each stage is labeled in terms of a conflict that besets the child. Resolution of this conflict is assumed to result in the development of a specific sense of competence essential for adapting to and coping with social reality. These stages are listed here with corresponding Freudian psychosexual stages. Freud's description of child development identifies a number of distinct stages differentiated primarily on the basis of those objects or activities that then serve as principal sources of sexual gratification.

Erikson: Psychosocial Development	Freud: Psychosexual Development	Very Approximate Ages
Trust versus mistrust	oral	First year
Autonomy versus shame and doubt	anal	1– 2 or 3 years
Initiative versus guilt	phallic	2 or 3 – 6 years
Industry versus inferiority	"latency"	6 – 10 or 11 years
Identity versus identity diffusion	puberty ⎫	
Intimacy and solidarity versus isolation	genital ⎭	10 or 11 onward
Generativity versus self-absorption		
Integrity versus despair		

Principle 10

Development usually proceeds at the rate at which it started. A child who learns to walk and talk at a very early age is more likely to be intelligent as an adult

---

* PPC suggestion: "Better indicate that these labels are not to be taken seriously. OR ARE THEY?! (How old is the bear?)"

than another who begins developing more slowly. Data to support this contention are relatively difficult to find since early measures of intelligence are notably unreliable; however, Bloom (1964) has recently surveyed a large number of studies that, taken as a whole, suggest that human characteristics are remarkably stable. In other words, there is relatively little change after the initial period of rapid development that characterizes most physical and intellectual qualities of human beings.

Principle 11

Development is directional. It proceeds from the general to the specific, or from undifferentiated to differentiated awareness.

This principle can be illustrated most clearly by reference to a child's early perceptual development. It is widely assumed that the neonate's world is a "blooming, buzzing mass of confusion"—that infants cannot differentiate among sights, sounds, smells, and so on; that, in short, they react reflexively to stimulation but cannot sort out their impressions. Slowly things begin to be differentiated; figures are sorted from background; noise is isolated as a sensation; touch becomes distinct, and the world turns into the vast, bewildering collection of specifics that we have put into it.

Development is directional in another sense. Fetal development is said to be **proximodistal** and **cephalocaudal**—*proximodistal* meaning from near to far, and *cephalocaudal* meaning from head to tail. Interestingly, fetal development does proceed from the early formation of both internal (proximal) organs and the head—complete with eyelashes at a very early age—to much later development of the extremities. Even more interesting, physical control in the early postnatal period follows the same general directional trend. The first controlled movements are of the head, the eyes, and the mouth. Eventually control is extended to the large muscles—the relatively "proximal" parts of the limbs. Only later does the child achieve control over fingers. Few ever achieve significant control over their toes.

Summary
Principle—A Definition

Development is the extremely complex process through which little humans progress in their quest to achieve an adequate adaptation to the world.

Review and Implications

The study of children presents a vast and complex assortment of topics, not easily contained within the pages of one or two chapters. Accordingly, this chapter is concerned principally with an overview of the most important and most clearly valid statements that can be made about developmental processes. These are admittedly not all-inclusive. Many of the topics touched on in this chapter are discussed in more detail in other chapters, where their implications are more apparent. Thus, as was mentioned earlier, moral development is discussed in connection with classroom management and discipline rather than in isolation. Similarly, Piaget's theoretical formulations and their educational implications form the substance of Chapter 10; the relative contributions of heredity and environment to the developmental process are discussed in Chapter 11, where their relationship to such important personality characteristics as intelligence and creativity are made more apparent. In short, then, the most important instructional implications of a study of child development are yet to come.

Summary of Chapter 9

Chapter 9 has presented a sketch of the history of the study of child development, and a sketch of development as well. The first sketch has dealt with changes in parental attitudes toward children and with historical positions organized around the nature-nurture question. The second sketch was in the form of a series of "principles" describing the present state of knowledge and conjecture in developmental psychology.

Main Points in Chapter 9

1. Human development does not begin at birth; it begins approximately 266 days earlier. Developmental psychology is concerned with explaining the systematic changes that individuals undergo in the course of growing up.

2. Development can be viewed as comprising all changes attributable to maturation, to growth, and to learning. Maturation refers to a natural unfolding, whereas learning refers to the effects of experience. Growth is defined by physical changes.

3. Among significant events in the formation of a science of the child were changes in parental attitudes toward children, advances in industry, discoveries in medicine, and the work of such people as Darwin, Hall, Freud, and Piaget.

4. Historically, developmental positions can be classified in terms of whether they see nature or nurture as the most significant factor in development. *Preformationistic* and *predeterministic* positions are on the nature side; *tabula rasa* positions are on the other. Both approaches are dead, but the winner has not been declared.

5. Some of Bruner's notions can be viewed as illustrating a modified recapitulation theory. He describes the development of representational systems (enactive, iconic, symbolic) as roughly paralleling the recent evolution of humans.

6. Language plays a crucial role in the development of children. It is closely related to achievement and to intelligence.

7. Both genetic and environmental factors are important in development (Principle 1).

8. Development takes place at different rates for different features of the organism (Principle 2).

9. Environmental changes will be most effective during the period of fastest growth and least effective during slowest growth (Principle 3).

10. Development follows an orderly sequence (Principle 4).

11. Development is continuous rather than discrete (Principle 5).

12. There is evidently a great deal of variability among human beings (Principle 6).

13. Any breaks in the continuity of development will generally be due to environmental factors (Principle 7).

14. Correlation and not compensation is the rule in development (Principle 8).

15. Development may be described in terms of arbitrarily demarcated stages (Principle 9).

16. Development usually proceeds at approximately the rate at which it started (Principle 10).

17. Development is directional (Principle 11).

18. Development is the extremely complex process through which little humans progress in their quest to achieve an adequate adaptation to the world.

Suggested Readings

For further elaboration and greater clarification of the principles outlined in this chapter, the reader is referred to the following three references. The book by J. McV. Hunt presents a highly documented, but very readable, review of the literature on the relative effects of experience and heredity on child development. Its thesis is clearly that early experiences are crucial in the later development of the child. The Lefrancois book is a standard reference in child development. The little book by Mussen is an easy-to-read primer for developmental psychology.

Hunt, J. McV. *Intelligence and Experience.* New York: Ronald Press, 1961.

Lefrancois, G. R. *Of Children: An Introduction to Child Development* (2nd Edition). Belmont, Calif.: Wadsworth, 1977.

Mussen, P. H. *The Psychological Development of the Child.* Englewood Cliffs, N.J.: Prentice-Hall, 1963.

The following book by Reese and Lipsitt is probably the most comprehensive and detailed account of the state of research in child psychology. Although it is not a book of readings, various sections were written by some of the outstanding people in the field.

Reese, H. W. and L. P. **Lipsitt.** *Experimental Child Psychology.* New York: Academic Press, 1970.

For a very readable, relatively nonacademic description of developments in the education of very young children, the reader is referred to the book by Maya Pines. A journalist, she has captured the current interest in the education of the young child in this intensely provocative book.

Pines, Maya. *Revolution in Learning: The Years from Birth to Six.* New York: Harper & Row, Publishers, 1966.

Development: The Theory of Jean Piaget

Piaget, the Man · Scope of the Theory · Piagetian Terminology · Orientation
· Intelligence · Structure · The Stage Theory · Piaget's Position in Review
· Evaluation of Piaget · Implications for Education ·
Summary · Main Points ·

If a little knowledge is dangerous, where is
the man who has so much
as to be out of danger?
(Thomas Henry Huxley)

And if ignorance is bliss . . . ?

Advance Organizer There is probably no theory that has had as much impact on the study of children in recent years as that of Jean Piaget. This chapter presents a relatively simple account of some of the more important aspects of this comprehensive and some- times highly complex theory. A substantial portion of the chapter is devoted to examining the educational implications of Piaget's theory.

A twenty-five-year-old man sat in his home in Geneva watching his wife breast- feed their first child. On his knee he had a notebook in which he wrote furiously. Every few minutes he would stop and peer intently at the baby, craning his neck from left to right in order to get a better view. He would then resume writing for a short while, before returning to his examination of the proceedings before him. The man's name was Jean Piaget. He was to become one of the foremost developmental psychologists of this century. He was also destined to become a member of the French *Légion d'Honneur*.

Piaget, the Man

Jean Piaget was born at Neuchâtel, Switzerland, on the ninth of August, 1896. By his own admission (Piaget, 1952a), he was a studious child. At the age of ten he had already given some indication of the prolific career that was to be his. At that young age he published his first paper—a one-page note on a partly albino sparrow he had found. Interestingly, his early inclination was toward the biological sciences. His doctorate, which he received at the age of twenty-two, was in that area—his dissertation being on molluscs. By the age of thirty, he had already pub- lished twenty-five papers on molluscs and related topics.

Piaget's interest in psychology came about almost accidentally. Shortly after leaving the University of Neuchâtel with his Ph.D., he took a position in Binet's laboratory in Paris. This was the Binet who originated the well-known intelligence scale. Piaget's duties while at the laboratory included administering reasoning tests to elementary school students. It was probably this that marked the beginning of his interest in children. Shortly thereafter he was appointed director of the *Institut Jean-Jacques Rousseau* in Geneva. This institution was succeeded by the *Institut des Sciences de l'Education*, of which he is still director. In addition, he is the founder of the *Centre d'Epistémologie Génétique*, which probably produces as much develop- mental research data and theory as any other center in the world today. Piaget also edits numerous journals and periodicals. His stature in the field of developmental psychology is unequalled.*

---

* It should be pointed out here that throughout a large part of his career Piaget's closest associate and collaborator has been Barbel Inhelder. She continues to coauthor a large number of their publications and to read many of the papers which they present jointly.

Scope of the Theory

Piaget's theory is contained in more than twenty books and 200 different articles. It would be highly presumptuous, then, to attempt to reduce the entire system to one chapter. The present chapter is something less than highly presumptuous—only some aspects of the theory are discussed.

The scope of Piaget's theory is extremely broad. It deals, first, with intelligence, and second, with perception; but in the course of treating these two topics, it touches on almost every facet of human functioning. Among the specific subjects that Piaget deals with in his books and articles are language (1926), causality (1930), time (1946a), velocity (1946b), movement (1946b), judgment and reasoning (1928), logic (1957b), number (1952b), play (1951), imitation (1951), and physics (1957a). The treatment of each separate subject is consistent with certain unifying concepts; these form the essence of Piaget's developmental theory. This chapter discusses these unifying concepts with illustrations drawn from Piaget's writings. The bulk of his work is written in French and remains untranslated. A number of excellent summaries* of this work have been prompted by the tremendous increase in popularity which Piaget's ideas are currently undergoing.

Piagetian Terminology

A student who is just being introduced to Piagetian theory faces a very real problem posed by the vocabulary employed. For this reason you are now advised to return to Chapter 4 and study the thirty-eight-frame linear program on Piagetian terminology presented there.

Orientation

Consistent with his early training, Piaget's approach to the study of children stems very directly from a biological orientation. His theory is much easier to understand when viewed from that perspective. Biologists have two overriding interests, each of which can be expressed in the form of a question:

1. What are the characteristics of organisms that enable them to adapt to their environments?
2. What is the simplest, most accurate, and most useful way of classifying living organisms?

Obviously much of the effort expended in the biological sciences has been directed toward answering these two questions. Any zoology student who has had to

---

* Among these summaries are articles by Berlyne (1957), Tuddenham (1966), and Lefrancois (1967); and books by Flavell (1963), Phillips (1969), Furth (1970), and Ginsberg and Opper (1969).

memorize classifications can attest to that. Interestingly, the same questions can be asked about human beings:

1. What are the characteristics of children that enable them to adapt to their environment?

2. What is the simplest, most accurate, and most useful way of classifying or ordering child development?

Piaget's attempts to answer these two questions can be seen as comprising his entire system. The answers are therefore very complex in detail, but in principle they can be simplified as follows:

1. *Characteristics that permit adaptation.* The answer to the first question is simply that a child's adaptation to the world is accomplished through a combination of the only two ways a human being has of interacting with the environment: *assimilation* and *accommodation*. Both of these are biological terms defining adaptation. Assimilation involves making a response that has already been acquired; accommodation is the modification of a response. Whenever an organism responds in terms of some activity it already *knows*, it is said to be assimilating. On the other hand, when a change in behavior is required, accommodation is said to take place. Adaptation involves both assimilation and accommodation since new behavior must always stem from previous learning. This is only the beginning of Piaget's answer to the first question. Much of the remainder of the present chapter is a further explanation of these processes.

2. *Classifying behavior.* The answer to the second question can only be outlined here—the details are given later in this chapter. Piaget conceives of human development as consisting of a series of stages, each of which is characterized by certain specific criteria. These criteria take the form of the characteristics of mental functioning typical of children at that stage of development. Piaget's descriptions of what he terms the "broad characteristics of intellectual functioning" comprise his answer to the second question. Put very simply, Piaget's theory classifies human development by describing the characteristics of the child's behavior at different ages. This description can be valuable in helping teachers understand their students.

Intelligence

The easiest and clearest way of describing Piaget's basic theory is to summarize it. This can be done by discussing his views on intelligence. Unlike many of his contemporaries, who have defined intelligence as a relatively fixed and measurable quality, Piaget describes it as existing in the activity of individuals, and as changing continually. In a sense, intelligence is seen as the *process* of adapting rather than as the level of adaptive behavior. As a process it is not easily defined or measured, but it can be described.

If intelligence is the process of adapting, and if adaptation is the result of the interaction of assimilation and accommodation, then intelligence can be defined in terms of assimilation and accommodation. These processes can be illustrated quite simply. As the young Piaget was intently observing his son sucking at his mother's breast, he was making notes that described assimilatory and accommodatory activity. Their interaction in the total process of sucking is clearly adaptive. To begin with, children already know how to suck—in fact, this is one of a fairly limited number of reflexes with which they are born. They are not born knowing precisely how to suck any particular nipple, however. Indeed, they can only make relatively ineffective sucking movements at the very beginning. These are assimilatory behaviors. Children can be said to assimilate the nipple to the activity of sucking. But they soon learn to curl their lips around the nipple, and to elongate their mouths if the nipple is long, or pucker them if it is short—in other words, they learn to accommodate to the specific demands of the environment. Assimilation and accommodation are, therefore, simply ways of interacting with the environment. As methods of interacting, they do not change from childhood to adulthood; hence they are referred to as *invariant* functions, or, more often, as *functional invariants*. What *does* change, however, is the activity itself—and the change is effected through accommodation. Development, then, does not consist of changes in function, since these are invariant, but consists instead of changes in behavior. The behavior itself is labeled *content*. As content (behavior) changes, the inference is made that those properties of intellect which govern behavior must also change. These properties are termed *structure*. Only one other term needs to be introduced here. Why does structure change? Because the individual functions in relation to the *demands* of the *environment*. These four components—content, structure, function, and environment—comprise what is not only a representation of intelligence, but also a simple model of Piaget's basic theory. This representation is given in Figure 10.1.

What does the model say? Beginning at the bottom, it can be interpreted as follows: The environment is reacted to by an individual when she assimilates aspects of it to structure or when she accommodates to it. In the first case, her behavior is determined by structure (properties that govern behavior); in the second, her struc-

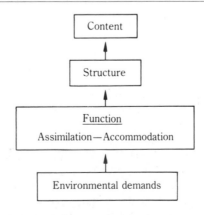

Figure 10.1 *Intelligence in Action*

ture is modified by the environment. The result of this interaction is content (behavior).

While this is a simple statement of Piagetian theory, it is only part of the total picture. Another part can be completed by discussing the meaning of the term *structure* in more detail.

Structure

Structure has been defined as those properties of intellect which govern behavior. They are inferred rather than "real" properties—that is, it is not possible to isolate a structure and look at it.

At the earliest level, structure can be defined in terms of reflexes since these are the first "governors" of behavior. Piaget labels reflexes *schemas*. Schemas become more firmly established as the child assimilates objects to them and change as he accommodates to objects. The schema is usually named in terms of the activity it represents. For example, there is a sucking schema, a looking schema, a reaching schema, a grasping schema, and, unfortunately, a wailing schema. Structure in later stages of development, usually after age seven or eight, is defined in terms of less overt acts. By this age the child has internalized his activities—that is, he can represent activities in *thought*. In addition, "thought" is subject to certain rules of logic. These rules, which are discussed in connection with the stage of concrete operations, define the term **operation.**

Structure governs behavior; changes in behavior are what define stages of development; therefore, Piaget's description of development is really a description of structure at different ages. The details of these developmental changes compose the next section of this chapter.

The Stage Theory

The aspects of Piaget's work that have received the most attention, particularly on the part of educators, are those describing differences among children at different ages. These descriptions are found in the many books and articles where he investigates the child's increasing competence in various areas.

The developmental stages described by Piaget (1961), together with the approximate ages to which they correspond, are as follows:

	Stage	*Age*
1.	Sensorimotor	0 – 2 years
2.	Preoperational	2 – 7 years
	a. Preconceptual	2 – 4 years
	b. Intuitive	4 – 7 years
3.	Concrete operations	7 – 11 years
4.	Formal operations	11 – 15 years

The characteristics of children in each of these stages are described below.

A Preliminary
Comment on Piaget's Methods

Konorski (1967) has argued that the data of **subjective** experience should be as valid in the scientific investigation of human behavior as the more **objective** data that commonly form the basis of that science. In order to discover something as obvious as, for example, the fact that a connection is formed between the smell of turkey and the image of that noble bird, he contends that one need not assemble a group of hungry subjects. Probably, however, the volume of printed *research* often depends on the use of objective rather than subjective data. Imagine the amount of prose that could result from a detailed analysis of the salivation of twenty hungry subjects allowed to catch a whiff of turkey from the laboratory kitchen. To this might be added a detailed examination of changes in subjects' pupil size, and a correlation of these changes with eyeball movements. The conclusion reached—twenty pages, $4,000, and five months later—might well be: "There is evidence to suggest that in some cases, perhaps, some degree of measurable change in pupil size results from turkey-whiffing. These changes are not correlated with either salivation or eye movements. There is also some tentative evidence that salivation increases as subjects undergo the turkey-whiffing test." The original question, interestingly, was whether or not a whiff of turkey would evoke an image of turkey. Subjective experience says clearly that if people have been exposed to turkey often enough, its odor "reminds" them of it.

The intriguing and difficult thing about studying children is that there cannot be any subjective verification of the inferences that one makes about them. Adults all have some intuitive notions about how adults feel and think. But few adults have any idea how children feel and think—and such ideas, in any case, could only be verified in very indirect ways. Here, then, one must rely on relatively objective data.

Jean Piaget has developed a method for studying children that permits the investigator to be both flexible and relatively precise. This, in fact, is one outstanding feature of his work. The technique is known as the **méthode clinique.** It is an interview approach, where the experimenter has a clear idea of the questions to ask, and of how to phrase them, but where many of the questions are determined by the child's answers. Hence it provides for the possibility that the child will give unexpected answers and that further questioning will lead to new discoveries about thinking.

Piaget is sometimes criticized for basing a great deal of theory on the study of very few children. While this may be a valid scientific criticism, further research has, in fact, seldom contradicted his early findings. It is true, however, that much of his work, particularly with very young children, has not been systematically replicated. Perhaps that is because the original work took Piaget the better part of a lifetime. In any case, his findings and theory are generating a great deal of interest and research, as is evident from perusing most contemporary journals of developmental psychology.

Sensorimotor Intelligence:
Birth to 2 Years

Learning probably begins before birth, but the young Piaget started his investigations by studying the activities in a child's repertory at birth. These include the acts of looking, reaching, and sucking. The last received much initial attention, since in some ways it is easiest to observe.

Piaget labeled the first two years of life the period of sensorimotor intelligence. This was because it seemed to him that, until the child developed some way of representing the world "mentally," intelligent activity would be confined to sensorimotor functions. The child's world at birth is a world of the here and now. Objects exist when they can be seen, heard, touched, tasted, or smelled; when they are removed from the child's immediate sensory experience they cease to be. One of the child's major achievements during this stage is the acquisition of what Piaget calls the **object concept**—the notion that objects have a permanence and identity of their own and that they continue to exist even when they are outside the child's immediate frame of reference.

Piaget conducted an interesting experiment (1954) to trace the evolution of the object concept. It can easily be replicated by any parent. It involves showing a bright, attractive object to an infant, and then hiding it. At the earliest level, children will not even look for the object. Later they will begin to search for it if they saw it being hidden. Interestingly, it is usually not until around the age of one that children will search for an object they have not just seen.

There is no language early in the sensorimotor period, but there is the beginning of symbolization. Piaget contends that the internal representation of objects and events is brought about through imitation. Thought is defined as internalized activity. It begins when children can represent to themselves (in a sense, imitate) a real activity. The first step in this process of internalization involves activities relating to objects or events that are present before the child. At a later stage, that of **deferred imitation,** the child can imitate in the absence of the object or event. This internal imitation is a symbolic representation of aspects of the environment. It is also the beginning of language, since eventually words will come to replace more concrete actions or images as representors. From this simple relationship of activity and environment, imitation, symbol formation, and language, an inference of tremendous importance for parents and teachers can be drawn. Hunt (1961) summarizes it in this way:

> . . . *the more new things an infant has seen and the more new things he has heard, the more new things he is interested in seeing and hearing; and the more variation in reality he has coped with, the greater is his capacity for coping. (p. 262)*

In other words, the amount and variety of stimulation a child receives is instrumental in determining adaptation.

Piaget describes the evolution of thought structures in the child from birth to two years in terms of six substages. These are summarized here. The ages given should be considered as approximations.

Substage 1: 0 to 1 Month During the first month, the infant does little obvious learning, but spends most waking hours exercising the ready-made schema (reflexes) that were present at birth. Flavell (1963) says that there is an intrinsic need for schemas to be exercised once they are established. This is how activity becomes perfected. By the age of one month, children can fixate on objects, reach, suck, and grasp. They cannot, however, both look and reach at the same time, or reach and grasp in sequence. In other words, these motor activities are isolated, noncoordinated behaviors. They are nevertheless the "building blocks of intelligence."

Substage 2: 1 to 4 Months After the first month, children begin to acquire new behaviors. That is, through accommodation they adapt to new environmental situations. These early adaptations are referred to as **primary circular reactions**—primary because they center on the child's body, and circular because they can be described in terms of an S-R model where the response serves as its own stimulus. Figure 10.2 gives an example of a circular reaction in a child's babbling

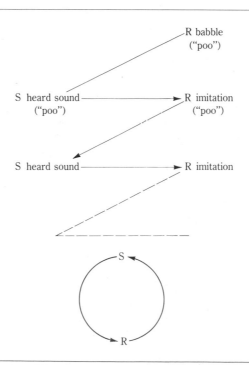

Figure 10.2 *A Circular Reaction*

behavior. The infant says "poo." As she says "poo," she hears the word, and, hearing it, she repeats it. As she repeats it, she hears it again, and therefore repeats it once more and then . . . An example of *primary* circular reaction is provided by the activity of thumb-sucking, an activity sometimes developed while the child is still in the womb. The sensation caused by the sucking movement is a stimulus for the repetition of that movement.

Two characteristics of primary circular reactions at this stage are especially noteworthy: In the first place, a reflex is involved; in the second place, the initial behavior is accidental rather than intentional. A third point is that while children will, in a sense, imitate their own behavior, they will not imitate the behavior of others.

Substage 3: 4 to 8 Months Behavior during the third stage is also characterized by circular reactions. In this case, however, the reactions are *secondary* rather than *primary*. This means that the behaviors in question are centered less on the child's body than on the environment. Piaget gives this stage the intriguing title, "behavior designed to make interesting sights and sounds last"—a title which amply describes third substage behavior. A **secondary circular reaction** occurs when, for example, a child accidentally does something that has a desired effect on the environment. The effect then serves as a stimulus for the repetition of the act. A child who is given his first rattle at the age of six months does not shake it because he knows that rattles are intended for shaking. Rather, he shakes it accidentally, but the effect that this activity has is pleasing and therefore leads to a repetition of the response.

What appear to be the crude beginnings of intention become evident at this stage. A child who has dropped his rattle, but continues to shake his hand, appearing all the while to be waiting for it to make a noise, might seem to be displaying intention. He has not, however, succeeded in separating the means from the end. The shaking movement is not differentiated from the effect that it has. According to Piaget, this behavior is therefore not clearly intentional.

Substage 4: 8 to 12 Months By the age of eight months, children have learned to coordinate various previously isolated activities. They can now reach toward the objects they are looking at; they can grasp as they reach, and perhaps they can crawl as they look. In other words, they are able to coordinate activities and subordinate them to the attainment of goals. They can now display behavior that is unequivocally intentional.

The ability to use signs in order to anticipate events also emerges in this period. Putting on a jacket, for example, now means "bye-bye"; the opening of the refrigerator means milk; pajamas mean bed; and big brother means hide.

Substage 5: 12 to 18 Months This is referred to as the stage of **tertiary circular reactions.** It is the stage at which children begin to experiment actively with the environment. It is this experimentation that distinguishes between tertiary and secondary circular reactions. It will be recalled that the latter involved the exact repetition of behaviors that produced interesting sights or sounds. A tertiary circular reaction also involves the repetition of a behavior that has an interesting effect, but the repetition is not exact—the child deliberately varies the response in order to see what change there will be in its effect. For example, a child who accidentally drops a spoon from a high chair will probably drop the spoon again, since it made a very interesting sound (it probably also elicited some intriguing responses from the adults who were around). The next time she drops the spoon, however, she may raise or lower her hand, or she may throw it rather than simply dropping it. Perhaps a clearer example of a tertiary circular reaction is provided by the babbling of a fifteen-month-old child. In the interests of science, the author took copious notes of his son's babbling very early one morning. A typical sequence, which shows clear evidence of a circular reaction with variations, is the following:

> . . . *ballooh, ballooh, ballooh, balloooh, balloooh, billoooh, billooh, billo, billo, billo, billo, billo, bilooooooooh, balooo, balooo, baloooo, bloooo, blooo, BLAH.*

One of the major differences between activity at this stage and the type of activity that precedes it is that children are not simply exercising the schemata that they are developing. This is no longer activity for the sake of activity, but activity *to see* what the environment is like and how it can be reacted to. In other words, this is more clearly instrumental behavior.

Substage 6: 18 to 24 Months The last substage of the sensorimotor period is, in a sense, a transition between a motoric intelligence and a symbolic intelligence. Early in life, children know objects in terms of the overt activities they perform in relation to them—looking, walking, touching, throwing, and so on. Toward the end of the second year, they have learned to represent objects and events through internalized acts. They have also come to the point where they can manipulate these acts in order to anticipate their outcomes. In this way, they can actually solve problems in a manner which is less overtly trial-and-error based. The sixth substage is often titled "the invention of new means through mental combinations" (Flavell, 1963). Piaget (1952a) describes how Lucienne, his daughter, approached a closed door with a blade of grass in each hand and found that she had to set one down before she could turn the knob. This she did, but it became immediately apparent to her that the door would sweep the blade of grass away as it swung open. With little hesitation she picked up the grass and moved it out of the door's path, thereby solving the problem. The solution had apparently been arrived at mentally.

Summary of Characteristics
of Sensorimotor Stage

Baldwin (1967) describes three accomplishments of the sensorimotor period. The first is the acquisition of internally controlled schemas. This may be more simply described as the establishment of controlled internal representations of the world. In other words, by the age of two children have made the transition from a purely perceptual and motoric representation of the world to a more symbolic representation. They have begun to distinguish between perception and conceptualization, but they will not have perfected this distinction until much later.

The second accomplishment is the development of a concept of reality. Much of a child's development can be viewed in terms of how he or she organizes information about the world. It is evident that this information will be very much a function of what the child thinks the world is. As long as children do not know that the world continues to exist even in their absence, they are not likely to have any very stable representation of it. Or perhaps it would be more accurate to say that, as long as children do not have a stable representation system for the world, they cannot conceive of it when they are not actually experiencing it. In either case, the development of some notion of object constancy is absolutely essential for the child's further development. The acquisition of a concept of reality is really nothing more than the development of the object concept.

The third accomplishment of this period is the development of some recognition of cause and effect. This is a logical prerequisite for the formation of intention, since intention is manifested in behavior that is engaged in deliberately because of its effect. Piaget sees intention as being inseparably linked with intelligence. For him, intelligent activity is activity that is, in fact, intentional.

While these three accomplishments describe a child at the end of the period of sensorimotor intelligence, they are not the general characteristics of that period.

Those are implicit in the label given to the stage—sensorimotor. In general, the first two years of a child's life are characterized by an enactive (Bruner, 1966) or motoric representation of the world. The next stage progresses from the perceptual-motor realm to the conceptual.

The Preoperational
Period: 2 to 7 Years

The preoperational period is so called because children do not acquire operational thinking until around the age of seven. Prior to that time their fumbling attempts at conceptual behavior are replete with contradictions and errors of logic. More important from Piaget's point of view, their thought does not yet possess true **reversibility.** This means that a preoperational child cannot consistently undo or reverse actions (thoughts) and govern thinking according to the logical outcome of this reversibility. An action is reversible when the child realizes that the inverse action necessarily and logically nullifies it.

The preoperational period is often described in terms of two substages— the period of preconceptual thought and the period of intuitive thought. Each is discussed below.

The Period of Preconceptual Thought: 2 to 4 Years The period of preconceptual thought is not "preconceptual" in the sense that children do not utilize concepts, but rather in the sense that the concepts they employ are both incomplete and sometimes "illogical." Piaget describes as an example of this his son's reaction to a snail. He had taken the boy for a walk one morning, and they had seen a snail going north. This humble creature had occasioned an expression from the child that can be imagined to have been phrased in the following manner:

"*Papa! Cher Papa! Mon cher Papa!*" (Swiss children like their fathers.) "*Papa! Papa! Papa!*" he repeated. "*Voici un escargot.*"

To which Piaget probably replied, "*Mon fils, mon fils, mon cher fils! Oui, mon fils, c'est un escargot!*"

It was an interesting conversation, as father and son conversations go, but it was not remarkable. It happened, however, that a short while later they chanced upon another snail, whereupon the boy again turned to his father and said, "*Papa! Cher Papa! Mon cher Papa! Mon Papa! Voici encore l'escargot! Regarde! Regarde!*"

This, Piaget says, is an example of preconceptual thinking. In the same way, a child who is shown four different Santa Clauses in four different stores all on the same day, and who still thinks there is *one* Santa Claus, is manifesting preconceptual thinking. She evidently knows something about the concept "Santa Claus," since she can recognize one; but she does not know that objects with similar characteristics can all belong to the same class, yet each having an identity of its own. A young child who sees another with a toy identical to one he has at home can hardly be blamed for insisting that he be given *his* toy.

Another feature of thinking in the preconceptual stage is called **transductive reasoning.** Whereas inductive reasoning proceeds from particular instances to a generalization, and deductive reasoning begins with the generalization and proceeds toward the particulars, transductive reasoning goes from particular instances to other particular instances. It is not a "logical" reasoning process, but it does occasionally lead to the right answer. Consider, for example, the following transductive process:

> A gives milk.
> B gives milk.
> Therefore B is an A.

If A is a cow and B is also a cow, then B is an A. If, however, A is a cow but B is a goat, B is not an A. Surprising as it might sound, children do appear to reason in this way. When a young child calls a dog a kitty, she is also likely to call a bear a cow, and a rabbit a kitty.

The Period of Intuitive Thought: 4 to 7 Years After the age of four, the child's thinking becomes somewhat more logical, although it is still largely dominated by perception rather than reason. It is labeled intuitive because intuition, governed by perception and by egocentricity, plays an important role in the child's thinking. Piaget describes, for example, the answers made by children to this simple problem. Two dolls are placed side by side on a string. One is a girl doll, and the other is a boy (naturally). A screen is placed between the child and the experimenter, who are facing one another. The experimenter holds one end of the string in each hand. He hides the dolls behind the screen and asks the child to predict which doll will come out first if he moves the string toward the right. Whether or not the child is correct, the doll is moved out, and then hidden again. The question is repeated—again the doll will come out on the same side. This time, or perhaps next time, but almost certainly before very many more trials, the subject will predict that the *other* doll will come out. If asked why, he might say, "Because it's her turn. It isn't fair."

This experiment clearly illustrates the role of **egocentrism** in the child's problem solving at the intuitive stage—the problem is interpreted only from the child's point of view. An example of the role of perception is provided by the following experiment.

A child is asked to take a bead and place it in one of two containers. As she does so, the experimenter places a bead in another container. They repeat this procedure until one of the containers is almost full. To confuse the child, the experimenter has been using a low flat dish, whereas the child's container is tall and narrow. The question asked is: "Who has more beads, or do we both have the same number?" The child will probably say that she has more, since they come up to a higher level, but she might say that the experimenter has more, since his cover a wider area. In either case she will be answering in relation to the appearance of the containers. This reliance on perception where it conflicts with thought is one of the major differences between children and adults.

Another striking characteristic of children's thinking during the intuitive period is their inability to classify. While they can group objects in simple collections, they cannot nest these collections one within another—that is, they cannot reason about two classes if one is part of the other. The following classical Piaget experiment illustrates this. A five-year-old child is shown a collection of wooden beads, of which ten are brown and five are yellow. He admits that all of the beads are wooden, but when asked whether there are as many, fewer, or the same number of *brown* beads as *wooden* beads, he says there are more. Piaget's explanation of this phenomenon is simply that when the child is asked to consider the subclass, this destroys the larger class for him. In other words, children at this level understand that classes may contain many different but similar members (they would not make the preconceptual "escargot" error), but they do not yet understand that classes can be "nested" one inside the other in hierarchies (even as the class of brown beads is nested within that of wooden beads, each being separate but related).

The child's problem solving in this period is largely intuitive rather than logical. Whenever possible, mental images rather than rules or principles are utilized in arriving at answers. A striking illustration of this is provided by asking five- or six-year-old children to solve the rotated-bead problem. Three different colored beads are placed on a wire and the wire is then inserted into a tube so that the child can no longer see them. She knows, however, that the red one is on the left, yellow in the middle, and blue on the right. She is then asked what the order of the beads will be if the tube is rotated through 180°, 360°, 540°, 720°, and so on. Younger preoperational children are likely to be thoroughly confused by the question, and older children will solve it correctly as long as they can imagine the actual rotations—but they will *not* apply any rule to the solution of the problem (even versus odd number of turns, for example).

In summary, the thought processes of the intuitive period child are egocentric and perception-dominated. In addition, the ability to classify or to apply rules of logic rather than motor or imaginal representations for problem solving has not yet been acquired. A final, very significant difference between thought at this period and thought during the period of concrete operations is that only at this latter stage does the child acquire the ability to conserve. (See Figure 10.3 for a summary of preoperational thought).

A Break

STOP! It would probably be wise for the reader who is not already familiar with Piaget to stop at this point. If you have available an electroencephalograph machine, a cardiograph, a thermometer, and a pupillometer, as well as any other graph or meter, these should be connected and read at once. Alpha waves, together with decelerated heart rate, abnormal temperature, and reduced pupil size are symptoms of imminent **jargon shock.** This condition in advanced stages can be highly detrimental to concentration and learning. Several hours of sleep usually bring about a significant improvement.

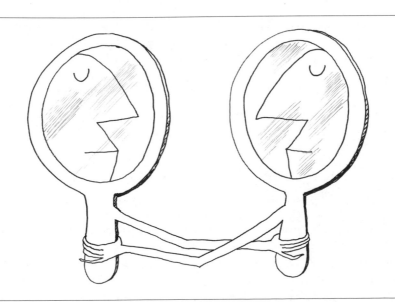

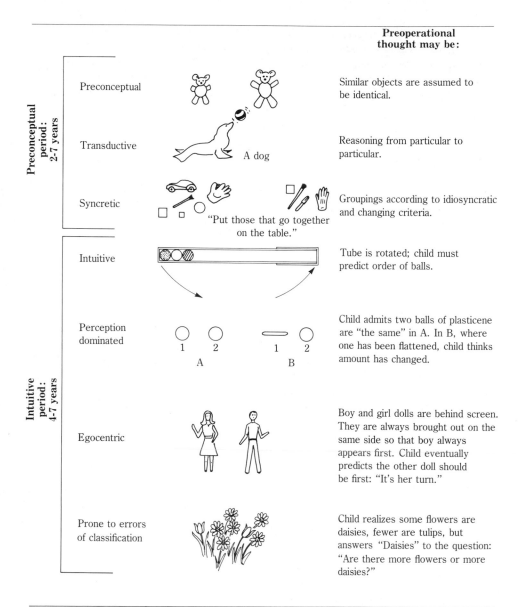

Figure 10.3 *Experiments Concerned with Preoperational Thought*

If you don't have any of this sophisticated electronic gadgetry readily available, you can substitute a hand mirror. Hold the mirror up to your face and look at your eyes. If they are closed you are probably in the terminal stage of "jargon shock."

Concrete Operations:
7 to 11 or 12 Years

The key feature of the period of concrete operations is activity in relation to the environment. At this stage the child develops operations for the manipulation of *objects* rather than for the manipulation of hypotheses or propositions (a proposition is simply any statement which can be true or false—for example, "Johnny West has a long nose"). The surest criterion for the appearance of concrete operations is the development of the ability to conserve.

The Conservations The definition of **conservation** is "the realization that quantity or amount remains invariant when nothing has been added to or taken away from an object or a collection of objects, despite changes in form or spatial arrangement" (Lefrancois, 1966, p. 4). In the experiment cited earlier, where the child is asked whether the two containers have the same number of beads, he does not demonstrate conservation behavior until he realizes that they do. A correct response to a conservation problem not only marks the end of the preoperational period, but signals the beginning of concrete operational thought. It is a direct manifestation of a number of rules of logic that now govern and limit the child's thinking. Among these rules are *reversibility* and *identity*. The former specifies that for every operation (internalized, *reversible* action) there is an inverse operation that cancels it. **Identity** is the rule that states that for every operation there is another that leaves it unchanged. Both reversibility and identity can be simply illustrated by reference to the number system. The operation of adding two numbers can be reversed (and nullified) by subtraction (for example, $2 + 4 = 6$; $6 - 4 = 2$). The identity operator for addition is 0 (i.e., $2 + 0 + 0 + 0 = 2$); for multiplication it is 1 (i.e., $2 \times 1 \times 1 \times 1 = 2$). The relevance of the operational rules to the thinking of a child at the concrete operations stage can be illustrated by reference to any of the conservation problems. The child who has placed one bead in a long container for every bead placed by the experimenter in a flat container, and who now maintains that there are the same number in each despite their appearances, may be reasoning as follows: (1) If the beads were taken out of the containers and placed again on the table, they would be as they were before (reversibility); or (2) nothing has been added to or taken away from either container, so there must still be the same number in each (identity).

There are as many conservations as there are perceptible quantitative attributes of objects. There is conservation of number, length, distance, area, volume, continuous substance, discontinuous substance, liquid substance, and so on. None of these is achieved prior to the period of concrete operations—even then, some (volume, for example) will not be acquired until very late in that period.

The experiments are interesting, and the results are often very striking. Several experimental procedures for conservation are described below, together with the approximate ages of attainment. (Note: These ages are, in fact, nothing more than *very approximate approximations*.)

1. *Conservation of number* (6 or 7)

Two rows of counters are placed in one-to-one correspondence between the experimenter (E) and the subject (S):

    0   0   0   0   0
    0   0   0   0   0

One of the rows is then elongated or contracted:

        0   0   0   0   0
    0   0   0   -   0   0

S is asked which row has more counters or whether they still have the same number.

2. *Conservation of length* (6 or 7)

E places two sticks before the subject. The ends are well aligned:

S is asked if they are the same length. One stick is then moved to the right:

The question is repeated.

3. *Conservation of substance or mass* (7 or 8)

Two plasticine balls are presented to S. She is asked if they have the same amount of plasticine in them. If S says no, she is asked to make them equal. (It is not at all uncommon for a young child to simply *squeeze* a ball in order to make it have less plasticine.) One ball is then deformed.

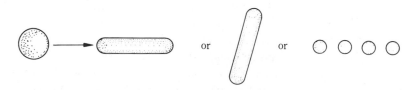

S is asked again whether they contain the same amount.

4. *Conservation of area* (9 or 10)

S is given a large piece of cardboard, identical to one that E has. Both represent playgrounds. Small wooden blocks represent buildings. S is asked to put a building on his playground every time E does so. After nine buildings have been scattered throughout both playgrounds, E moves his together in a corner.

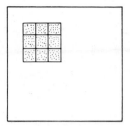
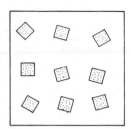

S is asked whether there is as much space (area) in his playground as in E's.

5. *Conservation of liquid quantity* (6 or 7)

S is presented with two identical containers filled to the same level with water.

One of the containers is then poured into a tall thin tube, while the other is poured into a flat dish.

S is asked whether the amount of water in each remains equal.

6. *Conservation of volume* (11 or 12)

S is presented with two identical containers filled to the same level with water,

and two weights, identical in volume but highly disparate in weight.

1″ sq.   1″ sq.

1 oz.   7 oz.

S is asked to predict the level to which the water in the second container will rise if the heavier weight is now placed in it.

One of the intriguing things about conservation is that children can be made to contradict themselves many times without ever changing their minds. After experiment 5, for example, the experimenter can pour the water back into the original containers and repeat the question. The subject now admits they they have the same amount—but the moment the water is again poured into the tall container and the flat one, the decision is reversed.

Other Abilities Children acquire three new, distinct abilities as they come into the stage of concrete operations. These are the ability to classify, to seriate, and to deal with numbers.

Classification: To classify is to group objects according to their similarities and differences. The process involves incorporating subclasses into more general classes, all the while maintaining the identity of the subclasses. This process leads to the formation of what Piaget calls nested hierarchies of classes (Piaget, 1957b). An example of a nested hierarchy is given in Figure 10.4. The preoperational child's inability to deal with classes was illustrated in the experiment involving the ten brown and five yellow wooden beads. It will be recalled that at that stage the child thought there were more brown than wooden beads, even though the child knew that all the beads were wooden.

This error is no longer made after the child reaches concrete operations.

Seriating: The ability to order objects in terms of some attribute is essential for an understanding of the properties of number. One experiment that Piaget conducted to investigate the understanding of **seriation** involves presenting children

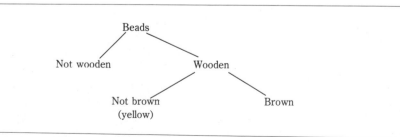

Figure 10.4 *A Nested Hierarchy of Classes*

with two corresponding series: one containing dolls, the other canes. (See Figure 10.5.) The problem is simply to arrange these as shown in Figure 10.5. When the objects are presented in random order, preoperational children cannot arrange a single series in sequence. Typically, they compare only two objects at a time, and fail to make an inference that is almost essential for the solution of the problem. This inference is that if A is greater than B, and B is greater than C, then A must be greater than C. Preoperational children do not hesitate to put C before B if they have just been comparing A and C.

Figure 10.5 *Two Ordered Series*

Number: The ability to deal with numbers is simply a by-product of classification and seriation activities. A number involves classes in the sense that it represents a collection of objects (cardinal property of numbers); it involves seriation in the sense that it is ordered in relation to larger and smaller numbers (ordinal property of numbers).

Summary of Concrete Operations Thinking Children at the stage of concrete operations can apply rules of logic to classes, to relations (series), and to numbers. In addition, their thinking has become relatively decentered—that is, it is no longer so egocentric or so perception-bound. They are still incapable, however, of applying rules of logic to objects or events that are not concrete. In other words, they deal only with the real or with that which they are capable of imagining. Their ready answer to the question "What if Johnny West had a short nose?" is "Johnny West does *not* have a short nose!"

Formal Operations: 11
or 12 to 14 or 15 Years

The final stage in the evolution of thought structures is labeled formal operations—*formal* because the subject matter with which children can now deal may be completely hypothetical. To it they can apply a *formal* set of rules of logic. This chapter does not include an account of the actual logical model employed by Piaget to describe thinking at this stage. Its relevance to educational practice is remote; in addition, the model is complex both in detail and in level of comprehension required. An excellent summary of Piaget's use of logic can be found in *The Pupil's Thinking* by Peel (1960), or in Piaget's *Logic and Psychology* (1957).

A clear example of the difference between the thinking of a child at the formal operations level and one at the concrete level is provided by an item from Binet's reasoning test. The item in question deals with abstract relations: Edith is fairer than Susan; Edith is darker than Lilly; who is the darkest of the three? (If the reader has difficulty with this . . .) The complexity of this problem does not reside in the fact that it involves seriation, since seriation has already been mastered in the stage of concrete operations, but is due, instead, to the nature of the events that are to be ordered. It is obvious that if Edith, Susan, and Lilly were all standing in front of a ten-year-old subject the subject could easily say, "Oho! Edith is fairer than Susan, and she is darker than Lilly—and so Susan is the darkest. Susan dyed her hair." When the problem is not a *concrete* but a *verbal* one, however, it becomes insoluble until the child can handle propositions logically.

A second experiment that illustrates a distinction between formal and concrete thinking involves a number of colored disks. If subjects are asked to combine each color of disk with every other in all possible ways (that is, by twos, threes, etc.), a complete and systematic solution will not be achieved until formal operations. Prior to this stage, the child will arrive at a large number of combinations, but will not do so systematically, and will therefore not exhaust all possibilities. Piaget refers to the thought processes involved in the solution of this and of similar problems as *combinatorial thinking*.

The development of formal operations in the schoolchild is of particular significance since prior to this stage the child will understand many concepts only very incompletely or not at all. Such concepts as proportion and heat (see Lovell, 1968), which are said to require *second-order* operations, are ordinarily beyond the comprehension of a child at the level of concrete operations. A *second-order* operation refers to the sort of thought process required when the problem goes beyond a consideration of empirical reality (first-order operations), involving, instead, the products of first-order thinking. For instance, consider the problem of proportionality posed by the statement 2 : 5 as 6 : 15. Understanding this statement requires knowledge of the relationship between each pair (2 is ⅓ of 6; 5 is ⅓ of 15) and establishing an equivalence relationship between these two relationships. Realizing that 2 is ⅓ of 6 may be considered a first-order operation. Relating this to the knowledge that 5 is ⅓ of 15 is an operation performed on another operation—hence a second-order operation.

An important feature of formal operations that results from the child's ability to deal with the hypothetical is an increasing concern with the ideal. Once children are able to reason from the hypothetical to the real or from the actual to the hypothetical they can conceive of worlds and of societies which, hypothetically, have no ills. Having just discovered this boundless freedom of the mind to envisage the ideal, adolescents create their Utopias and rebel against the generation which has as yet been unable to make its Utopias a reality.

Piaget's Position in Review

Piaget's theoretical position and his description of the characteristics of children at different stages can be summarized in a number of ways. One is simply to list, compare, and contrast characteristics of thought. Another is to discuss development in terms of the interplay of assimilation and accommodation. A third is to first describe the world in terms of the objects and events that it comprises and in terms of the relationships that are possible among these objects and events. Then ontogenetic development can be examined in the light of the question "How suitable are the child's thought processes for understanding this world?" The preceding portion of this chapter can be interpreted as a discussion of part of Piaget's answer to this question.

Evaluation of Piaget

This chapter began with the assertion that Piaget's stature in developmental psychology is unequalled. It is nevertheless true that he has many critics as well as many devoted followers. A rather standard criticism, which was discussed earlier, is that Piaget has not employed sufficiently large samples, sophisticated analyses, or adequate controls. As was pointed out, the value of this criticism can only be assessed in terms of whether replications support his findings.

Among the many contributions that various authors ascribe to Piaget are the following: Hunt (1961) recognizes that he has helped clarify the role of variety of stimulation in the development of intelligence. Marx and Hillix (1963) see his interdisciplinary approach (combining biology, logic, mathematics, epistemology, and psychology) as being particularly worthwhile. Isaacs (1961) praises his systematically planned inquiries, and Lefrancois (1967) draws attention to the depth and comprehensiveness of his work.

Implications for Education

Piaget's work has direct educational implications for three facets of the teaching-learning process: the acceleration of development, the derivation of specific principles for teaching, and the measurement of development.

Can Development
Be Accelerated?

This question has been of little direct concern to Piaget. He has been occupied more with the elaboration and description of the specific details of growth than with the factors that cause developmental changes. By implication, however, his theory would clearly support the notion that an enriched experiential background should lead to the earlier appearance of the thought structures characteristic of different stages.

Direct attempts to accelerate development have generally been aimed at the teaching of conservation behavior to young children (see, for example, Smedslund, 1961a, b, c, d, e; Sawada and Nelson, 1967; Carlson, 1967; Lefrancois,

1968; and Travis, 1969). The results of the many studies conducted to this end are not uniform. Early attempts to teach conservation (e.g., Smedslund) were not often successful. What appears to be one of the easiest teaching tasks possible, simply convincing a five-year-old child that an amount of plasticine does *not* change unless something is added to or taken away from it is next to impossible. I once asked five teachers who were attending an evening course to teach their own children conservation of substance. Two reported that they had been completely unsuccessful. The other three claimed that their youngsters would now answer correctly, but none of these three was convinced that the children really *believed* what they had learned. They were then asked to test the stability of the learning either by varying the procedure (e.g., breaking the ball into pieces instead of elongating it) or by testing the subjects for conservation of number. None of the children was successful. Several systematic training procedures (for example, Lefrancois, 1968; Côté, 1968; and Mermelstein et al., 1967) have been shown to accelerate the acquisition of conservation behavior in young children. No evidence has yet been provided that this has a generally beneficial effect on other aspects of intellectual functioning. It is true, however, that the lack of experimental evidence should not be interpreted as meaning that accelerating in conservation does not benefit the child in other ways.

Educational Principles

Although Piaget's research has stimulated a great deal of thinking among educators, it is still true that much research needs to be undertaken in order to determine how best to apply his findings to actual classroom practice and curriculum development. A number of preschool programs have been based on Piaget's writings (see, for example, Kamii, 1972; Weikart et al., 1969; Weber, 1970), and are currently being evaluated. Their impact is still limited, and the final evaluation is pending.

Beard (1969) attempted to derive educational implications from Piaget's work. She cites four main areas of development during the school years to which Piaget has drawn particular attention: the function of language, the formation of concepts, the translation of concrete experiences into symbolic forms, and the development of logical thinking. In each of these areas, Piaget's findings have definite, though rather global, implications. To the extent that language facilitates and guides thought processes, children should be given ample opportunity to interact verbally not only with teachers but with each other; to the extent that concepts arise from sensing and acting upon the environment, children should be *involved* in numerous, real, and relevant activities; insofar as development proceeds from activity to the apprehension of the concrete and finally to the symbolic, a reasonable argument can be advanced for structuring curricula from activity to the concrete and finally to the symbolic (recall that Bruner similarly advocates proceeding from the enactive to the iconic and then to the symbolic); and, to the extent that teachers understand the progression of logical thought forms from the beginning to the end of the school years, they can provide activities that are appropriate to the child's developmental level but that, on occasion, challenge the child sufficiently that some small accommodations are required.

These general instruction-related observations have been made slightly more specific by a number of writers. Athey and Rubadeau (1970) describe Piaget-inspired, classroom-related research, and a number of principles for teaching are discussed by Ginsberg and Opper (1969), Phillips (1969), and Furth (1970b), among others. The following sections present brief summaries of these principles. They are not intended as a collection of related recipes for classroom practice, but rather as guiding principles that might eventually contribute to recipes (for those who need and want them).

Respect of Differences While it has always been recognized that there are some important differences between children and adults, Piaget, more than anyone, has demonstrated precisely what some of these differences are. For example, when a child says that there is more water in a tall container than in a short flat one, she *truly believes* what she is saying. When a row of disks is made shorter than a corresponding row, and the child changes his mind and says that now there are fewer disks in that row, he is *not really contradicting himself* since he sees no error and therefore no contradiction. When a second grade student becomes completely confused in the face of a verbal seriation problem—for example, "Stan Twolips has a shorter nose than Johnny West, and Johnny West has a longer nose than John George. Who has the longest nose?"—she is not being unintelligent.

These and other discoveries about the world of the young child should help teachers to (1) accept more easily the limitations of children's thought and (2) communicate more effectively with children.

Action The ability to deal with classes, relations, and numbers results from the activities of associating, dissociating, and setting up correspondences between real objects during the preoperational stage. These new abilities will continue to be exercised in relation to real or potentially real objects and events in the environment. It follows that since a child's natural method of learning and of stabilizing what he knows involves activity, much classroom learning should likewise involve activity. While this might seem to contradict the still widely prevalent bench-bound, passive approach to learning, it need not be so interpreted. Activity, for Piaget, is not only physical activity but *internalized* mental activity as well. The point of this principle is twofold:

1. Provision should be made for a relatively large amount of *physical* activity in school, but obviously *mental* activity should be provided for as well.
2. Provision should be made for relating learning to real, concrete objects and events, particularly before the formal operations stage.

Optimal Difficulty Assimilation and accommodation are still the child's two ways of interacting with the world. All activity involves both. Assimilation occurs when new objects or events can be reacted to largely in terms of previous learning;

accommodation involves modification of structure. It follows from Piaget's more basic theories that assimilation will take place only if the new situation is somewhat familiar and that accommodation will take place only if it is, at the same time, somewhat strange. This principle holds that there is an optimal discrepancy between new material and old learning (a point corroborated by other theoretical positions— for example, those of Ausubel and Bruner). By knowing a student's level of functioning, a teacher can more effectively and realistically determine which learning experiences are best for the individual. This obviously requires a great deal of individualized instruction.

Knowledge of Limits This is related to the first principle. A teacher should be aware of the limitations of children at different ages. Concepts of proportion cannot easily be taught to seven-year-old children— nor can conservation of volume be taught to a five-year-old. Even if this statement were proven false, it would probably still be true that the amount of time required to teach five-year-olds conservation of volume might better have been spent teaching them to read. This is particularly true since they would probably have acquired conservation of volume by themselves. They would be less likely to learn to read without instruction.

Social Interaction One of the chief factors in the decentering of thought is social interaction. An egocentric point of view is essentially one that does not recognize the views of others. Through social interaction at both a physical and a verbal level, the child is made aware of the ideas and opinions of peers and of adults. Piaget contends that the socialization of thought, the development of moral as well as of game rules, and even the development of logical thought processes are highly dependent upon verbal interation. The implication for teaching is that instructional methods should provide for learner-learner as well as for teacher-learner interaction.

Implications for Testing

Detailed accounts of Piaget's experimental procedures as well as of his findings provide the classroom teacher with a great many informal and easily applied suggestions for assessing students' thought processes. It is not particularly difficult or time-consuming, for example, to ascertain whether a child has acquired conservation of number or the ability to seriate. Both of these abilities are critical for early instruction in mathematics.

A second, more formal, implication for testing that derives from Piaget's theory has to do specifically with the construction of intelligence tests. Pinard and Laurendeau (1964) have developed a preliminary test based on Piaget's theory. It consists of a series of items that relate directly to developmental levels and that are sequenced in such a way that the subject's answer determines what the next question will be. In this sense, the test is considerably less structured than most conventional "intelligence" tests. In addition, wrong answers are taken into account as well as correct ones. The emphasis is on the quality of the child's thinking rather than on the derivation of a score.

The Goldschmid and Bentler tests (1968) are also based on Piaget. These deal largely with the development of concepts of conservation, and are appropriate for students from kindergarten to grade 2.

Summary of Chapter 10

This chapter has presented a synthesis of some of the work of Jean Piaget. His basic theory, his views on intelligence, and his description of the broad characteristics of intellectual functioning at different ages were discussed. In addition, some of the implications of his theory for teaching were indicated.

Main Points in Chapter 10

1. Piaget's early training and interests centered mainly on biology. This orientation is evident in his approach to human development.

2. This theory can be viewed in terms of the answers it provides to two biology-based questions: What are the characteristics of children that allow them to adapt to their environment? What is the simplest, most accurate, and most useful way of classifying and ordering child development?

3. The basic theory can be summarized by referring to Piaget's views on intelligence. Intelligent activity is the result of the interaction of assimilation and accommodation (functioning) in response to the environment, and in accordance with mental structure (schemas). Behavior (content) occurs as a result of this process; its occurrence justifies the inference that structure exists. Changes in that behavior justify the inference that functioning has occurred.

4. Piaget describes development as proceeding through four major stages. Each stage is qualitatively different from every other, but each results from the one that preceded it, and prepares the child for the one that follows.

5. Piaget employed a "father-experimenter," clinically oriented, verbal questioning method almost exclusively in his earlier work. It is true, however, that some of his recent work makes greater use of a more standardized and somewhat less flexible approach.

6. The sensorimotor period (birth to two years) is characterized by a motoric representation of the world. Among the child's major achievements during this period are the development of language, the development of the *object concept*, the development of control of schemas, and the recognition of cause and effect relationships.

7. The preoperational period (two to seven years) is divided into two substages: the preconceptual (two to four years) and the intuitive (four to seven years). During the preconceptual period, the child's reasoning is characteristically transductive—that is, it proceeds from particular to particular. At the intuitive stage the child's reasoning is egocentric, perception-dominated, and irreversible.

8. Three new abilities mark the period of concrete operations (seven to eleven or twelve years): the ability to classify, to order, and to deal with numbers. It is in this stage, too, that the child acquires a variety of conservations.

9. During the formal operations stage (eleven or twelve to fourteen or fifteen years), the child acquires thought structures that are as sufficient for dealing with the world as they will ever be. The child becomes freed from concrete objects and events and can now deal with the hypothetical. This is advanced as one of the reasons for the idealism of adolescence.

10. While it is doubtful that contrived experiences can ever be sufficient to alter significantly the course and rate of development, specific abilities (e.g., conservation of mass) can sometimes be taught prior to the age at which they would normally appear.

11. Among the principles for teaching that can be derived from Piaget's work are the following: teacher recognition of differences between children and adults can enable them to communicate more effectively. Provision should be made for activity in instructional procedures. There is an optimal level of difficulty for new learning, which can be determined on the basis of what the student already knows. A teacher should be aware of the limits of children's abilities—some concepts *are* too difficult at certain ages. Social interaction is an important variable in the decentering of thought and should be provided for in schools.

12. Teachers can employ Piaget's findings and experimental procedures directly in assessing the quality of their students' thinking. In addition, the Montreal Intelligence Scale, developed by Pinard and Laurendeau, may be of considerable value for this purpose.

Suggested Readings

Owing to the tremendous recent impact of Piagetian theory on North American child psychology, a wide variety of books and articles is available on the subject. Among the most readable, interesting, and authoritative articles on Piaget's basic theory are the following:

Berlyne, D. E. Recent developments in Piaget's work. *British Journal of Educational Psychology,* 1957, 27, 1–12.

Tuddenham, R. D. Jean Piaget and the world of the child. *American Psychologist,* 1966, 21, 207–217.

Three paperback books provide useful accounts of the theory of Jean Piaget. All are similar in content; each contains valuable information on the application of Piagetian principles to classroom practice.

Furth, H. G. *Piaget and Knowledge.* Englewood Cliffs, N.J.: Prentice-Hall, 1969.

Ginsberg, H. and S. **Opper.** *Piaget's Theory of Intellectual Development.* Englewood Cliffs, N.J.: Prentice-Hall, 1969.

Phillips, J. L. *The Origins of Intellect.* San Francisco: W. H. Freeman, 1969.

Although Piaget's own books are relatively difficult reading, and much more suitable for the advanced student than the novice, the following book by Inhelder and Piaget is something of an exception. It is of particular value in understanding the logical thought processes of children in the concrete operations and formal operations stages.

Inhelder, B. and J. **Piaget.** *The Growth of Logical Thinking from Childhood to Adolescence.* New York: Basic Books, 1958.

The following book by John H. Flavell is highly rewarding for the serious student of Jean Piaget. It is easily the most comprehensive and most authoritative book on the subject, but also probably one of the more difficult.

Flavell, J. H. *The Developmental Psychology of Jean Piaget.* New York: Van Nostrand, 1963.

The following text by Furth is a short, teacher-oriented book which attempts to relate Piaget's theorizing to school practice. It is written in the form of fifteen letters addressed to educators and designed to show them how Piaget can be useful in the classroom.

Furth, H. G. *Piaget for Teachers.* Englewood Cliffs, N.J.: Prentice-Hall, 1970.

There are several collections of the writings of Piaget and of researchers who have replicated or extended Piaget's work. Among these collections of readings the one edited by Athey and Rubadeau is useful for the prospective teacher.

Athey, I. J. and D. O. **Rubadeau** (eds.). *Educational Implications of Piaget's Theory.* Waltham, Mass.: Ginn-Blaisdell, 1970.

Delayed implantation is one of the common features of brown and polar bears, badgers, mink, and a small number of other animals. The fertilized egg does not become implanted in the uterine wall shortly after conception, but may remain dormant for weeks and sometimes months. Although delayed implantation clearly has survival value, ensuring that the young will be born at the optimal time of the year, the mechanisms which delay embryonic development and later serve to trigger it are not understood (Matthews, 1969).

Creativity and Intelligence

Intelligence · Creativity · The Relationship between Creativity and
Intelligence · Guilford · Summary · Main Points ·

> I will not Reason and Compare:
> My business is to Create.
> (William Blake)

And can one not reason, compare, and create?
Is the creative mind truly akin to madness?

Advance Organizer *Creativity and intelligence, nebulous and ill-defined characteristics, are among the most prized of our "possessions"—and perhaps among the most useful as well. This chapter examines the meanings of these terms, the forces that shape the qualities they represent, and some of the methods that have been devised to assess them. In addition, the chapter looks at the relationship between creativity and intelligence. Is it possible to be creative but stupid? To be intelligent, but totally devoid of creative talent?*

We generally assume that, of all the animals on earth, we are by far the most intelligent and the most inventive. As evidence, we point proudly to our increasing mastery of nature and contrast with this the perennial struggle for survival of those less gifted than we are.* So viewed, we appear to be the creature who has adapted best to the environment—and this, the ability to adapt, may be considered an accurate, though global, definition of intelligence.

It is interesting to consider that we, the self-admitted *wise ones,* do not have the largest brain of the earthly species. Indeed, the adult male brain weighs a mere three and one-quarter pounds. The female brain weighs approximately ten percent less—not even three pounds. This, compared with the thirteen-pound elephant brain or the brain of a whale, which in some cases weighs nineteen pounds, is relatively unimpressive. However, given the strong likelihood that the absolute weight of the brain is less related to intelligent behavior than is the ratio of brain to body weight, we still retain the advantage. Our brain-to-body ratio is approximately 1 to 50; that of the whale and elephant approaches 1 to 10,000. It should be pointed out, however, that some small monkeys have even better brain-to-body-weight ratios—as high as 1 to 18. But in these cases, the absolute size of the brain is so small that it probably cannot do much more than handle simple physiological functioning.

The dolphin, on the other hand, is not inordinately large—in fact, it often weighs no more than an adult man. Yet its average brain weight is a full three and three-quarters pounds. This fact has led to a great deal of speculation and research on the dolphin's intelligence—research that has not yet succeeded in determining how intelligent the dolphin really is.

Although a fairly accurate ranking of species in terms of intelligence may be based on their brain-to-body-weight ratios, such a crude indicator of intelligence does not appear to be of any real value in gauging the subtle but significant differences that exist between geniuses and less gifted persons within the human species. For this, instruments labeled intelligence tests are commonly employed, and these tests are not only generally unsuitable for nonhumans but are often suitable only for very specific groups within the human race. Problems associated with the fairness of tests for different cultures have given rise to considerable research (see, for example, Jensen, 1968). The present chapter examines intelligence by defining it and

---

* And we point, less proudly, to our dwindling supply of irreplaceable resources, to our idiotic penchant for polluting the environment, and to our unreasoning failure to control our numbers.

by giving examples of tests employed to measure it. This is followed by a discussion of creativity. Chapter 12 is concerned with the promotion of creative behavior in schools and, to a lesser extent, with the development of intelligent behavior.

Intelligence

The second most frequently employed and least understood term in education is intelligence. First place must be granted to the term *creativity*. I once interviewed a number of people in order to discover what the common meaning of intelligence is, if indeed it has a common meaning. Surprisingly, there is a great deal more agreement among nonexperts than among the so-called experts. The question asked was simply, "How can you tell whether or not someone is intelligent?" Most nonexperts (service station attendants, ticket sellers, fans at hockey games, and undergraduate students) gave some variation of the following answer: "Intelligent people are the ones who do well at school (university)." Presumably, then, unintelligent people would be those who do less well at school. The experts (educational psychologists!), on the other hand, had a variety of beliefs about intelligence. When pressed to answer the simple question "How can you tell whether or not someone is intelligent?" a few replied that intelligent people would do well on school achievement tests. Others said that intelligence would be reflected in performance on intelligence tests. A number of experts also discussed some of the definitions given in this section.*

Definitions of Intelligence

1. "Intelligence is what the tests test" (Boring, 1923, p. 35).
2. "The global and aggregate capacity of an individual to think rationally, to act purposefully, and to deal effectively with his environment" (Wechsler, 1958, p. 7).
3. Intelligence A: "The innate potential for cognitive development" (Hebb, 1966, p. 332). Intelligence B: ". . . a general or average level of development of ability to perceive, to learn, to solve problems, to think, to adapt" (Hebb, 1966, p. 332).
4. To Hebb's definition, MacArthur and West have added another dimension, labeled Intelligence A': ". . . the present potential of an individual for future development of intelligent behavior, assuming optimum future treatment adapted to bring out that potential" (West and MacArthur, 1964, p. 18).

The first definition (what the tests measure) is not meant to be facetious. It is at once an admission that intelligence is an extremely difficult concept to define and an assertion that so-called "intelligence" tests are useful providing they are related to

---

* By far the most striking difference between the experts and nonexperts was the length of the answer given by the experts. At least seven nonexperts can be interviewed while one expert gives the *introduction* to his response. Verbal fluency is one of the criterial attributes of educational psychologists.

success on tasks requiring "intelligence." Whatever they measure can then be called intelligence even if its exact nature is unknown.

The second definition (global and aggregate capacity) defines intelligence in terms of clear thinking, purposeful activity, and effective interaction with the environment. Wechsler sees intelligence as a "global" capacity. This view is advanced in distinction to the view held by Spearman (1927) and Thurstone (1938), among others, that intelligence is not a single trait but consists of a number of separate abilities or factors. Guilford (1959), whose work is reviewed in the section on creativity, advances a similar view.

The third and fourth definitions make some useful conceptual distinctions among different types of intelligence. On the basis of the evidence, it is reasonable to assume that people are, in fact, born with different potentials for development. This, then, is Type A intelligence. Conventional estimates of intelligence, however, assess intelligence B rather than intelligence A. That is, what is measured is usually the present level of development.

Correlation

A brief introduction to **correlation** will make it easier to interpret the following sections. Two or more **variables** (properties that can vary) are correlated if there is some correspondence between them. Size of shoe is correlated with size of sock; income is correlated with standard of living; size of house is correlated with number of windows; and drunkenness is correlated with alcohol consumption. These are all examples of **positive correlation** since as one variable increases so does its correlate. On the other hand, the inverse relationship may hold. Number of wild animals is correlated with number of people; amount of pollutants in water is correlated with number of fish; and sobriety is correlated with alcohol consumption. In each of these cases, as one variable increases the other decreases; therefore each is an example of **negative correlation.**

The index (or coefficient) of correlation most often employed ranges in value from −1.00 to +1.00. Each of the extremes indicates perfect positive or negative correlation, while 0 indicates complete lack of relatedness (see Figure 11.1). The symbol employed for a correlation coefficient is usually r.

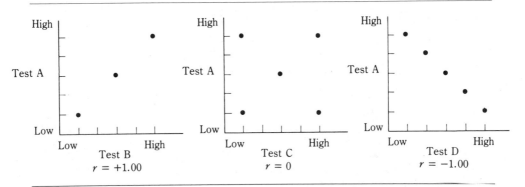

Figure 11.1 *Representations of Correlation*

The reader must be cautioned against making any inference of causality on the basis of indexes of correlation. Any two variables that covary are correlated. Variation in one, however, does not necessarily cause the other to vary. It is true, for example, that there is a very high positive correlation between the number of liquor outlets in urban areas and the number of churches in those same areas. Some people would prefer to think that one does not cause the other.

Intelligence and Achievement

One of the assumptions underlying the construction of most intelligence tests is that intelligence is related to successful performance of school tasks. It is almost inevitable, therefore, that these tests will correlate relatively highly with measures of school achievement. Tyler (1965) reports that the correlation between academic achievement and measured intelligence varies between .30 and .80 over a large number of studies. It would appear, then, that knowledge of a student's score on an intelligence test may be of considerable value to a teacher. The score can be used to predict how well a student should do, and can therefore help the teacher arrive at some reasonable **expectation** for that student. Intelligence test scores can also be employed for grouping students for instruction and counseling purposes. Whatever uses they are put to (if any), those uses should be tempered by the teacher's awareness of their limitations and of the myths that frequently surround the concept of I.Q. Some of these myths and limitations are listed briefly below:

1. It is widely assumed that all individuals have an I.Q.—an assumption that is implicit in the question "What's your I.Q.?" or the expression "My I.Q. is. . . ." It is also assumed that I.Q. is constant since it is a magical (or sometimes not so magical) number *possessed* by someone. The fact is, the numerical index of intelligence known as the I.Q. is simply a score that has been obtained by an individual in a specific testing situation and on a specific "intelligence" test. Quite apart from intelligence tests' sometimes disputable validity (a test is valid to the extent that it measures what it claims to measure; hence an intelligence test is valid if it measures intelligence and nothing else), none has perfect reliability.* The accuracy (reliability) with which intelligence tests measure whatever it is that they do measure varies considerably. This variation, technically known as the error of measurement, is such that any teacher looking at a specific intelligence quotient should say to himself, "This score of 130 means that this student probably has a measured I.Q. that ranges somewhere between 120 and 140."

2. It is also widely believed that I.Q. is highly related to success; however, Thorndike and Hagen (1961) and Cohen (1972) point out that, although the correlation between intelligence test scores and school achievement is substantial, previous achievement correlates even more highly with future achievement than does I.Q. In addition the correlation is considerably higher for some subjects (those requiring verbal or numerical skills) than it is for others. Hence the I.Q. is not necessarily related to success; it depends on the field in which success is being measured.

3. Intelligence tests measure relatively limited kinds of abilities—typically the ability to work with abstract ideas and symbols. They seldom tap interpersonal skills, athletic ability, creativity, and a variety of other desirable human attributes.

4. Most intelligence tests are culturally biased. That is, they tend to favor children whose backgrounds are similar to that of the sample upon which the test was normed. In America that sample has usually consisted of white, middle-class children, a fact that explains why the majority of intelligence tests are unfair for a variety of minority groups. A limited number of tests—none of them widely used in practice, though some are used more extensively in research—attempt to minimize cultural bias. Such tests, sometimes labeled *culture fair,* or, more accurately, *culture reduced,* are typically nonverbal. They attempt to tap intellectual functions through problems involving pictures or abstract designs (for example, the Ravens Progressive Matrices Test).

Measuring Intelligence

A wide variety of intelligence tests are available. Most of these yield a score referred to as the *intelligence quotient* (I.Q.). The average I.Q. of a randomly

---

* See Chapter 15 for a discussion of reliability and validity.

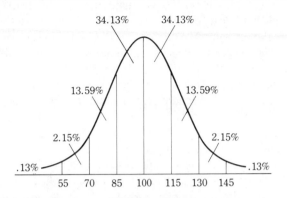

34.13%   34.13%

13.59%   13.59%

2.15%   2.15%

.13%   .13%

55   70   85   100   115   130   145

Figure 11.2 *A Normal Curve Depicting the Theoretical Distribution of I.Q. Scores among Humans (average score is 100; 68.26 percent of the population score between 85 and 115; only 2.28 percent score above 130)*

selected group of people on most tests is around 100. Approximately two-thirds of the population score between 85 and 115. About 11 percent score above 120, and 1.6 percent above 140.

Figure 11.2 gives some arbitrary descriptive labels that may be applied to intelligence test scores ranges, and Table 11.1 depicts the distribution of measured intelligence in a normal population.

Types of Tests There are two general types of intelligence tests: group and individual. The former are administered simultaneously to a group of testees; the latter require individual administration. Typically, **group tests** are, of necessity,

Table 11.1 Classification by I.Q.

Classification	I.Q. Range	% of Population
Very superior	140 – 169	1.6
Superior	120 – 139	11.3
High average	110 – 119	18.1
Normal	90 – 109	46.5
Low average	80 – 89	14.5
Borderline defective	70 – 79	5.6
Mentally defective	30 – 69	2.6

(Terman and Merrill, 1960, p. 18) Reprinted by permission of Houghton Mifflin Company.

paper and pencil tests. There are a great many more of them than there are **individual tests,** probably because group tests are inexpensive and widely used. Individual tests, on the other hand, are much more expensive in terms of both equipment and tester time. The scores they yield are sometimes more reliable, however, and often provide greater insight into the functioning of the subject's mind. They are particularly valuable in diagnosing specific learning problems in children. It is relatively rare, for example, to find school systems that base decisions to put students in "special" classrooms simply on a group assessment. Typically, an individual assessment is required after initial screening with a group measure. This is partly to determine whether the test has been *fair* to the student.

Group tests can usually be administered and scored by any reasonably intelligent classroom teacher. The administration of individual tests, with few exceptions, requires a great deal of training and skill. Brief descriptions of some of the most commonly used group and individual tests are given below. (For more information, the reader is referred to the current issue of the *Mental Measurements Yearbook,* or of *Tests in Print,* both edited by O. K. Buros.)

Individual Tests

1. *Peabody Picture Vocabulary Test (PPVT)* This is probably the most easily administered and scored individual intelligence test. It is an untimed test, usually requiring fifteen minutes or less per subject. It consists simply of having the subject point to the one picture out of four that represents a word that has been read by the examiner. The words are arranged from easiest to most difficult. After six consecutive failures the test is discontinued. An intelligence score can then be computed on the basis of subject's age and the level of the last response.

2. *The Revised Stanford-Binet* This is one of the best known and most widely used individual measures of intelligence. A relatively high degree of training and competence is required for its successful administration. It consists of a wide variety of different tests graded in difficulty so as to correspond to various age levels. It yields a score that can be converted to an I.Q.

3. *The Wechsler Intelligence Scale for Children Revised (WiscR)* This individual test is similar to the Stanford-Binet except that is is somewhat easier to administer. In addition, it yields scores on a number of specific tests (e.g., vocabulary, block design, digit span) and two major "intelligence" scores—one verbal and one performance. These can be combined to yield what is referred to as a full-scale I.Q. score. There is an adult version of this test (WAIS—Wechsler Adult Intelligence Scale), as well as a pre-school version (WPPSI—Wechsler Pre-school and Primary Scale of Intelligence). Various subtests of the Wechsler scales are described in Table 11.2.

Group Tests

1. *Draw a Man Test* This is an interesting measure of intelligence developed by Goodenough (1926) and later revised by Harris (1963). It is based on the assumption that children's drawings reflect their conceptual sophistication. The child is simply asked to draw the best man possible. No time limit is imposed. Drawings are scored primarily on the basis of

Table 11.2 The Wechsler Intelligence Scale For Children (WiscR)

Verbal Scale	Performance Scale
1. *General information.* Questions relating to information most children have the opportunity to acquire.	1. *Picture completion.* Child indicates what is missing on pictures.
2. *General comprehension.* Questions designed to assess child's understandings of why certain things are done as they are.	2. *Picture arrangement.* Series of pictures must be arranged to tell a story.
3. *Arithmetic.* Oral arithmetic problems.	3. *Block design.* Child is required to copy exactly a design with colored blocks.
4. *Similarities.* Child indicates how certain things are alike.	4. *Object assembly.* Puzzles to be assembled by subjects.
5. *Vocabulary.* Child gives meaning of words of increasing difficulty.	5. *Coding.* Child pairs symbols with digits following a key.
6. *Digit Span.* Child repeats orally presented sequence of numbers, in order and reversed.	6. *Mazes.* Child traces way out of mazes with pencil.

detail and accuracy according to a well-defined set of criteria (Harris, 1963). Tables for converting raw scores to I.Q. scores are provided for subjects aged three to fifteen.

    2. *Otis Quick-Scoring Mental Ability Tests* These consist of a number of forms suitable for all age levels from grades one to sixteen. Forms are machine scorable. The test yields verbal, nonverbal, and total I.Q. scores.

    3. *Lorge-Thorndike Intelligence Tests* These are multiform, multilevel paper and pencil tests suitable for grades one to twelve. They are currently in fairly wide use in various school systems. The scores derived from the test are either verbal or nonverbal I.Q.'s.

    4. *The California Test of Mental Maturity (CTMM) 1963* This is a widely used group test. Unlike the Lorge-Thorndike and the Otis, the CTMM gives eight specific subscores: logical reasoning, spatial relationships, numerical reasoning, verbal concepts, memory, language total, nonlanguage total, and total.

Uses of Intelligence Tests Intelligence tests are widely used in most school systems, as are a variety of other tests. Chief among the purposes for which they are employed are counseling, career guidance, class placement, and diagnosis for remedial or enrichment purposes. There is little doubt that, when skillfully administered and intelligently interpreted, they can be of considerable value for any and all of these purposes. Unfortunately, however, they are not always skillfully administered or intelligently interpreted.

    There are a number of very important cautions which should be kept in mind when one is interpreting the results of intelligence tests. Some of these have already been mentioned, but are summaried here again.

    1. The validity and reliability of *all* measures of intelligence are less than perfect. What this means, quite simply, is that an intelligence test provides a global

and imprecise index of what its makers consider to be "intelligence." If Johnny's measured I.Q. today is 120, and Frank's is 115, it would be foolish in the extreme to conclude that Johnny is more intelligent than Frank, and that he should therefore be granted the privelege of studying with the Orioles rather than with the White-Breasted Kites. It might well be that Johnny's measured I.Q. next month will be 110, or that Frank's measured I.Q. on another test today would be 130. It is, in fact, precisely the relative imprecision of measured I.Q. that has served to justify the secrecy that sometimes surrounds the I.Q. Unfortunately, the concept of the I.Q. is not at all well understood by parents; perhaps even more unfortunate, it is often not well understood by educators.

2. Measured I.Q. does not predict academic success nearly as well as is generally assumed. Recall that past success is usually more highly correlated with later success than is measured I.Q. (Cohen, 1972). Hence teachers would be well advised *not* to base their expectations of success for individual students solely on information derived from intelligence tests.

3. Intelligence, as it is measured by available tests, is not a fixed and unchanging characteristic. This observation is particularly true of tests administered in the preschool period. Anderson (1939) reports, for example, that the correlation between tests administered in the first two years of life and a Stanford-Binet adminis-tered at the age of five ranged from 0 (no relationship) to a modest .45. With

increasing age, however, measured I. Q. becomes increasingly stable (Bloom, 1964). This does not necessarily mean that it then predicts academic success more accurately. In addition, a high correlation can still admit to numerous individual exceptions. In other words, even though measured intelligence at the age of nine serves as a good predictor of I. Q. at the age of fifteen, there are a number of high-scoring nine-year-olds who may score relatively low at fifteen. The opposite is equally true.

In practice, what these cautions mean is that teacher decisions based on test results should be tentative and subject to continual review; that students should not be labeled on the basis of limited and changing samplings of their behavior; and that, in short, good sense should prevail here even as it should elsewhere.

Causes of Intelligence: A Debate

Intelligence is like a disease. It doesn't just happen; it is caused. It is probably obvious that the causes of intelligence are also the causes of stupidity, since one is the absence of the other. The assumption that human characteristics result from the interplay of heredity and environment has already been discussed (Chapter 9). If that assumption is valid, then the causes of intelligence are heredity and environment. The question that has puzzled psychologists for many years is: How much does each contribute to the development of intelligence? While the debate has by no means ended (see Jensen, 1968), a great deal of evidence has been gathered on both sides. It is clearly no longer an either-or question; it is a question of how much difference each makes.

The most important question from an educator's point of view is: Can intelligence be *increased* through the manipulation of experience? A sample of the research relevant to this question, and to the general nature-nurture question, is summarized below in the form of a debate between Watson and Galton—a debate replete with glaring anachronisms. In order to know all that they claim to know, Galton would have to be over 100 years old and Watson almost exactly 100.

> Galton: *My dear Watson, if you will simply open your mind to the problem, I can demonstrate for you beyond any doubt that heredity is the most powerful factor in development. As I said in 1869, "I have no patience with the hypothesis occasionally expressed, and often implied, especially in tales written to teach children to be good, that babies are born pretty much alike. . . ."*
>
> Watson: *Give me a dozen . . .*
>
> Galton: *You have said that before. Consider, if you will, the numerous twin studies that have been performed. As you know,* **identical twins** *are genetically exactly alike, whereas* **fraternal twins** *are as dissimilar as any two siblings. Burt's (1958) famous study shows that the intelligence test scores of identical twins, whether reared together or apart, display considerably higher correlation than the scores of fraternal twins. I have no doubt that if we had more reliable measures of intelligence, the correlations would be higher still. Bloom (1964) has recently summarized this study along with four others (p. 69). They all show the same thing.*

Watson: *Whoa now! That is a highly prejudiced interpretation. If you look at the Newman, Freeman, and Holzinger study (1937)—and that one too is included in Bloom's summary—if you look at that study you'll see just where environment comes in. Why do you suppose it is that the correlation for twins reared together is* always *considerably higher than for twins reared apart? Ha! What do you say to that?*

Galton: *I say that studies involving the measurement of intelligence in people are highly suspect. Now take rats, for example.*

Watson: *That is irrelevant!*

Galton: *It is not! Now you just hold on and listen here for a minute. Tryon (1940) did a fascinating study and it will prove you wrong. Do you know it?*

Watson: *You mean Tryon's study?*

Galton: *Yes.*

Watson: *No.*

Galton: *I thought not. You don't read much, do you? You're just a popularizer. What Tryon did was, he took 142 rats and ran them through a seventeen-unit maze nineteen times. The brightest rat made, I forget . . . about twenty errors (Author's note: he actually made exactly fourteen) and the dullest made 200 errors. (Author's note: Again Galton is wrong. The dullest rat made 174 errors.) The brightest rats were then bred with each other, whereas the dull males were given dull females. That usually happens to people, too. Heh! Heh! Well, after repeating the same procedure for only eight generations, a remarkable thing began to happen. The dullest rats in the bright group consistently made fewer errors than the brightest rats in the dull group. In other words, the brightest rats in the dull group were duller than the dullest rats in the bright group—or the dullest rats in the bright group were . . . you know. Imagine what we could do with people. John Humphrey Noyes would have done it if the American government hadn't outlawed polygamy. (Author's note: John Humphrey Noyes set up a religious, communal, free-love group in Oneida, New York, in the late nineteenth century. He practiced selective breeding with the aim of producing a superrace but had to disband the group when polygamy was outlawed in the 1880s.)*

Watson: *So that's the kind of ridiculous evidence you base your eugenic movement on. (Author's note:* Eugenics *is the term given to the practice of selective breeding.) Let me tell* you *about a rat study, seeing as you're the one who brought it up. Hebb (1947) and Krech et al. (1960, 1962, 1966) provide evidence that randomly selected rats can be significantly affected by environment. In the first case Hebb (1947) showed that rats reared as pets did better than laboratory rats on maze tests. Krech et al. (1962) even changed the brain chemistry of rats by enriching their environments. And if you don't think that's enough evidence, consider Heyns' (1967) work in South Africa. He's been affecting the intelligence of babies by using vacuum cleaners.*

Galton: *Whoa, there, whoa! Vacuum cleaners! You're going a little far.*

Watson: *That's what you think. It was reported in* Woman's World *(Feb. 4, 1967).*

Galton: *You read* Woman's World?

Watson: *My wife does. Anyway, what Heyns did is, he set up a decompression unit using a vacuum cleaner motor. He put this plastic bubblelike thing over the woman's abdomen and sucked the air out. It relieves all kinds of aches and pains and makes babies brighter, too.*

Galton: *It sounds like a gimmick to me. Jensen (1968) has recently been reviewing the research, and he has concluded that there is a powerful genetic factor in the determination of intelligence.*

Watson: *Well, the optimistic point of view for a teacher to have is certainly mine. You can't do anything about genetics but you can alter the environment . . . and that's what schools should be doing. That's what Head Start is all about—and that's what acceleration is, and television for kids and books and . . .*

Galton: *Don't get carried away, Watson. Your point of view might be more optimistic, but it's less accurate. I'm a scientist, not a philosopher.*

(The argument ends with Watson's wife calling him in to wash dishes.)

But the debate continues (see Jensen box), although most scientists now believe that both heredity and environment are important, that their relative influences cannot easily be separated, and that the important question in any case does not concern *what* the effects of these factors might be, but rather *how* they affect intelligence (Anastasi, 1958).

Probably one of the better analogies advanced to describe the relative influence of heredity and environment is the rubber band hypothesis. It compares innate potential for intellectual development to a rubber band. Intelligence at any point in time is reflected by the length of the band. Obviously a short piece (poorer genetic background) can be stretched—with a great deal of effort it can be stretched a long way. The forces that exert the pull on the band, or that fail to, are environmental. Hence genetic and environmental forces interact in such a way that less environmental stimulation may be required for average development if genetic endowment is

---

THE JENSEN HYPOTHESIS

The nature-nurture controversy has gained recent impetus through the writings of Arthur Jensen (1968, 1969). He has advanced a hypothesis based on comparisons among the performance of different racial groups on selected measures of intelligence, employing procedures designed to minimize the cultural bias inherent in most intelligence tests. Since most tests of intelligence are designed for middle-class white groups and standardized on these groups, they tend to yield inaccurate assessments for individuals from different cultures. One way of controlling for this cultural bias is to select different racial groups that have had highly similar cultural backgrounds—whites living among blacks, blacks living among whites, and Orientals living among whites or blacks. As a result of such studies, Jensen has reported that blacks typically perform less well than whites on intelligence tests. He has also reported that Orientals often do better than both of these groups, a finding that has been overlooked in the bitter racial argument following the publication of Jensen's findings. To account for these findings, Jensen hypothesizes that environmental factors alone cannot account for the observed differences—that part of these differences must be due to genetic factors. Critics have been quick to point out that Jensen has not proven his case. True. That, of course, is why he has advanced a hypothesis rather than a conclusion. The question remains unresolved. Indeed, it may never be resolved. I'm not certain that it's a very important question, anyhow. Are you?

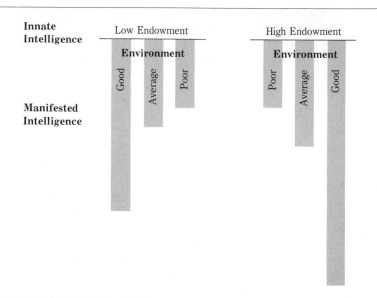

Figure 11.3 *The Stern Hypothesis (individuals with different potentials for intellectual development—low and high genetic endowment—can manifest poor, average, or good intelligence as a function of environmental forces)*

high. The reverse is also true. One of the functions of schools is to stretch rubber bands (see Figure 11.3).

In connection with the rubber band hypothesis, research indicates that the band (manifested intelligence) can more easily be stretched at younger ages. Recall the Lee (1951) studies, mentioned in Chapter 9, which found that those black children who had moved North at the youngest ages showed the least intellectual deficit relative to whites who had been born and brought up in more advantageous environments. Recall, too, Bloom's (1964) related assertion that the environment will have the most profound effect on a trait during its period of most rapid growth. The implication for educational practice points directly to the advisability of providing stimulating environments for children at the youngest possible age.

Additional evidence of the validity of these observations has recently been provided by Jensen (1977) in studies of *decrements* in measured I.Q. apparently as a function of environmental impoverishment. Large samples of black and white school children in rural Georgia were tested between the ages of five and eighteen. Results indicated that measured verbal and nonverbal I.Q. declined significantly between the ages of five and sixteen for those children whose environments could be described as deprived. Children in more advantaged environments exhibit no comparable decrements. Jensen's explanation, labeled a *cumulative deficit* hypothesis, maintains simply that environmental deprivation has a progressive and cumulative effect on measured intelligence so that decrements in I.Q. increase with age. It might well be that, in the same way that poor environments have a progressively deleterious effect, enriched environments might have a progressively beneficial effect. Put more simply, a rubber band is easier to stretch while it is new and highly elastic; with increasing age, it becomes less elastic, perhaps more brittle, and apparently less susceptible to those forces that might initially have served to stretch it.

Creativity

A great deal of work and attention has been devoted to the subject of creativity in the last two decades, particularly following the work of J. P. Guilford (1950, 1959, 1962). The central question in creativity research and speculation, however, remains largely unsolved. What *is* creativity? Few people agree on an answer.

While conversing with George Bernard Shaw, his biographer, Stephen Winsten (1949), alluded to the proverbial "hair's breadth" that separates genius from madness.

"The matter-of-fact man prefers to think of the creative man as defective, or at least akin to madness," Winsten said. To which Shaw replied, "Most of them are, most of them are. I am probably the only sane exception" (p. 103).

Though we no longer fear the creative person as openly as we might once have, there remains a certain uneasiness and uncertainty. Are creative people nonconformists, eccentrics, radicals, and fools, or are they ordinary people? The answer is probably that there are some of both, but that there really is no mystical or magical quality about creativity. Like intelligence, it is a quality of humans and of human behavior—a quality possessed by everyone. Just as very low intelligence is the typical idea of stupidity, so very low creativity is the typical idea of ordinariness. There are few geniuses as identified by tests of intelligence; there are also few very highly creative people.

Definitions

Creativity has been variously defined. Below are three of many possible definitions.

1. Creativity involves fluency, flexibility, and originality (Guilford, 1959; Lowenfeld in Parnes and Harding [eds.], 1962).

2. Creativity is ". . . the forming of associative elements into new combinations which either meet specified requirements or are in some ways useful. The more mutually remote the elements of the new combination, the more creative the process of solution" (Mednick, 1962, p. 221).

3. Creativity results in ". . . a novel work that is accepted as tenable or useful or satisfying by a significant group of others at some point in time" (Stein in Parnes and Harding [eds.], 1962, p. 86).

Consider these three cases:

1. René Choumard is a resident of a remote rural area. For the past three years he has been sitting on the porch of his dilapidated old shack, knitting himself purple mittens with no thumbs. He talks to himself incessantly about everything he has ever seen or done. Is he creative?

2. Joseph Lalonde is René's neighbor. Joseph is the local wit. His humor is also local humor. His jokes are expressions of associations between extremely remote ideas. They are never funny. Is Joseph creative?

3. In the course of routine procedure in a laboratory, a scientist accidently spills a small amount of chemical into a large vat filled with 700 gallons of sweet* cream. The cream immediately turns into four cows (a reversal phenomenon). Is this scientist creative?

In the first case, René was creative according to Guilford and Lowenfeld. His behavior was original and he manifested remarkable verbal fluency and flexibility. He was not creative, however, according to Mednick and Stein. Joseph, on the other hand, fulfilled Mednick's criteria for creativity—highly remote associations satisfying his own specifications. It could even be assumed that he was original, fluent, and flexible. But he did not produce anything "tenable or useful or satisfying." On the other hand, the scientist did. However, he did not behave in an original fashion but only in a clumsy fashion—nor did he make any remote associations whatsoever.

The above discussion is intended to highlight the confusion that exists in this area, making the assessment of creativity extremely difficult. The problem is partly resolved by accepting that *creativity* is, in fact, a global term, and that it does not necessarily represent only one event or quality. If we distinguish among the creative process, the creative product, and the creative person, many of the contradictions implicit in earlier formulations disappear. René, then, is a creative person who doesn't produce anything; Joseph employs a creative process, but also produces nothing creative; and the scientist neither is creative nor employs a creative process, but he produces something highly creative.

These distinctions, while useful, solve only part of the problem, since they are not reflected in current attempts to measure creativity. The inference continues to be made, at least implicitly, that creative personalities and processes can be judged on the basis of products that are deemed to be creative. Some ways of evaluating creativity in students are described below.

Measuring Creativity

One of the simplest (and most unreliable) ways of identifying creative talent is to have teachers rate students. Gallagher (1960) cites research indicating that teachers miss approximately 20 percent of the most highly creative students.

---

* PPC: "Wasn't that sour cream? Check the reference."
Author: "No."

Another simple method is to have individuals rate themselves. Taylor and Holland (1964) find this one of the most effective techniques.

A more popular method is that advanced by Guilford (1950) and developed in the Minnesota Tests of Creative Thinking (Yamamoto, 1964), and by Torrance (1966). This method is based on the assumption that creative ability comprises several separate factors, among which are fluency, flexibility, and originality. Tasks have been designed that allow the subject to produce a variety of responses, which can then be scored in terms of these and other factors. The most often cited example of such a test is the *unusual uses* test. Subjects are asked to think of as many uses as they can for an ordinary object, such as a brick or a nylon stocking. Responses are counted to arrive at an index of fluency. Flexibility is measured by counting the number of *shifts* between classes of response. For example, a brick might be used for building a house, a planter, a road, and so on. Each response scores for fluency, but not for flexibility. A shift from this category of uses to one involving throwing objects, for example, would illustrate flexibility. Originality is scored on the basis of the number of responses that are either statistically rare or are judged unusual by the experimenter. A statistically rare response might be one that occurs less than 5 percent of the time (see Table 11.3). A related test is the *Product Improvement Test,*

Table 11.3 Sample Answers and Scoring Procedure for One Item from a Test of Creativity

---

Item: How many uses can you think of for a nylon stocking?

Answers:	*	wear on feet
	§†*	wear over face
	*	wear on hands when it's cold
	†*	make rugs
	*	make clothes
	§†*	make upholstery
	†*	hang flower pots
	*	hang mobiles
	§†*	make Christmas decorations
	†*	use as a sling
	†*	tie up robbers
	§†*	cover broken window panes
	§†*	use as ballast in a dirigible
	†*	make a fishing net

Scoring:	*	Fluency:	14 (total number of different responses)
	†	Flexibility:	9 (number of shifts from one class to another)
	§	Originality:	5 (number of unusual responses—responses that occurred less than 5 percent of the time in the entire sample)

---

which requires subjects to think of as many ways as possible to improve a toy that is shown to them.

Several nonverbal measures of creativity are also included in the Minnesota Tests. These include a Picture Construction Task and a Figure Completion Task. The battery also includes tests of creative *writing* as opposed to creative *ability*. All of these are timed tasks. There is some evidence, however, that time limits on the writing tasks depress some students' scores (Peel, 1968).

The Relationship between Creativity and Intelligence

A classic study which highlights the distinction sometimes assumed to exist between creativity and intelligence is that reported by Getzels and Jackson (1962). They found that creative students were not necessarily the most intelligent, despite the fact that they achieved as well as those who were more intelligent. (Interestingly, however, the creative students were not as well *liked* by the teachers.) The study can be interpreted as implying a relatively low relationship between creativity and intelligence. It should be pointed out, however, that the subjects were selected from a private Chicago high school. The mean I.Q. rating in that school was 132. The mean I.Q. for the group designated as High Creative, Low I.Q. was a more than respectable 127. With such a limited range in intelligence test scores, it is doubtful that any relationship would be found even if it existed. In addition, the general findings of the study are probably not generalizable beyond this highly select group.

A related study (Wallach and Kogan, 1965) also identified four groups of students classified as high or low on intelligence and creativity, respectively. The purpose of this study was to identify characteristics that might be different among these four groups. Results of the study are summarized in Figure 11.4. While it is interesting to note that highly creative but less intelligent students are most frustrated with school and that highly intelligent but less creative students are addicted to school and well liked by their teachers, it should be kept in mind that these four groups represent relative extremes. The vast majority of students are not extreme. In addition, these general descriptions of school adjustment and personality characteristics are just that: general descriptions. Even with groups as highly selected as these there are numerous individual exceptions.

No conclusive statements can yet be made concerning the correlation between creativity and intelligence. Torrance (1962) has said, for example, that, "if we were to identify children as gifted simply on the basis of intelligence tests, we would eliminate from consideration approximately 70 percent of the most creative" (p. 5). Thorndike (1963) has summarized these and other findings by concluding that the correlation between creativity and intelligence ranges from 0 to .4. A number of investigators, on the other hand, maintain that there is a high relationship between creativity and intelligence. Meer and Stein (1955) claim that only above the ninety-fifth percentile do I.Q. scores cease to correlate with creativity. Wallach and Kogan

	Measured Intelligence	
	High	Low
Divergent Thinking (Creativity) High	high control over their own behavior; capable of adultlike and childlike behavior	high internal conflict; frustration with school; feelings of inadequacy; can perform well in stress-free environment
Low	addicted to school; strive desperately for academic success; well-liked by teachers	somewhat bewildered by environment; defense mechanisms include intensive social or athletic activity; occasional maladjustment

Figure 11.4 *Characteristics of Children Identified as High and Low on Measures of Intelligence and of Divergent Thinking (based on studies reported by Wallach and Kogan, 1965)*

(1965), Cropley (1965), and Pribram (1963) all see little real justification for treating creativity and intelligence as though they were distinct and separate. The last word has not been said.

Guilford

J. P. Guilford's (1959, 1967) model of the intellect (see Figure 11.5) provides an interesting and useful representation of human "intellectual" functioning. It can serve to illuminate the processes involved in both creativity and intelligence. The model is organized around three main aspects of human functioning: **operations, products,** and **content.** A specific ability involves a combination of all three. Hence there are 120 abilities, of which 80 have been identified through tests.

1. *Operations.* An operation is a major intellectual process. The term includes such things as knowing or discovering or being aware (cognition), retrieving from storage (memory), the generation of multiple responses (**divergent thinking**), arriving at a unique, accepted solution (**convergent thinking**), and judging the appropriateness of information or decisions (evaluation).

2. *Content.* An operation is performed upon certain kinds of information. This information is called *content,* and may be figural, symbolic, semantic, or behavioral. Figural content is concrete information, such as images. Symbolic content is information in the form of arbitrary denotative signs, such as numbers or codes. Semantic content is information in the form of word meanings. And behavioral content is nonverbal information involved in human interaction—for example, emotion.

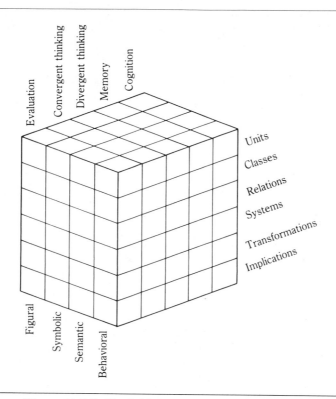

Figure 11.5 *Guilford's Model (J. P. Guilford, "Three faces of intellect,"* American Psychologist, *Vol. 14, 1959, pp. 469–479. Copyright 1959 by the American Psychological Association and reproduced by permission)*

3. *Products.* Applying an operation to content yields a product. The product is the form that information takes once it is processed. It includes single, segregated items of information (units), sets of items grouped by virtue of their common properties (classes), connections between items of information (relations), organizations of information (systems), changes of information (transformations), and extrapolations or predictions from information (implications).*

The two operations that have stimulated the most research and interest are those of convergent and divergent thinking. These are also the two operations most closely related to creativity and intelligence. Convergent thinking involves the pro-

---

* PPC: "Could specific examples be included? Nobody ever does, which leads me to suspect it is as hard for everyone else to explain how memory operates on semantic content to produce systems. (Go, Lefrancois!)"

Author: "You're right."

duction of one correct solution. It is a crucial factor in intelligence testing. Divergent thinking, on the other hand, involves the production of multiple solutions or hypotheses. It is central in the creative process. The phrase *divergent thinking* has, in fact, become almost synonymous with the phrase *creative thinking*.

Guilford's model is another example of a theoretical position premised on the assumption that intelligence is not a unitary trait but a conglomerate of separate abilities. This viewpoint resolves the apparent contradiction among the numerous studies that investigate the relationship between creativity and intelligence. If intelligence is defined in terms of the entire structure, and if creativity involves only some of the 120 abilities described in the model, it is inevitable that there should be some relationship between the two. At the same time, however, it is also inevitable that this relationship will vary from very low to very high according to the individual's pattern of abilities.

It is theoretically possible that, as instruments that measure specific human abilities are refined, educators will be able to assess intellectual weaknesses and strengths infinitely more precisely than they can now. The implications for remedial teaching and for acceleration and enrichment are limitless.

Summary of Chapter 11

This chapter has presented a discussion of creativity and intelligence. Definitions and tests were described for each. In addition, the nature-nurture question was reexamined in the form of a debate. The relationship between creativity and intelligence and Guilford's model of the intellect were also discussed. The next chapter looks at ways of increasing creativity.

Main Points in Chapter 11

1. Intelligence is defined in various ways, but generally implies a capacity for adapting well to the environment. A simple, useful definition is Boring's (1923): "Intelligence is what the tests test."

2. A correlation coefficient is an index of relationship between variables. It is a function of covariation—not of causal relatedness. The ordinary index (r) varies from -1.00 to $+1.00$.

3. Intelligence test scores correlate highly with performance in the academic world.

4. Intelligence tests usually yield a score referred to as an intelligence quotient (I. Q.). It ranges from perhaps 50 to 160 on some tests. The average population I. Q. is around 100.

5. Two types of instruments are commonly employed to measure intelligence: group tests and individual tests. The Otis, the California Test of Mental Maturity, and the Draw a Man tests are examples of group tests, whereas the Peabody Picture Vocabulary Test, the Stanford-Binet, and the WiscR are examples of individual tests.

6. Both creativity and intelligence appear to be a function of an interaction between heredity and environment.

7. Creativity is defined in various, apparently contradictory ways. Much of the contradiction disappears when the creative product, process, and person are considered separately.

8. Creativity may be measured using teacher or pupil ratings or by employing some of the tests developed for this purpose. Chief among these are the Minnesota Tests of Creative Thinking, which include verbal and nonverbal tasks as well as tests of creative writing ability.

9. Creativity and intelligence may or may not be highly related. It is likely that relatively high intelligence is required for superior creative effort. Above a certain point, however, personality and social factors are probably more important than purely intellectual ones.

10. Guilford's model of the structure of intellect is useful in understanding human abilities and the processes involved in intellectual activity. The terms *divergent* and *convergent* are derived from this model and serve to illustrate a broad distinction between creativity and intelligence.

Suggested Readings

For a more detailed discussion of the meaning of the term intelligence, *its development, and its measurement, the reader is referred to:*

Tyler, L. E. *The Psychology of Human Differences* (3rd Edition). New York: Appleton-Century-Crofts, 1965.

For a collection of classical articles on the development of psychological thought in the area of intelligence and its measurement, the student is referred to the following book, edited by Jenkins and Peterson. This text begins with Galton's strong stand for heredity in 1869 and concludes with J. P. Guilford's 1959 article.

Jenkins, J. J. and D. G. **Peterson** (eds.). *Studies in Individual Differences: The Search for Intelligence.* New York: Appleton-Century-Crofts, 1961.

For an introduction to the Jensen controversy, see the following reprint, which includes Jensen's original article and various rebuttals to it.

Environment, heredity, and intelligence. *Howard Educational Review.* Reprint Series No. 2, 1969.

Guilford's structure of intellect is described in the following article, which has been reprinted in countless books of readings:

Guilford, J. P. Three faces of intellect. *American Psychologist,* 1959, 14, 469–479.

Since Guilford's classic 1959 article, which has been interpreted as relating equally to creativity and intelligence, many books and articles have been written on the subject of creativity and on the problems associated with teaching creative behavior. Among these, two have been selected for this list of suggested readings. The first presents a provocative analysis of the relationship between creativity and intelligence. Although the research reported in this book has been criticized on methodological grounds, it may nevertheless be of considerable value for the classroom teacher.

Getzels, J. W. and P. W. **Jackson.** *Creativity and Intelligence.* New York: John Wiley, 1962.

The second text is intended as a guide for teachers concerned with their students' creative abilities. It is a highly readable and highly practical book.

Torrance, E. P. *Guiding Creative Talent.* Englewood Cliffs, N.J.: Prentice-Hall, 1962.

During hibernation, all the metabolic processes are slowed to an absolute minimum. The animal is exceedingly torpid, and approaches death as closely as possible without actually dying. Bears do not truly hibernate, although they do "den-up" during severe weather (Matthews, 1969).

12
Promoting Creativity and Intelligence

Promoting Ordinariness (or Stifling Creativity) · Promoting Creativity · Techniques for Creative Problem Solving · Implications of Research on Promoting Creativity · Classroom Climate and Creativity · Instructional Media and Creativity · Teaching Thinking · The Effects of Expectations on Intelligence and Achievement · Implications of Research on the Effects of Expectations · Summary · Main Points ·

Ah, yes! I wrote the "Purple Cow"—
I'm sorry, now, I wrote it!
But I can tell you, anyhow,
I'll kill you if you quote it!
(Gelett Burgess)

Advance Organizer Teachers too often define their roles as involving little more than is explicit in prescribed curricula. They see themselves as sources of information, and students as the recipients. Chapter 8 urged a greater recognition of the student as person, and highlighted the importance of teacher behaviors and attitudes in the student's development of self-concepts and attitudes. This chapter presents specific suggestions for increasing the basic abilities, skills, and attitudes that are represented by creativity and intelligence. Although the fundamental psychological characteristics that these represent probably cannot be taught directly (intelligence cannot be "taught"), certain behaviors and attitudes that relate to the characteristics can be.

This chapter presents a number of suggestions for enhancing creativity and intelligence in students. Like all other practical suggestions made in this text, these are no more than a few of the possible classroom applications of psychological knowledge (nor are they necessarily the best). The first part of the chapter deals with creativity; the second with intelligence and, indirectly, with achievement.

Promoting Ordinariness
(or Stifling Creativity)

Creativity is that special quality in students that *other* teachers in *other* classrooms stifle. Other teachers are rigid, rule-bound, and authoritarian. They reward students for sitting properly in well-aligned, straight-rowed desks with their feet firmly on the floor and their heads some considerable distance below the clouds. They stifle creativity by insisting on excessive conformity to arbitrary regulations, by giving high grades for neat, correct, unimaginative solutions to problems, executed and reported in exactly the prescribed manner, and by refusing to admire the mistakeful gropings of a child reaching toward the unknown. They stifle creativity by forbidding spontaneity and rewarding mediocrity. They crush the joyful inquisitiveness of young children by not hearing or not answering their questions. They are dry, sober, humorless keepers of the culture of their ancestors. Their generation is of another age. But those are *other* teachers in *other* classrooms. Today's teacher is very different from the teacher described above.

Promoting Creativity

An assumption implicit in this and in the last chapter is that to be creative, or intelligent, or both, is a good thing. The validity of the assumption is not usually questioned but is accepted as axiomatic. It is true, nevertheless, that were it not for our tendency to create, to innovate, and to change, much of the social unrest characteristic of this age would probably cease to be. At the same time, however, were it not for our creativity, we would still be living in caves and killing wild animals or being killed by them. As the world's problems multiply, the need for creativity

becomes ever more pressing and more apparent. The question of whether schools should deliberately try to encourage creative behavior in students is very much tied up with the question of whether stability and order are valued more highly than change and progress. This analysis, however, is somewhat superficial and over-simplified. It is widely assumed that change *is* progress. Is it, necessarily? It is also assumed that stability and order are incompatible with change. Are they? While it might be more comfortable and secure to live in a world of satisfied, uncreative people, I think it imperative not to. For this reason, it is essential for teachers to learn how schools can contribute to the development of creativity in students. And that goes considerably beyond taking steps to ensure that creativity is not stifled; it must also be encouraged. If you don't water your horse, you are not preventing it from living. But you might well kill it in any case. Confusing? Substitute "fertilize your yam" for "water your horse."

In the following discussion, creativity in children is defined as curiosity, as willingness to explore and to experiment, as the production of novel responses to problem situations, as sensitivity to problems, and as a concern for their own creative behavior.

Techniques for
Creative Problem Solving

Industry has long been concerned with creativity. Its emphasis, however, has been less on the development of creative *people* than on the production of creative *things* or *ideas*. Interestingly, those techniques which have been shown to contribute to creative production also seem to enhance creativity in people (see, for example, Meadow and Parnes, 1959, or Lefrancois, 1965). Five of these techniques are described below.

Brainstorming

The most common group approach for solving problems creatively is probably Alex Osborn's (1957) **brainstorming.** Osborn describes brainstorming as a *principle* rather than a *technique*. As such, it involves something as simple as *deferred evaluation;* as a technique, it offers certain rules for the conduct of problem-solving sessions.

The principle of deferred evaluation is implicit in most techniques developed to solve problems creatively. It involves producing a wide variety of solutions while deliberately suspending judgment about the appropriateness of these solutions. This is an extremely difficult thing for inexperienced problem solvers to do, but it seems to be highly conducive to creative production. Parnes (1962) reports, for example, that individuals working alone produce from 23 to 177 percent more *good-quality* solutions when deferring judgment than when simply following instructions to "produce good ideas" (p. 284). Delaying evaluation allows much greater scope in the responses emitted. Evaluation during production has a dampening effect on both groups and individuals.

Brainstorming, as a technique, employs the principle of deferred judgment. In addition, three other rules are closely followed (Haefele, 1962, p. 142):

1. Criticism of an idea is absolutely barred (deferred evaluation).
2. Modification or combination with other ideas is encouraged.
3. Quantity of ideas is sought.
4. Unusual, remote, or wild ideas are sought.

A brainstorming session may last for two or more hours. It usually involves anywhere from five to twelve people, who often come from a wide variety of backgrounds. If the members of the group are new to brainstorming, the leader begins by explaining the procedural rules. The specific problem that is to be dealt with is then described for the group, and the session begins. Ideally, it is a free-wheeling, wide-ranging affair with ideas coming very rapidly from all sources. All forms of evaluation are forbidden. Evaluative comments like "that sounds good" or "no, that won't work," ridicule, laughter, or nonverbal expressions of either admiration or disgust are stopped immediately. Habitual offenders may even be removed from the group.

During the course of a brainstorming session, a number of specific aids to creativity are employed. The most common of these are checklists of ways to deal with problems. Parnes (1967) had adapted one such list from Osborn's (1957) book, *Applied Imagination.* It is described below, with illustrations based on the problem of what to do with a class whose teacher cannot maintain discipline. The illustrations are not necessarily solutions; they are merely suggestions.

1. *Put to other uses:* The class might be used as something other than a learning situation. For example, it might be given the responsibility of entertaining the school at a social evening.

2. *Adapt:* Adaptation involves using ideas from other sources. Perhaps a school could be run like a factory, like a prison, or like a playground.

3. *Modify:* This suggests changing the composition of the class, changing teaching methods, or changing the approach to discipline problems. This entire checklist could be applied to any of these changes; it would suggest possible forms for them to take.

4. *Magnify:* Class size could be increased, as could number of teachers, number of assignments, or magnitude of punishment or reinforcement.

5. *Minify:* Class size could be decreased, as could number of assignments, number of reprimands, or number of school days.

6. *Substitute:* A new teacher might be substituted, the entire class might be exchanged, or a few members of the class might be replaced by students from other classes.

7. *Rearrange:* The seating plan could be rearranged so as to separate troublemakers, as could the physical arrangement of the room. Perhaps the desks should all face toward the rear.

8. *Reverse:* The last idea came one point too early. However, the teacher might face the front as a sort of reversal. Another reversal would be to have the students take turns teaching.

9. *Combine:* This suggests, first, that a combination of the previous suggestions might provide a solution; and second, that the teaching-learning function might possibly be combined with other functions, such as entertainment, problem solving, or the discussion of noncurricular topics of interest.

Several other checklists have been developed by other researchers. All are designed to stimulate the production of ideas. If the brainstorming session slows down, the chairperson will often make suggestions based on such a checklist: "How can we modify this?" "Magnify it?"—and so on. The suggestions are evaluated only after the session is over.

Research has shown that simply being involved in brainstorming sessions may increase scores on tests designed to measure creativity (Anderson, 1959, and Haefele, 1962).

The uses to which brainstorming can be put in a classroom are infinite. Quite apart from facilitating creative behavior, it can be used to solve numerous day-to-day classroom problems, particularly in this age of "participatory democracy." There is no reason why students and teachers cannot or should not use it to produce suggestions for planning courses and assignments, for conducting social and athletic events, or for involving themselves in local, national, and international projects.

The Gordon Technique

The **Gordon technique,** a slight modification of brainstorming, is based on the work of William J. J. Gordon (1961), who developed a process called "Operational Creativity." The major difference between the Osborn and the Gordon approaches is that the former presents the participants with a complete, detailed problem, often before the session itself, while the latter presents them only with an abstraction. In a Gordon group, for example, if the problem is one of parking cars in Montreal, the chairman might begin by saying, "The problem today is one of storing things. How many ways can you think of for storing things?" The author has used this example as an illustration in several classes. Below is a list of some of the responses that college students make to this question.

1. Put them in bags.
2. Pile them up.
3. Put them in rows.
4. Can them.
5. Put them on hangers.
6. Convey them on belts to storage areas.
7. Cut them up.
8. Fold them.
9. Put them in your pocket.
10. Put them in boxes.
11. Disassemble them.
12. Put them on shelves.

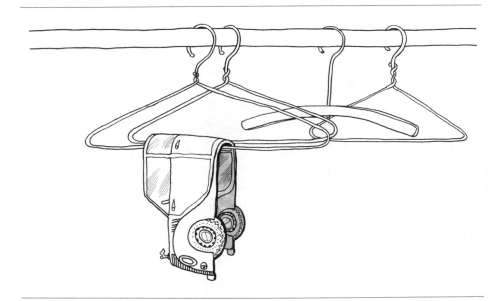

After a time, the chairman of the group begins to narrow the problem down. The next step might be to say, "The things that have to be stored are quite large." Later, more restrictions will be specified. "The objects cannot be folded or cut up," and so on.

The argument for the Gordon technique is that presenting an extreme abstraction may lead to many ideas that would not ordinarily be thought of. Consider, for example, the idea of hanging cars. This idea would probably not come easily in relation to parking cars—but in relation to the question of storing things, it is a relatively ordinary suggestion. Consider, also, the idea of moving objects to storage areas on conveyor belts. This one might have merit!

Morphological Analysis

This procedure, described by Osborn (1957) and Arnold (1962), is ascribed to Dr. Fritz Zwicky, Aero-Jet Corporation. It involves dividing a problem into a number of independent variables, thinking of as many solutions or ideas as possible for each one, and combining the result in all possible ways. Arnold illustrates **morphological analysis** using the problem of developing a new type of vehicle. Three different aspects of this problem are: (1) the type of vehicle, (2) the type of power, and (3) the medium in which the vehicle will be used. Each of these aspects lends itself to various solutions. For example, the type of vehicle might be a cart, a sling, a rocket, a box, and so on. Figure 12.1 presents 180 possible solutions for the problem. There are thousands more. Some of these have already been invented; some are completely impractical; others might be worth pursuing. Imagine, for

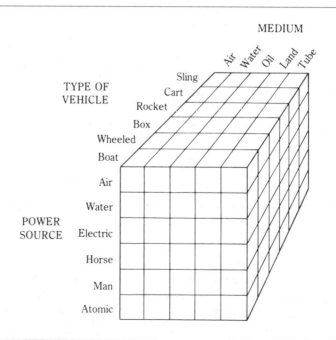

Figure 12.1

example, a sling-type vehicle, drawn by horses, going through oil, or an atomic-powered rocket going through a tube.

CNB Method

Haefele (1962) describes what he calls the *Collective Notebook* method, which can be employed in a factory (or probably anywhere else). It consists of presenting a problem, together with some possible solutions, on the first page of a notebook. These notebooks are then distributed to everyone in the factory. As individuals arrive at possible solutions for the problem, they write them down or diagram them in their books. At the end of a specified period of time the notebooks are collected and solutions are evaluated. The originators of worthwhile ideas are rewarded.

One argument advanced in favor of the notebook method is that it allows more time for incubation. Worthwhile ideas may occur to people at strange times—sometimes in the middle of the night, in the bathtub, in court, or even in school. If a person has a notebook handy, the pearl of wisdom may be recorded for posterity.

CBB Method

The *Collective Bulletin Board* method, devised by me (Lefrancois, 1965), is a combination of brainstorming and the CNB method, designed for use in a classroom.

One of the major advantages of group brainstorming over an individual method such as the CNB technique is that it allows members of the group to profit from each other's ideas. One of its major disadvantages is that the more vocal and uninhibited members of the group often monopolize the proceedings. The Collective Bulletin Board method was developed to allow individuals to benefit from each other's ideas, while maintaining complete freedom to express their own. It consists of placing a description of a problem, and of possible solutions, on a bulletin board in a classroom, rather than in a notebook. Students are then encouraged to add their own solutions to the board and to adapt ideas already on it. The method was employed over a ten-week period with two different classes. At the end of that time, it was found that participants in the CBB program did significantly better on tests of creative thinking than did comparable control groups (Lefrancois, 1965).

Individual Brainstorming

Brainstorming, as a principle, need not be restricted to groups; it is, in fact, highly recommended for individuals (Parnes, 1962). As a principle, brainstorming is the deferment of evaluation. Hence an individual employing this approach will simply try to think up as many ideas as possible, writing them all down or taping them, while deliberately withholding any decision about their worth.

Implications of Research
on Promoting Creativity

The preceding section has discussed various techniques developed largely in industry and designed specifically to lead to the production of ideas that are of real and immediate industrial value. One fairly obvious implication of this work is that the techniques themselves are valuable and should probably form the basis for instruction in problem solving, perhaps even in elementary grades. A second, less obvious, implication is that creative behavior in students can be increased by having them participate in creative problem-solving exercises. In this connection, Parnes (1967) had developed a particularly valuable workbook (*Creative Behavior Workbook*, Charles Scribner's Sons, 1967).

Classroom
Climate and Creativity

A question of great practical interest for educators concerned about creativity is: To what extent does the atmosphere of a classroom relate to creative behavior in students? A brief summary of literature relating to this question is given below.

Several studies have dealt with this problem directly. Haddon and Lytton (1968) contrasted two types of schools, which they labeled *formal* and *informal*. The formal schools were characterized by an authoritarian approach to learning and teaching, whereas the informal schools tended to emphasize self-initiated learning and greater student participation. Not surprisingly, students in informal schools consistently did better on measures of creative thinking than did students of comparable intelligence and socio-economic status who attended the more formal schools.

Related to this is Adams' finding (1968) that students tested under noncompetitive conditions scored higher on tests of spontaneous flexibility than did those tested under competitive conditions. Further, if the examiner were warm and receptive, students did even better. Turner and Denny (1969) also found that warm, spontaneous teachers were more likely to encourage creative behavior in their students than were teachers characterized as being highly organized and businesslike.

Torrance (1962) gives a list of suggestions for teacher behavior designed to promote creativity in students. These appear to be valuable and are therefore reproduced below. The reader is invited to consider how each might be implemented.

1. Value creative thinking.
2. Make children more sensitive to environmental stimuli.
3. Encourage manipulation of objects and ideas.
4. Teach how to test each idea systematically.
5. Develop tolerance of new ideas.
6. Beware of forcing a set pattern.
7. Develop a creative classroom atmosphere.
8. Teach children to value their creative thinking.

   9. Teach skills for avoiding peer sanctions.
   10. Give information about the creative process.
   11. Dispel the sense of awe of masterpieces.
   12. Encourage self-initiated learning.
   13. Create "thorns in the flesh" (i.e., awareness of problems).
   14. Create necessities for creative thinking.
   15. Provide for active and quiet periods.
   16. Make available resources for working out ideas.
   17. Encourage the habit of working out the full implications of ideas.
   18. Develop *constructive* criticism—not just criticism.
   19. Encourage the acquisition of knowledge in a variety of fields.
   20. Develop adventurous-spirited teachers.*

This chapter opened with a section devoted to the topic of promoting ordinariness. It described the kind of teacher who might be likely to stifle creativity. As a supplement to that section, other inhibitors of creativity are listed below (Hallman, 1967):

   1. Pressure to conform.
   2. Authoritarian attitudes and environments.
   3. Rigid teacher personality.
   4. Ridicule and sarcasm.
   5. Overemphasis on evaluation.
   6. Excessive quests for certainty.
   7. Hostility toward divergent personalities.
   8. Overemphasis on success.
   9. Intolerance of play attitudes.

It follows that, if these behaviors serve to discourage creativity, then their opposites might serve to promote it. This list suggests what *not* to do—as opposed to the Torrance list, which suggests what a teacher *should* do. Both, taken in combination, can serve as useful guides for teacher behavior.

Instructional
Media and Creativity

The argument is often advanced that teachers who are not themselves very creative cannot easily encourage creativity in their students. There is really little evidence to support this contention. Any teacher can make an effort to recognize and reward creativity in students and can provide opportunities for it to occur. This section discusses specific suggestions for creating such opportunities. They are selected from a list of 112 ideas reported in Taylor and Williams' (1966) book,

---

* PPC: "Want to give us some dope on how to implement the twentieth suggestion?"

   Author: "Not dope; spirit."

Instructional Media and Creativity. This book deals specifically with the creative use of media (films, film strips, television). The ideas selected are those which appear most directly relevant to the classroom. Their application, obviously, need not be restricted to the use of media alone; it can also be effective in more conventional instructional procedures.

     1. *Design media depicting creative individuals making a work of art out of their lives* (*p. 367*). This involves presenting creative individuals as models for students. These models can be described by the teacher or can be presented live. There is no reason why local people who *are* creative cannot be brought into schools to talk about their work and their lives—nor is there any reason why students should not occasionally leave the school and visit places where creative products and/or people are available.

     2. *Design media around the mystery of things—for example, birth, the universe, hypnotism, intuition,* **insight** (*p. 368*). There is something perennially fascinating about the unknown, for children as well as for adults. In fact, children are probably fascinated by many more things than adults are, since there are so many more unknowns for them. The teacher can capitalize on this characteristic to stimulate the students' curiosity and imagination.

     3. *Locate a group of very creative teachers and find out what and how they teach* (*p. 368*). This is a practical suggestion for people who are actually teaching. It is sometimes amazing how little communication there is among teachers about the instructional methods they employ and about which ones they find most effective. Exchanging this kind of information could easily prove to be tremendously valuable for teachers.

     4. *Produce two companion instructional media devices (films), one to be used for showing the classroom teacher how to produce a need to create, followed by a second one for students containing rich sensory inputs for releasing their creative abilities. Both should be used together in a school* (*p. 368*). This recommendation implies presenting lessons designed in such a way as to elicit creative behavior. This involves two stages: the first stage creates a need, while the second provides an opportunity to satisfy that need. An important aspect of the suggestion is that rich sensory input should be provided for the student. This can be put to good use in a writing class, for example, where the subject the students are writing about can be described and illustrated using a variety of approaches, so as to facilitate the creative process.

     5. *Design media which purposely present knowledge having incomplete gaps—for example, knowns as well as unknowns of a field* (*p. 369*). This can be interpreted as a suggestion for teaching via any instructional mode available. The point is that a teacher should not always close all the gaps, but should occasionally try to present the limits of human knowledge in a given area. Bruner strongly advocates a related approach, where the learner is given relevant information but is asked to discover the relationships within this information (see Chapter 6 for a more detailed discussion of this topic).

     6. *Design and use media for teaching children how to live with change—how to change the environment rather than just simply adjust to the environment* (*p. 369*). The necessity for developing this attitude in today's children is evident. As it becomes progressively more necessary to change the environment in order to survive, it becomes more essential that children learn the consequences of mere adjustment.

     7. *Show the conclusion of a film and have students guess what the beginning was. Choose a film that poses a problem and solves it, but only show the solution and have students define the problem—or vice versa* (*p. 369*). This is a practical suggestion that can be applied to oral or written presentations as well.

The Taylor and Williams book contains 105 practical ideas in addition to those discussed here, as well as 38 research ideas. The interested reader might find them valuable.

Teaching Thinking

After you have been teaching for a while, it might be a good idea to pause and ask yourself what it is that you have been teaching. If you are as honest as most teachers are (and like most teachers in other ways), you will probably find that you have been teaching information relating to one or more conveniently labeled and categorized bodies of knowledge that we call subjects, and perhaps a number of practical skills such as reading, writing, and manipulating numbers. Hopefully, you might also note that some of your students, some of the time, have also begun to learn how to understand and appreciate; how to analyze and synthesize. Some will show signs of being able to compare and summarize, will perhaps even know how to interpret and criticize, how to find and test assumptions, how to observe and classify. Sadly, however, unless you are one of those rare teachers who has taken pains to work toward these ends, most of this learning will have occurred incidentally—almost accidentally. In spite of the fact that we have long paid lip service to the desirability of developing creative and thinking skills in students, schools have paid little attention to programs deliberately designed to foster these skills. In fact, we have naively assumed that the abilities involved in creating and thinking are largely innate. Worse yet, we have assumed that systematic exposure to increasingly large bodies of information and increasingly difficult problems and concepts would automatically develop the ability to think. With respect to creativity, we have been less certain, and have preferred, instead, to assume that some have it and others don't. At the same time, we have assumed that the worst thing that a teacher might do with respect to creativity is to stifle it, and, sadly, that the best thing a teacher might do is *not* stifle it.

The preceding section of this chapter is meant not only to imply but to affirm that creative behavior can and should be fostered. It is not sufficient simply to generously refrain from those behaviors that might stifle it. It should come as no surprise that the same holds true for the thinking skills that are involved in analyzing, comparing, summarizing, criticizing, hypothesizing, and so on (Raths et al., 1967). Indeed, in all fairness to teachers, it must be pointed out that many of the practical suggestions offered by writers such as Raths et al. (1967) and de Bono (1976) designed specifically for fostering thinking have long been employed by teachers. But not all teachers have been aware of the fact that, in so doing, they have been *teaching for thinking.*

Lateral Thinking

De Bono (1970) suggests that, if one wants to dig a hole deeper, it is necessary to dig vertically. If, however, the object is to dig a hole in another place,

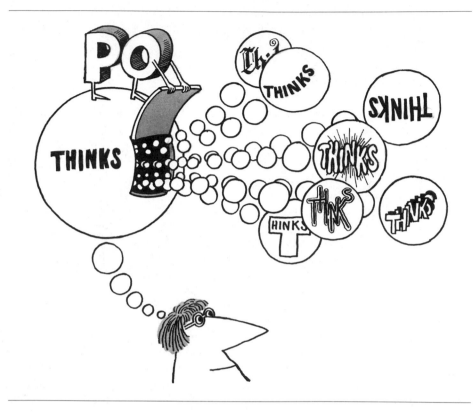

then it is necessary to dig laterally. In the same way, if the object is to discover more about something, or to arrive at a conventional, accepted, "convergent" solution to a problem, vertical thinking is entirely appropriate; but if the object is to find unusual, divergent, creative solutions for problems, *lateral thinking* is indicated. Superficially, then, lateral thinking would seem to be simply a different term for what has traditionally been called creative thinking. But de Bono (1970) argues that lateral thinking is a way of using the mind that *leads* to creative thinking and to creative solutions, but that is not the same thing. He maintains that lateral thinking is closely related to insight, creativity, and humor, but that these last three can only be prayed for whereas lateral thinking can deliberately be developed. Accordingly, he has devised a program for teaching lateral thinking, as well as one simply designed to teach "thinking" (de Bono, 1976).

Unlike brainstorming and other specific techniques designed to foster creative behavior, de Bono's program for teaching lateral thinking does not require students to solve specific problems, but encourages them instead to develop new ways of approaching all problems. More precisely, it attempts to teach lateral rather than vertical approaches. Many of the exercises are similar to items that have been employed on various tests of creativity. Students might be presented with various geometric designs, for example, and asked to describe them in as many ways as possible. Other activities are designed to encourage students to ask why, to suspend judgment, to identify and challenge assumptions, to brainstorm, to produce analogies, and so on. Throughout, emphasis is on the creation of new ideas, and the challenging of old ideas, but care is taken to assure that the learner does not overemphasize the negation of the old. De Bono suggests that negation is one of the principal techniques in vertical thinking—that "logical" thinking is based on negation and selection, with the major role being played by rejection. Hence the centrality of a word such as *no* in logical (vertical) thinking. Lateral thinking does not have a central word—that is, it didn't. In addition to offering a large number of specific exercises, de Bono also presents his students with a new word: *po. Po* is intended to be to lateral thinking what *no* is to vertical thinking. The word *yes* is clearly unsuitable, since it implies uncritical acceptance. But the word *po* is entirely suitable. It means nothing and everything. It is a word that permits us to do or say anything, a word that requires no justification, a word that, in de Bono's words, is the laxative of language and thinking. More simply, *po* is neither an affirmation nor a negation; it is simply an invitation to think laterally. As such, it is an invitation to examine, to challenge, to modify, combine, brainstorm, or analogize. *Po* might have some place in your teaching.

More Vertical Thinking

Other programs designed to teach thinking include Raths et al.'s (1967) detailed and highly specific exercises and activities designed to improve the many component skills involved in thinking but not ordinarily taught in any systematic fashion in the schools. As mentioned earlier, these skills include classifying, finding and testing assumptions, analyzing, comparing, summarizing, and so on. Applications are provided for each skill at both elementary and secondary levels, as are teaching guidelines. These are too numerous and too varied to be easily summarized in a textbook such as this. The interested reader is strongly advised to consult the original de Bono and Raths et al. books listed at the end of this chapter.

The Effects of Expectations on Intelligence and Achievement

Shapiro (1960), tracing the history of the use of placebos in medicine, describes the discovery of a toothache cure by Professor Ranieri Gerbi of Pisa. It seems that in 1794 Professor Gerbi discovered that a small **worm,** later aptly named *Curculio antiodontaligious* (whatever that is), could effectively cure toothaches and prevent their recurrence for at least a year. The cure involved crushing the worm between the thumb and the forefinger and applying it gently to the afflicted tooth. Gerbi made such extravagant claims for his worm-cure that an investigatory body was set up to assess their validity. This body later reported that of hundreds of toothaches studied a full 68.5 percent succumbed to the worm. It is interesting that these "cures" occurred despite the fact that the chemical composition of the worm could not account for its effectiveness. Quite simply, the cure illustrates a "self-fulfilling prophecy."

A striking illustration of this same phenomenon is provided by the school-teacher who found on his desk a list of I.Q. scores for the students in his class. He copied them down in his record book for future reference. During the course of that year, the teacher often noticed how well the students with high I.Q.'s did when compared to those with low I.Q.'s. At the end of the year, being a good, industrious, and well-educated teacher, he computed a correlation coefficient for I.Q. and achievement scores, and found that the correlation was .80. In order to show how well he had taught, he brought this information to his principal. It was with some embarrassment that he learned that no I.Q. tests had been given to his class, but that the list of scores that he had found was nothing other than locker numbers.

It would appear from these illustrations that expectations can be instrumental in determining the outcomes of behavior. It has been intuitively suspected for some time that school achievement, as well as performance on less intellectual tasks, could probably be affected by communicating high expectations to students, verbally or nonverbally. The magnitude of this effect has remained largely undetermined, although several recent studies shed some new light on it.

A study of the effects of expectations reported by Rosenthal and Jacobson (1968a, 1968b) has tremendous implications for teacher behavior. These investigators worked in "Oak School"—a lower-middle-class institution. Teachers in this school were told they were participating in the validation of a new test designed to predict academic "blooming." They were told that children, particularly slow achievers,

often show sudden spurts in their intellectual development, and that the new test could identify these "spurters." The tests that the Oak School children were given were actually intelligence tests (the Flanagan Tests of General Ability). These were administered in the spring. The only experimental treatment undertaken was to give the teachers, the following September, information ostensibly about the test results. In fact they were given, casually to be sure, the names of a group of students randomly chosen from the entire school, but designated "late spurters." This group comprised about 20 percent of the school population. The only difference, then, between the "spurters" and the control groups was that the teachers had reason to expect increased performance on the part of the "spurters."

Not surprisingly, their expectations were fulfilled. What is more surprising is that not only did academic achievement—which is to some degree under teacher control—increase, but so did intellectual ability as measured by the Flanagan tests. The most dramatic "spurts" were for first grade students. These were probably the ones who had the greatest room for improvement. In addition, indications are that intelligence is more malleable at an earlier age.

The results of the Rosenthal and Jacobson study have since been questioned by a number of reviewers. Barber and Silver (1969a, 1969b) have critically examined conclusions derived from thirty-one studies cited by Rosenthal and Jacobson. In particular, they criticize the analyses employed in these studies, and what they allege is frequent misjudging, misrecording, and misrepresentation of data. As a result they conclude that the majority of the studies do not demonstrate the effects of experimenter bias. Rosenthal (1969) has replied to the Barber and Silver criticisms, pointing out that they had omitted relevant details in some of the experiments reviewed, and that a reanalysis of the original data still led to the same conclusions. A second rejoinder by Barber and Silver (1969b) attempts to show that the Rosenthal (1969) reply is "erroneous or misleading."

Implications of Research on
the Effects of Expectations

Obviously, the conclusion that teacher expectations undeniably and consistently affect pupil behavior is not fully warranted by the evidence. It is likely, nevertheless, that the phenomenon described by Rosenthal and Jacobson does occur occasionally in schools. How expectations function to affect behavior is still a matter for speculation. Nevertheless, the research on expectations has clear implications for teacher behavior.

In the first place, high achievement may well be no more susceptible than low achievement to the effects of increased expectations. For ethical reasons, this contention cannot be experimentally investigated since, if it were correct, the result would be to depress performance. Anecdotal observations support it, however. Consider the plight of slum children entering school. It is not at all unlikely that the teacher's expectations of low achievement for these children will be at least partly responsible for their inferior performance. Obviously, however, teachers cannot honestly expect high achievement from every student. Nevertheless, they should guard against the stereotype that associates children of less advantaged backgrounds with lower achievement. This precaution could prevent much educational injustice.

In the second place, the effect of teacher expectations need not be restricted to a few students. Conceivably, it can include the whole class. It is relatively simple, particularly where there are multiple sections of one class, for the teacher to communicate to the students that this is the best class she has ever taught. The effect can be quite remarkable.

Summary of Chapter 12

This chapter has discussed a number of techniques and programs that can be useful in increasing creative behavior and fostering thinking skills. In addition, the effect of expectations on intelligence and academic achievement was examined. The inference was made that creativity could also be affected by teacher expectations.

Main Points of Chapter 12

1. Industry has developed a number of techniques for increasing creativity. The commonest of these is Osborn's brainstorming technique. The key to the production of worthwhile ideas in a brainstorming session appears to be deferred evaluation.

2. Brainstorming groups comprise small numbers of people who are encouraged to think up as many wild ideas as they can for solving a specified problem. They are encouraged to emit *many* ideas and to modify other people's ideas freely.

3. The Gordon technique is a slight modification of Osborn's brainstorming. Instead of a detailed, specific problem, an abstraction of the problem is presented to the group. For example, the problem of developing a new can opener might begin with a discussion of "openness" (Osborn, 1957, p. xx).

4. Morphological analysis, another approach for making groups creative, involves dividing a problem into its attributes and brainstorming these. The ideas thought up in connection with attributes are then combined in all possible ways. An incredibly large number of solutions can be arrived at in this way.

5. The CNB (Collective Notebook) method was devised by Haefele. It consists of presenting participants with notebooks, on the first page of which a problem is presented together with some possible solutions. As members think of additional solutions, they jot them down in the book, which is later returned for evaluation.

6. I have devised a modification of the CNB method and brainstorming—the CBB (Collective Bulletin Board) method. This technique provides for individual participation together with the sharing of ideas as a group.

7. Classroom climate is related to creative behavior. Students in formal schools are characterized by lower scores on creativity measures than their counterparts in informal schools; warm, receptive teachers are more likely to encourage creativity; and severe competition is detrimental to creative performance.

8. Torrance, Hallman, and Taylor and Williams provide useful lists of do's and don'ts for promoting creative behavior in students.

9. De Bono and Raths et al. present a number of practical suggestions for developing skills involved in lateral (creative) and vertical (logical) thinking.

10. There is evidence to suggest that teacher expectations can serve as self-fulfilling prophecies. As such, they can increase scores on tests of academic achievement, of intelligence, of physical performance, and probably of creativity as well. It is also very likely that low expectations can have the opposite effect. The generality of this *effect* has been questioned.

Suggested Readings

The following three references should be of particular value for teachers concerned with the creative behavior of their students. The first has been translated into many different languages; it is undoubtedly the largest selling book in this area in recent years.

Osborn, A. *Applied Imagination.* New York: Charles Scribner's Sons, 1957.

The second reference is to an article by Maltzman that describes a procedure for training students for originality.

Maltzman, I. On the training of originality. *Psychological Review,* 1960, 67, 229–242.

The third reference is to a practical aid for actual use in the classroom. It consists of a collection of carefully researched activities designed to enhance creative behavior in students.

Parnes, S. J. *Creative Behavior Workbook.* New York: Charles Scribner's Sons, 1967.

The following book, by J. McV. Hunt, serves to highlight the relationship between intelligence and experience:

Hunt, J. McV. *Intelligence and Experience.* New York: Ronald Press, 1961.

The highly controversial article and book by Rosenthal and Jacobson present a provocative, though perhaps biased, view of the possible effects of expectations on academic achievement. The feelings generated by reading either the article or the book should probably be tempered by following it with the Barber and Silver article. This article strongly criticizes some of Rosenthal and Jacobson's methods and conclusions.

Rosenthal, R. and L. **Jacobson.** *Pygmalion in the Classroom: Teacher Expectations and Pupils' Intellectual Development.* New York: Holt, Rinehart and Winston, 1968.

Rosenthal, R. and L. **Jacobson.** Teacher expectations for the disadvantaged. *Scientific American,* April, 1968.

Barber, T. X. and M. J. **Silver.** Fact, fiction and the experimenter bias effect. *Psychological Bulletin Monographs Supplement,* 1969, 70, 1–29.

Practical advice relating to teaching for thinking is presented in:

de Bono, F. *Lateral Thinking: A Textbook of Creativity.* London: Ward Lock Educational, 1970.

de Bono, E. *Teaching Thinking.* London: Temple Smith, 1976.

Raths, L. E., A. **Jonas,** A. **Rothstein,** and S. **Wassermann.** *Teaching for Thinking: Theory and Application.* Columbus, Ohio: Charles E. Merrill, 1967.

In the summer, a bear's heart normally beats approximately forty times per minute. In winter, when the bear is denned-up, heart rate may drop as low as ten beats per minute. Amazingly, extreme cold rouses the bear as readily as does warmth. If this were not the case, many bears would freeze to death, for it is necessary for the bear to awaken and warm up when the temperature drops too low (Matthews, 1969).

13
Motivation and Teaching

We can ask where we come from, where we are going, and why. These questions, the philosophers would have us know, are the grand roots of the existential dilemma.

And is that so different from wondering why you are here listening to me; and why I am here talking to you?

Why is the question . . . ?

Advance Organizer My grandmother, an astute observer of human affairs, spent much of her knitting and quilting time in quiet contemplation of human motives. "Why do geese go south and ravens stay?" she would mutter as her needles clicked. "Why did René go out in the storm?" "Why did Frank get so excited about it?" "Why doesn't Robert want to go to school anymore?" This chapter might have been of some value to her, although the questions it presents are surely no more important than the questions she asked. But it does provide some answers for why we do or don't do things, and some suggestions for teachers whose role in the motivation of students can hardly be overstated.

Frank Twolips and Johnny West are two seventh grade students. Johnny West has a long nose, like Stan the milkman, and a low I.Q. On the other hand, Frank Twolips is quite intelligent. Ordinarily Frank learns more easily and more quickly than does Johnny. On occasion, however, the reverse is true. For example, their teacher once spent an entire social studies period describing how great apes were hunted in the hilly regions of tropical Africa. He explained in great detail how the native guides would lead the hunters through the dark labyrinth of tunnels that the apes construct from interwoven branches; how, in the throbbing heat of the noonday jungle, the guide would stop at each intersection in the tunnel and attempt, with flared nostrils, to detect the pungent odor of the apes. He dwelt at length on the social customs of the apes, which have been described by DeVore and others, in order to explain why it is that when the hunter suddenly finds himself in the territory that has been claimed by an ape tribe, it is the largest and most ferocious male that unhesitatingly charges, beating his chest with great loud thumps. And at this point the teacher pierced the tense air of the classroom with the blood-curdling roar of an angry ape.

It is interesting to note that Johnny West received the highest mark in the quiz on the African unit; Frank Twolips received a modest grade. Obviously, any wise grandmother could have explained why. She would have said that Johnny was interested, since it is a well-known fact that he is an avid hunter, and that Frank was less interested, since he tends to faint at the sight of blood.

A more sophisticated psychologist might say the same thing in different words. She might say, "The observed difference in *learning* is due to *motivational* factors." Indeed, the incident described above illustrates the relationship between motivation and learning. The latter deals primarily with the acquisition of information, whereas the former refers to the "why" of learning.

Motivational theory poses four questions. The first is: What initiates action? In other words, why does behavior even begin? The second question is: What directs behavior? Given that there is behavior, why is it this specific kind of behavior? The third question is: Why is behavior learned? And the fourth is: Why does behavior stop?

The importance of motivational theory to education should be obvious. If we can discover at least some of the reasons why people learn, or why certain behaviors are engaged in by some but not by others, we will almost certainly be in a better position to influence learning. Indeed, answers to the questions of how one learns and why one learns are often very difficult to separate.

These answers have varied throughout the history of psychology. They are outlined in the present chapter.

Instincts

Sometime ago, my English setter, a one-and-a-half-year-old bitch, gave birth to her first litter. Two hours before the births, she began to tear up newspapers and arrange them in a pile in a secluded corner of the garage. I joined her at this point in a clean white shirt, armed with a stack of fresh towels, a pair of blunt scissors, two yards of antiseptic cord, three human obstetrics textbooks, one veterinary textbook, and a large bottle of liquid depressant (for medicinal purposes only).

Two hours later the first of the little pups emerged, encased in its sac. The bitch turned, began to lick vigorously, broke the sac, and released the pup. She then cleaned the mucus from its nose, dried its body, stimulated its breathing, and moved it toward a nipple. Three more pups were delivered in the same expert fashion by a bitch which, unlike her bleary-eyed master, had never read a medical textbook.

This is a good example of instinctual behavior patterns in an animal. The question is, do people engage in behavior that can be similarly explained in terms of instincts?

Among the earliest attempts to solve problems of motivation were the various instinct theories (McDougall, 1908; Bernard, 1924). **Instincts** were broadly defined to include any type of behavior that seemed to be generally human. For example, Bernard (1924) listed some 6,000 human instincts, ranging from those familiar to the layperson (sex, maternal, gregarious) to such remote inclinations as the tendency "to avoid eating apples that grow in one's own garden" (p. 212).

The obvious disadvantage of this approach is that the only behaviors that are ever explained are those for which an instinct has been named. In addition, of course, naming the instinct neither explains the behavior nor predicts it. At best, the whole process is entirely circular. If humans make love, it is obvious that we have an instinct for mating (or perhaps for making love—the point is never quite clear). Why, then, does one make love? Well, because one has this instinct, you see. How do we know about this instinct? Well, because people make love. Why is there an instinct for making love? For survival—propagation of the species and all that. Well then, there must be an instinct for survival, too. Of course. *Ad infinitum.*

Currently, the notion of instincts is applied more to animal than to human behavior (Thorpe, 1963). The term is also defined more precisely as *complex, species-specific, relatively unmodifiable behavior patterns.* A related term, **imprinting,** has been introduced by Lorenz (1952), Tinbergen (1951), and other ethologists (scientists, usually zoologists, engaged primarily in studying the behavior of lower animal forms) to explain some behaviors in animals. Imprinting refers to the appearance, particularly in birds, of complex behaviors apparently as a result of exposure to an appropriate object or movement (releaser) at a **critical period** in the animal's life. For example, newly hatched ducklings will follow the first moving object they encounter, and apparently become attached to it. Fortunately this object is usually the mother duck. Lorenz (1952) reports, however, the case of a greylag goose which imprinted on him and followed him around like a dog. Much to his embarrassment, when it matured it insisted on foisting its affections on him during mating season.

Although few complex human behaviors appear to be instinctual in the sense that many animal behaviors are, we may be born with potential instincts that are modified through experience. Perhaps a mother, left to her own devices, would instinctively know how to deliver and care for her child. Perhaps not. In any event, experience, culture, and evolution have so modified our behavior that the question of the existence of human instinct has become largely irrelevant.

Psychological Hedonism

A second approach used in accounting for the direction of human behavior has been to make what on the surface appears to be an entirely logical and obviously true statement: We act so as to avoid pain and obtain pleasure. This intuitively attractive explanation for human behavior is referred to as *psychological* **hedonism.**

But psychological hedonism does little to explain behavior, for it fails to specify those conditions which are pleasurable or painful. And this is necessary,

---

IN STINKS

There is a rather bad story about skunks that I often relate to my eager classes as we approach a discussion of instinct. It seems that a mother skunk had given birth to identical twin skunks—both female as it happened. Identical twin skunks, as you well know, are extremely difficult to tell apart. Yet this wise mother could always differentiate between her twins whom she had named, in a moment of whimsy, In and Out. When asked how she managed to tell In and Out apart, she said, sagely, "Instincts."

Instincts have been defined as "complex, species-specific, relatively unmodifiable behavior patterns." The definition is broken down and examined below.

"Complex": Since the behavior patterns that fall within the realm of instinct are complex, all simple behaviors are excluded. Thus eye-blinking in response to air blown in the eye, sucking behavior, and the host of other simple behaviors of which humans are capable at birth are not instincts. More precisely they are reflexes, the principal difference between reflexes and instincts being that the former involve some simple stimulus-response behavior as opposed to a chain of related behaviors.

"Species-specific": Instincts are not general across species, but are general within species. Thus all ducks are characterized by a migratory instinct and all bears by the urge to hibernate in winter.

"Relatively unmodifiable": It was long believed that instincts were impervious to environmental influences since they are largely innate. Research has now shown, however, that instincts can be modified by the environment. Female rats reared in deprived environments do not exhibit the maternal and nesting instincts characteristic of normally reared female rats. It remains true, nevertheless, that instincts are relatively unmodifiable.

because even if it is true that the pain-pleasure principle governs our activities, we can predict and control these activities only if we know what gives pleasure and what gives pain.

Need-Drive Theories

One attempt to answer this question has taken the form of **need-drive theories.** A need is a specific or general state of deficiency or lack within an organism. Drives, on the other hand, are the energies or the tendencies to react that are aroused by needs. For example, we have a need for food; this need gives rise to a hunger drive.

The relationship between the need-drive theories and a hedonistic interpretation of motivation is implicit in the assumption that to be in a state of need is unpleasant, while to satisfy a need is pleasant. It is often debated in esoteric academic circles whether the pleasure lies in the actual satisfaction of the need (e. g., the act of consumption in the case of food); or in the reduction in muscular tension that accompanies the reduction in drive that accompanies consumption. (See Hull, 1943, 1952.)

If one assumes that need satisfaction is pleasant while a state of need is unpleasant, the relationship between need theory and hedonism is obvious. The identification and description of needs simply makes clear the nature of pain and pleasure. A list of needs is a list of conditions that when satisfied are pleasant and when unsatisfied are unpleasant.

In a broad sense, needs can be divided into two categories: psychological and **physiological.** The latter are manifested in actual tissue changes, while the former are more closely related to mental functioning. Other differences exist between the two categories. Psychological needs are never completely satisfied, while physiological needs can be. In addition, psychological needs are probably more often learned than are physiological needs.

Physiological needs include the need for food, water, sleep and rest, activity, and sex. Psychological needs include the need for affection, belonging, achievement, independence, social recognition, and self-esteem.

Maslow

Needs may be classified in many ways; this list is but one example. Murray (1938) lists twelve physical (**viscerogenic**) and twenty-eight psychological (**psychogenic**) needs. On the other hand, Maslow (1970) proposes two general need systems: the basic needs and the meta-needs. The basic needs consist of:

physiological needs: the basic biological needs—for example, the need for food, water, and temperature regulation

safety needs: those needs which are manifested in people's efforts to maintain sociable, predictable, orderly, and therefore nonthreatening environments

love and belongingness needs: the need to develop relationships involving reciprocal affection; the need to be a member of a group

self-esteem needs: the need for cultivating and maintaining a high opinion of oneself; the need to have others hold one in high esteem

These needs are hierarchical in the sense that higher-level needs will be attended to only after lower-level ends are satisfied. While people need food, they are not likely to be concerned with love or with self-esteem. History provides striking examples of the prepotency of lower-level needs where, in hungry nations, thousands of children were abandoned while parents devoted themselves to their own survival. Such practices were prevalent in eighteenth-century Europe (see Kessen, 1965).

Maslow's basic needs are also termed *deficiency needs* since they motivate (lead to behavior) when the organism is deficient with respect to a need (i.e., lacks food or water). The meta-needs are termed *growth needs* since they motivate behaviors that do not result from deficiencies, but that result, instead, from our instinctual tendencies toward growth. Unlike the basic needs, the meta-needs are not hierarchical. All supersede the basic needs, and will be attended to only once the basic needs are reasonably satisfied. The meta-needs include aesthetic and cognitive urges associated with such virtues as truth and goodness, with the acquisition of knowledge, and with the appreciation of beauty, order, and symmetry (see Figure 13.1). The highest need in Maslow's system is our tendency toward self-actualization—the

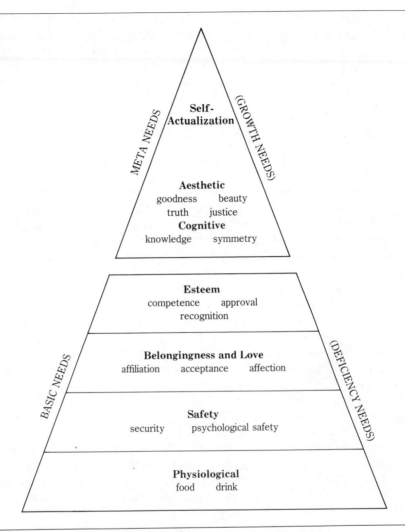

Figure 13.1 *Maslow's Hierarchy of Needs*

unfolding and fulfillment of self. Recall from Chapter 8 that self-actualization is a process rather than a state. It is a process of growth—of becoming—a process that most humanistic psychologists consider absolutely central to the healthy experience of being human. And although such abstractions as beauty, goodness, truth, and self-actualization are difficult to describe and even more difficult to examine in a scientific way, it is difficult to deny that they represent "moving" concerns and processes for a great many individuals. The occasional frustration of science with those more humanistically oriented relates more appropriately to the imprecision, abstractness, and mystery that define the human experience than to the humanistically oriented thinker.

Listing needs in this fashion may or may not lead to an accurate description of the human condition. In any case, one would probably have to admit that many human activities exemplify behaviors that are not tension-reducing but tension-inducing. This point is clarified later in this chapter.

Needs and Teaching

A great many human behaviors do not appear to result from efforts to satisfy needs. Nonetheless it is important for teachers to be aware of needs in their students. It is obvious, for example, that certain basic biological needs must be satisfied if the teaching-learning process is to be effective. A hungry or thirsty student is almost certain to find concentration difficult to maintain. By the same token, a hungry teacher is probably seldom as effective as his well-fed, smiling counterpart. Other basic needs, such as the need for sex, are not likely to present a very serious problem for younger students. Unfortunately (or fortunately perhaps?) the same cannot be said about a teacher—young or old.

Since, in our society, most children's basic needs are adequately taken care of, the teacher is not often called upon to walk around with a bag of cookies and a jug of milk. Psychological needs are quite another matter. It will be recalled that these include the need for affection, for belonging, for achievement, for social recognition, and for self-actualization. A useful exercise for a prospective teacher might be to consider what a "bag" filled with the wherewithal to satisfy these needs would look like. Teachers who, through their actions, can give each individual student a sense of accomplishment and belonging are probably carrying such a bag. (As the popular expression has it, "That's their bag.")

By now it should be apparent that teachers can make direct use of their knowledge of student needs for instructional purposes. Obviously many students can have their needs for achievement and self-actualization, among others, satisfied through school-related activities. Such activities must not be so difficult that success is impossible, nor so easy that success is meaningless. The meaningfulness of these activities, their relevance to the student's life, and the recognition that they will gain from peers, parents, and teachers are likewise of paramount importance.

It should also be mentioned that self-actualization, the process of becoming whatever one can through one's own efforts, can not only be facilitated (and, indeed, made possible) by a dedicated teacher, but can also become the very goal of the instructional process. This is the strongest motive behind the humanistic movement in education.

Arousal Theory

In the spring of 1969, a friend and I came down an eighty-mile stretch of river in a fifteen-foot fiberglass canoe. This river, for most of its length, runs a leisurely course displaying from its banks a vast panorama of peaceful, farm-dotted prairie. But on occasion it plunges in wild abandon over boulder-strewn rapids and around corners where, in the boiling maelstrom, no human and no beast can easily survive.

In the spring, the eighty-mile stretch of swollen river that courses from the foothills of the mountains to the prairies is almost entirely covered with white water which lashes in furious frenzy at floating beaver-cut logs as they tear among the precariously anchored rocks in its bed.

This was the stretch that we traversed by canoe and it was here that, in the blinding rain of a freezing May morning, we plunged through the hellish, roaring, watery chaos known on detailed maps as the Blue Rapids. And, at the height of that insane dash through the turbulent waters, my friend pierced the air with an animal scream of pure exhilaration.

In the spring of 1961, I sat in the back row of an introductory educational psychology course. The instructor, a nondescript, middle-aged man who had almost mastered the art of the monotone, was reading from page 87 in a psychology text. The instructor had begun, thirty-four minutes earlier, in the middle of the second paragraph on page 81, where he had been interrupted by the buzzer during the previous lecture. He would continue without pause until the next buzzer.

Between the thirty-fourth and the thirty-eighth minute, forty-two of the fifty-six students in that class yawned. Four of the others were visibly sleeping. I could not see the remaining ten (I was one of those who yawned).

These two incidents illustrate the two extremes of what is referred to as **arousal**—a concept with both physiological and psychological aspects, and one which is absolutely central to many contemporary theories of motivation.

Psychological Arousal

In one sense arousal refers to nothing more complicated than excitement. More precisely, however, arousal refers to such qualities of human responding as attention, alertness, or vigilance. In other words, level of arousal refers to an individual's degree of wakefulness.

Physiological Arousal

Arousal is one of the few variables studied in psychology for which there are observable physiological counterparts. These consist primarily of changes in the chemoelectrical aspects of the nervous system—changes which are indirectly observable through brain wave patterns (electroencephalograph recordings—eeg's). Deep sleep and some meditative states are sometimes accompanied by theta or delta waves. Low arousal (resting state) is characterized by slow, deep, regular waves (**alpha** type); high arousal is characterized by shallower, more irregular, and faster waves (**beta** type). Increasing arousal is also accompanied by changes in the electrical properties of the skin (usually increased conductivity, probably due to perspiration, and ordinarily measured on the palms—sometimes referred to as a galvanic skin response—gsr—or as electrodermal response), as well as by changes in respiration rate, heart rate, blood pressure, or blood vessel diameter (see Hebron, 1966; French, 1957).

Cue and Arousal Functions

Hebb (1958) identified the two functions of stimuli as the **cue function** and the arousal function. The term *cue* refers to the message associated with a stimulus. Whenever an individual reacts to a sight, a sound, a taste, a smell, or any sensation, that sensation must have some particular physical property that, when it is transmitted to some part of the brain, allows the individual to determine what it is that is being looked at, heard, tasted, or smelled. This property is the cue.

It appears that the cue function of a stimulus is transmitted relatively directly to the sensory areas of the cortex via neural pathways. At the same time, however, from each of the major nerve trunks going to the cortex, there are branching nerves going into the brain stem (Moruzzi and Magoun, 1949). The effect of stimulation is not restricted to the transmission of a simple message (cue) to the cortex. It includes the general activation of wide areas of the cortex via the brain stem—specifically, via that portion of the brain stem known as the *reticular activating system* (RAS) (French, 1957) or the nonspecific projection system (NSPS) (Hebb,

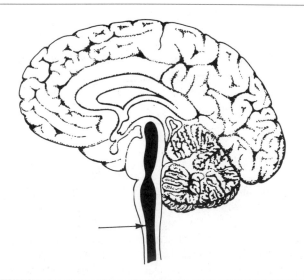

Figure 13.2 *The Reticular Activating System*

1955). This diffuse activation defines the arousal function of a stimulus (see Figure 13.2).

The normal living human being has been described as an organism whose state of "consciousness" (for want of a better term) varies from sleep to high excitement. This variation has been attributed largely to functioning of the RAS, which responds selectively to incoming impulses and in turn activates the cortex. Activation of the cortex is essential for normal wakeful functioning. Likewise, reduction of cortical activity is essential for sleep. When anxiety or pain keeps a person awake, it is because these conditions, acting through the RAS, prevent that reduction in cortical activity which would permit sleep.

Sources of Arousal

The primary sources of arousal are the **distance receptors** (hearing and vision), but arousal may be affected by all other sources of stimulation, including activity of the brain. An organism's level of activation is probably a function of the impact of all stimuli present at a given time. However, there is no direct relationship between amount of stimulation and arousal level. Some properties of stimuli (i.e., meaningfulness, intensity, surprisingness, novelty, complexity, and incongruity [Berlyne, 1960]) make them more arousal-inducing than others. Therefore, *amount* of stimulation is probably less critical in determining level of activation than are the above-mentioned variables.

BIOFEEDBACK

There are a host of fascinating and potentially useful experiments related to arousal (see Wallace, 1970, for example). Many are lumped under the heading "biofeedback experiments" since they involve providing subjects with instant information about arousal level so that they can control their own arousal. In a typical experiment subjects are connected to an electroencephalogram recorder (also called a polygraph or more popularly an alpha recorder). Simple alpha recorders differentiate between alpha (normal resting arousal level) and beta (more vigilant, excited) waves. The object of the experiment is to have the subject control brain functioning in order to increase the proportion of alpha to beta waves. It has repeatedly been demonstrated that this is quite feasible without any direct instructions. Indeed, the procedure used can be explained in terms of an operant conditioning model. Whenever subjects emit a sufficient proportion of alpha waves, a tone is heard. Since they have been told that the object is to keep the tone going as much as they can, the sound serves as reinforcement. Eventually most subjects find that they can reach the "alpha state" much more easily than was originally the case. Interestingly, practitioners of Zen, Yoga, and transcendental meditation can, through the practice of their respective meditative techniques, arrive at similar states of low arousal—a condition that is believed to be highly conducive to physical and mental health.
Inexpensive alpha recorders are currently on the market—some good and some less so. The tranquility and peace of ancient oriental meditative states may be within your reach!

Arousal and Motivation

The relationship between arousal and motivation can be seen more clearly when predicated on two assumptions, both of which appear to have considerable empirical support.

1. For any given activity there is a level of arousal at which performance will be optimal.

2. At any given time, an individual behaves in such a way as to maintain the level of arousal that is most nearly optimal for ongoing behavior.

The first assumption simply means that certain activities can best be performed under conditions of relatively high arousal, while others are best performed under conditions of lower arousal. It is evident that such activities as sleeping or resting, or activities involving routine, habitual responses such as counting one's fingers, driving a car, or asking for a raise (?) do not require a very high level of arousal. On the other hand, intense, concentrated activities such as writing examinations require higher levels of arousal. The relationship between arousal level and performance is illustrated in Figure 13.3.

As can be seen from Figure 13.3, the relationship between behavior and arousal level is represented by an inverted u-shaped curve (Hebb, 1955). At the lowest level of arousal, sleep, there is little or no response to external stimulation. Try asking a sleeping person what the capital of Iran is. Ask him again just as he is waking up. He may say "Pardon"—or he may respond in some less printable manner. As he becomes more fully awake, he may respond correctly (if he knows the answer). If, however, in your zeal for observing the relationship between arousal and behavior, you proceed to set your subject's house on fire, awaken him with a bucket of cold water, inform him that his house is on fire, and then ask him what the capital of Iran is, you will probably observe the ineffectiveness of behavior which accompanies too high arousal.

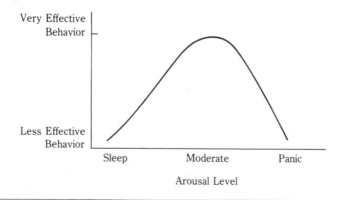

Figure 13.3

Persons under great stress often engage in inappropriate behavior. There was the woman in Dover, Delaware, who, after surprising the back of my car with her Volkswagen, hobbled around the cars eight times, dropping a "damn" at each of the four corners of her circle (??)—most inappropriate behavior. There was the trapper, who, waking to find his cabin on fire, ran to the door and proceeded to burn to death as he repeatedly tried to turn the doorknob. The door was locked, but the key was in the lock facing him. There are instances of students "freezing" when writing examinations, and responding by repeating their name several hundred times, or by not writing anything at all. There is stage fright which causes actors to forget their lines and professors to tell lies because they have forgotten the truth (not because they didn't know the truth). There are the tragic examples of panic-stricken people in crowds trampling each other to death in their haste to escape danger (Schultz, 1964). There are the studies of Marshall (cited by Bruner, 1957b), who found that fewer than one-quarter of the infantrymen in combat during World War II actually fired their rifles when under heavy fire. Fortunately, it is probable that the enemy did no better.

The second assumption is that people behave so as to maintain their arousal level somewhere near the optimal. In other words, if arousal level is too low the individual will seek to increase it; if it is too high she will attempt to lower it. If this is true, and if we know what factors increase or decrease arousal, we can perhaps

explain and predict some behaviors not easily explained in other ways. When a person faces a moment of great fear, her first reaction may well be to flee. The effect, if she succeeded in escaping, would be to remove the source of fear and consequently to reduce her arousal level. When a person is bored, her level of arousal is probably too low. She may then engage in more "stimulating" activity: reading, sports (participating or observing), or, if she is a student, daydreaming. The effect should be an increase in arousal level.

Arousal and Learning

Like effective behavior, maximally effective learning takes place under conditions of optimal arousal. Low levels of arousal are characterized by low attentiveness—a condition which, in a student, rarely leads to effective learning.

There is an experiment that can be conducted by any teacher to illustrate this point. Prepare a good lesson full of content, write it out, and read it to your class very slowly in a soothing monotone. Then deliver the same lesson to another comparable class in your usual exciting, stimulating style. Test the relative retention of your two classes.

Controlling Arousal

The relevance of arousal theory for education depends on the teacher's control over the variables that affect arousal. Ideally, all students in a given class should be working at their optimal levels. But there are a number of problems. Are all students at the same level? How does the teacher know the level of each student? How can arousal level be changed?

In the first place, all members of a class are probably not at the same level of arousal. In the second place, the teacher doesn't know the exact level of each student. Probably those who are asleep, nearing sleep, or just waking up are at low levels of arousal; those who show signs of panic and impending flight are at higher levels of arousal.

But the really central question for teachers is: How can arousal level be controlled? It has been pointed out that the primary sources of arousal are the distance receptors, but that all other sources of stimulation also have some effect. Furthermore, it is less the amount than the intensity, meaningfulness, novelty, complexity, and incongruity of stimulation that affect arousal. There are other factors as well. Degree of risk or personal involvement is probably directly related to arousal level, as is illustrated by the arousing effects of risk-taking behavior.

Teachers in a classroom are stimuli. They control a very significant part of all the stimulation to which the student will be reacting. The intensity, meaningfulness, and complexity of what teachers say, of what they do, of how they look, and of what they write all directly affect the attention (arousal) of their students. They can keep them at an uncomfortably high level of arousal by presenting material that is too complex—and the students may reduce that arousal by ceasing to pay attention. Teachers can also keep students at too low a level of arousal by failing to present meaningful material in a stimulating manner—and again students may cease to pay attention.

Since changes in stimulation are usually arousing, changes in voice should increase student attentiveness. The range of the human voice in terms of tone, volume, inflection, and so on is amazing. Given this range, it is also amazing that some teachers scarcely depart from the monotone. A useful exercise for teachers (or prospective teachers) is to monitor some of their presentations with a tape recorder in order to learn how effective their voice changes (if any) are. They might also use a video tape recorder in order to see themselves teaching. Since stimuli that emanate from a teacher consist not only of verbal signals but also of visual ones, changes in appearance, in posture, and in position together with the use of expressive gestures should affect students' arousal levels.

Many other specific examples could be mentioned. But the essential thing for the teacher to remember is that arousal increases in proportion to the intensity, meaningfulness, novelty, and complexity of stimulation. Consequently *all changes* in teacher behavior that tend to intensify these properties of stimuli may increase attention as well. The key word is, without doubt, *variety*.

A teacher's motivational problems seldom involve too high an arousal level. More often problems arise because teachers fail to awaken their students sufficiently, or because they actually put them to sleep. What can you do?

1. You can fire a miniature cannon. That is an intense and novel stimulus.

2. You can stand on your head, walk on your hands, jump in the air, holler "Yahoo," or, as one of my colleagues once did before he was dismissed, you can pound your fist on the desk and say very quietly, *"Nghaa."*

3. You can present problems of increasing complexity, interest, and meaningfulness.

4. You can involve students in projects. The personal involvement is accompanied by a risk of personal failure. This is probably arousing.

5. You can read this book for good ideas.

6. Think. . . .

THE PLEASURE CENTERS AND A
LITTLE SCIENCE FICTION

A rather striking procedure is sometimes employed in animal learning laboratories on university campuses. Electrodes are used to dupe animals into "thinking" that they have just engaged in a satisfying sexual experience or that they have eaten or drunk something equally satisfying. The electrodes are implanted in certain areas of the midbrain nuclei or in hypothalamus (Olds, 1956). The transmission of a mild current to these parts of the brain has been repeatedly proven to be highly rewarding. Hungry animals will ignore food in order to stimulate themselves (electrically). Some, when they have control over the stimulation (i.e., by pressing a lever a rat causes a mild current to be delivered to its hypothalamus) will engage in self-stimulation more than 2,000 times per hour for twenty-four consecutive hours (Olds, 1956). On the other hand, it is also possible to punish an animal by implanting the electrodes in a different part of the brain (lower parts of the midbrain system).

There are at least two relatively precise ways of controlling activity in the RAS other than by controlling external stimulation. One involves the use of drugs. Depressants have the effect of inhibiting activity in the reticular formation; stimulants have the opposite effect. The other is to utilize electrode implants to activate the RAS directly.

Imagine, if you will, 1984. The Dean of Academia awakens gently from a dreamless sleep when his reticular activator engages at .0005 ampere. He turns to his control panel, drops his nourishment pill down his throat, and flicks toggle switch number three. It controls stimulation of his own pleasure centers. He now thinks he has had a satisfying meal—or something!

He then turns to his wider responsibilities. Seven A.M. He depresses switch forty-two. Four million seven hundred thousand four hundred twenty-two seventh grade pupils receive a mild jolt and awaken. The current is increased and now 4,700,422 pupils are wide awake and in high gear. Away they go to school, where, if they learn, they will receive a mild zap in the hypothalamus—and if they don't, well, a mild zap below the midline. The ultimate reward is to control one's own activator.

Imagine tomorrow. Twenty thousand twelve-year-old children in academia awaken from dreamless sleeps, pop their daily dosage of bennies into their mouths, and go out looking for arousal jags—sex, dope, and good books. At night they pop their evening doses of tranquilizers into their mouths and sleep dreamlessly till morning. The ultimate reward is to control your own prescription.

The reader is invited to add to this list. He or she is also cautioned that even suggestions which seem facetious, whimsical, or absurd can sometimes be related directly to the content of a lesson and can then be employed with good results.

A Second Look at Motivation

Instincts. Pain and pleasure. Needs, drives. Arousal. An interesting assortment of explanations for human behavior, what? And valuable explanations, too, as has been shown in a number of places through the first part of this chapter. But their value is limited, as you might already have guessed, and the explanations they offer, only partial. There are other explanations as well, some very new and not yet firmly established. These explanations, as they are described here, are really very different from the explanations provided in the first part of this chapter. And the nature of that difference is very significant, for it is indicative of some major current movements in many areas of psychology.

Traditional accounts of motivation view the human organism as a passive being, unmoved and unmoving in the absence of those external or internal conditions that define needs, drives, and arousal levels, that trigger instinctual or primitive learned behavior, or that are clearly associated with pain or pleasure. In other words, psychology has, inadvertently or otherwise, described an organism that is highly *reactive*, often in unpredictable ways, but that is considerably less *active*. Put yet another way, we are seen as *reacting* to certain recognizable situations and states, but not as *acting* in their absence. Hence the contention that traditional theories have painted an overly passive and mechanistic picture of humans.

The "newer" approaches, collectively labeled *cognitive* positions for reasons that will be made clear shortly, present a contrasting view. Humans are seen not as the victims of internal or external prods moving them willy-nilly through their daily activities, but as organisms whose ongoing activity is mediated largely by conscious evaluation, anticipation, and emotion. Bolles (1974) makes the point that there are no unmotivated behaviors; hence motivation is not some special force that should be isolated and classified as needs are isolated and listed. It is quite simply a characteristic of ongoing behavior. The plea of the contemporary cognitive theorist is not that psychology begin to search for new subjects, but that psychologists turn their attention to ongoing behavior in natural situations, taking into account what may well be the single most important feature of human motivation: *our ability to delay gratification* (Mischel and Baker, 1975; Toner, 1974). So much of our behavior is motivated by our anticipations of distant outcomes that the analysis of human behavior in terms of those conditions that seem relevant to the behavior of rats and young children is often fruitless for school children and adults. We can delay gratification by virtue of some uniquely human abilities involved in thinking, imagining, and verbalization. It is through a study of these ongoing cognitive processes that the cognitive theorist searches for understanding and explanations.

*A Short History of
Cognitive Motivation Theories*

Cognitive theories often present bewildering arrays of facts and speculation, not easily organized or understood. We are, after all, a complex animal. Some of the principal ideas underlying cognitive theories, however, are relatively simple and potentially valuable. These ideas developed roughly as follows:

1. Almost half a century ago Tolman (1932) attempted to break from the behavioristic and "mechanistic" theories that then dominated psychology. In particular, he insisted that an organism's behavior is not affected solely by stimuli and related drives and needs, but that it is determined largely by the organism's *expectancy* of being rewarded, and by the *value* attached to that reward. Expectancy and value have become key terms in cognitive motivational theories.

2. Rotter (1954) developed a social-personality theory which describes people in terms of their tendencies to ascribe failure or success to internal or external causes. There are those who typically take responsibility for successes and failures. These are the internally oriented people, sometimes described as those with an *internal locus of control*. In contrast, there are those who attribute success or failure to external causes. Their locus of control is external; in other words, they look to external explanations for their successes and failures.

Subsequent investigations with the externality-internality dimension have established that it is a useful and valid way of classifying people's typical reactions to their own behavior (Rotter, 1966). It seems clear that some people are highly dependent on others and operate under varying degrees of "felt powerlessness" (externally oriented); others are considerably more independent and operate under varying degrees of "felt powerfulness" (internally oriented).

3. Heider (1958) elaborated Rotter's external-internal dimension into a motivational theory, arguing that there must be some interaction between "personal causality" and motivation. In particular, Heider argued that *intention* is what motivates behavior—that behavior cannot be said to be motivated by external or internal forces unless the organism *intends* to reach a goal. Thus, intention, expectancy, and value are central concepts in this cognitive explanation of behavior.

4. A more systematic motivational theory, premised on Tolman, Heider, and Rotter, is advanced and investigated by Weiner (1972, 1974). It is described in the following section.

Attribution and Achievement Motivation

Weiner begins with the assumption that people do attribute their successes and failures to internal or external causes. For purposes of analysis, he breaks these causes into separate areas. If, for example, I am internally oriented, I might attribute my successes and failures to my ability, to effort, or to some combination of the two. In either case, I am attributing my performance to causes for which I assume some personal responsibility. If, on the other hand, I am externally oriented, I will attribute my performance to factors for which I have no responsibility, and therefore over which I have no control: namely, luck or task difficulty. Thus, if I fail, I will assume

that the task was too difficult or that I was unlucky (or both); conversely, if I succeed, I will attribute my success to the easiness of the task or to luck (see Figure 13.4). Clearly, there are other causes to which performance can also be attributed (mood, illness, fatigue, for example), but these are more personal, more variable, and not amenable to scientific investigation.

The implications of this classification of personal attribution become clearer when considered in relation to what is known or suspected about *achievement motivation*. Several decades ago, McClelland (1953) and his associates began to investigate

External	Internal
Difficulty (task easy or too difficult)	Ability (intelligence, skill, or the lack thereof)
Luck (bad or good)	Effort (hard work, industriousness, self-discipline, or laziness, distractions, lack of time)

Figure 13.4 *Why did you fail or succeed? Research suggests that you will attribute the results of your behavior to one or more causes, and that this attribution reveals something about your personality and your achievement orientation.*

what appears to be an intuitively valid observation: Some individuals behave as though they have a high need to achieve, to be successful, to reach some standard of excellence; others behave as though they are more afraid of failing than desiring of success. Measures were then devised to identify those with high need for achievement (abbreviated nAch) and those with low need for achievement. The principal measure, still in use, particularly for research purposes, presents subjects with pictures from the Thematic Apperception Test (TAT). Pictures selected typically portray one or more individuals doing something (a boy playing the violin for example), and ask the subject to describe what is happening in the picture, what has happened in the past, and what will happen in the future. This *projective* test assumes that individuals *project* their personal feelings and thoughts into the descriptions. Thus, those individuals for whom achievement is an important motive provide descriptions replete with achievement imagery and themes. A count of these achievement-related references provides a crude measure of achievement orientation. Despite the problems associated with this type of measurement, research indicates that individuals who score high on this measure of need for achievement also tend to be the high achievers in school. Other relevant findings in this area are that high need achievers are typically moderate risk takers. They attempt tasks that are moderately difficult, thus providing themselves with a challenge but at the same time keeping their probability of success fairly high (McClelland, 1958). In contrast, low need achievers typically attempt tasks that are very difficult or very easy. The relevance of this finding was not immediately obvious, and did not become obvious until the elaboration of attribution theory. If I attempt a very difficult task and fail, I will probably attribute my failure to task difficulty, a factor over which I have no control; assume no personal responsibility; and therefore experience no negative affect (emotion). If I am successful, there will again be little positive affect, since my success is not due to factors over which I have any control, but to external factors. Moderate risk takers, on the other hand, can attribute success to skill or effort; similarly, they can still attribute failure to personal factors. In either case, there will be considerably more emotional involvement in the outcomes of their performances.

It appears reasonable to suppose, then, that high need achievers will tend to be internally oriented whereas low need achievers will more likely attribute their performance to external factors. This supposition is, in fact, borne out by research (Weiner et al., 1971; Weiner, 1974). Knowledge of the relationship between achievement orientation and causal attribution can, as is shown in a later section of this chapter, be of considerable value to the teacher. A second relationship among motivational factors is also of importance. It involves the notion of competence.

White (1959) advanced the notion that all humans are born with a need to strive toward competence. As he describes competence, it is not very different from the desire to meet certain standards of excellence that characterizes the high need achiever. Competence is manifested not only in the ability to perform, but in notions of the self that accompany successful performance. Chief among these self-notions are feelings of confidence, of worth—in short, of competence. Put another way, individuals are driven by a need to achieve competence; successful fulfillment of this need will be manifested in a positive "self-concept." In this connection, it is revealing that positive self-concept (good feelings about one's self and one's capabilities) are highly related to success both in school and in interpersonal affairs (Coopersmith, 1967; Coleman, 1966). It follows, then, that, if self-concept can be enhanced through school experiences, increased feelings of competence, more internal orientation, and a higher degree of achievement motivation might result.

Educational Implications

Assuming that high achievement needs are desirable, can these be increased in students, even if they result largely from early parent-child interaction? Research and common sense agree that they can. Alschuler (1972) and others (for example, McClelland and Winter, 1969) have devised achievement programs for use in schools and with adults in economically deprived circumstances. Details of these programs are beyond the scope of this text, although the interested reader can obtain more information by consulting the readings annotated at the end of this chapter. In general, such programs provide learners with a series of situations in which they are invited to take risks, make predictions about their performances, modify their predictions on the basis of ongoing feedback, and earn or lose points or token money on the basis of their performance. One of the objectives is simply to encourage learners to make use of information concerning their previous performance, to arrive at realistic goals, and to assume *personal responsibility* for their performance. Initial indications are that these programs can be quite successful in increasing measured need for achievement as well as in improving actual performance (Alschuler, 1972).

A more general and perhaps more speculative educational implication that can be derived from a combined consideration of achievement and attribution theory concerns the structuring of conditions that appear to be related to attribution. Weiner (1974) suggests that a number of specific factors are involved in an individual's evaluation of causes of success and failure. Clearly, the difficulty of a task might be determined by its objective nature. In practice, however, a student is likely to judge a task difficult or easy on the basis of previous experience with similar tasks and knowledge of other people's successes and failures. Ability is most often inferred from past failures and successes. Effort is judged relatively objectively in terms of time and energy expended on a task, and luck is inversely related to the control subjects assume they have over the outcomes of their behaviors.

In most school-related tasks, luck should have little bearing on performance, though there are those students who will invoke that lady repeatedly in any case. They blame her for the fact that they have "unluckily" studied the wrong sections, inadvertently misaligned their answer sheets, or had the misfortune of being presented with inferior teachers. Teachers can exercise some control over the other three major categories to which performance outcomes can be attributed (effort, ability, or task difficulty). It should come as no great surprise that repeated failures are likely to have a negative effect on self-concepts and on feelings of competence, and that those individuals who have failed more than they have succeeded will eventually be reluctant to attribute their failures to ability. Indeed, it appears reasonable to predict that repeated failures are likely to contribute to external attribution and concomitant feelings of powerlessness. By the same token, repeated successes, provided they represent tasks of moderate or high difficulty (rather than tasks too absurdly simple) are more likely to lead to positive self-concepts, feelings of competence, the acceptance of personal responsibility for performance, and high achievement drives. The key phrase is, undoubtedly, *personal responsibility*. To the extent that students accept personal responsibility for their performance, they will be emotionally involved, success will enhance their self-concepts, motivational forces will be largely intrinsic rather than extrinsic, and the problems of classroom management, discussed in the next chapter, will become interesting pedagogical problems rather than discipline problems.

Summary of Chapter 13

This chapter has presented several explanations of human behavior. Instinct theory, psychological hedonism, need-drive theories, and arousal theories were presented briefly, along with some instructional implications relating to each of these. Particular attention was paid to arousal theory. Attribution theory and its relationship to competence, achievement orientation, and self-concept were also discussed.

Main Points in Chapter 13

1. Theories of motivation attempt to answer questions dealing with the initiation, the direction, and the reinforcement of behavior. Obviously, these answers (if available and valid) are tremendously significant for education.

2. Instinct theory as applied to human behavior is largely of historical rather than contemporary interest. Instincts are complex unlearned patterns of behavior common to an entire species (e.g., nesting behavior in ducks or rats). Whatever human instincts remain have become so confounded by culture that the concept retains little explanatory value for a study of human behavior.

3. Psychological hedonism is an attempt to give theoretical recognition to the observation that people usually behave so as to achieve pleasure and avoid pain. Need theories offer one definition of pain and pleasure. The satisfaction of a need (physical or psychological) is assumed to be pleasant; not to satisfy a need is unpleasant.

4. Different theorists have advanced various lists of human needs. One such theorist is Maslow. His list is a hierarchical arrangement of need systems, with physiological needs at the lowest level and the need for self-actualization at the highest. The central assumption in Maslow's theory is that higher-level needs will be attended to only after low-level needs have been satisfied.

5. Arousal is a concept with physiological and psychological determinants. Physiologically, increasing arousal is defined by changes in respiration rate, in eeg, in gsr, and in blood pressure. The psychological symptoms of increasing arousal are increasing alertness or wake-fulness. With excessively high arousal, however, high anxiety and panic may result.

6. The primary sources of arousal are the distance receptors (vision and hearing); secondary sources include all other sensations. The amount, intensity, meaningfulness, sur-prisingness, and so on of stimulation are directly related to the level of arousal.

7. The relationship between arousal and motivation is expressed by two assump-tions: There is an optimal level of arousal for maximally effective behavior; the individual will behave in such a way as to maintain arousal level at or near the optimal.

8. The teacher in a classroom can be seen as the source of the stimulation that maintains student arousal at low or high levels. This view has extremely important implications for teacher behavior.

9. Traditional theories of motivation present a passive view of humans. More recent "cognitive" theories describe humans as active, exploring, evaluating organisms, capable of delaying gratification and of explaining the outcomes of their own behaviors.

10. Weiner's attribution theory of motivation is based on the assumption that individ-uals attribute their successes or failures to internal (ability and effort) or external (difficulty or luck) factors. Individuals having a high need for achievement tend to attribute their perfor-mances to internal factors, thus accepting personal responsibility for their successes and failures. Those having a lower need for achievement are more likely to attribute their perfor-mances to external factors over which they have no control.

11. Feelings of competence, of self-worth—in short, positive self-concepts—appear to be related to internal sources of attribution and consequent feelings of powerfulness. The key concept with respect to the educational implications of attribution theory is that of *personal responsibility*.

Suggested Readings

For a very simple and practical approach to motivating the classroom child, the reader is referred to:

Charles, Don C. *The Psychology of the Child in the Classroom.* New York: Macmil-lan, 1964, Chapter 1.

Fowler and Lindsley provide a more sophisticated and complex treatment of motivation. Lindsley's treatment deals largely with motivation and its neural correlates. Fowler's book is of value in understanding the development of recent approaches to motivation theory. His Chapter 4, which considers arousal theory in some detail, is especially relevant to the present chapter. The last part of the book contains fourteen of the more interesting and readable articles in motivation theory.

Lindsley, D. B. "Psychophysiology and motivation," in *Nebraska Symposium on Motivation,* ed. M. R. Jones. Lincoln: University of Nebraska Press, 1957.

Fowler, H. *Curiosity and Exploratory Behavior.* New York: Macmillan, 1965.

For a very popular and fascinating account of the relationship of instincts, imprinting, and behavior, the reader is referred to:

Lorenz, K. *King Solomon's Ring.* London: Methuen, 1952.

For an equally fascinating account of the effect of high arousal on human behavior, see:

Schultz, Duayne P. *Panic Behavior.* New York: Random House, 1964.

Cognitive theories of motivation are presented clearly but at a sophisticated level in the following collection:

Weiner, B. (Ed.). *Cognitive Views of Human Motivation.* New York: Academic Press, 1974.

Successful attempts to increase the need for achievement are described in:

McClelland, D. C. and D. G. **Winter.** *Motivating Economic Achievement.* New York: The Free Press, 1969.

Alschuler, A. S. *Motivating Achievement in High-School Students: Education for Human Growth.* Englewood Cliffs, N.J.: Educational Technology Publications, 1972.

The brown bear (Ursus arctos) *is still found in small numbers in very limited mountainous areas of western Europe, in Russia, Asia, India, and northern China, as well as in North America. It is extinct in the British Isles (Southern, 1964).*

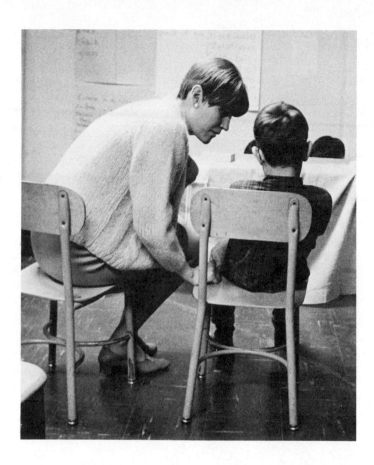

Discipline and Morality

Discipline: A Brief History · Discipline: A Definition · The
Ethics of Control · Preventive Strategies · Corrective Discipline ·
From Discipline to Morality · Moral Development ·
Summary · Main Points ·

As the twig is bent, so the tree will grow.
(A famous and prolific grandmother
named Anon.)

Indeed, should you be stupid enough
simply to watch it; else you might prune, graft,
bend in the other direction, and otherwise
shape its future so that even the wisest
of those so gifted would never know
how it was originally bent.

Advance Organizer It may not come as a surprise to you that one of the principal reasons for teacher unhappiness and premature retirement is discipline problems. This chapter, one of the more practically oriented chapters in this text, outlines a number of strategies and principles that might be effective in preventing and/or correcting disruptive behavior in the classroom. It looks too at the development of morality, and at the relationship between discipline and morality. The single most important point it makes is that here, as in medicine, prevention is far more valuable than correction.

In the second grade I tried to make a hole in my rubber eraser by holding a freshly sharpened pencil against it and hitting the pencil with my ruler. This was to be the last of a series of noisy experiments I had undertaken that day. The teacher interrupted me (not for the first time), called me to the front of the class, and administered "the strap" once on each of my small hands.

In the fourth grade I was detained after school and asked to scrub the inside walls of the outhouse, where someone had discovered an offensive scrap of graffiti penciled above the small hole (there was a larger one). I might have remained convinced to this day that God does watch all transgressors and reports directly to their teachers had I not remembered later that the spelling test we had been given that afternoon had contained most of the words found in the graffiti. In those days I spelled turkey "t-e-r-k-e-e."

In the eighth grade I had to write "I will not squirt ink on Louise" one hundred and fifty times. I don't remember why I had to write "I will not squirt ink on Louise," though it now strikes me that these words might be a nice title for a song.

I escaped unscathed from the tenth grade, having fallen in love with a sweet young thing who seemed to prize academic excellence, co-operation, and love of teachers. I co-operated, tried to excel, and almost succeeded in loving my teacher.

In eleventh grade, I fell out of love and into a small gang of village terrorists. We placed thumbtacks on our teacher's chair, glued her books to her desk, painted her class register, and aimed missiles at her back in between barely suppressed fits of hysterical giggles. Elsewhere we broke lightbulbs, "borrowed" horses for insane bareback romps along the lakeshore, and distributed dead chickens on various doorsteps in the middle of dark winter nights. Various unimaginative disciplinary measures did little to dampen our enthusiasm, though most of us eventually tired of regular noon-hour and after-school detention.

In college the registrar sent for me on one of those days when the geese would surely be flying. His message was a simple one: "Miss one more eight o'clock English and you will be removed." Removal not being one of my priorities at the time, I missed no more eight o'clock Englishes.

Discipline: A Brief History

Although the term *discipline* is in constant use among teachers, administrators, and students, it is not always the preferred word. Indeed, for quite a number of recent years, the more euphemistic expression "classroom management" has seemed less offensive and has consequently been more in vogue. Part of the reason for this lies in current philosophical movements in education. To the extent that "discipline" has been equated with yesterday's teacher, and to the extent that the activities most often associated with "disciplinary measures" are interpreted as being incompatible with the more permissive, more humanistic, and more child-centered beliefs of the present age, it has seemed more appropriate to exhort teachers to "manage" their classrooms rather than to "discipline" them.

It should also be noted that one of the more common meanings of the term *discipline* equates it with punishment of various kinds. Recall Thorndike's widely accepted "discovery" that punishment is not nearly as effective for its purposes as is reinforcement for opposite purposes; indeed punishment does not lead to the extinction of a response but merely to its suppression. It is hardly surprising that educators should have rejected punishment as a "control" technique. Nor is it surprising that "discipline" should also have fallen into disfavor, given its apparently close relationship with punishment. Hence the rise of "classroom management," a nebulous, ill-defined bag of topics, sometimes completely ignored by educational psychology textbooks, even as "discipline" is often ignored.

It is ironic that discipline as a research topic and as a legitimate area of concern for teacher trainees should have been so long neglected—ironic because classroom control is, in fact, one of the primary preoccupations of a great many teachers, and "discipline" problems are one of the principal reasons for teacher failure. Their role in student failure has not been negligible either. It is also ironic that the topic of punishment has been largely neglected by psychology and education, particularly in view of the fact that Thorndike's assertions have been seriously questioned by recent research, and also in view of the fact that various forms of punishment are employed routinely both by teachers and by parents *in spite of* any advice to the contrary that they might have been given.

Discipline: A Definition

Some of the various meanings of the term *discipline* are revealed in the following common statements:

"One of the reasons why she is a good teacher is because she has such good discipline."

"They had to be disciplined again after they released the pigeons in the classroom."

"Now Jack, for example, is a well-disciplined young man."

"What sort of discipline do you use in your classroom?"

A consideration of these statements reveals that discipline can refer to the degree of order or control that characterizes a group. Thus, a teacher is said to have good discipline when her students are obedient, well behaved, and friendly.

A second meaning relates to the techniques that might be employed to bring about order and control. When a teacher is asked to describe the "sort of discipline" he uses, he is being asked to reveal the methods by which order is established.

A third meaning refers to self-control. Thus, individuals are described as being highly disciplined when they appear to exercise firm control over their personal activities.

The final, and most common, meaning of the term *discipline* relates to punishment. When, for example, a teacher proudly claims to have successfully disciplined her class, the most obvious inference is that she has punished them, and has thereby apparently succeeded in achieving a higher degree of control. In fact, in the same way that the term *classroom management* has been employed as a euphemism for *discipline,* so the term *discipline* is often employed as a euphemism for *punishment*. In this text, the term *punishment* is employed freely. It was defined and discussed briefly in Chapter 3, and is considered in more detail later in this chapter.

For our purposes, *discipline* may be considered a global term descriptive of the variety of methods that might be employed to maintain the sort of classroom climate that is conducive not only to learning but to the healthy personal development of individuals within the class. It includes procedural strategies, instructional strategies, reward and punishment, and all other facets of teacher-learner interaction. This chapter deals with some of the ethical issues implicated in a discussion of discipline, with specific preventive and corrective disciplinary measures, with punishment, and with morality.

The Ethics of Control

The term *control* is highly, and unjustifiably, unpopular; some of its unpopularity can be traced to educational and philosophical writings that have improperly addressed issues of freedom, self-determination, self-worth, individuality, and other humanistic concerns. These concerns have unfortunately been equated with liberal and permissive child-rearing and educational methods. They are the concerns that define the spirit of these times. No teacher wants to be nonliberal and restrictive. And there is little doubt that the deliberate exercise of control is restrictive. Is control therefore unethical?

There is, of course, no simple answer. If there were, there would be little controversy, and behavioristic and humanistic concerns would have found relatively less about which to disagree.

Consider, first, that control is not only inevitable, but necessary. There is no doubt that teachers, both by virtue of their position and by virtue of the duties that are their responsibility, have control. Indeed, it is not at all unreasonable to insist, as Marland (1975) does, that the exercise of control is one of the teacher's most important duties. We are not speaking here of a type of fear-enforced control that might have been characteristic of some of yesterday's schools. Control can be achieved or at least facilitated in a variety of ways, some of which can be learned.

Parents too control their children, or at least try to. Part of the successful socialization process requires that children be prevented from engaging in behaviors that might be injurious to themselves or to others. Thus, parents do not permit their children to play with the dinner as it is cooking on the stove, to insert knives into electrical outlets, to jump off ladders, or to swim in dangerous waters. Less extreme instances of control involve the teaching of socially appropriate behavior, of values and morals—of "shoulds" and "should nots." It is less by accident than by virtue of parental control that children learn not to deface walls, to steal other people's property, or to kill the neighbor's dog. In short, there are certain standards of behavior that are learned at least partly as a function of parental control. Whether that control involves reinforcement, punishment, models, reasoning, or a combination of these and other strategies does not hide the fact that control is being exercised.

The classroom situation is not really very different. Teachers have often been described as acting *in loco parentis* —in the place of parents. More precisely, teachers have been urged to act in all ways as might a wise, judicious, and loving parent. And there is, in fact, no great incompatibility between values held in highest esteem by those who describe themselves as being humanistically oriented and the more precise techniques of behavior control that have been described by science. Love, empathy, warmth, genuineness, and honesty might go a long way toward ensuring that a classroom climate remain conducive to learning and development. In spite of these highly desirable qualities, however, discipline problems are not uncommon in most classrooms. That a teacher should judiciously administer rewards and punishment in an effort to maintain the type of environment most conducive to the goals of the educational process does not mean that she cares less for her students; indeed, it might well indicate that she cares more.

Preventive Strategies

In the classroom, as in medicine, there is little doubt that prevention should be valued more highly than correction. It is perhaps unfortunate that research has not paid a great deal of attention to the methods by which teachers might prevent the occurrence of discipline problems. Considerably more research has been devoted to corrective measures and their effectiveness. Speculation, however, is seldom hampered by lack of research evidence. Accordingly, it is not difficult to find advice addressed to teachers and intended to help them with the management of the classroom in order to avoid discipline problems. Much of this advice is based on the collective experience of successful teachers, and on the systematic observation of teachers in their classrooms. For what it might be worth to you, a distillation of advice is presented in this section. Bear in mind, however, that the teacher's personality is probably the single most important factor in the classroom situation. It is in the combination of elusive and abstract qualities that define personality that students find reasons to like or to dislike teachers. There are other reasons as well. Some traits can be learned; but desirable personality characteristics cannot, and are not discussed further in this chapter. Not everybody should be a teacher. If you do not genuinely love children . . . please.

Elements of the Craft

Among the valuable classroom management strategies that can serve as preventive discipline and that can be learned, Marland (1975) describes the following:

1. Teachers should learn pupils' names as soon as possible. More important, perhaps, they should also learn as much as they can about individual students. Relevant knowledge can be obtained in conversations with other teachers (but beware of their prejudices and the consequent expectations that you might develop), from records, through involvement in extracurricular activities, and from parents and others. The children you teach should be more than names and faces. The extent to which you care about them will be reflected in the knowledge and understanding that you have of each. And evidence suggests that the depth of your caring will affect how much they care about you and about each other. As is pointed out in a later section of this chapter, the development of morality may well be a function of the development of *care for others*.

2. Rules should be consistent, and should be enforced in a consistent manner. This does not mean that infractions of rules should never be tolerated. Last week two of my children were allowed, with their classmates, to leave their room in the middle of a class period because someone had noticed a strange darkening outside. It was a rare eclipse of the sun, which the teachers allowed their students to look at very briefly. Both teachers then availed themselves of this opportunity to discuss the effects of ultraviolet light on the retina and the movements of planetary

bodies. The incident reminded me of a time when we lived in California. It snowed one morning—the first time in more than a decade. Only the most unwise and the most unfeeling of teachers and administrators did not permit students to run outside and stand in the few flakes that survived their fall.

3. Marland (1975) advises, as well, that teachers arrange situations so that they can make frequent but *legitimate* use of praise, and that they observe some simple guidelines concerning the use of praise and criticism. Praise, given its effect on self-esteem and self-concept, should be public. On occasion, it should be communicated to parents and other interested adults as well. Criticism, on the other hand, also because of its effects on self-esteem and self-concept, should be given privately. In addition, both praise and criticism should be specific rather than general. Research in the area of learning demonstrates rather clearly that praise and punishment that are not contingent on behavior or that are not clearly related to a specific behavior are much less likely to be effective. Thus, Marland suggests that a student should not be admonished in general terms such as "Behave yourself," or "Be good." Instead, students should be directed to engage in a specific behavior *and* given a reason for that behavior. For example, instead of saying "Behave yourself," the teacher might say, "Please put down your water pistol and your hunting knife because you are disturbing the class." Presumably, the rule relating to the inadvisability of disturbing the class will already have been explained and justified, and the penalties for repeated infraction of that rule will have been made explicit.

Pertinent advice relating to the prevention of discipline problems can be gleaned from many writings. Our list of suggestions continues.

4. The effectiveness of humor is often overlooked by teachers who do not consider themselves spontaneously humorous. And faculties of education have not gone far out of their way to encourage prospective teachers to learn how to make others laugh and, perhaps most important, to learn how to laugh at themselves. Potentially explosive confrontations can often be avoided by turning aside an implied student challenge with a skillful humorous parry. Consider, for example, Ms. Howard, who, because of her reputation for maintaining order in the classroom, has been assigned 9b, a class that might generously be described as predelinquent. Less generous descriptions are entirely inappropriate in a textbook as polite as this one. On the first day of class, she is challenged. One Rodney Phillips, closely modeled after a popular television personality who is himself modeled after a stereotype of the 1950s, finds an excusable error in Ms. Howard's arithmetic computations on the chalkboard. "She can't even add proper and they call her a teacher," he says for the benefit of his classmates. Whereupon Ms. Howard immediately falls to her knees and in an amateurish imitation of the television hero, prays loudly to some undisclosed source to "Make me perfect again like I used to be!" Laughter that might otherwise have been directed *at* her is now *with* her. Ms. Howard simply has the knack of not taking herself and her responsibilities too seriously.

5. Kounin (1970) rated several hundred hours of videotaped classroom lessons in an attempt to identify those qualities of teacher behavior that appear to be most closely related to good classroom management. One factor that was found to be

common in most successful teaching situations was that teachers in these classrooms seemed to be more aware than less successful teachers of what was going on in their classrooms, of who was responsible for infractions of rules, and of when intervention was necessary. Accordingly, Kounin argues that a quality best described as *"with-it-ness"* is important for maintaining order in the classroom. A teacher who is "with it" knows what is going on, and is more likely to be respected by students. Similarly, Kounin found that those teachers who were most successful were able to handle more than one behavior problem at one time, all the while maintaining the direction and momentum of ongoing classroom activities. Unfortunately, little practical advice can be offered the apprentice teacher with respect to the cultivation of "with-it-ness." It is not unlikely, however, that simple awareness of the desirability of this quality will contribute to its development.

6. Since all that is involved in teacher-learner interaction and in the teaching-learning environment can facilitate or impede classroom discipline, preventive measures might also be directed toward the environment itself. In this connection, Marland (1975) suggests that there are various ways in which the learning environment can be personalized. More specifically, there is something impersonal and cold about what once was the traditional, dominating position of the teacher's desk, at the front, center of the class, where God intended the teacher's desk to be. Similarly, student desks were to be aligned in straight, even-length rows with uniform spaces front back, and side. Eyes front.

There are, of course, certain definite advantages to this traditional placement, not the least important of which is the fact that there must be some focal point for student attention, and that it is considerably easier and more natural for students to look to the front to see their teacher than to have to look to the rear. My eleventh grade teacher did move her desk to the back of the room, not because she was experimenting with ways to personalize the classroom environment, but because she could more easily watch those among us who were overly dedicated to mischief and other innocent amusements. We suspected as well that she had tired of being bombarded with our crude, elastic-propelled spitballs.

Marland's (1975) advice that the learning environment be personalized goes beyond a search for a more "personal" arrangement of desks, but includes as well those small decorative touches that are often more visible in the early rather than the later grades. Posters, charts, wall hangings, and other instructional and/or decorative objects need not be provided solely by the school and by teachers, but might also be provided by students.

Classroom climate is more than physical environment, as was shown in Chapter 12. Recall that creativity, for example, appears to be fostered in certain climates (defined loosely in terms of "atmosphere" and describable as warm, friendly, cold, and so on), and can be impeded in others. So, too, certain classroom climates are more conducive to preventive discipline than are others. Glasser (1969), for example, suggests that discipline problems will be minimized in those environments where all students are accepted as being capable, and where schools are warm and personal places.

Democratic Discipline

Webster (1968) describes a number of principles intended to guide teachers in their efforts to maintain a nonautocratic form of classroom order. One of the primary goals of these principles is to promote the development of self-discipline in students. The principles themselves are based on what Webster describes as the three Ks of good discipline: reason, respect, and relevance. That is, discipline should be rational (reasonable) and interpreted as such by students; it should reflect one of the most important of society's values, namely, respect for individuals; and disciplinary measures invoked by teachers should be relevant to the behaviors giving rise to disciplinary action.

Among the principles listed by Webster are the following (p. 50):

1. Teachers must make sure that all students understand rules and standards, and the reasons for their existence.
2. First violation of a rule should lead to a warning, a discussion of alternative ways of behaving, and clarification of the consequences of repeated infraction.
3. Teachers should endeavor to discover the causes underlying misbehavior.
4. Whenever possible, teachers should address students in private regarding their misbehavior.
5. Sarcasm, ridicule, and other forms of discipline that lead to public humiliation should be avoided.
6. When teachers make mistakes (if they ever do), they should apologize.
7. The punishment should fit the crime. Minor infractions should not attract harsh punishment.
8. Extra classwork and assignments, academic tests, and other school-related activities should never be employed as a form of punishment.

While there is little that is surprising, obscure, or difficult about the advice presented by Webster, it is nevertheless valuable advice. It is all too easy to act "instinctively" when faced with a discipline problem. And although the teacher's instincts might often be entirely appropriate, there might be occasions where other behaviors would have been considerably more appropriate. Perhaps knowledge of these principles can increase instances of appropriate reaction.

Several Final
Words about Prevention

The preceding sections concerning strategies designed as preventive disciplinary measures are by no means exhaustive. Indeed, much that teacher preparation programs attempt to teach about the preparation of lessons, their delivery, the establishment of classroom routines, the use of eyes, voices, and hands, and so on relates directly to prevention. More simply, all that relates to good and effective teaching also relates to the maintenance of classroom order.

Corrective Discipline

But even good, effective teachers are sometimes called upon to deal with disturbances and disruptions in the classroom. That this should be the case does not necessarily mean that the teacher is a failure, that the system is at fault, or that teacher training institutions have been remiss. Though each of these might be wholly or in part responsible for the trouble, the point is not to lay the blame but to deal with the situation. And in dealing with any disciplinary problem, two concerns are of paramount importance. The first is that the individual not be harmed, that whatever is done, it be done in the best interests of the student, with full consideration of that person's self-esteem and humanity. The second consideration is that those disciplinary measures which are invoked should also be applied in the interests of the entire group. In short, the teacher as a humanitarian practitioner of skills (with a little art to be sure) must strike a delicate balance between the well-being of the group and that of the individual. The resolution is not always simple.

There are a variety of corrective strategies available to the teacher. Since the immediate objective of corrective discipline is to change or eliminate a particular behavior, these strategies might appropriately be labeled behavior modification techniques. Recall that behavior modification generally refers specifically to those strategies that are predicated on behaviorist learning theory. These include the use of reinforcement, of models, of extinction, and of punishment. Each of these strategies is discussed below with specific reference to discipline problems. In addition, *reasoning,* a widely employed corrective and preventive measure, is also dealt with.

Reasoning

Reasoning presents one of the most important alternatives to the more direct forms of corrective intervention. Essentially, to reason is to provide rational explanations; hence reasoning as a corrective strategy involves presenting children with reasons for not engaging in deviant behavior and/or reasons for engaging in some alternative behavior. There is a fundamental difference between saying to a student, "Don't snap your fingers because you are distracting the others and making it difficult for them to study," and saying, "Don't snap your fingers or you will have to stay after school." The first employs reasoning; the second involves a threat of punishment. It might be noted, however, that the first statement, while appealing to reason, might also be interpreted as implying a threat, depending on the child's prior experience with the person attempting the correction. If children have learned through experience that the likely consequences of not acceding to authority's wishes, no matter how reasonably those wishes might be phrased, is some form of punishment, the effectiveness of "reason" might well be due to the implied threat.

Reasoning is considerably more appealing to parents and teachers than are most other disciplinary alternatives. It seems somehow more human to deal with children on an intellectual level than to deal with them from our positions of power as dispensers of rewards and punishments. And, happily, research and good sense both confirm our suspicions that reasoning can be an effective means of controlling or correcting student behavior.

A number of researchers have looked at the comparative effectiveness of various kinds of reasons that might be given children to prevent them from engaging in some behavior. In an experimental situation subjects are typically requested not to play with a toy and are then left alone with that toy so that they have no reason to believe that they will be apprehended if they do play with the toy. Investigations of reasoning techniques provide subjects with specific reasons for not playing with the toy. Parke (1974) reports that rationales which stress the object ("The toy might break") are more effective for younger children than are more abstract rationales relating to rights of possession (for example, "You should not play with toys that belong to others"). However, Hoffman (1970) found that for older children rationales that emphasize the consequences of their behavior for other persons (other-oriented induction) are more persuasive than are rationales that emphasize the consequences to the child. In other words, if the experimenter says, "Do not play with that toy because you will make the child it belongs to unhappy," subjects are more likely not to play with the toy than if the experimenter says, "Do not play with that toy because it might break and that would make you unhappy." Walters and Grusec (1977) argue that reasoning which arouses empathy for others is usually more effective than reasoning which focuses on personal consequences, particularly after the ages of six or eight. Thus, with advancing intellectual and moral development, children are more likely to respond to rationales relating to abstractions and ideals, and to become less concerned with immediate objective consequences. This observation is further corroborated by what is known about the sequence of moral development in children (see the section on moral development later in this chapter).

The implications of the foregoing observations are obvious. It would seem wise to provide younger children with specific, concrete reasons for requests that are made of them. After school age, however, more abstract rationales are preferable. Perhaps most important, rationales that are other-directed, and that consequently arouse empathy for others, appear to be most effective.

In addition to humanitarian and ethical considerations which clearly favor reasoning over punishing, there are several practical reasons why reasoning is preferable to punishment. First, a punishing agent provides a model of aggressiveness for the learner. In effect, the punisher's activities signify that one acceptable method of dealing with difficult situations is through the assertion of power in punitive form. Reasoning provides a rather different model. To reason with a child, and to provide a rationale for required behavior, is to say, in effect, that one of the ways of coping with difficulty is through the deliberate application of thought.

A second advantage of a reasoning strategy is that such an approach lends itself naturally to the description of alternative acceptable behaviors. In other words, reasoning need not be restricted to providing rationales for why a behavior should *not* be engaged in, but can be directed toward explaining why certain behaviors *should* be undertaken. Various forms of altruistic and prosocial behavior (co-operation, sharing, helping) cannot easily be taught by punitive means, but lend themselves more easily to the use of models, of reasoning, of reinforcement, or of a combinations of these.

Reinforcement

Teachers have at their disposal a wide variety of potent reinforcers, not the least important of which are praise, smiles, grades, and attention. When these social reinforcers prove ineffective, more elaborate reinforcement systems might be established. The best known among these are token systems where students earn points or tokens for good behavior and sometimes lose them for less desirable behavior. These tokens can later be exchanged for more tangible reinforcers (see Chapter 4).

Applying positive reinforcement to a discipline problem simply requires that the problem be reinterpreted. Instead of focusing on the elimination of undesired responses, one focuses on the reinforcement of the opposite behavior. Consider the example of a student who continually disrupts classroom activities in order to gain the teacher's attention. A relatively easy, and often effective, disciplinary measure is to pay attention to that student whenever he is not being disruptive and to ignore him when he is.

Psychology journals offer numerous examples of the use of positive reinforcement in the classroom (for example, Birnbrauer and Lawler, 1964; Birnbrauer et al., 1965; Quay et al., 1966; Wolf et al., 1964; O'Leary and Becker, 1967). The O'Leary and Becker (1967) report describes a study where a token system of reinforcement was employed in conjunction with social approval in order to eliminate deviant responses and to encourage acceptable classroom behavior. Subjects were seventeen "average" nine-year-olds. (In effect, while these students were of "aver-

age" intelligence, they had been classified as emotionally disturbed and placed in a special classroom.) The experimental procedure, which lasted for a year, involved writing a number of instructions on the chalkboard (e.g., desk clear, face the front, do not talk) and each day assigning every student a score based on his observance of the rules. The scores ranged from 1 to 10. They were entered in a record book on each student's desk and could be totaled and exchanged for manipulatables at any time. Additional reinforcement was provided for each child by the teacher's comments as she entered scores in the record books (e.g., "I like the way you held your hand up before talking today"). The success of the project was evaluated by comparing incidents of deviant behavior prior to the program and at its completion. The evidence suggests that it was highly effective.*

Although the effectiveness of reinforcement in establishing and maintaining acceptable behaviors can hardly be disputed, there are a number of problems involved in the systematic use of token systems. The establishment of such a system requires a great deal of time and care, and presents some real problems in selecting reinforcers for which tokens may be exchanged. In addition, several studies have found tokens to be ineffective for some students, and to be distracting for others (Kazdin and Bootzin, 1972). Some students spend so much time counting and sorting their tokens that they experience considerable difficulty attending to those tasks and behaviors that are desired of them.

One frequently used alternative to token systems, described earlier as the *Premack principle,* simply allows those students who have behaved appropriately (or who have not behaved inappropriately) to engage in some reinforcing activity—some activity that the child enjoys. Thus, one child might be permitted free time for reading, another for painting, another for running around the gym.

Another interesting alternative is presented by Nay et al. (1976), who used tape to demarcate an area of approximately one square yard around each student's desk. These areas were described as the students' personal space, to be named and decorated by them, and to be occupied by them alone. In the experiment in question, two types of deviant behaviors were addressed: leaving one's desk at inappropriate times and speaking out. Unambiguous signals were placed at the front of the class to indicate when leaving one's territory or speaking were not allowed. In the first case, a red light was put up; in the second, a figure with the lips closed. When walking quietly around the room, obtaining supplies, or leaving personal territory for some other reason was permitted, a green light replaced the red light; similarly, when children were permitted to talk quietly, a figure with the lips open was placed at the front. The implicit assumption is, quite simply, that being allowed to remain in one's territory is reinforcing, particularly if infractions of rules result in one's removal from that territory. Accordingly, desks were set aside in an area labeled "no-man's land," and children guilty of leaving their seats or of talking when those activities were prohibited were sent to one of these desks for a twenty-minute period. Further infractions in "no-man's land" resulted in a longer exile from home territory. Strik-

---

* The procedure described here involved both positive reinforcement and extinction. In fact, most programs based on behavior modification make use of a combination of techniques.

ingly, after several weeks disruptive behavior had virtually been eliminated in a classroom that had previously threatened to pose some severe discipline problems.

The varieties of reinforcers available to teachers (extrinsic and instrinsic, for example) and the conditions under which they are best administered are discussed in considerably more detail in Chapter 4. That chapter also presents a detailed account of other behavior modification techniques that can be employed in the classroom. For that reason, these techniques are illustrated briefly here, but are not discussed in detail. The interested reader is invited to return to relevant portions of the fourth chapter.

Modeling

Teachers make unconscious use of the various effects of models throughout their teaching careers. It is, in fact, inevitable that they should present models to their charges. The deliberate and systematic use of models is perhaps rarer, though these too can be used to good advantage.

The use of modeling for discipline is likely to involve attempts to eliminate undesirable behavior and to replace it with behavior that is appropriate. One illustration of modeling is provided by the following anecdote.

John George was a young, full-blooded Indian lad who attended the same rural school as I did. The school was in fact run by my father. On the morning when John George first came to school, he was a quiet, withdrawn boy who didn't speak a single word of English. It was not expected that he could possibly be a discipline problem. It happened, however, that in the middle of that warm, brown September morning, John George felt the strong call of nature. Quite openly and unashamedly he left his desk and walked slowly to the far corner of the open schoolyard. And there, to the roaring delight of an entire student body, he squatted and attended to that call.

My father, a resourceful and very capable teacher, took it upon himself to walk to the corner of the yard and try to explain to John George, using various interesting gestures, that the little edifice in the other corner was equipped to handle problems like the one John George had just solved. There are some sign explanations that are not universally understood by frightened six-year-old boys whose pants have settled around their ankles.

The discipline problem here is evident. This kind of behavior, if continued, was likely to have a very disruptive effect on classroom proceedings. The solution finally arrived at was to have me serve as a model and demonstrate for John George where *it* was and what *it* was for. I did.

Recall that one of the effects of models involves the suppression or reappearance of previously suppressed deviant behavior. This effect, labeled the inhibitory-disinhibitory effect (see Chapter 4) apparently occurs as a result of seeing a model being punished or rewarded for deviant behavior. Not surprisingly, the intended application of the inhibitory effect is extremely common in schools. Whenever a teacher punishes any student in a class, she makes the implicit assumption that other students will inhibit any tendencies that they might have had to engage in the punished behavior. Whenever a teacher singles out for punishment one offender from among a group of offenders, she hopes that the effects of the punishment will spread to the remainder of the group. This is why leaders are often punished for the transgressions of their followers. Interestingly, the punishment may have a "secondhand" effect, as does reinforcement. The reinforcement that an observer derives from seeing a model reinforced is termed *vicarious* reinforcement; the similar effects of punishment could also be termed vicarious.

Extinction

Animal studies indicate that responses that are maintained by reinforcement can usually be eliminated through the complete withdrawal of reinforcement. Thus, a pigeon that has been taught to peck at a disk for its food should soon cease to peck when food is no longer provided as a contingency of disk pecking. In fact, however, many pigeons will continue to peck at the disk indefinitely, even when the experimenter no longer provides reinforcement. A humanist might simply insist that to be a pigeon is to peck, that a fully actualized pigeon gets high by pecking disks and remains unmoved by the crass material rewards that might move other pigeons. A behaviorist would analyze the situation differently, insisting that a pigeon continues to peck because there is something instrinsically reinforcing about the act of pecking. Whatever the reason might be, it remains true that not all behaviors can be extinguished through the removal of reinforcement. Furthermore, it should be noted that many disruptive behaviors in the classroom are reinforced by peers rather than by teachers. To the extent that teachers are not in control of relevant reinforcers, there is little that they can do to remove them.

More optimistically, there are a number of disruptive behaviors that appear to be maintained by teacher attention, in which case it might be a relatively simple matter to cease paying attention. On the other hand, the matter might not be quite as simple if the behavior in question is highly disruptive of class activities. But there are other alternatives, the most common of which is punishment.

Punishment

Punishment can take a variety of forms. Recall that there are, in principle, two distinct types of punishment: The first involves the presentation of a noxious (unpleasant) stimulus and is well illustrated by a frozen boot; the second involves the removal of a pleasant stimulus and was illustrated in the Nay et al. (1976) study in which students were *removed* from their territories for infraction of rules.

Specific punishments employed by teachers include subtle facial gestures of disapproval, reprimands, detention, unpleasant activities, "timeout," and, occasionally, physical punishment. There are many passionate objectors to the use of punishment, and a number of practical objections as well. At the same time, there is a need to reexamine the effectiveness of various forms of punishment.

The Case Against

In addition to some obvious ethical and humanitarian objections to punishment, there are a number of more practical objections. Among these is the observation that punishment, by itself, draws attention to socially undesirable behavior but does not illustrate suitable alternatives. It should be noted that punishment used in conjunction with reasoning and other corrective measures need not be subject to the same objection.

There is evidence as well that punishment sometimes has effects opposite to those intended. This is particularly obvious where parents or teachers attempt to eliminate aggressive or violent behavior through punishment (Sears et al., 1957). In effect, parents who punish violence with violence provide a model of violence for the child—a model which might be interpreted to mean that aggressiveness is permissible under certain circumstances.

Other objections to the use of punishment are described by Clarizio and Yelon (1974, p. 50) as follows: First, punishment does not eliminate an undesirable response, although it might result in its suppression, or in a reduction in its frequency. Second, punishment may have unpleasant emotional side effects which are themselves maladaptive (for example, fear, anxiety, tension). Finally, punishment is a source of frustration and may therefore lead to other undesirable or maladaptive behaviors.

The Case for Punishment

It should be noted that most of these objections apply only to one type of punishment: namely, that involving the presentation of unpleasant stimuli. Furthermore, these objections are most applicable to physical punishment and much less applicable to verbal punishment. Those forms of punishment which involve the removal of pleasant stimuli (for example, loss of privileges) are not subject to the same parental, academic, and philosophical objections, and should be considered legitimate methods by which teachers can maintain the degree of control that is essential for humane and personal teaching.

The case to be made for punishment can be based on a number of recent studies which have demonstrated that punitive methods can be effective in suppressing disruptive and sometimes dangerous behaviors (Parke, 1970). Some situations demand immediate and decisive intervention, and do not lend themselves to the more gentle strategies of reinforcement, modeling, and reasoning. A child who persists in lighting matches and touching them to the family drapes may be reasoned with and physically removed; but if he insists on firing the drapes at every opportunity, punishment may well be in order.

It should be noted as well that, although reinforcement, modeling, and reasoning have proven highly effective for promoting desirable behaviors, it is sometimes extremely difficult for a child to learn about unacceptable behaviors simply by generalizing *in reverse* from situations that have been reinforced (Ausubel, 1957). In many cases, then, punishment *of specific behaviors* can be highly informative. And while there is considerable evidence that punishment administered by an otherwise warm and loving parent is more effective than that administered by a parent who is habitually cold and distant (Aronfreed, 1968), there is in fact no evidence that punishment administered by a loving parent serves to disrupt affectional bonds between parent and child (Walters and Grusec, 1977).

One of the often quoted theoretical objections to the use of punishment is, quite simply, that it does not work—that while it might serve to suppress behavior or reduce its frequency, it does not lead to the elimination of a response. Consider, however, that a punisher's intent is clearly *to suppress* a behavior. Complete elimination is, in fact, absolutely irrelevant. If Johnny has been punished for burning curtains, we should not dare hope that he will, as a result, have forgotten how to burn curtains. But we are justified in hoping that he will refrain from doing so in the future.

Interestingly, most of the data that we have regarding punishment is derived from the animal laboratory. For obvious reasons, it is easier to do research with animals than with children, although even the lowly rat is now treated with considerably more respect than was once the case. Nevertheless, it is possible to administer electric shocks to animals; there are no directly comparable stimuli that can (or indeed should) be employed with children. Hence, controlled research of the effects of punishment typically use such "annoyers" as loud buzzers. Evidence from a number of studies suggests that these annoyers can be effective in suppressing unwanted behavior (in many of these experiments children are asked not to play with a toy; the buzzer sounds if they do).

This section is not meant to minimize the dangers of punishment. Several important points need to be made. The most important is that most researchers and theorists remain virtually unanimous in their rejection of physical punishment. Not only is physical punishment a humiliating violation of the person, but it presents a highly undesirable model. If your task were to teach children that the best way of obtaining what they want is by force, then excessive use of physical punishment might well be your best teaching method.

If we do reject physical punishment (in practice, the rejection is very far from complete), a number of alternatives remain. The least objectionable are those involving the withdrawal of reinforcement.

Punishment in the Classroom

If you are like most teachers, you are likely to make use of the two major types of punishment in your classroom: withdrawal of pleasant consequences and the administration of unpleasant consquences. A careful review of the punishment literature and of humanistic counterarguments reveals that there are perhaps three different forms of punishment that can be effective but that do not bring with them the disadvantages usually associated with our ordinary interpretations of punishment. These are verbal reprimands, timeout, and response cost. Each is discussed briefly and illustrated below.

Reprimands Reprimands can be mild or harsh; they can be verbal or nonverbal; and they can be administered by teachers, parents, or peers. A simple "no" is a verbal reprimand; a negative head shake is a nonverbal reprimand.

A series of studies dealing with reprimands (for example, O'Leary and Becker, 1968; O'Leary et al., 1974) have identified an important factor associated with their effectiveness: soft reprimands are considerably more effective than loud reprimands. When teachers were asked to reprimand children so that only the child being reprimanded could hear, disruptive behavior decreased dramatically. In contrast, teachers who continued to use loud reprimands (that is, reprimands spoken so that the entire class could hear) had classrooms with markedly higher incidences of disruptive behavior. Recall the advice given earlier with respect to praise and punishment. Specifically, because of their effects on the child's self-concept, praise should be public (loud) and criticism should be private (soft).

Timeout A timeout procedure is one in which students are removed from a situation where they would ordinarily expect reinforcement and are placed in situation where they cannot be reinforced. For example, if classroom activities are such that children *like* to be in class, being removed from the classroom (a timeout procedure) may be interpreted as a form of punishment. Although the procedure has been employed in several studies (for example, Birnbrauer et al., 1965), it has usually been used in conjunction with other methods (for example, reinforcement for good behavior). Hence, there is little research data that would be directly relevant to an evaluation of timeout procedures in an ordinary classroom.

Response-Cost When students have been given tangible reinforcers for good behavior, but stand to lose some of these reinforcers for disruptive behaviors, the loss is referred to as response-cost. It too comprises a mild form of punishment not dissimilar from preventing a child who has misbehaved from watching television. Response-cost systems are frequently used in token-reinforcement programs. An experiment reported by Kaufman and O'Leary (1972) clearly illustrates the difference between a response-cost method and a reinforcement system. The experiment was conducted in two classes in a children's unit of a psychiatric hospital. In one class, students earned points for good behavior (token reinforcement); in a second class, children were awarded all their points at the beginning of a class period, and had points subtracted from their total for specific misbehaviors. While both methods were highly effective in reducing disruptive behavior, one was not more effective than the other.

From Discipline to Morality

The first part of this chapter has intentionally emphasized preventive and management strategies rather than corrective strategies. Hopefully, with proper attention to those aspects of teacher-learner interaction that are conducive to enthusiasm, warmth, and caring, seriously disruptive behavior will be infrequent, and the need for corrective action rare. And hopefully, too, the teacher will have time and energy to address the larger but sometimes less visible problems of social adjustment, self-discipline, and moral development.

Rules and standards in a classroom might exist primarily to ensure the order necessary for the teaching-learning process, but they have other effects as well. School is more than preparation for later life; it is a fundamental part of the child's immediate life. And it is perhaps fortunate that, in many respects, schools mirror larger society. The penalties for infraction of school rules might not be as harsh as those which apply to the infraction of society's laws, but the rewards for compliance are no less. And although we might strenuously object that schools should not teach compliance, we must nevertheless admit that society would be incredibly more chaotic that it sometimes appears to be were it not for the fact that most of us have learned to live within social, legal, and moral prescriptions, that we have learned how to resolve a majority of our conflicts without resorting to knives, guns, and fists, and that we behave in morally acceptable ways most of the time.

It is probably highly presumptuous, and perhaps not a little remiss, of schools to assume that the development of high moral standards, the internalization of values, and the development of principles and ideals will result incidentally from the experiences that life provides for children—that nothing can, or should, be done deliberately to foster their development. In fact, it is likely that much is accomplished incidentally by wise and sensitive teachers who might accomplish much more were they to address themselves deliberately to the development of "character." Character is a global expression for values, moral strength, principles, and bags of virtues—an ill-defined and very unpopular term in today's social sciences. Consequently, these sciences have little advice to offer the teacher who might be concerned with more than classroom management and the curriculum-bound teaching-learning process.

Conflict Resolution

Humanistic approaches to education present several attempts to cater more directly to children's social and emotional needs, and to help them develop the sorts of social skills that are useful and sometimes necessary for effective interaction with others. The humanistic emphasis on affective education points clearly in this direction, as do the various group-process approaches that have become popular in humanistic schools. One additional example is described briefly here.

Palomares and Logan (1975) have developed an extensive curriculum, both audio-visual and textual, for conflict management. Essentially, the curriculum is intended to teach children a variety of methods they can employ to resolve conflicts. Many of these conflicts are employed spontaneously by children and are learned incidentally as a function of the give-and-take of social interaction. However, a number of children experience more difficulty than others in acquiring these social skills. For these children, the program should prove particularly effective.

Among the conflict-resolution skills taught by the program are negotiation, compromising, taking turns, explaining, listening, apologizing, soliciting intervention, using humor, and invoking chance (i.e., flipping a coin). Seventeen specific strategies are developed, fourteen of them being primarily positive and clearly useful in adult interaction as well. Three are more negative, though they too might occasionally be resorted to (violence, flight, and tattling).

Intentionally or otherwise, schools do much to teach children how to get along with one another, even as they contribute a great deal to the development of self-discipline and morality. Webster (1968) claims, for example, that one of the more important contributions of discipline in schools is its effect on the development of personal control in students. By personal control he means morality. Accordingly, Webster argues that teachers should be aware of the child's level of moral development and of the ways in which morals are acquired. Similarly, Glasser (1968) argues that morality should be discussed in schools, that standards of conduct, ideals, and moral dilemmas should be examined by students so that they might have some basis for arriving at their own sets of moral rules. Accordingly, the final section in this chapter presents a brief summary of research on moral development.

Moral Development

Many decades ago Piaget (1932) interviewed children, asking them about rules and laws, right and wrong, good and evil. To no one's great surprise, he discovered that very young children do not operate within limitations imposed by abstract conceptions of right and wrong, but respond instead in terms of the im-

---

Table 14.1 *Kohlberg's Levels and Types of Morality*

Level I   Premoral

    Type 1   Punishment and obedience orientation
    Type 2   Naive instrumental hedonism

Level II   Morality of Conventional Role Conformity

    Type 3   Good-boy morality of maintaining good relations, approval of others
    Type 4   Authority maintains morality

Level III   Morality of Self-Accepted Principles

    Type 5   Morality of contract, of individual rights, and of democratically accepted law
    Type 6   Morality of individual principles of conscience

---

mediate *personal* consequences of their behavior. More simply, a very young child's morality is governed by the principles of pain and pleasure. Accordingly, children consider "good" those behaviors that have pleasant consequences and/or that do not have unpleasant consequences. Piaget's label for this initial stage of moral development is *heteronomy*. During this stage the child responds primarily to outside authority, authority being the main source of rewards and punishments. This initial stage is followed by the appearance of more autonomous moral judgments. During this stage of *autonomy* behavior is guided more and more by internalized principles and ideals.

Much later Kohlberg (1964) undertook detailed longitudinal investigations of moral beliefs and behaviors, eventually arriving at a detailed description of three sequential levels of moral orientation, each describable in terms of two stages (see Table 14.1). In principle, these stages are similar to Piaget's description of a progression from heteronomy to autonomy, though they are considerably more detailed. Each of the levels and stages is described briefly below.

Level I: Preconventional Level

Children respond primarily in terms of the immediate hedonistic consequences of their behaviors, and in terms of the *powers* of those who have authority over them.

Stage 1: Punishment and Obedience Orientation Behavior is designed to avoid punishment. Obedience is "good" in and of itself. Evaluation of the morality of an action is totally divorced from its more objective consequences, but rests solely on its consequences to the actor. Behavior for which one is punished is, ipso facto, bad; that for which one is rewarded must necessarily be good.

Stage 2: Instrumental and Hedonistic Orientation The beginnings of reciprocity (do for me and I will do for you). Strikingly, however, Stage 2 reciprocity is highly practical. Children will do something good for others only if they expect

Reciprocity

that their behaviors will result in someone doing something good for them in return. Quite simply, their moral orientation remains largely hedonistic (pain-pleasure oriented).

Level II: Conventional Level

A morality of conformity. Those behaviors which are "good" are those which maintain established social order.

Stage 3: Morality of Good Relationships Children's actions are judged largely in terms of their role in establishing and maintaining good relations with authority and with peers. A "good-boy, nice-girl" orientation. Approval is all-important, and is assumed to be the result of "being nice."

Stage 4: Morality of "Law and Order" Morality characterized by blind obedience. No idealistic rejection of established order. What is legal is, by definition, good. And the good person is the one who is aware of rules, and who obeys them unquestioningly.

*Level III: Postconventional
or Autonomous Level*

Individual makes deliberate effort to clarify moral rules and principles, and to arrive at self-defined notions of good and evil.

Stage 5: Morality of Social Contract and of Individual Rights This stage retains an important element of conformity to laws and legal systems, but with the important difference that legal systems are interpreted as being good to the extent that they guarantee and protect individual rights. The individual can now evaluate laws in terms of social order and individual justice, and is capable of reinterpreting and changing them.

Stage 6: Morality of Individual Principles of Conscience The final stage of moral development is characterized by individual-chosen ethical principles that serve as major unifying guides to behavior. Individual moral principles are highly abstract rather than concrete. They are not illustrated by the Ten Commandments, for example, but are implicit in deep-seated convictions that guide behavior—for example, beliefs in justice or equality.

Kohlberg's (1971) research suggests that progression through these stages is sequential and universal. That is, all children in all cultures progress through the stages in the same sequence. This does not mean, however, that all individuals eventually reach Stage 6 (self-determined principles) and operate only on that level. In fact, even after people are capable of making Stage 5 or Stage 6 moral judgments, their actual behavior may often be more illustrative of Levels I or II. Furthermore, other researchers have found that very few individuals ever reach Level III. Turiel (1974) found that few of his subjects reached the fifth stage until late adolescence. Kohlberg reports that only about 10 percent of his adults (twenty-four years old) were at Stage 6; another 24 percent were at Stage 5; and the remainder operated at lower levels.

Kohlberg's investigations of morality typically make use of stories depicting moral dilemmas to which the subject must respond. For example, a situation is described where a woman is dying, but can be saved if her husband can obtain a rare and very expensive drug. Since he is unable to pay for the drug, he is faced with the choice of letting his wife die or of stealing it. What should he do, and why? Level I responses might draw attention to the fact that he will miss his wife if she dies, or that he might be put in jail if he steals the drug. A Level II response might point out that it is illegal to steal, or that the druggist should be "nice and give the man the drug." A Level III response might place the value of a human life above adherence to legal rules.

Educational Implications

Knowledge of the progression of moral development might be of value in several ways. First, knowing how and why children judge things to be morally right or wrong relates directly to the types of rationalizations a teacher might offer children in exhorting them to "behave" and/or not to misbehave. Recall, for example, the fact that rationalizations which stress the object (the toy might break) are more effective for younger children than rationalizations that are more abstract ("you should not play with toys that belong to other children"). By extrapolation, the types of rationalizations that might be offered adolescents would be quite different from those offered younger children.

A second indirect application of knowledge of moral development relates to the actual teaching of morality. It is perhaps unfortunate that little research has been devoted to the question of whether or not moral development can be promoted or accelerated in children. This is partly because early studies (Hartshorne and May, 1928, for example) found little correspondence between actual behavior and moral and religious training. Specifically, these investigators found that such immoral behaviors as cheating were much less affected by religious training, apparent strength of conscience, and other abstract signs of "moral goodness" than by the probability of being caught. Given these widely accepted and highly pessimistic findings, it is not surprising that schools have traditionally paid little attention to the deliberate inculcation of virtues.

More recently, however, Fodor (1972) has found that children identified as delinquents operate at a much lower level on the Kohlberg scales than nondelinquent children. Similarly, Haan et al. (1968) report that subjects who score highest in terms of moral orientation are most likely to be politically and socially active. In other words, there does appear to be some correspondence between level of moral orientation and actual behavior. If this is the case, anything that the schools can do to promote progression through these stages might contribute directly to classroom control, and indirectly to the development of better individuals.

What, precisely, can be done? Unfortunately, suggestions remain rather abstract (perhaps Bear IV will be more concrete). Kohlberg (1964), for example, suggests that, while the content of moral rules can be taught, the attitudes that are necessary for behavior at each level result from a complex process of cognitive development and cannot themselves be taught. In addition, as Peters (1977) points out, Kohlberg's theory deals with the cognitive aspects of moral development, but does not consider the affective components of morality. Hence the theory itself does little to clarify the types of feelings that ought to be fostered if children are to develop morally. But other researchers have attempted to clarify this area.

Peters (1977) argues that caring for others is perhaps the most important attitude involved in progressing from primitive levels of morality to self-determined principles. Similarly, McPhail et al. (1972) have developed a teaching program for adolescents designed to foster empathy and concern. And Sullivan (1977) argues that the dimension of "care" often appears to be lost in contemporary society. He argues as well that the type of moral training most often characteristic of established, orthodox religions appears to serve as a motivator for attaining higher levels of moral reasoning (Sullivan and Quarter, 1972; Sullivan, 1977).

In the abstract, then, the implication of these findings and speculations is that one ought to attempt to develop in children care and concern for others and to encourage and reward behaviors that reflect virtues ordinarily associated with caring.

More concretely, Hoffman (1976) suggests four different kinds of experiences that can foster altruistic (caring) behavior in children. Some of these may suggest worthwhile classroom activities.

1. Situations in which children are allowed to experience unpleasantness rather than being overprotected.

2. Role-taking experiences in which children are responsible for the care of others.

3. Role-playing experiences in which children imagine themselves in the plight of others.

4. Exposure to altruistic models.

Summary of Chapter 14

This chapter examined the ethics of control and punishment, as well as their inevitability and frequent desirability. Special emphasis was placed on preventive disciplinary measures. In addition, a number of corrective measures were described and illustrated. Finally, the progression of moral development and how to foster its development in the classroom were discussed.

Main Points in Chapter 14

1. The expression *classroom management* is often a euphemism for discipline; discipline may be a euphemism for punishment.

2. In this text, *discipline* is a global term descriptive of the methods and practices conducive to establishing and maintaining the type of classroom climate and order that fosters learning and healthy personal development.

3. Despite some valid ethical and humanitarian objections to control, to the extent that teachers act *in loco parentis,* and to the extent that they *care* for their students, discipline is necessary.

4. Preventive strategies are of paramount importance in classroom discipline. These strategies include procedural routines, instructional methods, the use of humor, and an elusive quality labeled "with-it-ness."

5. With-it-ness is the ability to *see* what is going on in the classroom and to deal with it without disrupting the flow of ongoing activities.

6. Webster's *democratic discipline* is based on reason, relevance, and respect, and is guided by a number of obvious but often overlooked principles.

7. Corrective discipline is invoked when preventive discipline has not been successful in curbing the appearance of a disciplinary problem. It includes reasoning, reinforcement, the use of models, extinction, and punishment.

8. Reasoning, often in combination with other disciplinary measures, appears to be a highly effective and humane way of handling classroom problems. Concrete rationalizations appear to be more effective with younger children; abstract reasons work better with older children. In addition, rationalizations that appeal to the effect of behavior on others is particularly successful and may be important in developing higher levels of moral orientation.

9. Reinforcement is used extensively by teachers. In addition to natural social reinforcers such as approval and love, the Premack principle and a variety of token systems may be employed.

10. Models provide children with standards of appropriate behavior. On occasion, punished models may serve to inhibit deviant behaviors as well. Perhaps the most important of classroom models is the teacher.

11. Extinction involves an attempt to eliminate undesirable behavior through the withdrawal of reinforcement. It is frequently inapplicable when teachers do not have control over reinforcement, or when reinforcement is intrinsic or nonidentifiable.

12. Punishment involves the presentation of an unpleasant stimulus as a consequence of behavior, or the removal of a pleasant stimulus.

13. Among objections to the use of punishment are claims that it does not always work, that it presents an undesirable model of violence, that it might have undesirable emotional side effects, and that it might lead to maladaptive behaviors through the introduction of frustration.

14. Research indicates that punishment may suppress undesirable behaviors, and that it might be particularly appropriate in cases where it is necessary for a child to learn about behaviors that are *not* permitted.

15. Reprimands are among the most common of punishments. Verbal reprimands that are soft (heard only by the student being reprimanded) appear to be more effective than loud reprimands. In addition, they are less of a violation of the student's individuality and self-esteem.

16. Timeout punishment refers to the transfer of a student from a reinforcing situation to another nonpunitive, but nonreinforcing, situation.

17. Response-cost refers to that form of punishment in which previously earned reinforcers are removed as a consequence of undesirable behavior.

18. In addition to the attention that teachers must sometimes devote to maintaining classroom order, they should also devote attention to the development of social and affective skills in children. The withdrawn, nonparticipating child is in as much need of help as the rebellious, truculent discipline problem.

19. Moral development proceeds from a preconventional level, characterized by hedonistic concerns and obedience to authority, to a conventional level, characterized by conformity and a desire to maintain good relationships, and finally to a postconventional level, characterized by attention to individual rights and the development of individual principles of conduct and beliefs.

20. Knowledge of moral development might be of value in helping teachers determine the types of rationalizations that are most likely to be effective with different children. In addition, it might be possible to foster moral growth through systematic educational programs.

Suggested Readings

The following is a short, highly readable, and very practical discussion of specific methods by which teachers can achieve and maintain a high level of classroom control described by the author as being necessary for "personal" teaching.

Marland, M. *The Craft of the Classroom: A Survival Guide to Classroom Management in the Secondary School.* London: Heinemann Educational Books, 1975.

A collection of readings edited by Brown and Avery presents a comprehensive series of illustrations of behavior modification principles and techniques in classroom use. Of particular relevance is the fourth section, which deals solely with classroom applications.

Brown, A. R. and C. **Avery.** *Modifying Children's Behavior: A Book of Readings.* Springfield, Ill.: Charles C. Thomas, 1974.

A comprehensive and recent analysis of research on punishment, its effectiveness, and its uses is detailed in the following.

Walters, G. C. and J. E. **Grusec.** *Punishment.* San Francisco: W. H. Freeman, 1977.

Kohlberg's theory and relevant research is summarized in:

Kohlberg, L. and E. **Turiel.** *Research in Moral Development: A Cognitive Developmental Approach.* New York: Holt, Rinehart and Winston, 1971.

The Royal Guards who attended the coronation of Queen Elizabeth in 1953 wore shakos (military hats) made of the pelts of black bears. Seven hundred bears were killed around the little town of Lillooet, along the Fraser River in British Columbia, to make the three hundred shakos required.

15

Measurement and Evaluation

Have known the evenings, mornings, afternoons,
I have measured out my life with coffee spoons.
(T. S. Eliot)

And where, O teacher, are the coffee spoons
with which you would presume to measure
the educational lives of your charges?

Advance Organizer In spite of the intuitive appeal of "schools without failures," "schools without tests," and other hypothetical situations where everyone is highly motivated, absolutely dedicated, and deliriously happy, the nitty-gritty of classroom practice sometimes (perhaps frequently) requires assessment. This chapter describes the various methods by which student and teacher *performance can be measured and evaluated, the reasons why assessment might be important, and some of the abuses and misuses of assessment procedures.*

The observation could be made here that Johnny West has a striking nose. You will recall that Johnny is the boy who chewed up one of Piaget's nipples when he was a baby. That was why Stan Twolips presented Johnny's mother with a long nipple (for Johnny, of course) on the occasion of his first birthday. Stan Twolips also has a very long nose. His nose is four inches long! Galton and Watson wondered about that.

Measurement and Evaluation

The statement "Stan Twolip's nose is four inches long" illustrates a **measurement** procedure. The statement "Johnny West has a striking nose" is an example of **evaluation.** The former involves applying an instrument to gauge the length of the nose (a nosemeter in psychological terms). The latter is simply the formation of a judgment about the appropriateness of the nose; it is a more subjective reaction.

Both measurement and evaluation are important parts of teaching, contrary to the popular notion that tests serve only to help the teacher assign grades. This can be seen by examining the teaching model presented in Chapter 1. That model describes teaching as decision making about instructional strategies on the basis of educational goals, implementing these strategies, and assessing their effectiveness in relation to the goals. Obviously the assessment stage will require either measurement or evaluation or both. The use of a test to determine whether students have learned what they were intended to learn is *measurement.* Deciding whether they have learned well is *evaluation*.

Evaluation need not be based on measurement. Indeed, much teacher assessment of student behavior is not based on measurement. The countless value judgments made by teachers about the abilities of students, their motivation, their persistence, their pleasantness, and so on are often examples of evaluation without mesurement. *One of the major premises of this chapter is that evaluation should be based on measurement, and, consequently, that the measuring instruments should not only be the best possible, but that they should also be used intelligently.* It is possible to use them with something less than great wisdom. In order to simplify and clarify the content of this chapter, the term measurement will be predominant throughout. It should be kept in mind, however, that evaluation often follows measurement.

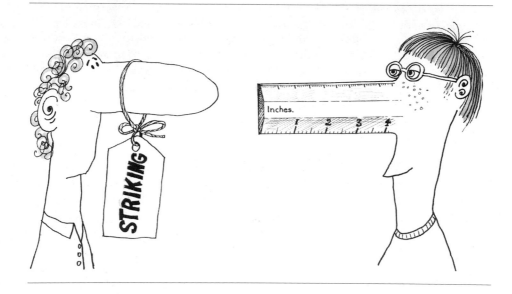

Measurement and Goals

The relationship between measurement in schools and educational goals is obvious. Less obvious, judging from general practice, is that the specification of these goals is essential to good measurement. It is difficult to imagine how teachers can assess the effectiveness of instructional procedures unless they know precisely what those procedures were intended to do. It is equally obvious that they will not know what procedures to employ unless they have already made a decision about the outcomes desired. A simple representation of the act of teaching comprises only three processes: the specification of goals, the implementation of procedures to attain these goals, and evaluation of the effectiveness of these procedures.*

Goals

Goals are outcomes which are desired. School-related goals include not only the specific instructional goals of a teacher, but also the wider objectives of curricula, programs, principals, and communities. However, because questions relating to the wider objectives of education have traditionally been in the domain of philosophy rather than psychology, and because evaluation seldom goes beyond the goals of the classroom teacher, we will discuss only the specific instructional goals of the teacher here. Three approaches to specifying instructional objects are discussed below.

---

* See Chapter 7, "Instructional Objectives," for a discussion of goals.

General Objectives It is sometimes useful to begin the preparation of a unit or of an entire course by specifying in general terms what the final desired outcome of the instruction is. Such a statement may be of value in assessing the general effectiveness of the entire course or of a portion thereof. It is *not* likely to be of any real value, however, in determining the adequacy of specific instructional procedures or of particular lessons. For example, the general objectives of a unit in the natural sciences may include a statement such as this:

> *The students should be familiar with the flora and fauna of the Rocky Mountains and adjoining foothills in North America.*

While this statement of general objectives might serve as a guide for teachers, indicating to them that they need to prepare lessons related to wild fruit and animals as well as to all the flora and fauna of that area, it is not specific enough to serve as a *blueprint* for the construction of measuring instruments.

Specific Objectives On the other hand, a specific instructional objective such as the following suggests means for evaluating the effectiveness of specific instructional procedures.

> *After the unit, the student should be able to recognize a lynx, a grizzly bear, a cougar, an elk, a mountain sheep, and a moose when presented with these animals.*

Any enterprising teacher can easily obtain bears, cougars, moose, lynx, elk, and sheep, and use these both for instruction and for assessing the attainment of goals.

A useful exercise in the preparation of any lesson is to list specific objectives at the very outset. Not only are these useful for evaluative purposes, but they also often serve to clarify the teacher's thinking.

Bloom's Taxonomy Bloom et al. (1956) and Krathwohl, Bloom, and Masia (1964) have provided an exhaustive and useful list of educational objectives in the cognitive and affective domains. The usefulness of these lists of objectives (referred to as *taxonomies*) is that they can serve as guides in determining what the goals for a lesson or course are. The taxonomy of objectives for the cognitive domain (Bloom et al., 1956), for example, describes a class of objectives, a list of educational objectives which correspond to this class, and test questions which illustrate it. The six hierarchical classes of objectives in that domain are, from the lowest to the highest level: **knowledge, comprehension, application, analysis, synthesis, and evaluation.** Each of these is also broken down into subdivisions. The reader is referred to the handbook of objectives (Bloom et al., 1956) for a detailed consideration of a taxonomy of educational objectives (and to the boxed insert for a preview of that detail).

Scales of Measurement

The crudest scale of measurement is a **nominal scale.** The numbers on the backs of football players or descriptive categories such as blue-red or house-barn are all examples of nominal measurement. A more precise level is the **ordinal scale.** It permits the ranking of individuals or objects with regard to certain attributes. For example, individuals can be ranked by height or by length of nose. The third level of measurement, the **interval scale,** is the one most frequently employed in education and psychology. An interval scale varies so that the distances between points on the scale are equal. For example, temperature is measured by means of an interval scale. The difference between 35° and 34° is the same as that between 37° and 36°. The zero point on an interval scale is arbitrary. It is for this reason that changes on an interval scale can only be compared qualitatively. In other words, while the change from 50° to 60° is the same as that from 20° to 30°, there is no basis for saying that 60° is twice as hot as 30°. Scales which permit this type of comparison are referred to as **ratio scales.** These have a true zero point which allows the computing of ratios. For example, weight and age have true zeros.

While most measurement in education employs an interval scale, virtually none of it is direct. That is, no instruments have been devised yet which measure knowledge directly, as a ruler measures distance or a scale measures weight. Measurement in education is like the estimation of temperature. The latter is based on inferences that are made from the observation that a column of mercury or alcohol rises or descends in a hollow glass tube. The former derives from inferences based on changes in behavior. Put very simply, knowledge as a cognitive phenomenon is not yet measurable; but the assumption can be made that some of its effects on behavior are.

Characteristics of a
Good Measuring Instrument

Validity

It might appear somewhat platitudinous to say that a good test must measure what it is intended to measure. It is true, however, that many tests probably do not measure exactly what they are intended to measure or that they measure many other things as well and are therefore difficult to depend on. Obviously **validity** is the most important characteristic of a measuring instrument since, if it does not measure what it purports to, then the scores derived from it are of no value whatsoever.

Several indicators of validity are helpful to teachers in constructing tests. One of these is *content validity*. It is assessed by making a careful analysis of the content of test items and relating these to the objectives of the course, lesson, or unit. A test designed to measure a student's comprehension of the ecology of the

---

REMEMBERING AND THINKING

The six classes of objectives described by Bloom et al. (1956) can be further divided into two broad classes: those which involve remembering and those which require thinking. Only the knowledge objectives fall into the first category (knowledge of specifics, knowledge of ways and means of dealing with specifics, and knowledge of the universals and abstractions in a field). All of these emphasize remembering. Most teachers prefer to teach for understanding (comprehension, application, and so on) as well as for recall. Yet few know clearly the precise skills involved in such intellectual (thinking) activities as comprehension, application, synthesis, analysis, or evaluation. The two most frequently confused skills involve comprehension and application. Put quite simply, comprehension is the lowest level of understanding, implying no more than the ability to apprehend the substance of what is being communicated without necessarily relating it to other material (Bloom et al., 1956). It can be tested through items that require the students to translate (change from one form of communication to another, express in their own words), interpret (explain or summarize), or extrapolate (predict sequences or arrive at conclusions). Application, on the other hand, requires that learners be able to use what they comprehend, that they abstract from one situation to another. Application cannot be tested simply by asking that students interpret or translate; they must also be required to abstract the material in order to see its implications.

Two final points should be made. The first is simply to urge you to familiarize yourself with this taxonomy because of its implications both for teaching and for testing. The second is a reiteration of a very obvious point: Your instructional objectives (what you want of your students) are communicated very directly and very effectively to your students through your measurement devices. Even if you emphasize repeatedly that you want to teach for comprehension and other high-level skills, you will probably not be successful unless you construct achievement tests that reflect these objectives.

Kingdom of Sweetgrass Landing but comprised only of items such as the following does not possess content validity:

	True	False
1. A Korug is a blue fruit which grows in a snrape hole.	_____	_____
2. Doraboturs have tails that are at least three feet long.	_____	_____

The items measure knowledge of specifics rather than comprehension. Better items might have been the following.

	True	False
1. If snrape holes were all filled by Congurs, doraboturs would probably become extinct.	_____	_____
2. The snrape is important to the survival of doraboturs.	_____	_____

It should be noted, however, that these last two items measure comprehension only if the student has not been explicitly taught that doraboturs would probably become extinct if snrape holes were filled, since the snrape is important to the survival of the dorabotur. In other words, it is easy to teach principles as specifics, in which case items that require students to identify principles do not require comprehension so much as simple recall. What an item measures, therefore, is not inherent in the question itself, but resides in the relationship between the material as it has been taught to the student and what it is that the item requires.

A second indicator of validity is the extent to which a test *predicts* what it is intended to predict. If, for example, scores in grade four year-end tests are intended to predict success in grade five, a direct measure of the validity of these tests can be obtained when students have reached the end of the fifth grade. In the same way, college entrance examinations are not utilized simply to eliminate applicants, but to select those for whom success in college can reasonably be predicted. A numerical index of predictive validity can be arrived at by computing the correlation between the predictor test and later achievement (see Chapter 11 for a discussion of correlation). Here you are; someone has predicted that you would succeed!

Reliability

A second requirement of a good measuring instrument is that it be **reliable.** This means that the test should measure consistently whatever it does measure. An intelligence test which yields a score of 170 for a student one week and a score of 80 the next week is probably somewhat unreliable (unless something has happened to the student in between the tests). An instrument which is highly unreliable cannot be valid. In other words, if a test measures what it purports to *and* that attribute does not fluctuate erratically, then the test will yield similar scores on different occasions. Hence, one way of assessing reliability is to correlate results obtained from a repetition of a test. Another way is to divide the test into two halves and correlate the scores obtained on each half. If all items are intended to measure the same things, the scores on the halves should be similar.

While a test cannot be valid without also being reliable, it can be highly reliable without being valid. Consider the following *intelligence* test.

The Lefrancois Scale of Intelligent Behavior

Instructions
Join the dot to the square with four *separate straight* lines.

Scoring
Minimum score: *100*

Add
50 for half an answer _____
25 for another half _____
Total (maximum 175) _____

Interpretation
If you scored:

100—you are very bright
150—you are a genius
175—God

This intelligence test has been demonstrated to be extremely reliable (as well as extremely democratic). Bright people usually score 100; geniuses, 150; and Gods, 175. (The reader can be the judge of its validity.)

Tests

A test is a collection of tasks (items or questions) assumed to be a representative sample of the behaviors which the tester wishes to assess. Given that human beings vary in countless ways, there are countless types of tests and countless

examples of each type. A few examples of some *psychological* (creativity and intelligence tests) tests were given in Chapter 11. The remainder of this chapter is
concerned primarily with teacher-made achievement tests. It should be kept in mind,
however, that self-made tests are not the only alternative open to a teacher. Numerous standardized achievement tests are readily available. In addition some school
boards provide year-end tests for their teachers.

Teacher-made Tests

Teacher-made tests are of two kinds: good and bad. They can be employed
for a variety of purposes, only one of which is the assigning of grades. Other than
this, a test can be employed to determine whether students are *ready* to begin a unit
of instruction, to indicate to the teacher how effective instructional procedures are,
to identify learning difficulties, to determine what students know as well as what they
don't know, and to predict their probability of success on future learning tasks.

Teacher-made tests are almost always of the *paper-and-pencil* variety. Only
occasionally can a sample of nonverbal behavior be employed on a test. For example,
in physical education, in art, in drama, and in some workshop-type courses students
are sometimes asked either to produce something or to perform. In most other
courses they will be given either an *objective* or an *essay* test (or both). The latter
typically involves a written response of some length for each question.

Objective items, on the other hand, are items which normally require very
little writing and in which the scoring procedure is highly uniform (hence objective).
The four major types of objective test items are *completion, matching, true-false,* and
multiple choice. Examples of each are given below:

1. *Completion*

   Doraboturs are often found in _____ holes.

2. *Matching*

   _____ 1. Korug   a. blue
   _____ 2. dorabotur   b. red
   _____ 3. snrape   c. purple and pink

3. *True-False*

   _____ 1. Sweetgrass Landing is a republic.
   _____ 2. Congurs have orange-colored feelers.

4. *Multiple Choice*

   The easiest way to bag a mature dorabotur in Sweetgrass Landing is

   a. by using a high-powered rifle.
   b. by using a low-powered rifle.
   c. by looking for tails in snrape holes.
   d. by using a bag.

Essay versus Objective Tests

While each of these tests possesses some advantages and some disadvantages, either can be used to measure almost any significant aspect of student behavior. It is true, however, that some behaviors are more easily measured with one type of test than the other. Several of the major differences between essay and objective tests are given below. These can serve as a guide in deciding which to use in a given situation. Very often a mixture of both can be employed to advantage.

1. It is somewhat easier to tap higher-level processes (analysis, synthesis, and evaluation) with an essay examination, although it is quite possible to do the same thing with objective items. Essay examinations can be constructed to allow students to organize knowledge, to make inferences from it, to illustrate it, to apply it, and to extrapolate from it.

2. The content of essay examinations is very often more limited than is that of the more objective tests. Since the former usually consist of fewer items, the range of abilities or of information sampled is necessarily reduced. The objective question format, on the other hand, permits coverage of more content per unit of testing time. While a student's range of knowledge is often apparent in an essay test, the absence of that knowledge may not be so readily apparent.

3. Essay examinations allow for more divergence. It is not unreasonable to expect that students who do not like to be restricted in their answers will prefer them over more objective tests. There is considerable evidence, however, that very few students consistently do well with one format and poorly with the other (despite individual exceptions). In general those students who do well on objective examinations also do well with essays, and vice versa.

4. Constructing an essay test is considerably easier and less time-consuming than making up an objective examination. In fact, an entire test with an essay format can often be written in the same length of time as it would take to write no more than two or three good multiple choice items.

5. Scoring essay examinations requires considerably more time than scoring objective tests. This is especially true where tests can be scored electronically (as objective tests are in most larger universities and in an increasing number of schools). The total time involved in making and scoring a test is less for essay examinations if classes are small (twenty students or less, perhaps) but is considerably less for objective tests as the number of students increases (see Figure 15.1).

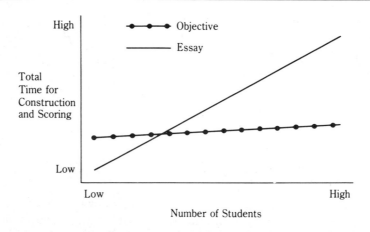

Figure 15.1 *A Hypothetical Representation of the Relationship between Size of Class and Test Construction and Scoring Time*

6. The reliability of essay examinations is very much lower than that of objective tests, primarily because of the subjectivity involved in their scoring. Numerous studies attest to this well-known fact. In one (Educational Testing Service, 1961), three hundred essays were rated by fifty-three judges on a nine-point scale. Slightly over one-third of the papers

---

TO BE OBJECTIVE OR SUBJECTIVE?

The question is purely rhetorical. Not only does it have no answer, but it deserves none. Very few teachers will ever find themselves in situations where they *must* always use either one form of test or the other. Some class situations, particularly where size is a factor, may lend themselves more readily to objective test formats; in other situations, essay formats may be better; sometimes a combination of each may be desirable. The important point is that both have advantages and disadvantages. You as a teacher should endeavor to develop skills necessary to constructing good items in a variety of formats without becoming a passionate advocate of one over the other.

received all possible grades. That is, each of these papers received the highest possible grade from at least one judge and the lowest possible grade from at least one other. In addition, each received every other possible grade from at least one judge. Another 37 percent of the papers each received eight of the nine different grades; 23 percent received seven of the nine.

Other studies have found that a relatively poor paper read after an even poorer one will tend to be given a higher grade than if it is read after a very good paper; some graders consistently give moderate marks whereas others give very high and very low marks, although the average grades given by each might be very similar; knowledge of who wrote the paper tends to affect scores, sometimes beneficially and sometimes to the student's detriment (halo effect); if the first few answers on an essay examination are particularly good, overall marks tend to be higher than if the first answers are poor.

There are a number of methods for increasing the scorer reliability of essay examinations, not the least of which is simply being aware of possible sources of unreliability. Some of the suggestions given below may be of value in this regard.

Suggestions for Constructing Tests

The advantages of a particular type of test can often be increased if the items of which it is comprised are carefully constructed. By the same token the disadvantages can also be made more severe through faulty item construction. Essay examinations, for example, are said to be more amenable to the measurement of "higher" processes. Consider the following item:

List the animals which live in Sweetgrass Landing.

If the tester's intention were to sample analysis or evaluation, this item has no advantage over many objective items—for example:

Given that doraboturs eat congurs whenever they can, that congurs like to hide in snrape holes, and that snrape holes are very shallow, where would you expect to find doraboturs?

> *a. in snrape trees*
> *b. in congur caves*
> *c. in snrape holes*
> *d. in collections of trees*

Several specific suggestions are given below for the construction of essay tests and of multiple choice tests. The latter are discussed since they are the most preferred among objective item forms.

Essay Tests The following suggestions are based in part on Gronlund (1968).

1. Essay questions should be geared toward sampling processes not easily assessed by objective items (for example, analysis, synthesis, or evaluation).

2. As for all tests, essay questions should relate directly to the desired outcomes of the learning procedure. This should be clearly understood by the students as well.

3. The questions should be specific if they are to be easily scorable. If the intention is to give marks for illustrations, the item should specify that an illustration is required.

4. A judicious sampling of desired terminal behavior should comprise the substance of the items.

5. If the examiner's intention is to sample high-level processes, sufficient *time* should be allowed for students to complete the questions.

6. The weighting of various questions as well as the time that should be allotted to each should be indicated for the student.

7. The questions should be worded so that the teacher's expectations are clear both to the student and to the teacher.

Other suggestions for making the scoring more objective are also available. One of these is to outline model answers before scoring the test (that is, write out an answer that would receive full points). Another is to score all answers for one item before going on to the next. The purpose of this is to increase uniformity of scoring. A third suggestion is simply that the scorer should intend to be objective. For example, if poor grammar results in the loss of five marks on one paper, perhaps grammar that is half as bad should result in the loss of two and a half marks on another paper.

Multiple Choice Items A multiple choice item consists of a statement or series of statements (called the *stem*) and of three to five alternatives, only one of which is the correct or best solution. The other alternatives are referred to as *distractors*. Each of the distractors is intended to be a response which will appear plausible *if students do not know the answer*. If they know the correct answer, distractors should, of course, appear less plausible. Below are a number of suggestions for writing multiple choice items. Most of them are common sense, which makes them no less valid.

  1. Both stems and alternatives should be clearly worded, unambiguous, grammatically correct, specific, and at the appropriate level of comprehension.
  2. Double negatives are highly confusing and should be avoided. Single negatives are not recommended either.
  3. The items should sample a representative portion of subject content, but they should not be taken verbatim from the textbook. This is defensible only where the intention is clearly to test memorization.
  4. All distractors should be equally plausible so that answering correctly is not simply a matter of eliminating highly implausible distractors. Consider the following example of a poor item:

> $10 + 12 + 18 =$
> a. 2146
> b. 7,568,482
> c. 40
> d. 10

  5. Unintentional cues need to be avoided. Ending the stem with *a* or *an* often provides a cue:

> A dorabotur is an
> a. tree
> b. animal
> c. small congur
> d. huge biped

  6. Specific determiners such as *never, always, none, impossible,* and *absolutely* should be avoided in distractors (though not necessarily in stems). They are almost always associated with incorrect alternatives. Words such as *sometimes, frequently,* and *usually* are most often associated with correct alternatives. In stems they tend to be ambiguous because people interpret them differently.

  Numerous other useful suggestions are provided by Thorndike and Hagen (1977) and Mehrens and Lehmann (1969).

Reporting Test Results

  Having constructed, administered, and scored a test, the teacher is faced with the responsibility of making the wisest possible use of the information derived from it. Obviously, some of these uses are separate from the actual reporting of test results to students or parents; they are concerned instead with instructional decisions that the teacher must make. Are the students ready to go to the next unit?

Should they be allowed to study in the library again? Should educational television be employed? Should a review be undertaken? Should the teacher look for another job?

Even if the test is primarily intended to enable the teacher to make decisions relative to questions such as those given above, results should also be reported to the students. The feedback which students receive about their learning can be of tremendous value in guiding future efforts. It can also be highly reinforcing in this achievement-oriented society.

While raw scores can be reported directly to the student, they are of little or no value unless they are related to some scale about which value judgments can be made. A score of 40 on a test where the maximum possible score is 40 is different from a score of 40 on a test where the ceiling is 80. The traditional way of giving meaning to these scores is to convert them either to a percentage or to a letter grade which has clearly defined, though arbitrary, significance. Advanced students should probably be given more information than simply a percentage or a letter grade. To begin with, it is useful to know precisely the areas of weakness as well as the strengths. In addition even a percentage score is relatively useless unless the student has some knowledge about the scores obtained by other students. A simple way of giving a class this knowledge is to report the arithmetical average (**mean**) as well as the range of scores (low and high scores). It might be even more useful to show the distribution of scores for the entire class in addition to the average of those scores, particularly since the "average" score is not always near the middle (**median**) of that distribution. The point which should always be kept in mind regarding the use of tests and test results is that they should not be employed simply to enable teachers to categorize students but should serve as an integral part of the instructional process. (See Figure 1.1, A Teaching Flow Chart.)

Criterion-Referenced Testing

There is a small kingdom hidden in the steamy jungles of South America. One of its borders is the Amazon, which describes a serpentine half-circle around most of the perimeter of this kingdom. Its other border consists of an impenetrable row of harsh mountains. The inhabitants of the kingdom are therefore trapped by the river on one side, since they dare not try to cross it; and by the mountains on the other, for although they can climb the mountains to their very tops, the other side presents an unbroken row of vertical cliffs attaining dizzying heights of no less than 8,000 feet at any location. In this kingdom there are numerous and very ferocious man-eating beasts. Fortunately, all are nocturnal. I say fortunately because, although the human inhabitants of the kingdom live on the mountain sides well beyond where their enemies can climb, they must descend the mountain every day to find food.

There is in this kingdom, then, a test that is given to all able-bodied men, women, and children, each day of their lives. It is a simple test. Before nightfall, each must succeed in climbing the mountain to a point beyond the reach of the predators. Failure to do so is obvious to all, for the individual who fails simply does not answer roll call that evening. Success is equally obvious. The situation, however, is not parallel to the ordinary testing practices of most schools. Passing the test does not require that an individual be the first to reach safety; it doesn't even require that he be among the first 90 percent to do so. Indeed, he will have been just as successful if he is the very last to reach the fire. He will be just as alive as the first (and perhaps he will be less hungry).

Consider the situation in schools where testing is of the traditional **norm-referenced** variety. Assume that all students are expected to attain a certain level of performance in a variety of subjects, a level of performance that we will denote by the symbol X. In the course of the school year, teachers prepare a number of intelligent examinations and determine, probably relatively accurately, that certain individuals typically do better than others on these examinations. These are, in effect, students comparable to those in the aforementioned kingdom who typically reach safety first. They are the students that the teacher can rightly assume have reached X or even gone beyond it. But in assessing student performance and reporting grades, teachers probably don't ask themselves which students have reached X and which haven't. They compare each child to the average performance of all children and on that basis make judgments about the relative performance of students. Thus, in a very advanced class, students who have in fact reached X, but who fall well below average performance are assigned mediocre marks. In a less advanced class, these same students might be assigned much higher grades.

Norm-referenced tests are therefore tests where the student's performance is judged and reported in terms of some standard or norm that is derived from typical student performance on that test. In other words, the results of such a test are based on comparisons among students.

There is a second alternative—one exemplified in the South American kingdom—where students are not compared one to the other, but where performance is judged only in relation to a criterion. In that example, the criterion is simply the ability to climb beyond the reach of predators; success is survival and failure is death.

Criterion-referenced testing can also be employed in schools. If teachers are able to specify what is involved in achieving X in terms of precise behavioral objectives (see Chapter 6), then they can judge whether a student has reached that criterion without having to compare that student to any other student. Obviously, it is frequently difficult and certainly very time-consuming to define X with directly measurable objectives. On the other hand, it is quite possible to define aspects of X in those terms, in which case criterion-referenced tests can be employed. The teacher can decide, for example, that all fifth grade students should be able to read a selected passage within five minutes and subsequently answer three predetermined factual questions relating to the content of the passage. This amounts quite simply to establishing a criterion. Students can then be tested to determine whether they have reached the criterion.

The principal difference between criterion-referenced tests and norm-referenced tests lies not in the nature of the tests themselves, but in the use that the teacher makes of them. In criterion-referenced testing, the student's performance is compared to a criterion; in norm-referenced testing, an individual's performance is compared to that of other students. Individual differences are of no importance in criterion-referenced testing. Indeed, the objective is to have all students succeed.

Literature on educational testing has recently become preoccupied with a minor controversy surrounding the relative merits of these two approaches to testing. Advocates of criterion-referenced testing point to the inherent justice of their approach. No student need consistently fail for performing less well than others after a fixed period of time. When students reach the criterion, they will have succeeded. Indeed, at that point, they will be as successful on that particular task as all others. And those students who have more to learn at the onset of instruction will not fail simply because they begin at a different place and consequently lag behind others in the beginning. If they reach the mountain heights before the beasts, they will also have succeeded. Criterion-referenced testing argues strongly for the individualization of instruction and of evaluation; it encourages students to work toward the goals of the system rather than against other students, and it forces teachers to make those goals explicit.

But criterion-referenced testing has certain limitations, as others have been quick to point out. While it is relatively simple to specify that after taking typing lessons for six weeks a student should be able to type thirty words per minute with no more than two errors, it is considerably more difficult to determine precisely what it is that a student should know after sitting in a social studies class for six weeks. A criterion-referenced test is clearly appropriate in the first situation, but much less so in the second.

A second limitation, though perhaps a minor one, is that some students can perform better than criterion. Some educators fear that exclusive reliance on criterion-referenced testing may thwart student incentive.

One final advantage of norm-referenced testing is that it provides both students and those who would counsel them with very valuable information concerning their likelihood of success in situations where they will, in fact, be required to compete with others. Such might be the case, for example, where a student is trying to decide whether she should go to college and become a doctor, or whether she should take over her father's bus line.

What should *you* do while the controversy rages around you? Very simply, both. There are situations where norm-referenced tests are not only unavoidable, but also very useful. There are also many situations where students will respond very favorably to the establishment of definite criteria for success and where both their learning and your teaching will benefit as a result. Here, as elsewhere, there is no either-or question; your decisions should be based on the fundamental purposes of your instructional procedures in specific situations.

The Ethics of Testing

Assessment, a global term for measurement and evaluation, is a fundamental part of the teaching-learning process. Its potential benefits to both teacher and learner are, as we have seen in earlier parts of this chapter, rather important. Deale

(1975) suggests that teachers need to assess students for the following reasons: to determine whether what has been taught has also been learned, how well, and by how many; to monitor the progress of individual students as well as of groups; to evaluate instructional materials and procedures; to amass and retain accurate records of student attainment; and to aid learning. For each of these purposes, teachers may employ their own teacher-made tests or standardized tests complete with administration, scoring, and norming procedures.

Several important words of caution are appropriate at this point. With the increasing use of tests, particularly of the standardized variety, and with increasing concern for privacy, individual rights, and equality, some of the ethical issues implicit in the administration and use of tests have become matters of political and social concern. Tests are frequently seen as a threat, as a violation of privacy, and as unjust. Unfortunately, these concerns are not entirely unfounded. For example, personality tests can violate privacy when they probe into areas that would not ordinarily be publicly revealed; tests can be threatening when school placement, job opportunities—indeed, success and failure—depend upon their results; and they can be patently unjust when employed for purposes for which they were not intended, or with groups for whom they were not designed.

It is reassuring to note that increasing concern with the ethics of testing and records has recently been reflected in a public law in the United States affecting all schools funded by the Office of Education. Among other things, this law (Public Law 93-380) grants parents of children under eighteen the right of access to education records kept by schools and relating to their own children, the right to challenge the accuracy and appropriateness of these records, the right to limit public access to these records and to receive a list of individuals and/or agencies that have been given access to them, and the right to be notified if and when the records are turned over to the courts of law. All these parental rights become the student's rights after the age of eighteen or after the student enters a postsecondary, educational institution.

None of these observations is intended as justification for abandoning the use of teacher-made and standardized tests in the schools; they are intended as an argument for the sane and restrained use of tests and the results obtained therefrom.

Summary of Chapter 15

This chapter has presented a discussion of measurements and evaluation in schools. Essay and objective tests were compared, and guidelines were provided for constructing each. Suggestions for the uses of test results were given, and criterion-referenced tests were compared with norm-referenced tests.

Main Points in Chapter 15

1. Measurement involves the use of an instrument (ruler, thermometer, nosemeter, test) to gauge the quantity of a property or behavior. Evaluation is the making of a decision about goodness or appropriateness; it should be based on the results of careful and thoughtful measurement.

2. A teaching model can be represented in terms of goals, instructional strategies, and assessment. Educational goals are important in determining both strategies and assessment.

3. Goals or objectives can be very general or more specific. Specific goals are usually more amenable to testing. Bloom's taxonomy can be of value both in setting up educational objectives and in designing tests to determine the extent to which these goals have been obtained.

4. Measurement can be nominal (categorical), ordinal (using ranks), interval (employing equidistant scales but with an arbitrary zero point), or ratio (based on a true zero). Educational measurement at least pretends to be on an interval scale (usually).

5. Good measuring instruments need to be both valid and reliable. A valid instrument measures what it purports to measure. If it is reliable as well, it measures it consistently.

6. Teacher-made tests are most often of the paper-and-pencil variety. These are either objective (true-false, completion, matching, or multiple choice) or essay type.

7. Both essay and objective tests have advantages and disadvantages. They should be employed together whenever possible.

8. Raw scores on achievement tests are usually quite meaningless. They are sometimes given meaning by converting them to percentage scores or letter grades. The average score, the range of scores, and the class distribution are also useful for both teachers and students.

9. Schools have traditionally employed norm-referenced tests—tests where student performance is judged in relation to the performance of other students.

10. Criterion-referenced tests judge students by comparing their performance to a preestablished criterion rather than to the performance of other students.

11. Both norm-referenced and criterion-referenced tests should be employed in schools.

12. Caution should be exercised in the administration, interpretation, and use of tests. On occasion they represent a violation of privacy; at times they can also be highly unjust.

Suggested Readings

The following short bulletin presents a clear and useful account of assessment procedures in the secondary school. Of particular importance are the many suggestions given for designing tests and interpreting test results.

Deale, R. N. *Assessment and Testing in the Secondary School.* London: Evans/ Methuen, 1975.

Among the most comprehensive measurement and evaluation books for teachers is the following:

Sax, Gilbert. *Principles of Educational Measurement: An Evaluation.* Belmont, Calif.: Wadsworth, 1974.

Purring among suckling young has been reported in the black bear. Growling among adult bears has also been reported (Ewer, 1973).

We have now come the full circle, and in the manner of that wonderful design we are ready to begin again. For it was somewhere near the beginning that the reader was given a word of caution. This same caution is equally fitting at the end. A science of humanity tends to dehumanize. It transforms living, breathing beings into *organisms;* it reduces our indescribably complex behavior to stimuli and responses and the activity of our mind to hypothetical structures that behave in a hypothetical fashion. At the beginning we said that students are more than all this—at the end we say again that they are much more. Psychology has only begun to understand; the last word has not been said or written. . . .

Yet something has been said in the pages of this text. On fifteen occasions, that something was reduced to a set of statements which were referred to as Main Points. Here, in this epilogue, these Main Points are further abstracted to fifteen summary statements—one for each chapter—and, finally, to a single point which is close to the very essence of the book.

Summary Statements

1. Evolution has equipped humans poorly for physical survival in an animalistic sense. On the other hand, our superior intelligence has allowed us to extend our adaptability by amplifying our capacities. The role of psychology is to explain our adaptation to the environment. The purpose of education is to facilitate that adaptation.

2. Among the instructional implications that may be derived from S-R positions are suggestions relating to the value of repetition, reinforcement, and activity.

3. Most significant human behaviors are probably of the operant variety. It is partly for this reason than an analogy between a Skinner box and a classroom is not entirely inappropriate.

4. Bears always face toward the front of their tracks.

5. Since a great deal of social learning appears to result from the observation of models, an awareness of the effects of imitation is important for teachers.

6. Learning may be viewed as consisting of the formation of cognitive structures (coding systems or subsumers). This view highlights the importance for instruction of integrating subject matter.

7. Statements of instructional objectives should specify what the learner must do as well as the criteria of acceptable performance.

8. One way of defining self-actualization is to say that it involves a continuing effort to achieve the maximum development of an individual's potentiality. The process is assumed to be related to healthy and creative functioning. It is facilitated by *student-centered* schools.

9. Development is the extremely complex process through which little humans progress in their quest to achieve an adequate adaptation to the world.

10. Among the principles for teaching that can be derived from Piaget's work are the following: Teacher recognition of differences between children and adults can enable them to communicate more effectively. Instructional procedures should provide for student activity. There is an optimal level of difficulty for new learning, which can be determined on the basis of what a student already knows. A teacher should be aware of the limits of children's abilities—

some concepts *are* too difficult at certain ages. Social interaction is an important variable in the decentering of thought and should be provided for in schools.

11. Both creativity and intelligence appear to be a function of the interaction of heredity and environment.

12. Creativity can be hampered through the employment of rigid, highly structured, nonpermissive, evaluation-conscious, dogmatic teachers; it may be fostered by teachers and schools less structured and less dogmatic.

13. The teacher in a classroom can be viewed as a source of stimulation that maintains arousal at low or high levels in students, a view which has important implications for instruction since it may be assumed that there is an optimal level of arousal for maximally effective behavior and that students will behave so as to maintain arousal level at or near the optimum.

14. The control of a class through attention to learning rather than through attention to discipline is highly desirable.

15. A teaching model can be represented in terms of goals, instructional strategies, and assessment. Educational goals are important in determining both strategies and assessment.

Main Point of the Book

The following is the main point of this book. It is derived from the preceding fifteen main points; these, in turn, were derived from the various Main Points that summarized each of the fifteen chapters. This is, then, the Final Main Point. It is not a summary of the content of the book, but is merely a true, obvious, and sensible observation. And it is an observation that may be of value for prospective teachers.

A Bear Always Faces the Front of Its Tracks*

The relevance of this statement to teaching cannot easily be explained in anything shorter than a full-length book. Since the present book is now concluding, suffice it to say that a teacher should endeavor to behave as sensibly as a bear, who persistently faces the front of its footprints. Teaching has been described as an art and a science. The comment was made in Chapter 1 that where science fails art should be employed. The point being made here is that both the art and the science partake heavily of common sense.

---

* In 1972 I had no doubt that this statement was entirely and absolutely true, but by 1975 I had realized that it is only a very stupid bear who does not occasionally look behind itself. Accordingly, the second edition of this work (that is a euphemism) loudly proclaimed "A bear ~~always~~ usually faces the front." Truth is a precarious luxury. It now seems fairly definite that many bears spend much of their time facing backwards. This does not appear to be accomplished by walking backwards. And they *do* sometimes face the front!

Bibliography

Adams, John C., Jr. The relative effects of various testing atmospheres on spontaneous flexibility, a factor of divergent thinking. *Journal of Creative Behavior,* 1968, 2, 187–194.

Agnew, N. McK. and S. W. **Pyke.** *The science game: an introduction to research in the behavioral sciences.* Englewood Cliffs, N.J.: Prentice-Hall, 1969.

Allen, K. and F. **Harris.** Elimination of a child's excessive scratching by training the mother in reinforcement procedures. *Behaviour Research and Therapy,* 1966, 4, 79–84.

Alschuler, A. S. Motivating achievement in high-school students: education for human growth. Englewood Cliffs, N.J.: Educational Technology Publications, 1972.

American Psychological Association. Guidelines for psychologists conducting growth groups. *American Psychologist,* 1973, 28, 933.

Ames, Louise B. The sequential patterning of prone progression in the infant. *Genetic and Psychological Monographs,* 1937, 19, 409–460.

Ammons, R. B. Effective knowledge of performance: a survey and tentative theoretical formulation. *Journal of Genetic Psychology,* 1956, 54, 279–299.

Anastasi, A. Heredity, environment, and the question "how"? *Psychological Review,* 1958, 65, 197–208.

Anderson, H. H. (ed.). *Creativity and its cultivation.* New York: Harper & Row, 1959.

Anderson, L. D. The predictive value of infant tests in relation to intelligence at five years. *Child Development,* 1939, 10, 202–212.

Anderson, R. C. and G. W. **Faust.** The effects of strong formal prompts in programed instruction. *American Educational Research Journal,* 1967, 4, 345–352.

Arnold, John E. "Useful creative techniques," in *A sourcebook for creative thinking,* eds. Sidney J. Parnes and Harold F. Harding. New York: Charles Scribner's Sons, 1962, 251–268.

Aronfreed, J. "Aversive control of socialization," in *Nebraska symposium on motivation,* ed. D. Levine. Lincoln: University of Nebraska Press, 1968.

Athey, Irene J. and Duane O. **Rubadeau** (eds.). *Educational implications of Piaget's theory.* Waltham, Mass.: Ginn-Blaisdell, 1970.

Ausubel, D. P. *Theory and problems of child development.* New York: Grune & Stratton, 1958.

Ausubel, D. P. Use of advance organizers in the learning and retention of meaningful material. *Journal of Educational Psychology,* 1960, 51, 267–272.

Ausubel, D. P. *The psychology of meaningful verbal learning.* New York: Grune & Stratton, 1963.

Ausubel, D. P. "Introduction," in *Readings in the psychology of cognition,* eds. R. C. Anderson and D. P. Ausubel. New York: Holt, Rinehart and Winston, 1965, 3–17.

Ausubel, D. P. *Educational psychology: a cognitive view.* New York: Holt, Rinehart and Winston, 1968.

Ausubel, David P. and Floyd G. **Robinson.** *School learning: an introduction to educational psychology.* New York: Holt, Rinehart and Winston, 1969.

Ayllon, T., S. **Garber,** and K. **Pisor.** The elimination of discipline problems through a combined school-home motivational system. *Behavior Therapy,* 1975, 6, 616–626.

Azrin, N. H. and O. R. **Lindsley.** The reinforcement of cooperation between children. *Journal of Abnormal and Social Psychology,* 1956, 52, 100–102.

Baldwin, Alfred L. *Theories of child development.* New York: John Wiley, 1967.

Bandura, Albert. "Social learning through imitation," in *Nebraska symposium on motivation,* ed. N. R. Jones. Lincoln: University of Nebraska Press, 1962, 211–269.

Bandura, Albert. *Principles of behavior modification.* New York: Holt, Rinehart and Winston, 1969.

Bandura, Albert, Dorothea **Ross,** and Sheila **Ross.** Imitation of film mediated aggressive models. *Journal of Abnormal and Social Psychology,* 1963, 66, 3–11.

Bandura, Albert and Richard **Walters.** *Social learning and personality development.* New York: Holt, Rinehart and Winston, 1963.

Barber, T. X. and M. J. **Silver.** Fact, fiction, and the experimenter bias effect. *Psychological Bulletin Monographs Supplement,* 1969, 70, 1–29(a).

Barber, T. X. and M. J. **Silver.** Pitfalls in data analysis and interpretation: a reply to Rosenthal. *Psychological Bulletin Monographs Supplement,* 1969, 70, 48–62(b).

Beard, R. M. An Outline of Piaget's Developmental Psychology for Students and Teachers. New York: Basic Books, 1969.

Berlyne, D. E. Recent developments in Piaget's work. *British Journal of Educational Psychology,* 1957, 27, 1–12.

Berlyne, D. E. *Conflict, arousal and curiosity.* New York: McGraw-Hill, 1960.

Berlyne, D. E. Curiosity and exploration. *Science,* 1966, 153, 25–33.

Bernard, Harold W. *Human development in western culture* (2nd Edition). Boston: Allyn and Bacon, 1966.

Bernard, Luther L. *Instinct: a study in social psychology.* New York: Holt, Rinehart and Winston, 1924.

Bernstein, B. Language and social class. *British Journal of Sociology,* 1961, 11, 271–276.

Bigge, M. L. *Learning theories for teachers.* New York: Harper & Row, 1964.

Bijou, S. W. Patterns of reinforcement and resistance to extinction in young children. *Child Development,* 1957, 28, 47–55.

Bijou, S. W. and P. S. **Sturges.** Positive reinforcers for experimental studies with children—consumables and manipulatables. *Child Development,* 1959, 30, 151–170.

Birnbrauer, J. S. and Julia **Lawler.** Token reinforcement for learning. *Mental Retardation,* 1964, 275–279.

Birnbrauer, J. S., M. N. **Wolf,** J. D. **Kidder,** and C. E. **Tague.** Classroom behavior of retarded pupils with token reinforcement. *Journal of Experimental Child Psychology,* 1965, 2, 219–235.

Bitterman, M. E. Toward a comparative psychology of learning. *American Psychologist,* 1960, 15, 704–712.

Bitterman, M. E. Thorndike and the problem of animal intellience. *American Psychologist,* 1969, 4, 444–453.

Bloom, Benjamin S. *Stability and change in human characteristics.* New York: John Wiley, 1964.

Bloom, Benjamin S. et al. (eds.). *Taxonomy of educational objectives: handbook I: cognitive domain.* New York: David McKay, 1956.

Bolles, R. C. Species-specific defense reactions and avoidance learning. *Psychological Review,* 1970, 77, 32–48.

Bolles, R. C. "Cognition and motivation: some historical trends," in *Cognitive views of human motivation,* ed. B. Weiner. New York: Academic Press, 1974, 1–20.

Boring, E. G. Intelligence as the tests test it. *New Republic,* 1923, 35, 35–37.

Borton, T. Reach, touch, and teach: student concerns and process education. New York: McGraw-Hill, 1970.

Bower, G. H. "Educational applications of mnemonic devices," in *Interaction: readings in human psychology,* ed. K. O. Doyle, Jr. Lexington, Mass.: D. C. Heath and Co., 1973, 201–210.

Bowlby, J. *Maternal care and mental health.* Geneva: World Health Organization, 1952.

Brackbill, Y. Extinction of the smiling response in infants as a function of reinforcement schedule. *Child Development,* 1958, 29, 115–124.

Brackbill, Y. and M. N. **Koltsova.** "Conditioning and learning," in *Infancy and early childhood,* ed. Y. Brackbill. New York: The Free Press, 1967, 207–286.

Breland, K. and M. **Breland.** A field of applied animal psychology. *American Psychologist,* 1951, 6, 202–204.

Breland, K. and M. **Breland.** The misbehavior of organisms. *American Psychologist,* 1961, 16, 681–684.

Bruner, J. S. "On going beyond the information given," in *Contemporary approaches to cognition.* Cambridge: Harvard University Press, 1957(a).

Bruner, J. S. On perceptual readiness. *Psychological Review,* 1957, 64, 123–152(b).

Bruner, J. S. The act of discovery. *Harvard Educational Review,* 1961, 31, 21–32(a).

Bruner, J. S. *The process of education.* Cambridge: Harvard University Press, 1961(b).

Bruner, J. S. *On knowing: essays for the left hand.* Cambridge: Harvard University Press, 1963.

Bruner, J. S. The course of cognitive growth. *American Psychologist,* 1964, 19, 1–15.

Bruner, J. S. The growth of mind. *American Psychologist,* 1965, 20, 1007–1017.

Bruner, J. S. *Toward a theory of instruction.* Cambridge: Harvard University Press, 1966.

Bruner, J. S. *Processes of cognitive growth: infancy.* Worcester, Mass.: Clark University Press, 1968.

Bruner, J. S., J. J. **Goodnow,** and G. A. **Austin.** *A study of thinking.* New York: John Wiley, 1956.

Bruner, J. S., Rose R. **Olver,** and Patricia N. **Greenfield.** *Studies in cognitive growth.* New York: John Wiley, 1966.

Buros, O. K. (ed.). *The seventh mental measurements yearbook.* Highland Park, N.J.: Gryphon, 1970.

Buros, O. K. *Tests in print II.* Highland Park, N.J.: Gryphon, 1974.

Burt, C. L. The inheritance of mental ability. *American Psyhologist,* 1958, 13, 1–15.

Cameron, A. W. *A guide to Eastern Canadian mammals.* Ottawa: Department of Northern Affairs and National Resources, 1956.

Carlson, J. S. Effects of instruction on the concept of conservation of substance. *Science Education,* 1967, 4, 285–291.

Carment, O. W. and C. G. **Miles.** Resistance to extinction and rate of lever pulling as a function of percentage of reinforcement and number of acquisition trials. *Canadian Journal of Psychology,* 1962, 64, 249–252.

Charles, Don C. *The psychology of the child in the classroom.* New York: Macmillan, 1964.

Cherry, E. C. Some experiments on the recognition of speech, with one and with two ears. *Journal of the Acoustical Society of America,* 1953, 25, 975–979.

Cherry, E. C. and W. K. **Taylor.** Some further experiments on the recognition of speech with one and two ears. *Journal of the Acoustical Society of America,* 1954, 26, 554–559.

Chomsky, N. *Syntactic structures.* The Hague: Mouton, 1957.

Chomsky, N. *Aspects of the theory of syntax.* Cambridge, Mass: MIT Press, 1965.

Clarizio, H. F. and S. L. **Yelon.** "Learning theory approaches to classroom management: rationale and intervention techniques," in *Modifying children's behavior: a book of readings,* ed. A. R. Brown and C. Avery. Springfield, Ill.: Charles C. Thomas, 1974, 44–56.

Cohen, D. K. Does IQ matter? *Current,* 1972, 141, 19–30.

Coleman, J. S. et al. *Equality of educational opportunity.* Washington, D.C.: U.S. Department of Health, Education, and Welfare, 1966.

Cook, John O. "Superstition" in the Skinnerian. *American Psychologist,* 1963, 18, 516–518.

Cook, John O. and M. E. **Spitzer.** Supplementary report: prompting versus confirmation in paired-associate learning. *Journal of Experimental Psychology,* April, 1960, 59, 275–276.

Coombs, A. W. *The professional education of teachers.* Boston: Allyn and Bacon, 1965.

Coon, C. L. *North Carolina schools and academies.* Raleigh, N.C.: Edwards and Broughton Printing Co., 1915.

Coopersmith, S. *The antecedents of self-esteem.* San Francisco: W. H. Freeman, 1967.

Côté, A. D. J. Flexibility and conservation acceleration. Unpublished Ph.D. dissertation, University of Alberta, Edmonton, Alberta, Canada, 1968.

Craig, R. C. Directed versus independent discovery of established relations. *Journal of Educational Psychology,* 1956, 47, 223–234.

Cropley, A. J. Originality, intelligence, and personality. Unpublished Ph.D. dissertation, University of Alberta, Edmonton, Alberta, Canada, 1965.

Crowder, N. A. "Automatic tutoring by intrinsic programming," in *Teaching machines and programmed learning,* eds. A. A. Lumsdaine and R. Glaser. Washington, D.C.: National Education Association, 1960, 286–298.

Crowder, Norman A. "Characteristics of branching programs," in *Conference on program learning,* ed. D. P. Scannell. Lawrence: University of Kansas, Studies in Education, 1961, 22–27.

Crowder, Norman A. On the differences between linear and intrinsic programming. *Phi Delta Kappan,* 1963, 44, 250–254.

Dale, E. "Historical setting of programed instruction," in *Programed instruction, the sixty-six yearbook of the National Society for the Study of Education,* part II, ed. P. C. Lange. Chicago: The University of Chicago Press, 1967, 28–54.

Darwin, C. A biographical sketch of an infant. *Mind,* 1877, 2, 287–294.

Deale, R. N. *Examinations bulletin 32: assessment and testing in the secondary school.* London: Evans/Methuen, 1975.

de Bono, E. *Lateral thinking: a textbook of creativity.* London: Ward Lock Educational, 1970.

de Bono, E. *Teaching thinking.* London: Temple Smith, 1976.

DeCecco, J. P. *Educational technology: readings in programmed instruction.* New York: Holt, Rinehart and Winston, 1964.

DeCecco, J. P. *The psychology of learning and instruction: educational psychology.* Englewood Cliffs, N.J.: Prentice-Hall, 1968.

de Garzia, A. and D. **Sohn** (eds.). *Programs, teachers and machines.* New York: Bantam Books, 1962.

Dennis, Wayne. Causes of retardation among institutional children: Iran. *Journal of Genetic Psychology,* 1960, 96, 47–59.

Dennison, G. *The lives of children.* New York: Vintage, 1969.

Deutsch, M. Facilitating development in the preschool child: social and psychological perspective. *Merrill-Palmer Quarterly,* 1964, 10, 248–263.

Ebbinghaus, H. *Memory.* Trans. H. A. Ruger and C. E. Bucenius. New York: Teachers' College, 1913. Reissued as paperback. New York: Dover, 1964.

Educational Testing Service. Judges disagree on qualities that characterize good writing. *ETS Development,* 1961, 9, 2.

Ellis, Albert. *Reason and emotion in psychotherapy.* New York: Lyle Stuart, 1962.

Environment, heredity and intelligence. *Harvard Educational Review.* Reprint series No. 2, 1969.

Ewer, R. F. *The carnivores.* Ithaca, N.Y.: Cornell University Press, 1973.

Feldhusen, J. F. Taps for teaching machines. *Phi Delta Kappan,* 1963, 44, 265–267.

Ferster, C. B. and B. F. **Skinner.** *Schedules of reinforcement.* New York: Appleton, 1957.

Festinger, L. *A theory of cognitive dissonance.* Stanford: Stanford University Press, 1957.

Festinger, L. Cognitive dissonance. *Scientific American,* October, 1962.

Flavell, John H. *The developmental psychology of Jean Piaget.* New York: Van Nostrand, 1963.

Fodor, E. N. Delinquency and susceptibility to social influence among adolescents as a function of level of moral development. *Journal of Social Psychology,* 1972, 86, 257–260.

Fowler, H. *Curiosity and exploratory behavior.* New York: Macmillan, 1965.

Fowler, William. Cognitive learning in infancy and early childhood. *Psychological Bulletin,* 1962, 59, 116–152.

Fowler, William. The effect of early stimulation: the problem of focus in developmental stimulation. Paper presented at a symposium on Heredity and Environment at the Annual Meeting of the American Educational Research Association, New York, February 16, 1967.

French, J. D. The reticular formation. *Scientific American,* May, 1957.

Frick, W. B. *Humanistic psychology: interviews with Maslow, Murphy, and Rogers.* Columbus, Ohio: Charles E. Merrill, 1971.

Furth, Hans G. *Piaget and knowledge.* Englewood Cliffs, N.J.: Prentice-Hall, 1970(a).

Furth, H. G. *Piaget for teachers.* Englewood Cliffs, N.J.: Prentice-Hall, 1970(b).

Gage, N. L. "Theories of teaching," in *Theories of learning and instruction: the sixty-third yearbook of the National Society for the Study of Education,* ed. E. R. Hilgard. Chicago: The University of Chicago Press, 1964, 268–285.

Gagné, R. M. The acquisition of knowledge. *Psychological Review,* 1962, 69, 355–365.

Gagné, R. M. *The conditions of learning* (1st Edition). New York: Holt, Rinehart and Winston, 1965.

Gagné, R. M. Learning hierarchies. *Educational Psychologist,* 1968, 6, 1–9.

Gagné, R. M. *The conditions of learning* (2nd Edition). New York: Holt, Rinehart and Winston, 1970.

Gagné, R. M. Domains of learning. *Interchange,* 1972, 3, 1.

Gagné, R. M. *Essentials of learning for instruction.* Hinsdale, Ill.: Dryden Press, 1974.

Gagné, R. M. and N. E. **Paradise.** Abilities and learning sets in knowledge acquisition. *Psychological Monographs,* 1961, 75, 14 (Whole No. 518).

Gallagher, James J. *Analysis of research on the education of gifted children.* State of Illinois: Office of the Superintendent of Public Instruction, 1960.

Galton, F. *Hereditary genius: an inquiry into its laws and consequences.* London: Macmillan, 1869.

Getzels, J. W. and P. W. **Jackson.** *Creativity and intelligence.* New York: John Wiley, 1962.

Ginsberg, Herbert and Sylvia **Opper.** *Piaget's theory of intellectual development.* Englewood Cliffs, N.J.: Prentice-Hall, 1969.

Glasser, W. *Schools without failure.* New York: Harper & Row, 1969.

Goldschmid, M. L. and P. M. **Bentler.** *Conservation concept diagnostic kit: manual and keys.* San Diego, Calif.: Educational and Industrial Testing Service, 1968.

Goodenough, F. *Measurement of intelligence by drawings.* New York: Harcourt, Brace & World, 1926.

Gordon, T. *T.E.T.: Teacher effectiveness training.* New York: Peter H. Wyden, 1974.

Gordon, William J. J. *Synectics: the development of creative capacity.* New York: Harper & Row, 1961.

Greenspoon, J. The reinforcing effect of two spoken sounds on the frequency of two responses. *American Journal of Psychology,* 1955, 68, 409–416.

Gronlund, N. E. *Constructing achievement tests.* Englewood Cliffs, N.J.: Prentice-Hall, 1968.

Guilford, J. P. Creativity. *American Psychologist,* 1950, 5, 444–454.

Guilford, J. P. Three faces of intellect. *American Psychologist,* 1959, 14, 469–479.

Guilford, J. P. Factors that aid and hinder creativity. *Teachers' College Record,* 1962, 63, 380–392.

Guilford, J. P. *The nature of human intelligence.* New York: McGraw-Hill, 1967.

Guthrie, E. R. *The psychology of learning* (1st Edition). New York: Harper & Brothers, 1935.

Guthrie, E. R. *The psychology of learning* (Rev. Edition). New York: Harper & Row, 1952.

Guthrie, E. R. "Association by contiguity," in *General systematic formulations, learning, and special process.* Vol. II of *Psychology: a study of the science,* ed. S. Koch. New York: McGraw-Hill, 1959, 158–195.

Guthrie, John T. Expository instruction versus a discovery method. *Journal of Educational Psychology,* 1967, 58, 45–49.

Haan, N., N. B. **Smith,** and J. **Block.** Moral reasoning of young adults: Political-social behavior, family background, and personality correlates. *Journal of Personality and Social Psychology,* 1968, 10, 183–201.

Haddon, F. A. and Hugh **Lytton.** Teaching approach and the development of divergent thinking abilities in primary schools. *The British Journal of Educational Psychology,* 1968, 38, 171–180.

Haefele, John W. *Creativity and innovation.* New York: Reinhold, 1962.

Hall, F. R. and K. R. **Kelson.** *The mammals of North America,* vol. II. New York: Ronald Press, 1959.

Hallman, Ralph J. Techniques of creative teaching. *Journal of Creative Behavior,* 1967, 1, 325–330.

Harris, D. *Children's drawings as measures of intellectual maturity.* New York: Harcourt, Brace & World, 1963.

Hart, B. et al. Effects of social reinforcement on operant crying. *Journal of Experimental Child Psychology,* 1964, 1, 145–153.

Hartshorne, H. and M. A. **May.** *Studies in the nature of character:* vol. 1, *Studies in deceit;* vol. 2, *Studies in self-control;* vol. 3, *Studies in the organization of character.* New York: Macmillan, 1928–1930.

Haslerud, G. N. and S. **Meyers.** The transfer value of given and individually derived principles. *Journal of Educational Psychology,* 1958, 49, 293–298.

Hebb, D. O. The effects of early experience on problem solving maturity. *American Psychologist,* 1947, 2, 306–307.

Hebb, D. O. *The organization of behavior.* New York: John Wiley, 1949.

Hebb, D. O. Drive and the CNS (conceptual nervous system). *Psychological Review,* 1955, 62, 243–354.

Hebb, D. O. *A textbook of psychology* (1st Edition). Philadelphia: W. B. Saunders, 1958.

Hebb, D. O. "A neuro-psychological theory," in *Sensory, Perceptual, and Physiological Formulations.* Vol. I of *Psychology: a study of the science,* ed. S. Koch. New York: McGraw-Hill, 1959, 622–643.

Hebb, D. O. *A textbook of psychology* (2nd Edition). Philadelphia: W. B. Saunders, 1966.

Hebron, Miriam E. *Motivated learning.* London: Methuen, 1966.

Heider, F. *The psychology of interpersonal relations.* New York: John Wiley, 1958.

Herbert, J. J. and C. M. **Harsh.** Observational learning by cats. *Journal of Comparative Psychology,* 1944, 37, 81–95.

Heron, Woodburn. The pathology of boredom. *Scientific American,* January, 1957.

Herrnstein, R. J. The evolution of behaviorism. *American Psychologist,* 1977, 32, 593–603.

Hewett, S. *The emotionally disturbed child in the classroom.* Boston: Allyn and Bacon, 1968.

Heyns, O. S. Treatment of the unborn. *Woman's Own,* February 4, 1967, 18.

Hicks, B. L. and S. **Hunka.** *The teacher and the computer.* Philadelphia: W. B. Saunders, 1971.

Higbee, K. L. *Your memory: how it works and how to improve it.* Englewood Cliffs, N.J.: Prentice-Hall, 1977.

Hilgard, E. R. "Learning theory and its applications," in *New teaching aides for the American classroom,* ed. W. Schramm. Stanford: Institute for Communications Research, 1960, 19–26.

Hilgard, E. R. and G. H. **Bower.** *Theories of learning* (3rd Edition). New York: Appleton-Century-Crofts, 1966.

Hill, W. F. *Learning: a survey of psychological interpretations* (Rev. Edition). New York: Chandler Publishing Company, 1971.

Hinde, R. A. and R. **Stevenson-Hinde** (eds.). *Constraints on learning: limitations and predispositions.* New York: Academic Press, 1973.

Hoffman, M. L. Conscience, personality, and socialization techniques. *Human Development,* 1970, 13, 90–126.

Hoffman, M. L. "Empathy, role-taking, guilt, and development of altruistic motives," in *Moral development and behavior,* ed. T. Lick. New York: Holt, Rinehart and Winston, 1976.

Hull, C. L. *Principles of behavior.* New York: Appleton-Century-Crofts, 1943.

Hull, C. L. *A behavior system.* New Haven: Yale University Press, 1952.

Hunt, J. McV. *Intelligence and experience.* New York: Ronald Press, 1961.

Hurlock, Elizabeth B. *Developmental psychology* (3rd Edition). New York: McGraw-Hill, 1968.

Inhelder, B. and J. **Piaget.** *The growth of logical thinking from childhood to adolescence.* New York: Basic Books, 1958.

Isaacs, N. *The growth of understanding in the young child.* London: The Education Supply, 1961.

Janos, O. Age and individual differences in higher nervous activity in infants. *Halek's Collection of Studies in Pediatrics,* 1965, No. 8.

Jenkins, J. J. and D. G. **Peterson** (eds.). *Studies in individual differences: the search for intelligence.* New York: Appleton-Century-Crofts, 1961.

Jensen, A. R. Social class, race and genetics: implications for education. *American Educational Research Journal,* 1968, 5, 1–42.

Jensen, A. R. How much can we boost I.Q. and scholastic achievement? *Harvard Educational Review,* 1969, 39, 1–123.

Jensen, A. R. Cumulative deficit in IQ of blacks in the rural South. *Developmental Psychology,* 1977, 13, 184–191.

Johnson, Nicholas. Through the video screen darkly. *The Christian Science Monitor,* February 28, 1969, sec. 2.

Johnson, Ronald C. and Gene R. **Medinnus.** *Child psychology: behavior and development* (2nd Edition). New York: John Wiley, 1969.

Jones, M. C. A laboratory study of fear: the case of Peter. *Pedagogical Seminary and Journal of Genetic Psychology,* 1924, 31, 308–315.

Kaess, W. and D. **Zeaman.** Positive and negative knowledge of results on a Pressey-type punchboard. *Journal of Experimental Psychology,* 1960, 60, 12–17.

Kamii, C. "A sketch of the Piaget-derived preschool curriculum developed by the Ypsilanti early education program," in *History and theory of early childhood education,* ed. S. J. Braun and E. Edwards. Worthington, Ohio: Charles A. Jones, 1972.

Kasatkin, N. I. and A. N. **Levikova.** On the development of early conditioned reflexes and differentiations of auditory stimuli in infants. *Journal of Experimental Psychology,* 1935, 18, 1–19.

Kass, N. and H. P. **Wilson.** Resistance to extinction as a function of percentage of reinforcement, number of training trials, and conditioned reinforcement. *Journal of Experimental Psychology,* 1966, 71, 355–357.

Katona, G. *Organizing and memorizing.* New York: Columbia University Press, 1940.

Kaufman, K. F. and K. D. **O'Leary.** Reward, cost, and self-evaluation procedures with schizophrenic children. Unpublished manuscript, State University of New York. Cited in O'Leary, K. D. and S. G. O'Leary. *Classroom management: the successful use of behavior modification.* New York: Pergamon Press, 1972, Chapter 1.

Kazdin, A. E. and R. R. **Bootzin.** The token economy: an evaluative review. *Journal of Applied Behavior Analysis,* 1972, 5, 343–372.

Keller, F. S. *Learning: reinforcement theory* (2nd Edition). New York: Random House, 1969.

Kelly, F. J. and J. J. **Cody.** *Educational psychology: a behavioral approach.* Columbus, Ohio: Charles E. Merrill, 1969.

Kendler, H. H. and T. S. **Kendler.** Effect of verbalization on reversal shifts in children. *Science,* 1961, 141, 1919–1920.

Kessen, William. *The child.* New York: John Wiley, 1965.

Kimble, G. A. *Hilgard and Marquis' conditioning and learning.* New York: Appleton-Century-Crofts, 1961.

Kintsch, Walter. *Learning, memory, and conceptual processes.* New York: John Wiley, 1970.

Koch, J. The development of a conditioned orienting reaction to humans in 2–3 month infants. *Activatas Nervosa Superior,* 1965, 7, 141–142.

Kohl, H. R. *The open classroom.* New York: Vintage, 1969.

Kohlberg, L. "Development of moral character and moral ideology," in *Review of child development research,* vol. 1, ed. M. L. Hoffman and L. W. Hoffman. New York: Russell Sage Foundation, 1964, 383–432.

Kohlberg, L. "Stages of moral development as a basis for moral education," in *Moral education: interdisciplinary approaches,* ed. C. Beck, E. V. Sullivan, and B. Crittenden. Toronto: University of Toronto Press, 1971.

Komoski, Kenneth P. (ed.). *Programmed instruction material, 1964–65: a guide to programmed instruction materials for use in elementary and secondary schools as of April, 1965.* New York: Institute of Educational Technology, Teachers' College, Columbia University, 1965.

Konorski, Jerzy, M. D. *Integrative activity of the brain.* Chicago: The University of Chicago Press, 1967.

Kounin, J. S. *Discipline and classroom management.* New York: Holt, Rinehart and Winston, 1970.

Krathwohl, D. R., B. S. **Bloom,** and B. B. **Masia.** *Taxonomy of educational objectives, the classification of educational goals. Handbook II: affective domain.* New York: David McKay Co., 1964.

Krech, D., M. **Rosenzweig,** and E. L. **Bennett.** Effects of environmental complexity and training on brain chemistry. *Journal of Comparative and Physiological Psychology,* 1960, 53, 509–519.

Krech, D., M. **Rosenzweig,** and E. L. **Bennett.** Relations between brain chemistry and problem solving among rats raised in enriched and impoverished environments. *Journal of Comparative and Physiological Psychology,* 1962, 55, 801–807.

Krech, David, Mark R. **Rosenzweig,** and Edward L. **Bennett.** Environmental impoverishment, social isolation, and changes in brain chemistry and anatomy. *Physiology and Behavior,* 1966, 1, 99–104.

Krutch, J. W. *The measure of man.* Indianapolis: Bobbs-Merrill Co., 1953.

Landreth, C. and K. H. **Read.** *Education of the young child: a nursing school manual.* New York: John Wiley, 1942.

Lange, P. C. What's the score on programmed instruction? *Today's Education,* 1972, 61, 59.

Lee, E. S. Negro intelligence and selective migration: a Philadelphia test of the Klineberg hypothesis. *American Sociological Review,* 1951, 16, 227–233.

Lefrancois, G. R. Developing creativity in high school students. Unpublished M.Ed. thesis, University of Saskatchewan, Saskatoon, Saskatchewan, Canada, 1965.

Lefrancois, G. R. The acquisition of concepts of conservation. Unpublished Ph.D. dissertation, University of Alberta, Edmonton, Alberta, Canada, 1966.

Lefrancois, G. R. Jean Piaget's developmental model: equilibration-through-adaptation. *Alberta Journal of Educational Research,* 1967, 13, 161–171.

Lefrancois, G. R. A treatment hierarchy for the acceleration of conservation of substance. *Canadian Journal of Psychology,* 1968, 22, 277–284.

Lefrancois, G. R. *Psychological theories and human learning: Kongor's report.* Belmont, Calif.: Brooks/Cole, 1972.

Lefrancois, G. R. Of children: an introduction to child development (2nd Edition). Belmont, Calif.: Wadsworth, 1977.

Lenneberg, E. H. On explaining language. *Science,* 1969, 164, 635–643.

Levine, J. N. Prompting and confirmation as a function of the familiarity of stimulus materials. *Journal of Verbal Learning and Verbal Behavior,* October, 1965, 4, 421–424.

Lindsley, D. B. "Psychophysiology and motivation," in *Nebraska symposium on motivation,* ed. M. R. Jones. Lincoln: University of Nebraska Press, 1957.

Logan, F. A. *Fundamentals of learning and motivation* (2nd Edition). Dubuque, Iowa: William C. Brown, 1976.

Lorenz, K. *King Solomon's ring.* London: Methuen, 1952.

Lovell, K. *An introduction to human development.* London: Macmillan, 1968.

Lumsdaine, A. A. and R. **Glaser** (eds.). *Teaching machines and programmed learning: a sourcebook.* Washington, D.C.: Department of Audio-Visual Instruction, National Education Association, 1960.

Luria, A. R. *The role of speech in the regulation of normal and abnormal behavior.* New York: Liveright, 1961.

MacArthur, R. S. Some differential abilities of northern Canadian youth. *International Journal of Psychology,* 1968, 3, 43–51.

Mager, R. F. *Preparing instructional objectives.* Palo Alto, Calif.: Fearon Publishers, 1962.

Maier, N. R. F. Reasoning in humans: I. On direction. *Journal of Comparative Psychology,* 1930, 10, 115–143.

Maltzman, I. On the training of originality. *Psychological Review,* 1960, 67, 229–242.

Markle, S. M. *Good frames and bad: a grammar of frame writing.* New York: John Wiley, 1964.

Marland, M. *The craft of the classroom: a survival guide to classroom management at the secondary school.* London: Heinemann Educational Books, 1975.

Marquis, D. P. Can conditioned responses be established in the new-born infant? *Journal of Genetic Psychology,* 1931, 39, 479–492.

Marquis, D. P. Learning in the neonate: the modification of behavior under three feeding schedules. *Journal of Experimental Psychology,* 1941, 29, 263–282.

Marx, Melvin H. and William A. **Hillix.** *Systems and theories in psychology.* New York: McGraw-Hill, 1963.

Maslow, Abraham H. *Motivation and personality* (2nd Edition). New York: Harper & Row, 1970.

Matthews, L. H. *The life of mammals,* vol. I. New York: Universe Books, 1969.

McCarthy, J. J. and S. A. **Kirk.** *Examiner's manual—ITPA.* Urbana: University of Illinois Press, 1964.

McClelland, D. C. "Risk taking in children with high and low need for achievement," in *Motives in fantasy, action, and society,* ed. J. W. Atkinson. Princeton, New Jersey: Van Nostrand, 1958, 306 – 321.

McClelland, D. C., J. W. **Atkinson,** R. A. **Clark,** and E. L. **Lowell.** *The achievement motive.* New York: Appleton-Century-Crofts, 1953.

McClelland, D. C. and D. G. **Winter.** *Motivating economic achievement.* New York: The Free Press, 1969.

McDougall, William. *An introduction to social psychology.* London: Methuen, 1908.

McNeil, Elton B. *Human socialization.* Belmont, Calif.: Brooks/Cole, 1969.

McPhail, P., J. R. **Ungoed-Thomas,** and H. **Chapman.** *Moral education in the secondary school.* London: Longmans, 1972.

Meacham, M. L. and A. E. **Wiesen.** *Changing classroom behavior: a manual for precision teaching.* Scranton, Penn.: International Textbook Co., 1969.

Meadow, Arnold and Sidney **Parnes.** Evaluation of training in creative problem solving. *Journal of Applied Psychology,* 1959, 43, 189 – 194.

Mednick, S. A. The associative basis of the creative process. *Psychological Review,* 1962, 69, 220 – 232.

Meer, Bernard and Morris L. **Stein.** Measures of intelligence and creativity. *Journal of Psychology,* 1955, 39, 117– 126.

Mehrens, W. A. and I. J. **Lehmann.** *Standardized tests in education.* New York: Holt, Rinehart and Winston, 1969.

Melton, A. W. (ed.). *Categories of human learning.* New York: Academic Press, 1964.

Mermelstein, E., E. **Carr,** D. **Mills,** and J. **Schwartz.** *The effects of various training techniques on the acquisition of the concept of conservation of substance.* Washington, D.C.: U.S. Office of Education Cooperative Research Project, No. 6 – 8300, 1967.

Merrill, M. D. Correction and review on successive parts in learning a hierarchical task. *Journal of Educational Psychology,* 1965, 56, 225– 235.

Michael, J. *Management of behavioral consequences in education.* Inglewood, Calif.: Southwest Regional Laboratory for Educational Research and Development, 1967.

Miller, G. A. The magical number seven, plus or minus two: some limits on our capacity for processing information. *Psychological Review,* 1956, 63, 81– 97.

Miller, N. E. and J. C. **Dollard.** *Social learning and imitation.* New Haven: Yale University Press, 1941.

Mink, O. G. *The behavior change process.* New York: Harper & Row, 1968.

Mischel, W. and N. **Baker.** Cognitive appraisals and transformations in delay behavior. *Journal of Personality and Social Psychology,* 1975, 31, 254– 261.

Morris, D. *The naked ape.* London: Jonathan Cape Ltd., 1967.

Moruzzi, A. G. and H. W. **Magoun.** Brain-stem reticular formation and activation of the EEG. *Electroencephalography and Clinical Neurophysiology,* 1949, 1:4, 455– 473.

Mowrer, O. H. *Learning theory and behavior.* New York: John Wiley, 1960.

Murray, Henry A. *Explorations in personality.* London: Oxford University Press, 1938.

Mussen, Paul H. *The psychological development of the child.* Englewood Cliffs, N.J.: Prentice-Hall, 1963.

Nay, W. R., J. A. **Schulman,** K. G. **Bailey,** and G. M. **Huntsinger.** Territory and classroom management: an exploratory case study. *Behavior Therapy,* 1976, 7, 240– 246.

Newman, H. H., F. N. **Freeman,** and K. J. **Holzinger.** *Twins: a study of heredity and environment.* Chicago: The University of Chicago Press, 1937.

Nichols, R. C. Heredity, environment and school achievement. A paper presented at a symposium on Heredity and Environment at the Annual Meeting of the American Educational Research Association, New York, February 16, 1967.

Norman, D. A. *Memory and attention: an introduction to human information processing.* New York: John Wiley, 1969.

Olds, James. Pleasure centers in the brain. *Scientific American,* October, 1956.

O'Leary, K. D. and W. C. **Becker.** Behavior modification of an adjustment class: a token reinforcement program. *Exceptional Children,* 1967, 637–642.

O'Leary, K. D. and W. C. **Becker.** The effects of a teacher's reprimands on children's behavior. *Journal of School Psychology,* 1968, 7, 8–11.

O'Leary, K. D., K. F. **Kaufman,** R. E. **Kass,** and R. S. **Drabman.** "The effects of loud and soft reprimands on the behavior of disruptive students," in *Modifying children's behavior: a book of readings,* ed. A. R. Brown and C. Avery. Springfield, Ill.: Charles C. Thomas, 1974, 168–186.

Osborn, Alex. *Applied imagination.* New York: Charles Scribner's Sons, 1957.

Osgood, C. E. "A behavioristic analysis of perception and language as cognitive phenomena," in *Contemporary approaches to cognition.* Cambridge: Harvard University Press, 1957(a).

Osgood, C. E. "Motivational dynamics of language behavior," in *Nebraska symposium on motivation,* ed. M. R. Jones. Lincoln: University of Nebraska Press, 1957, 348–423(b).

Osgood, C. E., G. P. **Suci,** and P. H. **Tannenbaum.** *The measurement of meaning.* Urbana: University of Illinois Press, 1957.

Palmares, U. and B. **Logan.** *A curriculum on conflict management.* Palo Alto, Calif.: Human Development Training Institute, 1975.

Parke, R. D. "Rules, roles, and resistance to deviation: recent advances in punishment, discipline, and self-control," in *Minnesota symposia on child psychology,* vol. 8, ed. A Pick. Minneapolis: University of Minnesota Press, 1974.

Parnes, Sidney J. "Do you really understand brain-storming?" in *A sourcebook for creative thinking,* eds. S. J. Parnes and H. F. Harding. New York: Charles Scribner's Sons, 1962, 283–290.

Parnes, Sidney J. *Creative behavior workbook.* New York: Charles Scribner's Sons, 1967.

Parnes, Sidney J. and Harold F. **Harding** (eds.). *A sourcebook for creative thinking.* New York: Charles Scribner's Sons, 1962.

Pavlov, I. P. *Conditioned reflexes.* London: Oxford University Press, 1927.

Peel, E. A. *The pupil's thinking.* London: Oldbourne, 1960.

Peel, Paul, Jr. Time effects on the creative writing of sixth grade children. Unpublished M.Ed. thesis, University of Alberta, Edmonton, Alberta, Canada, 1968.

Penfield, W. "Consciousness, memory and man's conditioned reflexes," in *On the biology of learning,* ed. K. H. Pribram. New York: Harcourt Brace Jovanovich, 1969, 129–168.

Perkins, H. V. *Human development and learning.* Belmont, Calif.: Wadsworth, 1969.

Perry, R. *The world of the polar bear.* Washington, D.C.: University of Washington Press, 1966.

Peters, R. The place of Kohlberg's theory in moral education. Paper presented at the First International Conference on Moral Development and Moral Education, August 19–26, Leicester, England, 1977.

Peterson, L. R. and N. J. **Peterson.** Short-term retention of individual verbal items. *Journal of Experimental Psychology,* 1959, 58, 193–198.

Phillips, John L. *The origins of intellect.* San Francisco: W. H. Freeman, 1969.

Piaget, J. *The language and thought of the child.* New York: Harcourt, Brace & World, 1926.

Piaget, J. *Judgement and reasoning in the child.* New York: Harcourt, Brace & World, 1928.

Piaget, J. *The child's conception of physical causality.* London: Kegan Paul, 1930.

Piaget, J. *The moral judgement of the child.* London: Kegan Paul, 1932.

Piaget, J. *Le développement de la notion de temps chez l'enfant.* Paris: Presses Univer. France, 1946(a).

Piaget, J. *Les notions de mouvement et de vitesse chez l'enfant.* Paris: Presses Univer. France, 1946(b).

Piaget, J. *Play, dreams, and imitation in childhood.* New York: Norton, 1951.

Piaget, J. "Autobiography," in *History of psychology in autobiography,* vol. IV, ed. E. G. Boring et al. Worcester, Mass.: Clark University Press, 1952, 237–256(a).

Piaget, J. *The child's conception of number.* New York: Humanities Press, 1952(b).

Piaget, J. *The origins of intelligence in children.* New York: International University Press, 1952(c).

Piaget, J. The child and modern physics. *Scientific American,* 1957, 196, 46–51(a).

Piaget, J. *Logic and psychology.* New York: Basic Books, 1957(b).

Piaget, J. The stages of the intellectual development of the child. *Bulletin of the Menninger School of Psychiatry,* March 6, 1961.

Piaget, J. Cognition and conservation: two views. *Contemporary Psychology,* 1967, 12, 530–533. (Part of a review of J. S. Bruner, Rose R. Olver, and Patricia M. Greenfield. *Studies in cognitive growth.* New York: John Wiley, 1966.)

Pinard, Adrien and Monique **Laurendeau.** A scale of mental development based on the theory of Piaget: description of a project, trans. A. B. Givens. *Journal of Research and Science Teaching,* 1964, 2, 253–260.

Pines, Maya. *Revolution in learning: the years from birth to six.* New York: Harper & Row, 1966.

Pinneau, S. R. The infantile disorders of hospitalism and anaclitic depression. *Psychological Bulletin,* 1955, 52, 429–462.

Postman, N. and C. **Weingartner.** *The soft revolution.* New York: Delacorte Press, 1971.

Premack, D. "Reinforcement theory," in *Nebraska symposium on motivation,* ed. D. Levine. Lincoln: University of Nebraska Press, 1965, 123–180.

Pressey, S. L. A third and fourth contribution toward the coming "industrial revolution" in education. *School and Society,* 1932, 36, 668–672.

Pressey, S. L. and John **Kinzer.** A puncture of the huge "programming" boom. *Teacher's College Record,* 1964, 65, 413–418.

Pribram, K. N. "The new neurology: memory, novelty, thought, and choice," in *EEG and behavior,* ed. C. N. Glaser. New York: Basic Books, 1963.

Purkey, William W. *Inviting school success: a self-concept approach to teaching and learning.* Belmont, Calif.: Wadsworth, 1978.

Quay, H. C., J. S. **Werry,** M. **McQueen,** and R. L. **Sprague.** Remediation of the conduct problem child in the special class setting. *Exceptional Children,* 1966, 32, 509–515.

Raths, L. F., A. **Jonas,** A. **Rothstein,** and S. **Wassermann.** *Teaching for thinking: theory and application.* Columbus, Ohio: Charles E. Merrill, 1967.

Reese, H. W., and L. P. **Lipsitt.** *Experimental child psychology.* New York: Academic Press, 1970.

Rogers, Carl R. *Client-centered therapy: its current practice, implications and theory.* Boston: Houghton Mifflin Co., 1951.

Rogers, Carl R. *Freedom to learn.* Columbus, Ohio: Charles E. Merrill, 1969.

Rogers, Carl R. and B. F. **Skinner.** Some issues concerning the control of human behavior: a symposium. *Science,* 1956, 124, 1057–1066.

Rosenthal, R. Experimenter expectancy and the reassuring nature of the null hypothesis decision procedure. *Psychological Bulletin Monograph Supplement,* 1969, 70, 30–47.

Rosenthal, R. and Lenore **Jacobson.** *Pygmalion in the classroom: teacher expectations and pupils' intellectual development.* New York: Holt, Rinehart and Winston, 1968(a).

Rosenthal, R. and Lenore **Jacobson.** Teacher expectations for the disadvantaged. *Scientific American,* April, 1968(b).

Rotter, J. B. *Social learning and clinical psychology.* Englewood Cliffs, N.J.: Prentice-Hall, 1954.

Rotter, J. B. Generalized expectancies of internal versus external control of reinforcement. *Psychological Monographs,* 1966, 80, no. 1.

Sarason, S. B. et al. *Anxiety in elementary school children.* New York: John Wiley, 1960.

Sarason, S. B. and G. **Mandler.** Some correlates of test anxiety. *Journal of Abnormal and Social Psychology,* 1952, 47, 810–817.

Satir, V. *Peoplemaking.* Palo Alto, Calif.: Science and Behavior Books, 1972.

Sawada, Daiyo and L. Doyal **Nelson.** Conservation of length and the teaching of linear measurement: a methodological critique. *Arithmetic Teacher,* 1967, 14, 345–348.

Schramm, W. *The research on programed instruction: an annotated bibliography.* Washington, D.C.: U.S. Government Printing Office, 1964.

Schultz, Duane P. *Panic behavior.* New York: Random House, 1964.

Schultz, Duane P. *Sensory restriction: effects on behavior.* New York: Academic Press, 1965.

Sears, Robert R., Eleanor P. **Maccoby,** and H. **Lewin.** *Patterns of child rearing.* Evanston, Ill.: Row, Peterson, 1957.

Seligman, M. E. P. and J. L. **Hager** (eds.). *Biological boundaries of learning.* New York: Appleton-Century-Crofts, 1972.

Seltzer, R. J. Effect of reinforcement and deprivation on the development of nonnutritive sucking in monkeys and humans. Unpublished Ph.D. dissertation, Brown University, Providence, R.I., 1968.

Shapiro, A. K. A contribution to a history of the placebo effect. *Behavioral Science,* 1960, 5, 109–135.

Sheppard, W. C. The analysis and control of infant vocal and motor behavior. Unpublished Ph.D. dissertation, University of Michigan, Ann Arbor, Mich., 1967.

Shirley, Mary. *The first two years: a study of twenty-five babies.* Vol. II of *Intellectual Development. Institute of Child Welfare Monographs* Series No. 7. Minneapolis: University of Minnesota Press, 1933.

Sievers, D. J. *Selected studies on the ITPA.* Urbana: University of Illinois Press, 1963.

Silberman, H. R., R. J. **Melaragno,** John E. **Coulson,** and D. **Estevan.** Fixed sequence versus branching auto-instructional methods. *Journal of Educational Psychology,* 1961, 52, 166–172.

Simon, S. B., L. W. **Howe,** and H. **Kirschenbaum.** *Values clarification: a handbook of practical strategies for teachers and students.* New York: Hart Publishing Co., 1972.

Singh, J. A. and R. N. **Zingg.** *Wolf-children and feral man.* New York: Harper, 1942.

Skinner, B. F. *Walden II.* New York: Macmillan, 1948.

Skinner, B. F. How to teach animals. *Scientific American,* December, 1951, 185, 26–29.

Skinner, B. F. *Science and human behavior.* New York: Macmillan, 1953.

Skinner, B. F. The science of learning and the art of teaching. *Harvard Educational Review,* 1954, 24, 86–97.

Skinner, B. F. *Transcripts of the New York Academy of Science,* 1955, 17.

Skinner, B. F. *Verbal behavior.* New York: Appleton-Century-Crofts, 1957.

Skinner, B. F. *Cumulative record* (Rev. Edition). New York: Appleton-Century-Crofts, 1961.

Skinner, B. F. Why teachers fail. *Saturday Review,* October 16, 1965, 80–81, 98–102.

Skinner, B. F. *The technology of teaching.* New York: Appleton-Century-Crofts, 1968.

Skinner, B. F. *Beyond freedom and dignity.* New York: Knopf, 1971.

Skinner, B. F. Herrnstein and the evolution of behaviorism. *American Psychologist,* December, 1977, 1006–1012.

Smedslund, J. The acquisition of conservation of substance and weight in children. I. Introduction. *Scandinavian Journal of Psychology,* 1961, 2, 11–20(a).

Smedslund, J. The acquisition of conservation of substance and weight in children. II. External reinforcement of conservation of weight and of operations of addition and subtraction. *Scandinavian Journal of Psychology,* 1961, 2, 71–84(b).

Smedslund, J. The acquisition of conservation of substance and weight in children. III. Extension of conservation of weight acquired normally and by means of empirical controls on a balance scale. *Scandinavian Journal of Psychology,* 1961, 2, 85–87(c).

Smedslund, J. The acquisition of conservation of substance and weight in children. IV. An attempt at extension of visual components of the weight concept. *Scandinavian Journal of Psychology,* 1961, 2, 153–155(d).

Smedslund, J. The acquisition of conservation of substance and weight in children. V. Practice in conflict situations without external reinforcement. *Scandinavian Journal of Psychology,* 1961, 2, 156–160(e).

Smith, M. E. An investigation of the development of the sentence and the extent of vocabulary in young children. *University of Iowa Studies in Child Welfare,* 1926, 3, No. 5.

Sokolov, A. N. "Studies on the problems of the speech mechanisms in thinking," in Vol. I of *Psychological Science in the U.S.S.R.,* ed. B. G. Anan'yev et al. Moscow: Scientific Council of the Institute of Psychology, Academy of Pedagogical Sciences, U.S.S.R., 1959, 669–704.

Soper, J. D. *The mammals of Alberta.* Edmonton, Alberta: Hamly Press, 1964.

Southern, H. N. *The handbook of British mammals.* Oxford: Blackwell Scientific Publications, 1964.

Spearman, C. E. *The abilities of man.* New York: Macmillan, 1927.

Spielberger, C. D. (ed.). *Anxiety and behavior.* New York: Academic Press, 1966.

Spitz, R. A. Hospitalism: an inquiry into the genesis of psychiatric conditions in early childhood. *Psychoanalytic Studies of the Child,* 1945, 1, 53–74.

Spitz, R. A. Hospitalism: a follow-up report. *Psychoanalytic Studies of the Child,* 1946, 2, 113–117.

Staats, A. W. and C. K. **Staats.** *Complex human behavior.* New York: Holt, Rinehart and Winston, 1963.

Standing, L. Learning 10,000 pictures. *Quarterly Journal of Experimental Psychology,* 1973, 25, 207–222.

Stolurow, L. M. "Social impact of programmed instruction: aptitudes and abilities revisited," in *Educational technology: readings in programmed instruction,* ed. J. P. DeCecco. New York: Holt, Rinehart and Winston, 1964.

Stolurow, L. M. Programmed instruction for the mentally retarded. *AV Communication Review,* 1966, 14, 151–152.

Stolurow, L. M. What is computer-assisted instruction? *Educational Technology,* 1968, 8, 10–11.

Sullivan, E. V. and J. **Quarter.** Psychological correlates of certain postconventional moral types: a perspective on hybrid types. *Journal of Personality,* 1972, 40, 2, 149–161.

Sullivan, E. V. A study of Kohlberg's structural theory of moral development: a critique of liberal social science ideology. Unpublished manuscript, Ontario Institute for Studies in Education, Toronto, Ontario, 1977.

Taber, Julian I., Robert **Glaser,** and H. H. **Schaeffer.** *Learning and programmed instruction.* Reading, Mass.: Addison-Wesley Publishing Co., 1965.

Taylor, C. W. and John W. **Holland.** Development and application of tests of creativity. *Review of Educational Research,* 1964, 33, 91–102.

Taylor, C. W. and F. E. **Williams** (eds.). *Instructional media and creativity.* New York: John Wiley, 1966.

Terman, L. M. et al. *Genetic studies of genius.* Vol. I: *The mental and physical traits of a thousand gifted children.* Stanford: Stanford University Press, 1925.

Terman, L. M. and M. A. **Merrill.** *Stanford-Binet intelligence scale.* Boston: Houghton Mifflin Co., 1960.

Thorndike, E. L. Animal intelligence: an experimental study of associative processes in animals. *Psychological Review,* Monograph Supplements, 1898, 2, No. 8.

Thorndike, E. L. *Animal intelligence.* New York: Macmillan, 1911.

Thorndike, E. L. *The psychology of learning.* New York: Teachers' College, 1913.

Thorndike, E. L. *Human learning.* New York: Appleton-Century-Crofts, 1931.

Thorndike, E. L. Reward and punishment in animal learning. *Comparative Psychology Monographs,* 1932, 8, No. 39.

Thorndike, E. L. A proof of the law of effect. *Science,* 1933, 77, 173–175.

Thorndike, E. L. *The psychology of wants, interests, and attitudes.* New York: Appleton-Century-Crofts, 1935.

Thorndike, E. L. *Selected writings from a connectist's psychology.* New York: Appleton-Century-Crofts, 1949.

Thorndike, E. L. et al. *The measurement of intelligence.* New York: Teachers' College, 1927.

Thorndike, R. L. The measurement of creativity. *Teacher's College Record,* 1963, 54, 422–424.

Thorndike, R. L. and E. **Hagen.** *Measurement and evaluation in psychology and education* (4th Edition). New York: John Wiley, 1977.

Thorpe, W. H. *Learning and instinct in animals* (2nd Edition). London: Methuen, 1963.

Thurstone, L. L. Primary mental abilities. *Psychometric Monographs.* Chicago: University of Chicago Press, 1938, No. 1.

Tinbergen, N. *A study of instinct.* Oxford: Clarendon Press, 1951.

Tolman, E. C. *Purposive behavior in animals and man.* New York: Appleton-Century-Crofts, 1932.

Tolman, E. C. Principles of performance. *Psychological Review,* 1955, 62, 315–326.

Toner, I. J. Maintenance of delay behavior in grade school children. *Psychological Reports,* 1974, 34, 1247–1250.

Torrance, E. P. *Guiding creative talent.* Englewood Cliffs, N.J.: Prentice-Hall, 1962.

Torrance, E. P. *Torrance tests of creative thinking.* Norms Technical Manual. Princeton, N.J.: Personnel Press, 1966.

Travis, L. D. Conservation acceleration through successive approximations. Unpublished M.Ed. thesis, University of Alberta, Edmonton, Alberta, Canada, 1969.

Tryon, R. C. Genetic differences in maze learning in rats. *Yearbook of the National Society for Studies in Education,* 1940, 39, 111–119.

Tuddenham, Read D. Jean Piaget and the world of the child. *American Psychologist,* 1966, 21, 207–217.

Turiel, F. Conflict in transition in adolescent moral development. *Child Development,* 1974, 45, 14–29.

Turner, Richard L. and David A. **Denny.** Teacher characteristics, teacher behavior, and changes in pupil creativity. *The Elementary School Journal,* 1969, February, 265–270.

Tyler, Leona E. *The psychology of human differences* (3rd Edition). New York: Appleton-Century-Crofts, 1965.

Ulrich, R. E. and N. H. **Azrin.** Reflexive fighting in response to aversive stimulation. *Journal of Experimental Analysis of Behavior,* 1962, 5, 511–521.

Verplanck, W. S. The control of the content of conversation: reinforcement of statements of opinion. *Journal of Abnormal and Social Psychology,* 1955, 51, 668–676.

Vygotsky, L. S. *Thought and language.* Translated from the Russian and edited by E. Hamsman and G. Vankan. Cambridge, Mass.: MIT Press, 1962.

Wallace, R. K. Physiological effects of transcendental meditation. *Science,* 1970, 167, 1751–1754.

Wallach, Michael A. and Nathan **Kogan.** *Modes of thinking in young children: a study of the creativity-intelligence distinction.* New York: Holt, Rinehart and Winston, 1965.

Walters, G. C. and J. E. **Grusec.** *Punishment.* San Francisco: W. H. Freeman, 1977.

Walters, R. H. and Thomas E. **Llewellyn.** Enhancement of punitiveness by visual and audiovisual displays. *Canadian Journal of Psychology,* 1963, 17, 244–255.

Walters, R. H., Thomas E. **Llewellyn,** and W. **Acker.** Enhancement of punitive behavior by audiovisual displays. *Science,* 1962, 136, 872–873.

Watson, J. B. Psychology as the behaviorist views it. *Psychological Review,* 1913, 20, 157–158.

Watson, J. B. *Behavior: an introduction to comparative psychology.* New York: Holt, Rinehart and Winston, 1914.

Watson, J. B. The place of a conditioned reflex in psychology. *Psychological Review,* 1916, 23, 89 – 116.

Watson, J. B. The unverbalized in human behavior, *Psychological Review,* 1924, 31, 273 – 280.

Watson, J. B. *Behaviorism* (2nd Edition). Chicago: The University of Chicago Press, 1930.

Watson, J. S. The development of generalization of "contingency awareness" in early infancy: some hypotheses. *Merrill-Palmer Quarterly,* 1966, 12, 132– 136.

Weber, E. *Early childhood education: perspectives on change.* Belmont, Calif.: Wadsworth, 1970.

Webster, S. W. *Discipline in the classroom: basic principles and problems.* New York: Chandler Publishing Company, 1968.

Wechsler, D. *The measurement and appraisal of adult intelligence* (4th Edition). Baltimore: Williams & Wilkins, 1958.

Wegmann, R. G. Classroom discipline: an exercise in the maintenance of social reality. *Sociology of Education,* 1976, 49, 71– 79.

Weikart, D. P., et al. *Ypsilanti-Carnegie infant education project: progress report.* Ypsilanti, Michigan: Department of Research and Development, Ypsilanti Public Schools, Sept. 1969.

Weiner, B. *Theories of motivation.* Chicago: Markum, 1972.

Weiner, B. (ed.). *Cognitive views of human motivation.* New York: Academic Press, 1974.

Weiner, B., I. **Frize,** A. **Kukla,** L. **Reed,** S. **Rest,** and R. M. **Rosenbaum.** *Perceiving the causes of success and failure.* New York: General Learning Press, 1971.

Weisberg, P. Social and non-social conditioning of infant vocalizations. *Child Development,* 1963, 34, 377– 388.

Weisberg, P. and E. **Fink.** Fixed ratio and distinction performance of infants in the second year of life. *Journal of the Experimental Analysis of Behavior,* 1966, 9, 105 – 109.

Wenger, M. A. An investigation of conditioned responses in human infants. *University of Iowa Studies in Child Welfare,* 1936, 12, no. 1.

West, L. W. and R. S. **MacArthur.** An evaluation of selected intelligence tests for two samples of Metis and Indian children. *Alberta Journal of Education Research,* 1964, 10, 17– 27.

White, R. W. Motivation reconsidered: the concept of competence. *Psychological Review,* 1959, 66, 297– 333.

Whorf, B. L. Science and linguistics. *Technology Review,* 1940, 54, 229– 231, 247– 248.

Whorf, B. L. "The relation of habitual thought and behavior to language," in *Language, culture, and personality,* ed. L. Spier. Salt Lake City, Utah: University of Utah Press, 1941.

Williams, D. R. and H. **Williams.** Auto-maintenance in the pigeon: sustained pecking despite contingent non-reinforcement. *Journal of the Experimental Analysis of Behavior,* 1969, 12, 511– 520.

Winsten, Stephen. *Days with Bernard Shaw.* New York: Vanguard Press, 1949.

Wittrock, M. C. Verbal stimuli in concept formation: learning by discovery. *Journal of Educational Psychology,* 1963, 54, 183– 190.

Wolf, M. N., T. R. **Risley,** and H. L. **Mees.** Application of operant conditioning procedures to the behavioral problems of an autistic child. *Behavior Research and Therapy,* 1964, 1, 305 – 312.

Wolpe, J. *Psychotherapy by reciprocal inhibition.* Stanford: Stanford University Press, 1958.

Worth, W. H., William T. **Fagan,** and Ethel **Kind.** *Before six: a report on the Alberta early childhood study.* Edmonton, Canada: The Alberta School Trustees Association, November, 1966.

Yamamoto, Kaoru. *Experimental scoring manual for Minnesota tests of creative thinking and writing.* Kent, Ohio: Bureau of Educational Research, Kent State University, May, 1964.

Zeaman, David and Betty J. **House.** "The role of attention in retardate discrimination learning," in *Handbook of mental deficiency,* ed. N. R. Ellis, New York: McGraw-Hill, 1963, 159 – 223.

Zubek, John P. *Sensory deprivation: fifteen years of research.* New York: Appleton-Century-Crofts, 1969.

This glossary defines the most important terms and expressions used in this text. In each case the meaning given corresponds to the usage in the text. For more complete definitions, the reader is advised to consult a standard psychological dictionary.

Accommodation Accommodation involves the modification of an activity or ability in the face of environmental demands. Piaget's description of development holds that assimilation and accommodation are the means by which individuals interact with their world and adapt to it. (See also *assimilation.*)

Adaptation Changes in an organism in response to the environment. Such changes are assumed to facilitate interaction with that environment. Adaptation plays a central role in Piaget's theory. (See also *assimilation, accommodation.*)

Advance organizers Introductory information given to learners intended to increase the ease with which they can understand, learn, and remember new material.

Affect (See *emotion.*)

Affective learning Changes in attitudes or emotions (affect) as a function of experience.

Aggression In human beings, a much studied characteristic that is generally defined as the conscious and willful inflicting of pain on others.

Alpha recorder An instrument designed to translate electrical brain activity into graphic or auditory form; a brain wave recorder.

Alpha waves Electroencephalograph brain wave recordings typical of individuals in states of rest.

Analysis Breaking down into component parts. As an intellectual activity it consists primarily of examining relationships among ideas in an attempt to understand them better. A relatively high-level intellectual skill in Bloom's taxonomy of educational objectives.

Application An educational objective described by Bloom. Consists primarily of the ability to use abstractions in concrete situations.

Arousal A term with both physiological and psychological connotations. As a physiological concept, arousal refers to change in such physiological functions as heart rate, respiration rate, electrical activity in the cortex, and conductivity of the skin to electricity. As a psychological concept, arousal refers to degree of alertness, awareness, vigilance, or wakefulness. Arousal varies from very low (coma or sleep) to very high (panic or high anxiety).

Assessment A global term for the processes involved in measurement and evaluation. A judgmental process intimately involved in the teaching-learning process. (See *measurement, evaluation.*)

Assimilation The act of incorporating objects or aspects of objects into previously learned activities. To assimilate is, in a sense, to ingest or to employ for something that is previously learned. (See *accommodation.*)

Associationism A point of view in learning theory that attempts to explain learning on the basis of the formation of associations.

Assumption A belief that is not directly and immediately amenable to objective verification but that is important for the formulation of theory or simply for the making of logical inferences.

Attributes Properties of objects or events that can vary from one object or event to another. (See also *values.*)

Auto-instructional device Any instructional device that is effective in the absence of a teacher. Common examples of such devices are programed textbooks and teaching machines.

Aversive control The control of human behavior, usually through the presentation of noxious (unpleasant) stimuli. This is in contrast to techniques of positive control, which generally employ positive reinforcement.

Avoidance learning A conditioning phenomenon usually involving aversive (unpleasant) stimulation, wherein the organism learns to *avoid* situations associated with specific unpleasant circumstances.

Bear The name given to the animal described in Chapter 4.

Behavior The activity of an organism. Behavior may be overt (visible) or covert (invisible or internal).

Behavior modification Changes in the behavior of an individual. Also refers to psychological theory and research that is concerned with the application of psychological principles in attempts to change behavior.

Behaviorism A general term for those theories of learning which are concerned primarily with the observable components of behavior (stimuli and responses).

Beta waves Relatively irregular and rapid brain waves that are characteristic of increasing arousal. May be employed as a physiological index of arousal.

Biofeedback Information that individuals receive about their physiological functioning. Biofeedback experiments typically provide subjects with information concerning respiration rate, heart rate, brain wave activity, and so on.

Black box A term employed by grandmothers to describe an object that is squarish and that appears black, usually as a result of having been painted with a substance of that color. In psychology the term is occasionally used to describe the "mind." The expression implies that the contents of the mind are unknown and perhaps unknowable.

Book A collection of words. (See also *textbook*.)

Brainstorming A technique popularized by Osborn and employed primarily in the production of creative solutions for a variety of problems. A brainstorming session usually involves a small group of people who are encouraged to produce a wide variety of ideas, which are evaluated later.

Branching program Programed material that, in contrast to a linear program, presents a variety of alternative routes through the material. Such programs typically make use of larger frames than do linear programs and frequently use multiple choices.

Categorization The act of placing stimulus input in categories. According to Bruner, the recognition of an object involves placing it in an appropriate category (categorizing it).

Category A term employed by Bruner to describe a grouping of related objects or events. In this sense a category is both a concept and a percept. Bruner also defines it as a rule for classifying things as equal. (See also *categorization, coding system*.)

Cephalocaudal A term for a direction of development beginning from the head and proceeding outward toward the tail. Early infant development is assumed to be cephalocaudal in the sense that children acquire control of their heads prior to acquiring control of their limbs.

Chaining That type of learning which involves the formation of links between stimulus-response bonds. Much human behavior that is describable in terms of S-R units is illustrative of chains since behavior is ordinarily so complex that it involves a large number of such S-R units.

Chains A term employed by Gagné to signify the learning of related sequences of responses. A chain is a series of stimulus-response bonds in that each response in the sequence serves as a stimulus for the next response. Motor chains are involved in my typing of this material.

Classical conditioning Also called learning through stimulus substitution, since it involves the repeated pairing of two stimuli so that eventually a previously neutral (conditioned) stimulus comes to elicit the same response (conditioned response) that was previously elicited by the first stimulus (unconditioned stimulus). This was the type of conditioning first described by Pavlov.

Client-centered therapy That type of patient-counselor relationship in which the counselor (therapist-psychiatrist) is not directive in the sense of telling clients how they should behave, but rather attempts to allow patients to express themselves and to discover within themselves ways of dealing with their own behavior. This therapeutic approach is generally contrasted with directive therapy. (See also *therapy, counseling, directive therapy.*)

Coding system A Brunerian concept. Refers to a hierarchical arrangement of related categories.

Cognitive learning Learning that, in contrast to affective and motor learning, involves the more psychological aspects of the organism. Cognitive learning is concerned primarily with the acquisition of information, with the development of strategies for processing information, with decision-making processes, and with logical processes.

Cognitive structure Refers to the organized totality of an individual's knowledge. (See *knowledge.*)

Cognitivism Includes those theories of learning that are concerned primarily with such topics as perception, problem solving, information processing, and understanding.

Combined schedules A combination of schedules of reinforcement.

Communication The transmission of a message from one organism to another. Communication does not necessarily involve language since some animals can communicate—usually through reflexive behaviors.

Comparative organizer A concept or idea that serves to facilitate the learning of new material by making use of the similarities and differences that exist between the new material and the previous learning.

Comprehension The lowest level of understanding in Bloom's hierarchy of educational objectives. Defined as the ability to apprehend the meaning of communication without necessarily being able to apply, analyze, or evaluate it.

Computer-assisted instruction (CAI) The use of computer facilities as autoinstructional devices. Computers may be employed simply to present information or to present complex branching programs. Some advantages include their almost unlimited storage capacities, their retrieval ability, their problem-solving capacities, and their versatility in terms of modes of presentation.

Concept A collection of perceptual experiences or of ideas that are related by virtue of their possessing common properties.

Concrete operations The third of Piaget's four major stages, lasting from age seven or eight to approximately eleven or twelve, and characterized largely by the child's ability to deal with concrete problems and objects, or objects and problems capable of being imagined in a concrete sense.

Conditioned response A response that is elicited by a conditioned stimulus. In some obvious ways a conditioned response resembles its corresponding unconditioned response. The two are not identical, however.

Conditioned stimulus A stimulus that, initially, does not elicit any response or elicits a global, orienting response, but that, as a function of being paired with an unconditioned stimulus and its response, acquires the capability of eliciting that same response. For example, a stimulus that is always present at the time of a fear reaction may become a conditioned stimulus for fear.

Conditioning A type of learning that is described in terms of changing relationships between stimuli, between responses, or between both stimuli and responses. (See also *classical conditioning, operant conditioning, instrumental conditioning.*)

Connectionism A theoretical explanation of learning that is concerned with the formation of bonds (connections) between stimuli and responses. The term is attributed to E. L. Thorndike.

Conservation A Piagetian term for the realization that certain quantitative attributes of objects remain unchanged unless something is added to or taken away from them. Such characteristics of objects as mass, number, area, and volume are capable of being conserved.

Content Piaget's term for the behavior of individuals. Content is "raw uninterpreted behavioral data."

Content A term employed by Guilford to describe the content of a person's intellect. Intellectual activity (operations) involves content and results in products. (See *operation, product.*)

Contiguity Simultaneous in time or in space. Contiguity is frequently used to explain the occurrence of classical conditioning. It is assumed that the simultaneity of the unconditioned and the conditioned stimulus is sufficient to explain the formation of the link between the two.

Continuous reinforcement That type of schedule of reinforcement where every correct response is followed by a reinforcer.

Convergent thinking A term employed by Guilford to describe the type of thinking which results in a unique, correct solution for a problem. It is assumed that most conventional tests of intelligence measure convergent thinking abilities rather than divergent thinking abilities. (See also *divergent thinking.*)

Correlation A statistical term employed to describe a relationship that exists between variables. (See *variable.*)

Correlative subsumption That type of learning which takes place when the new information is an extension of what was previously known and could not, therefore, have been derived directly from it. (See also *derivative subsumption.*)

Counseling This is literally the act of giving advice.

Counterconditioning A therapeutic technique that involves an attempt to condition an acceptable response as a replacement for one that is not acceptable. (See *threshold method, fatigue method,* as examples of counterconditioning techniques.)

Creative An adjective that may be used to describe people, products, or a process. The term *creativity* generally refers to the capacity of individuals to produce novel or original answers or products.

Criterial attribute An attribute or characteristic of an object that is employed in identifying it. For example, roundness is a criterial attribute for the category circle.

Criterion-referenced tests The use of test results in such a way that the student is competing relative to a criterion rather than relative to the performance of other students. The teacher decides beforehand the specific performance that is expected of the student and tests her to see whether she has reached this criterion.

Critical period A period in development during which exposure to appropriate experiences or stimuli will bring about specific learning much more easily than is the case at other times.

Cue function A term employed by Hebb to describe the message component of a stimulus.

Culture The pattern of socially acceptable behaviors that characterizes a people or a social group. It includes all of the attitudes and beliefs that the group has about the things it considers important.

Decision making The process of arriving at some inference or conclusion. May be either a perceptual or a cognitive process.

Deferred imitation The ability to imitate people or events in their absence. Deferred imitation is assumed to be critical in the development of language abilities.

Dendrite Hairlike extensions emanating from the cell body of a neuron. These are assumed to be involved in the transmission of impulses from one neuron to another.

Depressant A drug or event that has the effect of inhibiting activity.

Derivative subsumption That type of subsumption (or learning) which takes place when the new material could have been derived directly from what was already known. (See also *correlative subsumption*.)

Development A relatively global term employed to include both the maturational and the growth processes that transpire from birth to maturity.

Developmental theory A body of psychological theories concerned with the development of children from birth to maturity.

Differential reinforcement Describes the procedure of reinforcing only some responses and not others. Differential reinforcement is employed in the shaping of complex behaviors.

Directive therapy That type of counselor-client relationship in which the counselor takes major responsibility for directing the client's behavior.

Discipline Refers to the control aspects of teaching.

Discovery learning The acquisition of new information or knowledge largely as a result of the learner's own efforts. Discovery learning is contrasted with expository or reception learning, and is generally associated with Bruner, among others. (See also *reception learning*.)

Discriminated stimulus A stimulus that is perceived by the organism. In operant conditioning, the discriminated stimulus eventually comes to elicit the response.

Discrimination Processes involved in learning that certain responses are appropriate in specific situations, but inappropriate in other similar but *discriminably different* situations. Generalization is an opposite process. (See *generalization*.)

Dissociability A term used by Ausubel to indicate the ease with which material that is to be recalled can be separated (dissociated) from other related material that is also in memory.

Distance receptors Those senses which receive stimulation from a distance (for example, hearing and vision).

Divergent thinking An expression employed by Guilford to describe the type of thinking that results in the production of several different solutions for one problem. Divergent thinking is assumed to be closely related to creative behavior, and the term is often used interchangeably with the term creativity. (See also *convergent thinking*.)

Drive The tendency to behave that is brought about by an unsatisfied need.

Education Refers to formal attempts to maximize an individual's adaptability. Such attempts generally take place in schools or in similar institutions.

Educational psychology A science that is concerned primarily with the application of psychological knowledge (knowledge about human behavior) to problems of education.

Efferent pathway A neural pathway that emanates from the cortex and proceeds outward toward the effector systems (the muscular or glandular systems of the body).

Egocentrism A way of functioning that is characterized by an inability to assume the point of view of others. Early child thinking is largely egocentric.

Elicited response A response that is brought about by a stimulus. The expression is synonymous with the term *respondent*.

Eliciting effect That type of imitative behavior where the observer does not copy the model's responses but simply behaves in a related manner. (See also *modeling effect, inhibitory-disinhibitory effect.*)

Emitted response A response that is not elicited by a stimulus, but is simply emitted by the organism. An emitted response is, in fact, an operant.

Emotion Refers to the "feeling" or "affective" aspect of human behavior. The term *emotion* includes such human *feelings* as fear, rage, love, and desire.

Enactive A term employed by Bruner to describe young children's representation of their world. It refers specifically to the belief that children represent their world in terms of the activities that they perform toward it. (See also *iconic, symbolic.*)

Environmentalism (See *tabula rasa.*)

Escape learning A conditioning phenomenon where the organism learns means of *escaping* from a situation usually following the presentation of aversive (unpleasant) stimulation. (See *avoidance learning.*)

Evaluation In contrast to measurement, involves making a value judgment— deciding on the goodness or badness of performance. Also denotes the highest-level intellectual skill in Bloom's taxonomy of educational objectives. Defined as the ability to render judgments about the value of methods or materials for specific purposes, making use of external or internal criteria.

Excitation Refers to a state of physiological alertness. May be defined in terms of the activation of neurons.

Exemplary model A teacher.

Expectations Anticipated behavior. Teacher expectations are particularly important, since recent research tends to show that expectations significantly affect the behavior of some students.

Expository organizer An idea or a concept that serves as a description (exposition) of concepts that are relevant to new learning.

Extinction The cessation of a response as a function of the withdrawal of reinforcement.

Extinction rate The number of responses that are emitted prior to the cessation of a response following the withdrawal of reinforcement.

Fatigue method A technique for breaking habits (described by Guthrie). The fatigue method involves forcing the appearance of the undesirable response over and over again until the individual is so tired that he or she can no longer respond.

Feral children Children who have been abandoned by their parents and who have presumably been brought up by wolves.

Fixed schedule A type of intermittent schedule of reinforcement where the reinforcement occurs at fixed intervals of time, in the case of an interval schedule, or after a specified number of trials, in the case of a ratio schedule.

Forgetting The cessation of a response as a function of the passage of time. Not to be confused with extinction.

Formal operations The last of Piaget's four major stages. It begins around the age of eleven or twelve and lasts until the age of fourteen or fifteen. It is characterized by the child's increasing ability to employ logical thought processes.

Frame The label given to the unit of information that is presented in programed instruction. A frame not only presents information but typically requires the student to make a response as well.

Fraternal twins Twins whose genetic origins are two different eggs. Such twins are as genetically dissimilar as average siblings. (See also *identical twins.*)

Functioning A Piagetian term employed to describe the processes by which an organism adapts to its environment. These processes are, specifically, assimilation and accommodation.

Gating A term employed by Bruner to describe the process of sorting out stimulus input.

Generalization The transference of a response from one stimulus to a similar stimulus (stimulus generalization), or the transference of a similar response for another response in the face of a single stimulus (response generalization). A child who responds with fear in a new situation that resembles an old fear-producing situation is showing evidence of stimulus generalization.

Generalized reinforcer A stimulus that, like a secondary reinforcer, is not reinforcing prior to being paired with a primary reinforcer. Generalized reinforcers are those stimuli which are present so often at the time of reinforcement that they come to be reinforcing for a wide variety of unrelated activities. Such stimuli as social prestige, praise, and money are generalized reinforcers for human behavior. (See also *reinforcer, primary, secondary.*)

Gordon technique A creativity-enhancing technique very similar to brainstorming except that an abstraction of a problem rather than a specific problem is presented.

Group test A type of test, usually employed to measure intelligence, which may be given to large groups of subjects at one time. It is typically of the pencil-and-paper variety. (See also *individual test.*)

Growth Refers to the physical aspects of development. It is somewhat similar in meaning to the term *maturation,* although, unlike maturation, it does not refer to the appearance of nonphysical capabilities.

Gut A vulgar term that refers to the belly.

Habit A customary way of responding in a given situation. Some behaviorists (for example, Guthrie) refer to all learning as involving the formation of habits.

Hallucination An imagined experience that the subject believes is real. Often takes the form of visual impressions in the absence of appropriate stimulation.

Hardware A recent term in computer terminology. It refers to the actual mechanical and electronic systems that comprise computers.

Hedonism The belief that humans act in order to avoid pain and to obtain pleasure.

Higher mental processes What the average person commonly refers to as thinking. This includes such activities as are involved in problem solving, perception, decision making, and feeling.

Homeostasis The self-regulating process by which physiological and psychological systems maintain their equilibrium.

Humanism Describes the philosophical and psychological orientation that is primarily concerned with our humanity—that is, with our worth as individuals and with those processes that are considered to make us more *human*.

Iconic A stage in the development of the child's representation of his or her world. The phrase is employed by Bruner to describe an intermediate stage of development that is characterized by a representation of the world in terms of relatively concrete mental images. (See also *enactive, symbolic.*)

Identical twins Twins whose genetic origin is one egg. Such twins are genetically identical. (See also *fraternal twins.*)

Identification The relatively global term usually employed to describe the process of assuming the goals, ambitions, mannerisms, and so on of another person—of identifying with that person. (See also *imitation.*)

Identity A logical rule that specifies that certain activities leave objects or situations unchanged.

Imitation A relatively specific term that refers to the copying behavior of an organism. To imitate a person's behavior is simply to employ that person's behavior as a pattern. Bandura and Walters describe three different effects of imitation. (See also *modeling effect, inhibitory-disinhibitory effect,* and *eliciting effect.*)

Imprinting Unlearned, instinct-like behaviors that are not present at birth but that become part of an animal's repertoire after exposure to a suitable stimulus. Such exposure must ordinarily take place during what is referred to as a critical period. The "following" behavior of young ducks, geese, and chickens is an example of imprinting.

Impulse The label given to whatever-it-is that is transmitted by neurons. The effect of sensory stimulation.

Incompatible stimuli method A method for breaking habits, described by Guthrie. Involves presenting a stimulus that ordinarily brings about an undesirable reaction, and doing so at a time when the undesirable behavior is not likely to occur. (See also *threshold method, fatigue method.*)

Individual test A test, usually used to measure intelligence, that can be given to only one individual at a time. (See also *group test.*)

Inhibition The sophisticated grandmother's term for shyness. As a psychological term it often refers to the blocking of some sensory or neural function, or to the interfering effect of previous or subsequent learning on recall. (See *retroactive* and *proactive inhibition.*)

Inhibitory-disinhibitory effect That type of imitative behavior which results either in the suppression (inhibition) or appearance (disinhibition) of *previously acquired deviant behavior.* (See *modeling effect, eliciting effect.*)

Insight The sudden appearance of a solution for a problem. The phenomenon is often described in contrast to trial-and-error.

Instinct Complex, species specific, relatively unmodifiable behavior patterns such as migration in birds, hibernation in some mammals, and leadership behavior in fish.

Instruction The art and science of arranging learning situations in order to facilitate the modification of behavior in desired directions.

Instructional objective The goal or intended result of instruction. Objectives may be short range or long range.

Instructional strategy Relatively systematic behaviors engaged in by teachers in the teaching-learning process. Implies a conscious predetermined teaching approach for the attainment of specific instructional goals.

Instrumental conditioning A type of learning that is sometimes differentiated from operant conditioning, but that may also be considered a part of operant conditioning. It refers specifically to those situations in which a response is *instrumental* in bringing about a reinforcement, and in which a stimulus elicited the response in the first place and therefore becomes linked with the reinforcement.

Intelligence May be defined as a property measured by intelligence tests. Seems to refer primarily to the capacity of individuals to adjust to their environments.

Intermittent reinforcement A schedule of reinforcement that does not present a reinforcer for all correct responses. (See also *interval schedule* and *ratio schedule.*)

Interval scale A measurement scale that has no true zero point but on which numerical indicators are arbitrarily set. Intervals between numbers are assumed to be equal in such a scale (a thermometer scale, for example).

Interval schedule An intermittent schedule of reinforcement that is based on the passage of time. (See also *fixed schedule* and *random schedule.*)

Introspection A method of psychological investigation that involves simply examining one's own thoughts and emotions and generalizing from them.

Intuitive thinking One of the substages of preoperational thought, beginning around age four and lasting until age seven or eight. Intuitive thought is marked by the child's ability to solve many problems intuitively and by his or her inability to respond correctly in the face of misleading perceptual features of problems.

Invariants A term employed by Piaget to describe those aspects of development or of human functioning which do not change. Assimilation and accommodation, for example, as ways of interacting with the environment, are invariants. They are frequently referred to as the functional invariants of adaptation.

Jargon The unique, technical vocabulary of a discipline. The term implies that the vocabulary is not always essential.

Jargon shock The author's tongue was in his cheek in Chapter 10.

Knowledge A generic term for the information, ways of dealing with information, ways of acquiring information, and so on that an individual possesses.

Knowledge of results Refers to knowledge about the correctness or incorrectness of the student's response that is provided for him or her in programed instruction. Knowledge of results is usually immediate.

Lad A young man. Also the first letters of the hypothetical something that corresponds to grammar in the human brain (language acquisition device: Chomsky).

Language The use of arbitrary sounds in the transmission of messages from one individual or organism to another. Language should not be confused with communication. (See *communication.*)

Law of Effect A Thorndikean law of learning that states that it is the effect of a response that leads to its being learned (stamped in) or not learned (stamped out).

Law of Exercise A Thorndikean law of learning premised on the assumption that the repetition of a learned response increases the probability that it will be stamped in (learned). Repetitive "drill" exercises in schools illustrate a belief in the importance of this law.

Law of Readiness A Thorndikean law of learning which takes into account the fact that certain types of learning are impossible or difficult unless the learner is "ready." In this context, readiness refers to maturational level, previous learning, motivational factors, and other characteristics of the individual that relate to learning.

Learning Changes in behavior due to experience. Does not include changes due to maturation, fatigue, or drugs.

Learning theory A general term for psychological theories that are concerned primarily with questions relating to how people learn, how they acquire information, and how they behave.

Linear program The presentation of programed material in such a manner that all learners progress through the material in the same order. Linear programs typically make no provision for individual differences in learning, requiring all students to progress through the same material. That material, however, is broken up into very small steps (frames).

Match-mismatch mechanism Described by Bruner as that property of human functioning which enables humans to determine whether a stimulus input fits (matches) a category or does not fit (mismatches).

Maturation The process of normal physical and psychological development. Maturation is defined as occurring independently of particular experiences. (See also *growth, development.*)

Maze A complicated arrangement of pathways and barriers sometimes employed to study the learning behavior of rats.

Maze-bright An adjective employed to describe those rats who are able to learn to run through mazes very easily. A maze-bright rat is the counterpart of an intelligent person. (See also *maze-dull.*)

Maze-dull A derogatory adjective employed to describe a rat who has a great deal of difficulty in learning how to run a maze. A maze-dull rat is the counterpart of a stupid person. (See also *maze-bright.*)

Mean The arithmetical average of a set of scores. In distributions that are skewed (top or bottom heavy), the mean is not necessarily the best index of central tendency. That is, it is not necessarily at the middle of the distribution. (See *median.*)

Measurement The application of an instrument in order to gauge the quantity of something, as opposed to its quality. Assessing quality involves evaluation, not measurement.

Median In a distribution of scores, the point above and below which 50 percent of the scores respectively fall. The very center of a distribution in terms of rank. Often a better indicator of "average" performance than the mean. (See *mean.*)

Mediation A term used to describe processes that are assumed to intervene between the presentation of a stimulus and the appearance of a response.

Memory May be defined in terms of the effects that experiences are assumed to have on the human mind. Refers to the storage of these effects. (See also *retention, retrieval,* and *recall.*)

Mentalism Sometimes used in a derogatory sense to describe an approach in psychology that is concerned largely with discovering, through a process of introspection, how people feel or react emotionally. (See *introspection*.)

Méthode clinique Piaget's experimental method. It involves an interview technique in which questions are determined largely by the subject's responses. Its flexibility distinguishes it from ordinary interview techniques.

Modeling effect That type of imitative behavior that involves the learning of a *novel* response. (See also *inhibitory-disinhibitory effect, eliciting effect*.)

Morphological analysis A creativity-enhancing technique advanced by Arnold, involving the analysis of problems into their component parts and subsequent attempts to brainstorm each of these component parts.

Motivation theory A general label employed to describe psychological theories that are primarily concerned with the question of why human beings behave the way they do.

Motor capacity Capabilities relating to such physical activities as walking or doing things with one's hands.

Motor learning Learning that involves muscular coordination and physical skills. Such common activities as walking and driving a car involve motor learning.

Need Ordinarily refers to a lack or deficit in the human organism. Needs may be unlearned (for example, the need for food or water) or learned (the need for money or prestige).

Need-drive theory A motivational theory that attempts to explain human behavior on the basis of the motivating properties of needs. Such theories typically assume that humans have certain learned and unlearned needs, which give rise to drives, which in turn are responsible for the occurrence of behavior. (See also *need, drive*.)

Negative correlation That type of relationship that exists between two variables when as one increases the other decreases. Negative correlation is essentially an inverse relationship.

Negative reinforcer A stimulus that has the effect of increasing the probability of occurrence of the response which precedes it when it is removed from the situation. Negative reinforcement ordinarily takes the form of an unpleasant or noxious stimulus which is removed as a result of a specific response.

Neobehaviorism A division in learning theories that includes those theoretical positions which, while they are still concerned with stimuli and responses, are also concerned with events that intervene (mediate) between stimuli and responses.

Neuron (nerve cell) An elongated cell body that forms part of the nervous system. The main part of the neuron is labeled cell body, whereas the elongated part is labeled axon. (See also *dendrite, synapse*.)

Nominal scale A crude measurement scale that does no more than provide descriptive labels.

Nonsense syllable An arrangement of consonants and vowels to form a one-syllable word that has no referent in the English language. These are employed in studies of memory. The technique was pioneered by Ebbinghaus.

Norm-referenced test The use of test results in such a way that the student is competing relative to the performance of other students rather than in relation to some preestablished criterion of acceptable performance. (See also *criterion-referenced tests*.)

Object concept Piaget's expression for the child's understanding that the world is composed of objects that continue to exist quite apart from his or her perception of them.

Objective Adjective referring to research, theory, or experimental methods that deal with observable events. The implication is that objective observations are not affected by the observer.

Obliterative subsumption The incorporation of new material into preexisting cognitive structure such that the new material is eventually indistinguishable from what was already known (obliterated). In effect obliterative subsumption results in forgetting.

Observational learning A term employed synonymously with the expression "learning through imitation." (See *imitation*.)

Ontogeny The development of an individual from birth to maturity.

Operant The label employed by Skinner to describe a response not elicited by any known or obvious stimulus. Most significant human behaviors appear to be of the operant variety. Such behaviors as writing a letter and going for a walk are operants, since no known specific stimulus elicits them.

Operant conditioning A type of learning that involves an increase in the probability that a response will occur as a function of reinforcement. Most of the experimental work of Skinner investigates the principles of operant conditioning.

Operation A Piagetian term that remains relatively nebulous but refers essentially to a thought process. An operation is an action that has been internalized in the sense that it can be "thought," and that is reversible in the sense that it can be "unthought."

Operation A term employed by Guilford to describe a rather major kind of intellectual activity. Such activities as remembering, evaluating, and divergent and convergent thinking are operations. (See *divergent thinking, convergent thinking*.)

Ordinal scale A scale of measurement that permits no more than simple ranking. An ordinal scale does not have a true zero, nor are the intervals between units on the scale necessarily equal. Using an ordinal scale, it is possible to say that A is greater than B, and B greater than C, but never by how much.

Organism A generic biological term employed to designate a living being. The term *organism* can, therefore, include both *Homo sapiens* and rat, among others.

Organizer A term employed by Ausubel to describe that type of concept or idea which may be employed to facilitate the learning of new material. (See also *expository organizer, comparative organizer*.)

Paradigm A model or pictorial representation of some phenomenon. For example, the paradigm for classical conditioning is:

$$UCS \rightarrow UCR$$
$$CS \rightarrow CR.$$

Perception The translation of physical energies (stimuli-sensation) into neurological impulses that can be interpreted by the individual.

Personality theory A body of psychological theories primarily concerned with the adjustment of individual humans.

Phenomenal field The feelings, perceptions, awareness, and so on that an individual has at any given moment in time. Such humanistic theorists as Carl Rogers are particularly concerned with the phenomenal field.

Phenomenology Describes an approach primarily concerned with how individuals view their own world. Its basic assumption is that each individual perceives and reacts to the world in a unique manner, and that it is this phenomenological world that is of primary importance in understanding his or her behavior. (See also *phenomenal field.*)

Phylogeny The development of species from their origins through their evolutionary stages. Phylogeny is contrasted with ontogeny in the sense that it refers to species rather than to individuals.

Physiological needs Basic biological needs, such as the need for food and water.

Placebo A neutral treatment sometimes given to a control group in an experiment. Placebos are employed to ensure that experimental results are not a function simply of being in the experiment or of expecting changes to take place. In medicine, placebos often take the form of "sugar pills."

Pleasure centers A term employed by grandmothers to describe wicked, sin-filled places. In psychology, the label given to those parts of the brain which are assumed to be directly involved in sensations of pleasure.

Positive correlation That type of relationship which exists between two variables when as one increases the other does likewise.

Positive reinforcer A stimulus that increases the probability that a response will recur as a result of being added to a situation after the response has once occurred. Usually takes the form of a pleasant stimulus (reward) that results from a specific response.

Preconceptual thinking The first substage in the period of preoperational thought, beginning around age two and lasting till age four. It is so called because the child has not yet developed the ability to classify.

Predeterminism The belief that what the child will become as she develops is predetermined at birth. Predeterminism differs from preformationism in that it allows for some developmental changes. (See also *preformationism* and *tabula rasa.*)

Preformationism The invalid belief that the adult is completely preformed in the child—that is, that the child is a miniature adult complete in every detail except for size. (See also *predeterminism* and *tabula rasa.*)

Preoperational thinking The second of Piaget's four major stages, lasting from about two to seven or eight years. It consists of two substages: intuitive thinking and preconceptual thinking. (See also *intuitive thinking* and *preconceptual thinking.*)

Primary circular reaction An expression employed by Piaget to describe a simple reflex activity such as thumb-sucking. (See *secondary* and *tertiary circular reaction.*)

Primary reinforcer A stimulus that is reinforcing in the absence of any learning. Such stimuli as food and drink are primary reinforcers since, presumably, an organism does not have to learn that they are pleasant.

Proactive inhibition The interference of earlier learning with the retention of later learning.

Proboscis An elegant term for a nose. Employed primarily by erudite scholars in polite company.

Product A term employed by Guilford to describe the result of applying an operation on content. A product may take the form of a response. (See also *operation* and *content.*)

Programed instruction An instructional procedure that makes use of the systematic presentation of information in small steps (frames), usually in the form of a textbook, or employing some other device. Programs typically require learners to make responses and provide them with immediate knowledge of results.

Prompt A device employed in programed instruction in order to ensure that the student will probably answer correctly. It may take a variety of forms.

Proximodistal A term employed to describe a direction in development. It means, literally, from the near to the far. Fetal development is proximodistal in the sense that the inner organs are complete and functioning prior to the development of the outer limbs.

Psychogenic Refers to the psychological aspect of the human organism. Is often employed to describe psychological needs as opposed to physiological or physical needs.

Psychology The science that examines human behavior (and that of animals as well).

Psychotherapeutic Pertaining to psychotherapy. The treatment of mental disorders employing psychological techniques.

Punishment Involves either the presentation of an unpleasant stimulus or the withdrawal of a pleasant stimulus as a consequence of behavior. Punishment should not be confused with negative reinforcement.

Random schedule (also called **variable schedule**) A type of intermittent schedule of reinforcement. It may be of either the interval or the ratio variety, and is characterized by the presentation of rewards at random intervals or on random trials. While both fixed and random schedules may be based on the same intervals or on the same ratios, one can predict when reward will occur under a fixed schedule, whereas it is impossible to do so under a random schedule.

Rat A small rodent, the most important species of which originated in Norway. The rat was the hero of early twentieth-century psychology.

Rate of learning A measure of the amount of time required to learn a correct response, or, alternatively, a measure of the number of trials required prior to the emission of the correct response.

Ratio scale A measurement scale where there is a true zero and where differences between units on the scale are equal. Educational and psychological measurement does not involve ratio scales, although we sometimes act as though they do—as, for example, when we assume that the difference between a percentage score of 78 and 79 is the same as that between 84 and 85. Weight is measured on a ratio scale.

Ratio schedule An intermittent schedule of reinforcement that is based on a proportion of correct responses. (See also *fixed schedule* and *random schedule*.)

Ratiocinative capacities The intellectual or reasoning (cognitive) capabilities of humans.

Recall A synonym for the term *retrieval*. It appears obvious that what an individual can retrieve or recall from memory is less than the total amount of information that the individual has in memory.

Reception learning That type of learning which primarily involves instruction or tuition rather than the learner's own efforts. Teaching for reception learning often takes the form of expository or didactic methods. That is, the teacher structures the material and presents it to learners in relatively final form, rather than asking them to discover that form. Reception learning is generally associated with Ausubel (among others).

Reflex An unlearned, unconscious behavior of the respondent variety (see *respondent*). The knee jerk reaction, in response to a blow on the patella, is an example of a reflex. A second example is eye blink in response to air blown in the eye.

Reinforcement The effect of a reinforcer. That effect is specifically to increase the probability that a response will reoccur. (See also *reinforcer, reward, negative reinforcement*, and *positive reinforcement*.)

Reinforcer A stimulus that serves as reinforcement. The "thing" as opposed to its effect. (See *reinforcement* and *reward*.)

Reliability The consistency with which a test measures whatever it measures. A perfectly reliable test should yield the same scores on different occasions (for the same individual), providing what it measures hasn't changed. Most educational and psychological tests are severely limited in terms of reliability. (See *validity*.)

Remedial frame A frame in a branching program to which students are referred when they make an incorrect response. The purpose of the remedial frame is to provide information required for a subsequent correct response.

Respondent A term employed by Skinner in contrast to the term *operant*. A respondent is a response that is elicited by a known, specific stimulus. Unconditioned responses of the type referred to in classical conditioning are examples of respondents.

Response Any organic, muscular, glandular, or psychic process that results from stimulation.

Response rate The number of responses that are emitted by an organism in a given period of time. Response rates for operant behaviors appear to be largely a function of the schedules of reinforcement employed.

Retention A term often employed as a synonym for memory. (See *retrieval* and *recall*.)

Reticular activating system (RAS) That portion of the brainstem (also referred to as the nonspecific projection system) which is assumed to be responsible for the physiological arousal of the cortex. Its role in arousal-based theories of motivation is paramount.

Retrieval A term for the ability to bring items of information or impressions out of memory. It is often assumed that to forget is not to lose from memory but simply to lose the ability to retrieve from memory. (See also *recall*.)

Retroactive inhibition The interference of subsequently learned material with the retention of previously learned material.

Reversibility A logical property manifested in the ability to reverse or undo activity in either an empirical or a conceptual sense. An idea is said to be reversible when a child can unthink it and realizes that certain logical consequences follow from so doing.

Reward An object, stimulus, event, or outcome that is perceived as being pleasant and which may therefore be reinforcing.

Schedules of reinforcement The manner in which reinforcement is presented to organisms. (See also *continuous reinforcement* and *intermittent reinforcement*.)

Schema The label employed by Piaget to describe a unit in cognitive structure. A schema is, in one sense, an activity together with whatever structural connotations that activity has. In another sense, schema may be thought of as an idea or a concept.

Secondary circular reaction Infant responses that are circular in the sense that the response serves as a stimulus for its own repetition, and secondary since they do not center on the child's body, as do primary circular reactions. (See also *primary circular reactions* and *tertiary circular reactions*.)

Secondary reinforcer A stimulus that is not originally reinforcing but that acquires reinforcing properties as a result of being paired with a primary reinforcer.

Selective attention A characteristic of human attention evident in the observation that individuals cannot simultaneously attend to all stimuli that impinge upon them at any given moment. Only some aspects of the environment are selected and attended to.

Self-actualization The process or act of becoming oneself, of developing one's potentialities, of achieving an awareness of one's identity, of self-fulfillment. The term *self-actualization* is central in humanistic psychology.

Sensorimotor The first stage of development in Piaget's classification. It lasts from approximately birth to age two and is so called because children understand their world at that period primarily in terms of their activities in it and sensations of it.

Sensory capacities Abilities relating to each of the human senses (for example, vision, sight, hearing, and touch).

Sensory deprivation A term used synonymously with sensory restriction. Denotes conditions of unchanging or limited sensory stimulation.

Sensory restriction A condition in which an organism is subjected to limited and/or unchanging sensory stimulation. Such situations have been extensively investigated in the laboratory.

Seriation The ordering of objects in terms of one or more properties. To seriate is essentially to place in order.

Set Defined by Hebb as selectivity among motor outputs. Set is, in effect, a predisposition to react to stimulation in a given manner.

Sex An attribute employed to categorize people and other organisms. It is ordinarily dichotomous.

Shaping The term employed to describe a technique whereby animals and people are taught to perform complex behaviors that were not previously in their repertoires. The technique involves reinforcing responses that become increasingly closer approximations to the desired behavior. Also called the method of successive approximations, or the method of the differential reinforcement of successive approximations.

Signal learning The simplest type of learning in Gagné's classification system. It involves what Pavlov describes as classical conditioning.

Skinner box The label given to various experimental environments employed by Skinner in his investigations of operant conditioning. The typical Skinner box is a cagelike structure equipped with a lever and a food tray attached to a food mechanism. It allows the investigator to study operants (for example, bar-pressing) and the relationship between an operant and reinforcement.

Social learning The acquiring of patterns of behavior that conform to social expectations. Learning what is acceptable and what is not acceptable in a given culture.

Software A computing term employed in contrast to the term *hardware.* It refers to the programs that are employed by computers.

Speculation What grandmother says is her wisdom. Speculation is what psychologists say in the absence of obvious proof for what they believe.

Stages Identifiable phases in the development of human beings. Such developmental theories as those of Jean Piaget are referred to as stage theories, since they deal largely with descriptions of behavior at different developmental levels.

Stimulant A drug or event that has the effect of stimulating or increasing activity.

Stimulus (plural, **stimuli**) Any change in the physical environment capable of exciting a sense organ.

Stimulus substitution Describes the procedure involved in Pavlovian classical conditioning. Classical conditioning is sometimes referred to as learning through stimulus substitution. (See *classical conditioning.*)

Structure A phrase employed by Piaget to describe the organization of an individual's capabilities, whether they be motor or cognitive. Structure is assumed to result from interacting with the world through assimilation and accommodation. (See *schema.*)

Subjective A term used in contrast to the term *objective*. It refers to observations, theories, or experimental methods that are affected by the observer.

Subsumer The term employed by Ausubel to describe a concept, an idea, or a combination of concepts or ideas that can serve to organize new information. Cognitive structure is therefore composed of subsumers.

Subsumption Ausubel's term for the integrating of new material or information with existing information. The term implies a process in which a new stimulus input becomes part of what is already in cognitive structure. (See also *derivative subsumption, correlative subsumption,* and *obliterative subsumption.*)

Successive approximations (See *shaping.*)

Superstitious schedule A fixed interval schedule of reinforcement where the reward is not given after every correct response but rather after the passage of a specified period of time. It is so called because it leads to the learning of behaviors that are only accidentally related to the reinforcement.

Symbolic The final stage in the development of a child's representation of her world. The term is employed by Bruner and describes the representation of the world in terms of arbitrary symbols. Symbolic representation includes representation in terms of language as well as in terms of theoretical or hypothetical systems. (See also *enactive* and *iconic.*)

Symbolic model A model other than real-life person. Any pattern for behavior may be termed a symbolic model if it is not a person. For example, books, television, and written and verbal instructions are all symbolic models.

Synapse The space between the cell body of a neuron and the termination of the axon of an adjoining cell body. Neural transmission proceeds from a cell body outward along the axon and across the synaptic space of the dendrites of adjoining cells.

Syntax The grammar of a language.

Synthesis Putting together of parts in order to form a whole. Complementary to analysis. A high-level intellectual ability in Bloom's taxonomy of educational objectives.

Systematic desensitization A counterconditioning technique developed by Wolpe that attempts to bring about an acceptable response to a given stimulus through a process of gradually increasing the intensity of that stimulus. The technique is essentially the threshold method. (See *threshold method.*)

Tabula rasa The philosophical point of view, originally attributed to the British philosopher John Locke, that held that the mind is a "blank slate" at birth and that whatever the child becomes is entirely a function of the experiences to which he or she is subjected as he or she grows.

Task analysis The procedures of analyzing component tasks in a problem or subject area with a view to organizing them in hierarchical fashion. The hierarchy generally proceeds from the simplest to the most complex tasks, and is frequently based on the assumption that mastery of subordinate tasks is essential for successful performance of subsequent tasks.

Tertiary circular reaction An infant response that is circular in the sense that a response serves as a stimulus for its own repetition, but in which the repeated response is not identical to the first response. This last characteristic is what distinguishes a tertiary circular reaction from a secondary circular reaction. (See also *primary circular reaction* and *secondary circular reaction.*)

Textbook A collection of wise words. (See also *book.*)

Theory A body of information pertaining to a specific area, a method of acquiring and/or dealing with information, or a set of explanations for related phenomena.

Therapy Procedures or methods that are intended to correct undesirable situations, whether in physical or in mental health.

Threshold method A means for breaking habits (described by Guthrie). It involves presenting a stimulus so faintly that the undesirable response is not elicited. Gradually the intensity of the stimulus is increased.

Throat That part of most animals which connects the head to the remainder of the body. It is enclosed by the neck.

Tracking An instructional procedure that involves dividing the members of a classroom into groups according to their ability.

Transductive reasoning The type of semilogical reasoning which proceeds from particular to particular rather than from particular to general or from general to particular. One example of transductive reasoning is the following:

> Cows give milk.
> Goats give milk.
> Therefore goats are cows.

Transfer (See *generalization.*)

Trial-and-error An explanation for learning based on the idea that when placed in a problem situation an individual will emit a number of responses, but will eventually learn the correct one as a result of reinforcement. Trial-and-error explanations for learning are sometimes contrasted with insight explanations.

Type R conditioning A Skinnerian expression for operant conditioning. It is so called since reinforcement is involved in the learning and since response is also involved.

Type S conditioning A Skinnerian expression for classical conditioning. It is so called since stimuli are involved in classical conditioning.

Unconditioned response A response that is elicited by an unconditioned stimulus.

Unconditioned stimulus A stimulus that elicits a response prior to learning. All stimuli that are capable of eliciting reflexive behaviors are examples of unconditioned stimuli. For example, food is an unconditioned stimulus for the response of salivation.

Validity The extent to which a test measures what it says it measures. For example, an intelligence test is valid to the extent that it measures intelligence and nothing else. But educational and psychological tests are limited by their frequently low validity.

Values Variations in a single attribute. For example, the attribute "sides of a coin" has two values: heads and tails.

Variable A property, measurement, or characteristic that is susceptible to variation. In psychological experimentation such qualities of human beings as intelligence and creativity are referred to as variables.

Vicarious reinforcement That type of reinforcement that results from observing someone else being reinforced. In imitative behavior observers frequently acts as though they were being reinforced when in fact they are not being reinforced, but when they are aware, or simply assume, that the model is.

Viscerogenic Refers to physical aspects of the human being. For example, viscerogenic needs are those needs which relate to actual physiological changes in the body.

Worm A small, round, ugly, disgusting, frightening, low form of earth life. Some ancient grandmothers think that a particular greenish brown worm is effective in curing a toothache if correctly applied.

Index

399

To the owner of The Bear:

I hope that you have enjoyed **Psychology for Teaching: A Bear ~~Always~~ ~~Usually~~ Sometimes Faces the Front, Third Edition.** Your comments are valuable to me as an author and an educator. Would you care to share them?

School _____ Your instructor's name _____

1. What did you like *most* about The Bear? _____
   _____

2. What did you like *least* about it? _____
   _____

3. Were all the chapters of the book assigned for you to read?_____
   _____

   If not, which ones weren't? _____
   _____

4. How informative and helpful were the educational implications sections? _____
   _____

   In general, how practical did you find The Bear?_____

5. Did you use the Glossary, and how helpful was it? _____
   _____

6. How helpful were the illustrations? _____
   _____

7. Were any topics or concepts particularly difficult to understand?_____
   _____

8. Were there any topics on which you would have liked:
   More information?_____
   _____

9. Less information? _____
   _____

   Do you have any additional criticisms or suggestions to make? _____
   _____

Optional:

Your name _____   Date _____

May Wadsworth Publishing Company quote you, either in the promotion of *Psychology for Teaching,* Third Edition, or in future publishing ventures?

Yes _____   No _____

Thank you for your advice and comments.

Yours,

R.

FOLD HERE

CUT PAGE OUT

FIRST CLASS
PERMIT NO. 34
BELMONT, CA

BUSINESS REPLY MAIL
No Postage Necessary if Mailed in United States

Dr. Guy R. Lefrancois

Wadsworth Publishing Co., Inc.
10 Davis Drive
Belmont, CA 94002